CORPORATE SOCIAL RESPONSIBILITY

Corporate Social Responsibility

Adam R. Timpere
Editor

Nova Science Publishers, Inc.
New York

For permission to use material from this book please contact us:
Telephone 631-231-7269; Fax 631-231-8175
Web Site: http://www.novapublishers.com

LIBRARY OF CONGRESS CATALOGING-IN-PUBLICATION DATA

Corporate social responsibility / Adam R. Timpere (editor).
p. cm.
ISBN 978-1-60456-284-2(hardcover)
1. Social responsibility of business. 2.Social responsibility of business—Europe. I Timpere,Adam R.
HD60.C6912 2008
658.4'08—dc22
2007051992

Published by Nova Science Publishers, Inc. ✢ New York

CONTENTS

PREFACE

Corporate Social Responsibility (CSR) is a concept whereby organizations consider the interests of society by taking responsibility for the impact of their activities on customers, employees, shareholders, communities and the environment in all aspects of their operations. This obligation is seen to extend beyond the statutory obligation to comply with legislation and sees organizations voluntarily taking further steps to improve the quality of life for employees and their families as well as for the local community and society at large. This book presents new analyses of this very active field.

Chapter 1 - Ever since its foundation, the European Union (EU) has been incorporating aspects of the economic, social and environmental protection into its objectives; these have been reflected not only in several treaties, such as the Treaty Establishing the European Community in 1957, the Treaty on European Union in 1992 or the Treaty Establishing a Constitution for Europe in 2004, but also in various European Council conclusions. Until the Cardiff European Council in 1998, social cohesion and economic development had been jointly considered in the design and evaluation of European policies, but conservation of the natural environment seemed to have been dealt with under specific, independently conceived policies. It was only since the above-mentioned forum that environmental concerns have seen their integration into all other policies. At the Gothenburg European Council (2001), the EU specified a sustainable development strategy, establishing the principle of a coordinated examination of the economic, social and environmental effects of all policies as the basis for the European Union Sustainable Development Strategy (EU SDS).

In this European context, the main goal of the chapter is to analyse the effectiveness of the public funds in the European manufacturing sector from all three perspectives in accordance with the EU SDS. To account for this purpose, a prior extensive review of the state of the art on public policy evaluation has been realised. The study takes into consideration the importance of the subsidies historically received by industry.

In this vein, the authors follow the Gothenburg European Council principles of public policy assessment. This comprehensive evaluation system involves an impact analysis in terms of sustainability. In other words, it determines the extent to which public funds allocated to industries by way of direct financial resources contribute to making them economically viable, socially profitable, and environmentally responsible.

Chapter 2 - To date, corporate social responsibility (CSR) activities have been the responsibility of specialists in organizations. 'CSR' has been seen as a specialist activity, an add-on to the mainstream business, something nice to be 'seen' to be doing. Global events in

2006 changed the paradigm for organizations, for individuals and for countries. CSR has developed a momentum that is destined to lead to it being a mainstream business activity attitude and influence on organization decisions. The paper outlines the changes that are likely to be made within organizations as a result, in terms of three aspects – the organization/business strategy, operational changes and changes in measuring and reporting organizational performance. Through making these changes, CSR will become a part of the mainstream way of organizational thinking and behaving and organizations will think and act differently as a result.

Chapter 3 - Conducting business has become exponentially more complex because of the many rapid changes that have occurred over the last few decades. The contemporary customer or consumer is demanding high quality, swiftness and reliability in the delivery of products or services, all reflected in low pricing, good value and innovation. As organisations are now progressively performing in a global market, they need to be even more alert and competitive. Therefore, management in the twenty-first century needs to meet such challenges by ensuring to embrace the necessary tools and principles as well as integrate all business functions for long-term success. It also has to deal increasingly with diverse pressures, ranging from the more traditional productivity and efficiency dimensions to the more recent elements regarding societal responsibility and public image, as well as the whole 'package' of business risks.

As such, corporate strategy has considerably matured. According to Towells (2003), it has gone through the classical, evolutionary, processual and systemic approaches to today's more common known stage of resources and capabilities. Atkinson (2004) suggests that too many organisations have failed to create a strong business strategy to outwit their competitors, dominate market intelligence, retain existing customers and market share whilst, at the same time, attracting the loyalty of new customers. O'Regan & Ghobadian (2005) support this view by noting that, in the present turbulent business environment, managers increasingly need reliable navigational tools to achieve such a competitive advantage. Thus, when corporate objectives have been identified, it is necessary to develop viable strategies for implementation in a socially responsible manner. Management decision-making should not only focus on the outputs of the business process but should review, rethink its managerial practices and corporate structure and look further downstream to the outcomes of that process which relate to quality of life factors. Such a transformation in strategy should be performed effectively as well as efficiently in the pursuit of increased productivity and ameliorated reputation.

Chapter 4 - In the ongoing globalization of business, *transnational* industrial relations systems are emerging as complements to traditional *national* systems. Integral to the emergent transnational systems are international framework agreements (IFAs). This chapter shows that a previously unrecognised key aspect of IFAs is that they shift the locus of influence in the union movement from national unions to either global union federations or enterprise level unions. Based on a study of an IFA signing process, this chapter shows how this tension between different levels of the union movement affected both the IFA signing process and the IFA content. The outcome in the studied case was that the locus of influence was decentralized to the enterprise level union. This result challenges the prevalent argument that IFAs centralize influence to global union federations. Instead, this chapter proposes that the locus of influence will be decentralized to the enterprise level when: i) there is a trustful corporate-enterprise level union relation, ii) there is a distrustful corporate-global level union relation, and iii) the corporate driver for adopting an IFA is to foster its relations with its enterprise level union. On the other hand, the locus of influence will be centralized to the global level when: i) there is a distrustful corporate-enterprise level union relation, ii) there is a trustful corporate-global level union relation, and iii) the corporate driver for adopting an IFA is to improve its external legitimacy.

Chapter 5 - This chapter discusses the emergence of an embryonic form of pluralism in the negotiation of development projects between local communities and multinational mining companies (MNMCs) as part of (the latter's) corporate social responsibility (CSR) commitments in Papua New Guinea (PNG). The author draws on data gathered through long periods of fieldwork and observation of MNMCs, state and local communities interactions in the development and day to day operations of mines in PNG. The chapter identifies factors which have led to the emergence of eager and sometimes restless local communities which host large mining projects and their unrelenting pressures on developers for tangible development projects. This has led to the establishment of appropriate institutional arrangement and therefore legitimizing the entry of local communities into the pluralistic negotiation process. The background to mining, complexity characterizing PNG mining and CSR and discussion of three mines' CSR commitments are just some of the topics pursued in this chapter.

One theme is the pluralistic institutional framework facilitating local community participation and influencing in development agenda setting for MNMCs to honor whilst at the same time mining for ore. This unique arrangement giving unprecedented voice to formerly neglected spheres of state and MNMC concern has become exceptional for PNG local communities. This chapter contends that this mode of community participation at the peak decision making and influencing CSR function of MNMCs is both pluralistic and exceptional which is not common in most developing countries with mining economies. Therefore, Papua New Guineans have become active partners in mining development and had legitimized the process for a pluralistic approach to management and operation of mining projects in the country.

Chapter 6 - This chapter discusses how public relations is used to elicit greater corporate social responsibility (CSR) in support of U.K. regional and national cultures, culture-specific representations in electronic communication and, in particular, "endangered genres" in that country. It explores some of the prescient issues in this field and the technological and industry changes that have catalyzed U.K. activists. Its primary focus is on the strategies and impact of NGO viewer and listener broadcasting advocacy groups, community media associations, coalitions, and informal groups that seek to advance indigenous culture and get government and media corporations to both respond to these stakeholders and commit to policy and regulatory changes. The chapter also references pressure group activities with respect to the current crisis in children's television throughout the U.K.'s nations. Particular emphasis is placed on CSR structures and vehicles for cultural expression in the nations of Scotland and Wales, the North of England, and other underrepresented regions. It also examines if, and how, political devolution is intertwined with cultural agendas. Finally, it also touches on the larger crisis in children's television, which will have further impact across the U.K., and which is a growing arena of CSR for NGOs throughout the U.K.

Chapter 7 - Starting from the assumption that entrepreneurship does not occur in a vacuum but the external environment has relevant impacts on the entrepreneurial activity and is in turn affected by it, the chapter aims at exploiting the relational side of entrepreneurship proposing the stakeholder theory of the firm as a bridge between entrepreneurship and *business in society* research. It adopts a dual perspective considering the external environment as either an antecedent or as a *receptor* for entrepreneurial outcomes. The contribution of stakeholder theory to entrepreneurship is presented both in general terms using the concept of value as the common basis shared by the two fields and detailing the analysis along the three broad perspectives on stakeholder approach: normative, descriptive and instrumental lenses.

Chapter 8 - This chapter develops a cost benefit analysis model, which considers corporate social responsibility aspects of hydropower development projects. This cost benefit analysis model is empirically applied to controversial hydropower projects in Malaysia, Nepal and Turkey. The model emphasizes the importance of assessing not only economic impacts, but also environmental and social impacts in order to achieve sustainable hydro power development. The study covers diverse cases in terms of characteristics of the dams including size, their geographical locations, and the development stage in each country. According to the model results, the mean cumulative net present value at the 100th year of the analysis with the 5% discount rate for the Sharada-Babai dam in Nepal shows a positive figure, whereas the mean cumulative net present value after 100 years for both the Bakun dam in Malaysia and the Ilisu dam in Turkey are negative. The sensitivity analysis indicates that the significant positive impact of the generation capacity parameter on net present value for Bakun dam; and the parameter expressing initial expected increase in economic output for the Sharada-Babai dam and the Ilisu dam.

Chapter 9 - The Theory of Political Costs affirms that the information which a company provides is used to draft the regulations affecting them; as a consequence the executives of that company will attempt to choose the disclosure policies which most contribute to eliminating political interference and to producing a decrease in costs such as taxes, fees and regulated charges, as well as others. This chapter is an attempt to determine whether the reduction in costs is one of the goals pursued by companies when divulging information on Corporate Social Responsibility.

This information, established as a dependent variable, has been subjected to multivariate analysis, using a dependence model based on the estimation of a linear regression by ordinary least squares.

The independent variable was the measure of industrial concentration because the greater the monopolistic power of a firm, the greater the public scrutiny it is subjected to. Thus, in order to avoid or reduce political costs, companies would reveal more information with a view to showing their behavior to the State and to society at large.

Confirming the cases defended by the Theory of Political Costs, the results found indicate that companies with clearer monopolistic positions reveal a greater volume of unregulated information on Corporate Social Responsibility.

Chapter 10 - The concept of Corporate Social Responsibility (CSR) has a variety of definitions and, within the academic literature, there is some confusion about how CSR should be operationalized and measured (Godfrey & Hatch, 2006). In general, CSR refers to the obligations that organizations have toward society (Fisher, 2004). Considering the school as a particular but real formal corporation, this chapter explores the social responsibility related to the school "mission", that is, the accomplishment of school curriculum. The school (i.e., its legal representatives: teachers and headmasters) fulfils its social obligations when students achieve school goals. But what happens when students are not successful at school? Teachers are most directly responsible for learning, and the social contract assigns responsibility for education to schools (Del Schalock, H. 1998). This chapter identifies the relationship between causal and responsible ascription in the case of failure, stressing the role of effort as "cutting edge" in the discussion of accountability for student/pupil learning. Perceived social responsibility for failure in teachers and students is taken into account, and results of previous studies concerning teachers perceived responsibility in case of school failure are presented and discussed (Matteucci, 2007; Matteucci & Gosling, 2004). According to Weiner (1995) it is argued that effort attribution and responsibility ascription are mutually related, however teachers are reluctant to accept their responsibility for students' failure, thus assigning responsibility to the failing students. The issue of responsibility and accountability for student learning will be discussed, and implications of the results for teachers' work will be considered.

Chapter 11 - Devastating experiences can awaken social responsibility in companies as well as in individuals. A consultant of a Finnish company, Novetos Consulting Ltd, survived the Asian Tsunami in 2004. Her experience changed the course of Novetos Consulting, which started to organize responsible business high-altitude camps in Sri Lanka. These camps are called Scrub Brushes because Finnish business managers go there as hands-on groups to build something useful for local orphans. Many managers of small and medium-sized enterprises (SMEs) have embraced this initiative and learned a great deal about themselves, co-operation and mutual solidarity. They have then brought their individual sense of responsibility into their SME businesses. Unfortunately, managers of large companies seem to avoid individual involvement in social responsibility issues. Large companies only observe laws and donate relatively small amounts of money. It is suggested in this chapter that top managers' individual sense of responsibility could change the course of not only SMEs but also of large companies.

Chapter 12 - The main goal of corporate social responsibility is to make companies not only to act based on a purely economic point of view, but also to involve other aspects into business decisions – like the value of the natural environment or to create a workplace that pays attention to the needs and wishes of its employees. In this chapter, the authors focus on how another tool can assist CSR to achieve its goals. The other tool that we introduce is Futures Studies. It supports CSR with its long-term perspective that tries to investigate possible alternatives of the future more effectively, bringing new values into the decision-making process.

In: Corporate Social Responsibility
Editor: Adam R. Timpere
ISBN: 978-1-60456-284-2

Chapter 1

EUROPEAN UNION PUBLIC SUPPORT INSTRUMENTS TO INDUSTRY AS DRIVERS TO ACHIEVE SUSTAINABILITY RESULTS

María Jesús Muñoz-Torres and Juana M. Rivera-Lirio
University Jaume I. Castellón, Spain

ABSTRACT

Ever since its foundation, the European Union (EU) has been incorporating aspects of the economic, social and environmental protection into its objectives; these have been reflected not only in several Treaties, such as the Treaty Establishing the European Community in 1957, the Treaty on European Union in 1992 or the Treaty Establishing a Constitution for Europe in 2004, but also in various European Council conclusions. Until the Cardiff European Council in 1998, social cohesion and economic development had been jointly considered in the design and evaluation of European policies, but conservation of the natural environment seemed to have been dealt with under specific, independently conceived policies. It was only since the above - mentioned forum that environmental concerns have seen their integration into all other policies. At the Gothenburg European Council (2001), the EU specified a sustainable development strategy, establishing the principle of a coordinated examination of the economic, social and environmental effects of all policies as the basis for the European Union Sustainable Development Strategy (EU SDS).

In this European context, the main goal of the present article is to analyse the effectiveness of the public funds in the European manufacturing sector from all three perspectives in accordance with the EU SDS. To account for this purpose, a prior extensive review of the state of the art on public policy evaluation has been realised. The study takes into consideration the importance of the subsidies historically received by industry.

In this vein, we follow the Gothenburg European Council principles of public policy assessment. This comprehensive evaluation system involves an impact analysis in terms of sustainability. In other words, it determines the extent to which public funds allocated to industries by way of direct financial resources contribute to making them economically viable, socially profitable, and environmentally responsible.

INTRODUCTION

Enterprises have been considered crucial to the European Union's economic growth. The Union's commitment to the creation of a climate in which enterprise, industry and innovation can thrive is officially stated in EC Article 157. The main policy areas, which have historically been integrated in EU enterprise policy, are related to small and medium-sized enterprises (SMEs), innovation and competitiveness. To achieve these objectives, the EU has developed a series of policy instruments. In the context of our work, we pay special attention to public financial support of industry. All European Union and Member State business policy programmes systematically include a series of measures designed to improve the financial situation, as well as to offer a number of direct financial aid instruments, in order to facilitate access, at a lower cost, to capital markets and bank loans.

As reflected in Figure 1, the sector that has traditionally benefited most substantially from EU State aid is that of manufacturing. However, the amount of aid made available to each manufacturing sector varies from one EU State Member to another. During the period from 1992 to 2002, Greece, Italy, Denmark and Germany were the EU members that provided the greatest percentages of public funds on value added to this sector. Since 1995, EU statistics on Member State aid to manufacturing place Spain amongst the top six countries in this classification.

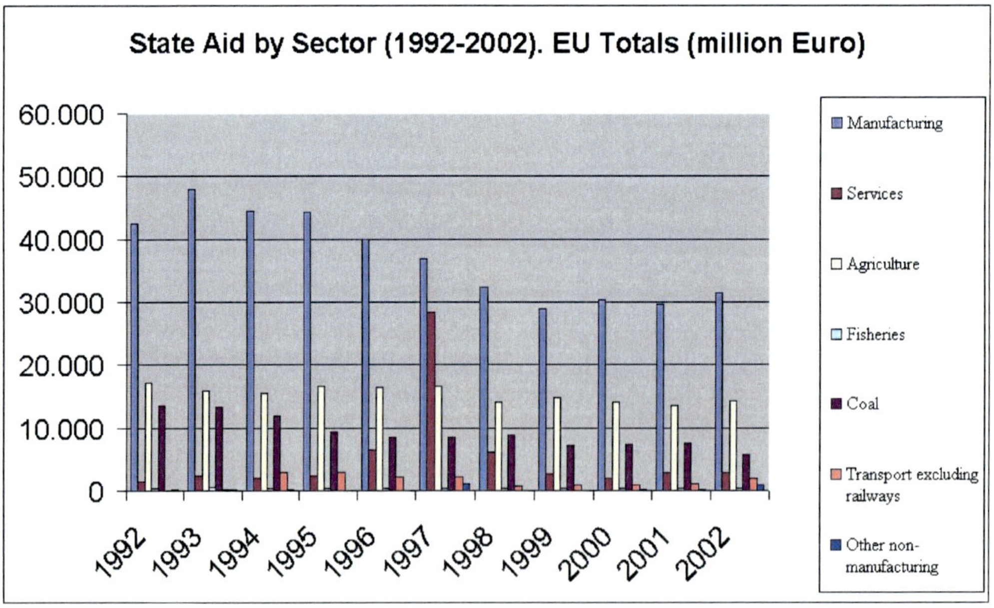

Source: DG Competition http://europa.eu.int/comm/competition/state_aid/scoreboard/

Figure 1. State Aid by Sector.

Most EU States tend to provide aid to manufacturing in the form of grants (European Commission, 2002a). Other aids are assigned in the form of tax exemptions, soft loans, tax deferral, state equity participation or guarantees.

Since its foundation, the EU has incorporated the aspects of economic, social and environmental protection into its objectives. These objectives have been reflected not only in several Treaties, such as the Treaty establishing the European Community in 1957, the Treaty on European Union in 1992 or the Treaty establishing a Constitution for Europe in 2004, but also in various European Council conclusions. Until the Cardiff European Council in 1998, social cohesion and economic development were jointly considered in the design and evaluation of European policies, whereas conservation of the natural environment seemed to be dealt with under specific, independently conceived policies. Following the European Council in 1998, environmental concerns began to be integrated into all other policies. At the Gothenburg European Council (2001), the EU specified a sustainable development strategy, adding an environmental dimension to the Lisbon strategy[1] (which until that date had only covered social and economic facets), and implanting the principle of a coordinated examination of the economic, social and environmental effects of all policies as the basis for the European Union Sustainable Development Strategy (EU SDS).

In this context, in accordance with the EU Strategy for Sustainable Development, and taking into account the importance of subsidies historically received by industry, the main empirical goal of this research paper is to carry out an exploratory analysis of the impact of the above mentioned public funds, where impact is understood not only as economic, but also as social and environmental. In this vein, we follow the Gothenburg European Council principles of public policy assessment. This comprehensive evaluation system involves an impact analysis in terms of sustainability; in other words, it determines the extent to which public funds allocated to industries by way of direct financial resources contribute to making them economically viable, socially profitable, and environmentally responsible.

To achieve the research objective we present a descriptive analysis based upon an array of company sustainable performance indicators, i.e. economic, social and environmental of a number of European Union countries and the evolution of the State aids transferred to industry.

In order to go in greater depth in the impact analysis of these financial instruments we analyse their social and environmental effectiveness by means of a sector study in the context of the Spanish industry results. An attempt is made to determine to what extent the most subsidised sectors show better results in economic, financial, social and environmental terms than the less subsidised ones.

This research comprises five sections. Section one provides a review of the relevant literature on and features of the European Union industrial policies; it also presents the sustainable approach to public policy evaluation that sets the framework for this study. Section two details the methodology, the data used and the variables analysed. Section three reports our findings and the final part exposes the conclusions drawn and provides bibliographical references.

---

[1] The main objective of the Lisbon strategy is to make the European Union the world's most competitive knowledge-based economy by 2010.

1. Industrial Policy Evaluation, State of the Art and New Approaches

The empirical literature on the evaluation of the public policies that support enterprise financing has centred upon different issues associated to the company's activities. One of the concerns that has provoked a major interest has been the impact of public aids in the private investment in the research and development area (see for example, Hujer and Radic, 2005; Hyytinen and Toivanen, 2005; Koga, 2005; Czarnitzki, 2006; Zhu et al., 2006, or the literature review by David et al, 2000 and Garcia–Quevedo, 2004). Some other analysed impacts of economic - financial nature refer to investment (Calomiris and Himmelberg, 1995; Fuest and Tillessen, 2005; Bronzini and de Blasio, 2006; Trovato and Alfó, 2006), productivity (Bergström, 2000; Pablo, 2004; Harris and Robinson, 2005), efficiency (Sakano et al. 1997; Calvo-Flores et al., 2004), or to growth (Becchetti and Trovato, 2002, Calvo-Flores et al., 2004 Hyytinen and Toivanen, 2005, Ohashi, 2005).

On the other hand, several studies incorporate socio-labour (Gabe and Kraybill, 2002; Girma et al. 2003; Görg and Strobl, 2006; Samaniego, 2006), or environmental (Popp, 2006) variables, though in the latter case the literature has primarily been focused on the environmental taxes evaluation (see for example Wagner, 2005; Clinch and Dunne, 2006; Glaziryna et al., 2006).

Conclusions drawn from the different studies vary according to study object, time period, geographical area, and even, as Samaniego (2006) denotes, to the beneficiary company's lifecycle stage. It should be underscored, therefore, that there are no concluding results that pertain to the economic, social and environmental performance generated by the company that benefits from public funds.

However, there is a noticeable lack of studies that carry out a general evaluation of public support policies in industry in order to assess their contribution according to the triple bottom line[2] principle.

1.1. Public Policy Evaluation in the European Sustainable Development Strategy Framework

The existence of a debate among different schools of economic thought about the role of the State in the economy, and therefore in the enterprise activity, depends on the historical context in which it takes place. Nowadays, the globalisation of the economy and the development of supranational government structures reduce the leadership and competence of governments, limiting their political and effective influence. Consequently, the current discussion focuses not on the dichotomy between State and market, but on the best way to achieve welfare through better policies that combine both structures (Albi 2000).

At the same time, poverty and underdevelopment are still widespread in many countries; even the so-called developed countries count the concerns of significant poverty and socially excluded groups. This, together with the presence of an increasing worry about environmental

[2] Reaching the so-called "triple bottom line" implies achieving economic results that allow financial viability, whilst doing so by means of sustainable actions from a social and environmental viewpoint (Elkington 1997).

deterioration, is changing the responsibilities to be assumed not only by government authorities, but also by the private sector. These liabilities are related to a new development approach known as sustainable development. Sustainable development is considered to be development that meets the needs of the present without compromising the ability of future generations to meet their own needs (World Commission on Environment and Development, 1987, commonly known as the Brundtland Report).

The European Union has gradually included the sustainable development concept in the design of its policies. As early as 1957, the aims of the Treaty establishing the European Community signatories were to ensure the economic and social progress of their countries by common action, and to promote, as the essential objective of their efforts, the constant improvement of the living and working conditions of their peoples, as well as to strengthen the unity of their economies and ensure their harmonious development by reducing the differences existing between the various regions and the backwardness of the less favoured regions.

Environmental action by the Community began in 1972, and was gradually adopted by various legislative initiatives, chiefly concerned with limiting pollution by introducing minimum standards, notably for waste management, water pollution and air pollution.

The 2nd Article of the Treaty establishing the European Community is related to these principles and was modified by the Treaty on European Union in 1992. The final version of the Article reads as follows: *"The Community shall have as its task, by establishing a common market and an economic and monetary union and by implementing common policies or activities referred to in Articles 3 and 4, to promote throughout the Community a harmonious, balanced and sustainable development of economic activities, a high level of employment and of social protection, equality between men and women, sustainable and non-inflationary growth, a high degree of competitiveness and convergence of economic performance, a high level of protection and improvement of the quality of the environment, the raising of the standard of living and quality of life, and economic and social cohesion and solidarity among Member States*".

However, the main lines of the EU Strategy for Sustainable Development were set out in the conclusions of the Gothenburg European Council in 2001. These conclusions affirm that the EU policies need to be consistent and should give priority to sustainable development. At the same time, they emphasise the need for an assessment of the potential economic, environmental and social benefits and costs of all these policies. In addition, the Treaty establishing a Constitution for Europe, signed in Rome on 29 October 2004, states that *"the Union shall work for the sustainable development of Europe based on balanced economic growth and price stability, a highly competitive social market economy, aiming at full employment and social progress, and a high level of protection and improvement of the quality of the environment*"[3]. To achieve these objectives, the European Commission (2002b) considers Corporate Social Responsibility (CSR) as the business contribution to Sustainable Development, where CSR is understood as the integration of social and environmental concerns in the enterprise operations and relations with its stakeholders (European Commission 2001). In this context, there is a growing attention and controversy surrounding the role of the State and the public policies in promoting domestic and global CSR. Several authors such as Fox, Ward and Howard (2002), Bell and Grinstein (2002), De la Cuesta and

[3] Part I, Title I, Article I-3, The Union's objectives.

Valor (2004) or the European Commission (2004), describe various public policies and actions designed to create a favourable climate in which enterprises may implement this philosophy[4].

1.2. CSR as a Tool for Generating Information about Companies' Sustainability

The origins of CSR date back to the final decades of the last century when a new entrepreneurial management model known as the socioeconomic model (Freeman, 1984 and Carroll, 1979) was defined. According to it, enterprises have responsibilities to society that go beyond traditional commitments to shareholder profit maximisation. CSR provides instruments for generating information related to the company's economic, social and environmental performance. Furthermore, CSR literature highlights the existence of positive relationships among the triple bottom line facets, and provides the main theoretical paths for justifying, in public enterprise policy terms, the possibility of achieving economic growth, social development and environmental protection, as underlined in the UE strategy. Margolis and Walsh (2003) carried out an empirical literature review of the existing studies from 1972 to 2002, related to the nature of the empirical relationship between the companies' socially responsible conduct and their financial performance. In the 127 studies analysed, 54 revealed a positive relationship between corporate social performance and financial performance. Only seven studies found a negative relationship; 28 studies reported non-significant relationships, while 20 recorded a mixed set of findings. Corporate social performance was included as a dependent variable, predicted by financial performance, in 22 of the 127 studies. In these, most of the results (16 studies) pointed to a positive relationship between corporate financial and social performance.

Therefore, the conclusions obtained from the economic research show that the aforementioned EU Sustainable Development Strategy objectives can be achieved. In this context, the main goal of this paper is to conduct an exploratory analysis of the impact industrial subsidies have in sustainability terms,; that is, to determine to what e extent public funds allocated to industries by way of direct financial resources contribute to this group being more economically viable, socially beneficial, and environmentally responsible (triple bottom line).

The CSR tools (European Commission, 2003a) available to generate company information in terms of its economic, social and environmental performance are very useful in the sustainability - conditioned company performance evaluation, since as Figge and Hahn (2004) affirm, "*the sustainability of a company is judged according to its economic, environmental and social performance*". Among those tools The Global Reporting Initiative Guide (GRI) stands out as widely accepted.

The GRI is an international standard voluntarily applied by the organisations to offer information on the economic, social and environmental dimensions of their activities, where each dimension is associated to a list of specific indicators. Currently, more than 800 organisations worldwide publish sustainability reports in accordance with the GRI 2000

[4] See these authors for a wider review of this issue.

Guide (data obtained from www.globalreporting.org on 22 August 2006). The new GRI G3 was introduced in October 2006.

The GRI guide has served as a reference basis for different investigation projects related to the integration of the sustainability concept in the organisations. (Azapagic, 2004; Kranjc and Glavič, 2005a, 2005b; Konrad et al., 2006; de la Cuesta-González et al., 2006; Moneva et al., 2007; Muñoz et al., 2007). Therefore it can be considered that the GRI indicators constitute a sound foundation for the evaluation of the industries' contribution to sustainable development and for the further determination of the possible effectiveness of the public aids received.

2. Data and Methodology

2.1. EU Countries Descriptive Analysis

To start with, the possible indicators of economic, social and environmental performance generated in reference to the European manufacturing industry have been extensively reviewed on the basis of the public information provided by official organisations (European Commission, Eurostat, OECD). In the presentation of the analysis - derived results the following premises have been considered: i) highest possible homogeneity of the studied period as far as the data availability for the different indicators is concerned, ii) data disaggregation by country (Member States EU-15), iii) a degree of adjustment to the previously commented GRI G3 Guide indicators (GRI, 2006) and iv) data referring to the manufacturing industry.

The available information reveals aspects related to the three sides of the results. However, it demonstrates an elevated heterogeneity, especially in terms of measurement units, time span and disaggregation by country. That is why the scope of this study has been limited to four European countries and to a few basic variables directly related to a GRI indicator or adapted to it as its proxy. Nevertheless, it has been considered that the basic incorporated variables of economic (table 1), social (table 2) and environmental (table 3) nature are representative enough of the company sustainability in order to draw conclusions from them. As far as the variable related to State aids for the European manufacturing industry is concerned (table 4) it has been based upon the information supplied by the European Commission via the State Aid Scoreboard (SAS) and includes grants and tax exemptions, equity participations, soft loans and tax deferrals and guarantees. The shortlisted countries of this study have been Germany, France, Spain and Italy and the time span surveyed stretches from 1997 to 2002. The variations that have occurred in the different indicators elaboration for each country in particular, especially in the economic performance area make the comparative analysis of the performance indicators difficult. That is the reason why the conclusions from this study are drawn according to the particular evolution of each country.

To solve the difficulty related to the disparity in measurement units employed by the core indicators, a process of normalization has also been applied before analysing the triple bottom line variables' evolution.

Table 1. Economic Performance Indicators

Variable	Indicator	Description	Data base	Sector	G3 2006 Indicator
Variation of the Gross value added at basic prices	EcEU1	*"Value added at basic prices is calculated from the production value plus subsidies on products less the purchases of goods and services (other than those purchased for resale in the same condition) plus or minus the change in stocks of raw materials and consumables less other taxes on products which are linked to turnover but not deductible. It represents the value added by the various factor inputs in the operating activities of the unit concerned. (...)Value added at basic prices is calculated "gross" because value adjustments (such as depreciation) are not subtracted."* (CODED, 2006). It has been expressed in variation terms.	Eurostat. European Commission	Manufacturing	G3, EC1
Research and development Intensity	EcEU2	$RDIP_i^k = \frac{ANBERD_i^k}{PROD_i^k} \times 100$ *"Where: ANBERD and PROD are the business enterprise Research and Development and production at current prices, respectively. For each country, this indicator expresses the R&D expenditures by sector relative to the production."* (OECD, 2006)	STAN Indicators database. OECD	Manufacturing	G3, EC9
Economic Profitability	EcEU3	BAIT/AT (AECA, 1998).	BACH Database. Directorate General for Economic and Financial Affairs. European Commission	Manufacturing	G3, EC1
Financial Profitability	EcEU4	BAT/FP (AECA, 1998).	BACH Database. Directorate General for Economic and Financial Affairs. European Commission	Manufacturing	G3, EC1
Operative Efficiency	EcEU5	Turnover/Total Assets (AECA, 1998).	Directorate General for Economic and Financial Affairs. European Commission	Manufacturing	G3, EC1

Table 2. Social Performance Indicators

Variable	Indicator	Description	Data base	Sector	G3 2006 Indicator
Labour Cost Index - Wages and salaries	SocEU1	Wages and salaries in cash and in kind that are part of Labour Costs (defined as core expenditure borne by employers for the purpose of employing staff). Data are presented in the form of annual growth rates (Eurostat, 2006).	Eurostat	Manufacturing	G3, LA2
Standardised incidence rate of accidents at work (severity: more than 3 days lost)	SocEU2	*"The incidence rate of serious accidents at work is the number of accidents at work resulting in more than 3 days' absence per 100 000 persons in employment"* (Eurostat, 2006).	Eurostat	Manufacturing	G3, LA7
Employment Growth	SocEU3	Employment growth rates calculated on annual basis according to data provided by ILO. Exception: France (there are no complete available data in ILO so the information used is first quarter data supplied by Eurostat).	ILO Eurostat	Manufacturing	G3, LA1
Female employment	SocEU4	Female employment in total employment. Idem SocEU3.	ILO Eurostat	Manufacturing	G3, LA7
Temporary employment	SocEU5	Annual variation of temporary employment in manufacturing, calculated upon second quarter data - available data for all the countries with the exception of France (first quarter)-.	Eurostat	Manufacturing	G3, LA1
Industrial disputes, Strikes and Lockouts.	SocEU6	National statistics on strikes and lockouts: Number of working days lost (1000).	Eurostat	Manufacturing	G3, LA7

Table 3. Environmental Performance Indicators

Variable	Indicator	Description	Data base	Sector	G3 2006 Indicator
Emission of greenhouse gases (Global warming potential, CO2 equivalent) in Gross value added at basic prices	EnvEU1	Following Eurostat (2006), the indicator is defined as an index of greenhouse gas (CO2, CH4, N2O, HFC, PFC and SF6) emissions normalized by the base quantity in CO2-equivalents (excluding land use changes and forestry). The base quantity is defined by the index of greenhouse gas emissions in the base year. The base year for the non-fluorinated gases (CO2, CH4 and N2O) is 1990, and 1995 for the fluorinated gases (HFC, PFC and SF6). Exceptions concern: France has 1990 as the base year also for the fluorinated gases; Emissions of the 6 greenhouse gases are weighted by their global warming potentials (GWPs) and aggregated to give total emissions in CO2 equivalents. Global warming potential (GWP) relates to the ability of the different greenhouse gases to contribute to global warming over a 100 year time horizon. GWPs are provided by the Intergovernmental Panel on Climate Change. GVA is expressed in million euros	Eurostat	Intergovernmental Panel on Climate Change (IPCC) sectors: -1.A.2 Manufacturing Industries and Construction -2.Industrial Processes	G3, EN16
Emission of acidifying pollutants (Acid equivalent) in Gross value added at basic prices	EnvEU2	*"Weighting factors are used to derive acid equivalents so that emissions of sulphur dioxide, nitrogen dioxide and ammonia can be combined in terms of their acidifying effect: sulphur dioxide = 1 / 32 , nitrogen dioxide = 1 / 46 and ammonia = 1 / 17"* (Eurostat, 2006). GVA is expressed in million euros	Eurostat	Intergovernmental Panel on Climate Change (IPCC) sectors: -1.A.2 Manufacturing Industries and Construction -2.Industrial Processes	G3, EN20

Variable	Indicator	Description	Data base	Sector	G3 2006 Indicator
Final energy consumption in Gross value added at basic prices	EnvEU3	*"Covers the consumption in all industrial sectors with the exception of the "Energy sector". The fuel quantities transformed in the electrical power stations of industrial autoproducers and the quantities of coke transformed into blast-furnace gas are not entered under overall industrial consumption but under transformation input"* (CODED, 2006). Expressed in 1000toe Thousands tons of oil equivalent (TOE). GVA is expressed in million euros	Eurostat	Non-ferrous metal industry Chemical industry Non-metallic mineral products industry Ore extraction (except fuels) industry Food, drink and tobacco industry Textile, leather and clothing industry Paper and printing industry Engineering and other metal industry Other non-classified industries	G3, EN3
% Investment related to pollution control (among others)	EnvEU4	Investment carried out this year and planned investment for next year is, or will be, of the following kind: "Other investment objectives (pollution control, safety, etc.)", different from: replacement of worn-out plant or equipment, extension of production capacity and investment designed to streamline production (Directorate General Economic and Financial Affairs, 2006).	Investment survey, European Commissi on	Manufacturing	G3, EN30

Table 4. State Aids to Manufacturing

Variable	Description	Data base
State Aids to Manu-facturing	State Aid for the manufacturing sector. *"For the purposes of the Scoreboard, the manufacturing sector includes aid for steel, shipbuilding, other manufacturing sectors, rescue and restructuring, aid for general economic development and aid for most horizontal objectives including research and development, SMEs, environment, commerce and energy saving"* (European Commission, 2003b). *"The Scoreboard covers State aid as defined under Article 87(1) EC Treaty that has been granted by the twenty-five Member States and has been the subject of a final Commission decision"* (State Aid Scoreboard, 2006). Data are expressed in million euro at constant 2000 prices.	State aid Scoreboard. Competition Directorate-General. European Commission

Following Krajnc and Glavič (2005a), we differentiate between indicators whose increase has a positive impact on sustainable development and those whose increase has a negative impact, where $I^{+}_{N,ijt}$, the normalized indicator *i* (with a positive impact) for a group of indicators *j* for time (year) *t* and $I^{-}_{N,ijt}$ the normalized indicator *i* (with a negative impact) for a group of indicators *j* for the same time (year) *t:*

$$I^{+}_{N,ijt} = \frac{I^{+}_{A,ijt} - I^{+}_{\min,jt}}{I^{+}_{\max,jt} - I^{+}_{\min,jt}} \qquad I^{-}_{N,ijt} = 1 - \frac{I^{-}_{A,ijt} - I^{-}_{\min,jt}}{I^{-}_{\max,jt} - I^{-}_{\min,jt}}$$

Thus in all cases values close to 1 have positive connotations in sustainability terms, while those close to 0 have negative ones.

2.2. Sector Analysis of the Spanish Industry

For the second part of the empirical analysis, i.e. a sector study of the economic, social and environmental effectiveness of these financial instruments through the analysis of the Spanish industry, the Global Reporting Initiative (GRI) Guidelines seem to be the most comprehensive tool that can be used for measuring the enterprises' sustainable performance as well. Consequently, variables and ratios were selected from the Spanish industry public databases, taking into account the work of the AECA (Spanish Association of Accounting and Business Administration) (1998), Margolis and Walsh (2003), Orlitzky et al. (2003) and Calvo-Flores et al. (2004), using the GRI (2002) variables' definition.

Bergström (2000) and Calvo-Flores et al. (2004) carried out comparative studies between subsidised and non-subsidised enterprises in order to evaluate the financial contribution of public funds to certain economic and financial enterprise parameters. In our analysis, we adopt this evaluation approach, but consider that in a sector context and with average or aggregate values, we cannot distinguish between subsidised and non-subsidised enterprises. Hence, the comparative dimension must be realised by differentiating between companies receiving higher - or lower- volume subsidies.

The sectorial information was obtained from several Spanish public databases compiled by the Central Balance Sheet Office of the Bank of Spain[5] (CBBE), the Spanish National Statistics Institute[6] (INE), the SEPI[7] Foundation (the Business Strategy Survey databases, ESEE) and the Ministry of Labour and Social Affairs[8] (MTAS). This variety of data sources is due to the lack of a single database that jointly provides the financial-economic, social and environmental information required to fulfil our research objectives.

In order to achieve our objective, we classified each sector according to whether the amount of capital subsidies received (CBBE SUB ratio) each year was above or below the population median for the period 1986-2002. We use the median statistic instead of the mean, because the median is less sensitive to extreme values. Results on the sectors with historically

---

[5] For more information about the sample's properties see http://bde.es/informes/be/cb/cb.htm
[6] For more information about the sample's properties see http://www.ine.es/inebase/cgi/um?L=0
[7] For more information about the sample's properties see http://www.funep.es/esee/esee1.asp
[8] For more information about the sample's properties see http://www.mtas.es/estadisticas/presenta/index.htm

a higher or lower volume of subsidies are shown in table 5. Each sector's classification is highlighted in bold.

The term capital subsidy has an accounting-related meaning; that is, non-refundable subsidies received for the establishment or fixed structure of an enterprise would be included in this concept. In this case, we have included an indicator of capital subsidies received over a certain period of time, in relative terms, according to the volume of aggregate liabilities of the sector analysed, in order to eliminate any possible influence of the CBBE sample size[9].

Table 5. Sectorial classification by volume of subsidies received 1986-2002

Sector		Classification
3	MAN. FOOD PROD, BEVE, TOBAC.	+
5	MANUFACTURE OF CHEMICALS	-
6	MAN. OTHER NON-METH MINERA.	+
7	MAN. BASIC MET.&METAL PRO.	+
8	MAN. MACHINERY EQUIPMENT	-
9	MAN. ELECT.&OPT. EQUIPMENT	-
10	MAN. TRANSPORT EQUIPMENT	+
11	MAN. TEXT. &TEXT. PRODUCTS	-
12	MAN. LEATHER & LEATH PROD.	-
13	MAN. WOOD AND CORK PRODUCT.	+
14	MAN. PULP, PAPER, PUBL, PRINT.	-
15	MAN. RUBBER & PLASTIC PROD.	-
16	MANUFACTURING N.E.C.	-

Table 6. Performance Indicators and variables, Spanish industry

Reference guide: GRI 2002	Variable	Description	Data Base
Economic performance indicators			
Customers			
EC1. Net sales	MS	Market share in the main market (%)	ESSE
EC2. Geographical breakdown of markets.	FS/NATOI	Foreign sales on net amount of turnover and other operating income	CBBE
	ExEn	Percentage of export enterprises	ESEE
Suppliers			
EC3. Cost of all goods, materials, and services purchased.	OE/NATOI	Operating Expenses on net amount of turnover and other operating income	CBBE

[9] CBBE database shows aggregate, not average data.

Table 6. Continued

Reference guide: GRI 2002	Variable	Description	Data Base
Employees			
EC5. Total payroll and benefits	Re	Remuneration per employee (personnel costs / average number of employees) (€)	CBBE
Providers of capital			
EC6. Distributions to providers of capital broken down by interest on debt and borrowings, and dividends on all classes of shares, with any arrears of preferred dividends to be disclosed.	DClt	Average Costs of the long term debt with credit entities	ESEE
	DCst	Present costs of the short term debt with credit entities	ESEE
	ORE	Ordinary return on equity (Ordinary net profit / equity)	CBBE
	DRA	Debt repayment ability [(depreciation + net result) / (short-term debt + long-term debt)]	CBBE
Indirect Economic Impacts			
EC13. The organisation's indirect economic impacts. Identify major externalities associated with the reporting organisation's products and services (includes R&D activities)	NoR&D	Percentage of enterprises that neither undertake nor outsource R&D activities.	ESEE
	R&D/TS	Percentage of R&D expenditures on total sales.	ESEE
	RP	Average of patents registered in Spain	ESEE
Others (NO GRI)			
	NATOI/TA	Net amount of turnover and other operating income on total assets.	CBBE
	NATOI/PC	Net amount of turnover and other operating income on personnel costs.	CBBE
	GVAfc/PC	Gross value added on personnel costs.	CBBE
	ORNA	Ordinary return on net assets [(ordinary net profit + financial costs) / Net assets].	CBBE
	IE	Investor Effort (% Investment on Sales)	ESEE
Environmental performance indicators			
Emissions, Effluents, and Waste			
EN8. Greenhouse gas emissions. (CO_2, CH_4, N_2O, HFCs, PFCs, SF_6).	SOx	SOx (tonne) on net amount of turnover and other operating income (1000)	INE
EN10. NOx, SOx, and other significant air emissions by type.	NOx	NOx (tonne) on net amount of turnover and other operating income (1000)	INE

Reference guide: GRI 2002	Variable	Description	Data Base
	CO	CO (tonne) on net amount of turnover and other operating income (1000)	INE
	NMVOC	Non-methane volatile organic compounds (tonne) on net amount of turnover and other operating income (1000)	INE
	CO2	CO2 (1000 tonne) on net amount of turnover and other operating income (1000)	INE
	CH4	CH4 (tonne) on net amount of turnover and other operating income (1000)	INE
	N2O	N2O (tonne) on net amount of turnover and other operating income (1000)	INE
Social performance indicators			
Employment			
LA1. Breakdown of workforce, where possible, by employment contract (indefinite or permanent/fixed term or temporary).	NE TE	Number of employees (1000) Percentage of temporary employment	INE ESEE
LA2. Net employment creation	EC	Yearly employment creation (%)	IN E
LA12. Employee benefits beyond legal requirements.	ExCon	Extra social contributions per employee (social costs apart from remunerations and National Insurance Contributions) (€)	CBBE
Labour/Management Relations			
LA4. Policy and procedures involving information, consultation, and negotiation with employees over changes in the reporting organisation's operations (e.g., restructuring).	EPER	Percentage of enterprises with steady employment reduction.	ESSE
Health and Safety			
LA5. Practices on recording and notification of occupational accidents and diseases	IRA	Standardised Incidence rate of accidents at work.	MTAS

Table 6. Continued

Reference guide: GRI 2002	Variable	Description	Data Base
Diversity and Opportunity			
LA11. Composition of senior management and corporate governance bodies (including the board of directors), including female/male ratio and other indicators of diversity as culturally appropriate.	FemER	Female employment rate.	INE

The sector classification was performed according to the historical volume of subsidies received by each of the sectors taking into account the date of Spain's entry into the EU, 1986. The period analysed for social and economic variables runs from 1992 to 2002 (see table 6). However, in terms of environmental information, the public data available runs from 1995 to 2000. To our knowledge, no further sector public information has been available that corresponds to our objective and period analysed.

We used the MS variable in relation to the monetary flows between the organisation and its customers. This variable is the average of the enterprise market share in its main market, and was preferred to the net sales value, since none of the databases provided information in average values and the results obtained would have been distorted. The AECA (1998) defines MS as the measure of the organisation's impact in the market. Moreover, this variable is considered by the economic literature as an entrepreneurial performance measure (Morgan and Strong 2003). We used ratios related to the companies' exporting activity as proxy variables to establish the geographical breakdown of markets belonging to both analysed samples. This performance indicator revealed the competitive capacity of both samples in the international markets. The economic performance indicators related to suppliers were expressed in our analysis by the ratio operating expenses on net amount of turnover and other operating incomes (OE/NATOI). The use of operating expenses as a financial-economic performance measure has been reflected in previous works such as those by Christmann (2000) or Klassen and Whybark (1999). On the other hand, economic indicators related to employees refer to a breakdown of total salary costs. Hence, we have attempted to reflect the wage differences that may exist between the samples analysed by considering the average remuneration per employee (Re). For capital providers, we have included ratios that refer to the debt cost with credit entities (DClt and DCst), enterprise financial risk (debt repayment ability, DRA, Calvo-Flores et al. 2004), and financial profitability (ordinary return on equity[10], ORE). With regard to the organisation's indirect economic impacts, special attention has been paid to those related to the samples' R&D activity.

In addition to the performance indicators outlined in the GRI Guidelines (2002), we have considered it appropriate to include a set of variables according to the objectives of some other studies outlined in reviewed literature. Consequently, productive efficiency, economic profitability and investor effort ratios have been added.

The GRI Guidelines (2002) accentuate that the environmental dimension of sustainability concerns an organisation's impacts on living and non-living natural systems, including ecosystems, land, air and water. In this vein, the lack of information on the companies' vis-à-vis environmental issues in the Spanish databases should be mentioned. As a result, our study has been limited and the scope of GRI environmental variables considered - reduced. Under these circumstances, we have only considered the INE's typology of pollutant gases, taking into account each sector's activity volume (expressed in terms of net amount of turnover and other operating incomes). Finally, the GRI Guidelines emphasize that the social dimension of sustainability concerns an organisation's impacts on the social systems within which it operates. According to these guidelines, we have analysed the variables related to employment, labour-management relations, health and safety at work and opportunity. In employment terms, the NE variable has been used to measure the number of employees in each sector. Employment stability was expressed by the TE ratio, which represents temporary employment as a percentage of total employment. The EC variable shows the yearly employment creation by each sector analysed in the sample; employment creation has been used as a social performance measure by other authors such as Bragdon and Karash (2002). ExCon enabled us to show some extra social contributions, i.e., social contributions other than wages and National Insurance Contributions received per employee. In addition, considering the available information, we have associated the variables related to labour conflicts with the indicators that measure the climate of labour-management relations. Here, the ratio used was the EPER, which expresses the percentage of enterprises with steady employment reduction due to special internal agreements. Health and safety at work was explained by the IRA index, which represents the rate of accidents at work and occupational illness per one thousand employees exposed to risk. Finally, the FemER variable indicates female employment as a percentage of total employment, and expresses a measure of diversity and equality of opportunities.

A one-way ANOVA test was performed on each variable to determine whether there was a significant difference between the means of the samples of the most and least subsidised sectors. In order to check whether the variables violate the one-way ANOVA test preliminary hypothesis (normality and variance homogeneity), we used the Kolmogorov-Smirnov test and the Levene test respectively. Thus if variables violated the abovementioned assumptions, greater reliance was then placed upon the difference in medians for the most and least subsidised sector groups. For this purpose the Kruskall-Wallis median test was applied.

According to the tests applied, the specific hypotheses to be verified are:

H_1: The more heavily subsidised an economic sector is, the better it performs in economic terms

H_0: The average values of the economic and financial ratios of more heavily subsidised sectors are better than the average values of the economic and financial ratios of less subsidised sectors.

H_1: The average values are worse or there are no significant differences in the averages.

H_2: Public financial support instruments have helped to improve the environmental impact of industry.

H_0: The average values of the environmental ratios of more heavily subsidised sectors are better than the average values of the environmental ratios of sectors with a lower volume of subsidies.

H_1: The average values are worse or there are no significant differences in the averages.

H_3: More heavily subsidised sectors have better results in social terms than less subsidised sectors

H_0: The average values of the social ratios of more heavily subsidised sectors are better than the average values of the social ratios of less subsidised sectors.

H_1: The average values are worse or there are no significant differences in the averages.

3. Results

3.1. EU Countries Descriptive Analysis

The analysis shows disperse results as far as the country premise is concerned. Since the data are context - dependent for each country for the period in focus, it is difficult to compare the different countries. Therefore, the present section of the analysis centres upon the contribution to sustainable development of each country´s manufacturing industry in accordance with its economic, social and environmental performance evolution. When analysing the graphics, the normalised nature of the presented variables should be kept in mind (see table 7). This means that values close to 1 bear positive connotations in terms of the indicator's evolution and the year-on- year variations are quite pronounced.

Spain

In the case of Spain (figure 2), in the period between 2000 and 2001, there was a reduction in the level of the aids granted to the manufacturing industry. It is in the year 2002 when the biggest volume of allocated aids can be appreciated, the period coinciding with the launching of the EU Sustainable Development Strategy (EU SDS).

Focusing on the evolution of the economic variables of the period, it is evident that it does not correspond, in financial terms, to the effort made by the administration. The only indicator to reach maximum values is the R&D "Research and Development Intensity" (EcEU2) one while EcEU1 "Variation of the Gross Value Added at Basic Prices", EcEU3 "Economic Profitability", EcEU4 "Financial Profitability" and EcEU5 "Operative Efficiency" report the lowest results.

As far as the environmental results are concerned, it can be observed that the "Final Energy Consumption" (EnvEU3) variable keeps a growing tendency independently from the level of the aids granted to the industry. There is a positive evolution, however, in the EnvEU1 "Emission of Greenhouse Gases" and EnvEU2 "Emission of Acidifying Pollutants" variables and an increase of the EnvEU4 "Percentage of Investment Related to Pollution control" one.

In social terms the variables display a disparate evolution. A number of them, such as the"Labour Cost Index - Wages and Salaries" (SocEU1), "Female Employment" (SocEU4), "Temporary Employment" (SocEU5) and "Industrial Disputes, Strikes and Lockouts" (SocEU6) ones present relatively satisfactory results in the periods of major aid allocation. There is no case, however, of aids destined to aspects such as "Standardised Incidence Rate of Accidents at Work" (SocEU2) and "Employment Growth" (SocEU3).

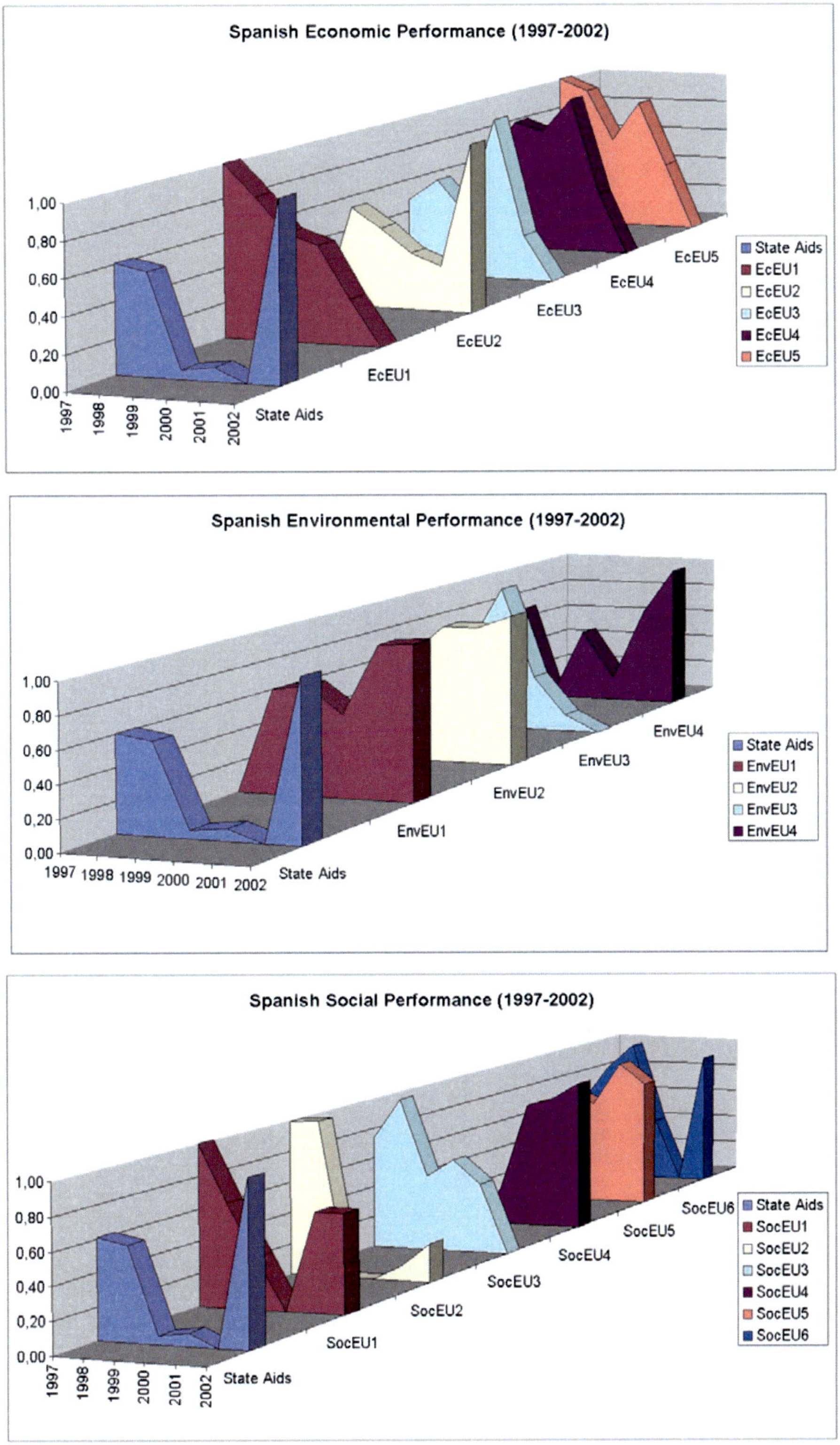

Figure 2. Spanish Sustanible Results.

Table 7. European Countries Performance Data

		Year / Indicator	Originals						MAX	MIN	Normalized					
			1997	1998	1999	2000	2001	2002			1997	1998	1999	2000	2001	2002
GERMANY	Economic	EcEU1	0.04	0.01	0.01	0.07	0.02	-0.02	0.07	-0.02	0.73	0.37	0.34	1.00	0.42	0.00
		EcEU2	2.49	2.52	2.64	2.56	2.52	2.61	2.64	2.49	0.00	0.18	1.00	0.47	0.21	0.83
		EcEU3	0.08	0.09	0.09	0.09	0.08	0.08	0.09	0.08	0.00	1.00	0.56	0.90	0.08	0.04
		EcEU4	0.16	0.17	0.16	0.16	0.11	0.12	0.17	0.11	0.79	1.00	0.76	0.82	0.00	0.21
		EcEU5	1.37	1.43	1.38	1.33	1.30	1.23	1.43	1.23	0.70	1.00	0.74	0.50	0.33	0.00
	Social	SocEU1	0.000	1.500	2.000	1.600	1.400	1.000	2.000	0.000	0.00	0.75	1.00	0.80	0.70	0.50
		SocEU2	4,865	4,761	4,639	4,455	4,206	3,672	4,865	3,672	0.00	0.09	0.19	0.34	0.55	1.00
		SocEU3	-0.007	-0.002	0.008	0.001	0.008	-0.015	0.008	-0.015	0.33	0.56	1.00	0.69	0.98	0.00
		SocEU4	0.280	0.283	0.283	0.283	0.283	0.280	0.283	0.280	0.00	0.85	0.99	0.79	1.00	0.13
		SocEU5	0.068	0.162	0.031	0.006	-0.040	-0.062	0.162	-0.062	0.42	0.00	0.59	0.70	0.90	1.00
		SocEU6	9.770	10.120	63.290	4.880	21.070	240.760	240.760	4.880	0.98	0.98	0.75	1.00	0.93	0.00
	Environmental	EnvEU1	0.408	0.371	0.350	0.331	0.326	0.334	0.408	0.326	0.00	0.46	0.70	0.94	1.00	0.91
		EnvEU2	2.3E-05	2.1E-05	2.0E-05	1.8E-05	1.8E-05	1.7E-05	2.3E-05	1.7E-05	0.00	0.38	0.54	0.85	0.96	1.00
		EnvEU3	0.114	0.113	0.109	0.112	0.109	0.110	0.114	0.109	0.00	0.35	1.00	0.41	0.98	0.77
		EnvEU4	11.900	9.000	9.000	9.000	12.000	15.000	15.000	9.000	0.48	0.00	0.00	0.00	0.50	1.00

		Originals						MAX	MIN	Normalized					
	Year / Indicator	1997	1998	1999	2000	2001	2002			1997	1998	1999	2000	2001	2002
FRANCE Economic	EcEU1	0.044	0.045	0.030	0.042	0.017	-0.006	0.045	-0.006	0.97	1.00	0.71	0.94	0.44	0.00
	EcEU2	2.221	2.158	2.198	2.049	2.115	2.291	2.291	2.049	0.71	0.45	0.61	0.00	0.27	1.00
	EcEU3	0.080	0.079	0.078	0.084	0.075	0.069	0.084	0.069	0.74	0.65	0.56	1.00	0.40	0.00
	EcEU4	0.132	0.133	0.149	0.170	0.134	0.121	0.170	0.121	0.23	0.24	0.57	1.00	0.27	0.00
	EcEU5	1.275	1.216	1.273	1.297	1.295	1.278	1.297	1.216	0.73	0.00	0.70	1.00	0.97	0.76
Social	SocEU1	1.100	1.100	2.000	3.500	3.500	1.600	3.500	1.100	0.00	0.00	0.38	1.00	1.00	0.21
	SocEU2	4,573	4,458	4,412	4,488	4,399	4,559	4,573	4,399	0.00	0.66	0.93	0.49	1.00	0.08
	SocEU3	0.013	0.025	0.008	0.029	0.012	-0.027	0.029	-0.027	0.71	0.92	0.63	1.00	0.70	0.00
	SocEU4	0.319	0.307	0.299	0.287	0.278	0.284	0.319	0.278	1.00	0.71	0.52	0.22	0.00	0.15
	SocEU5	0.083	0.179	-0.004	0.195	0.027	-0.175	0.195	-0.175	0.30	0.04	0.54	0.00	0.45	1.00
	SocEU6	258.180	216.040	295.710	420.440	246.360	128.570	420.440	128.570	0.56	0.70	0.43	0.00	0.60	1.00
Environmental	EnvEU1	0.532	0.493	0.442	0.402	0.396	0.389	0.532	0.389	0.00	0.27	0.63	0.90	0.95	1.00
	EnvEU2	4.8E-05	4.3E-05	3.8E-05	3.1E-05	2.9E-05	2.6E-05	4.8E-05	2.6E-05	0.00	0.25	0.48	0.77	0.86	1.00
	EnvEU3	0.139	0.136	0.128	0.118	0.122	0.122	0.139	0.118	0.00	0.15	0.56	1.00	0.81	0.81
	EnvEU4	35.100	33.300	33.000	31.300	33.400	36.700	36.700	31.300	0.70	0.37	0.31	0.00	0.39	1.00

Table 7. Continued

		Year / Indicator	Originals						MAX	MIN	Normalized					
			1997	1998	1999	2000	2001	2002			1997	1998	1999	2000	2001	2002
SPAIN	Economic	EcEU1	0.061	0.051	0.040	0.037	0.020	0.006	0.061	0.006	1.00	0.82	0.62	0.56	0.26	0.00
		EcEU2	0.550	0.636	0.619	0.599	0.589	0.695	0.695	0.550	0.00	0.59	0.48	0.34	0.27	1.00
		EcEU3	0.084	0.087	0.082	0.096	0.079	0.073	9.557	7.285	0.47	0.60	0.40	1.00	0.28	0.00
		EcEU4	0.127	0.145	0.141	0.154	0.118	0.096	0.154	0.096	0.54	0.84	0.78	1.00	0.39	0.00
		EcEU5	1.247	1.236	1.188	1.225	1.165	1.104	1.247	1.104	1.00	0.92	0.59	0.85	0.43	0.00
	Social	SocEU1	3.000	1.800	0.700	-0.400	1.700	1.700	3.000	-0.400	1.00	0.65	0.32	0.00	0.62	0.62
		SocEU2	7,770	7,758	8,983	8,977	8,861	8,674	8,983	7,758	0.99	1.00	0.00	0.00	0.10	0.25
		SocEU3	0.049	0.065	0.035	0.042	0.033	0.007	0.065	0.007	0.73	1.00	0.49	0.61	0.45	0.00
		SocEU4	0.227	0.223	0.230	0.249	0.250	0.254	0.254	0.223	0.14	0.00	0.23	0.83	0.89	1.00
		SocEU5	0.121	0.042	-0.006	0.007	-0.040	-0.018	0.121	-0.040	0.00	0.49	0.79	0.71	1.00	0.86
		SocEU6	484.300	295.800	173.560	581.970	889.670	226.310	889.670	173.560	0.57	0.83	1.00	0.43	0.00	0.93
	Environmental	EnvEU1	0.691	0.663	0.661	0.668	0.649	0.649	0.691	0.649	0.00	0.67	0.70	0.54	0.98	1.00
		EnvEU2	1.4E-04	1.2E-04	1.1E-04	1.0E-04	1.0E-04	1.0E-04	1.4E-04	1.0E-04	0.00	0.41	0.72	0.91	0.91	1.00
		EnvEU3	0.182	0.179	0.169	0.184	0.191	0.193	0.193	0.169	0.47	0.58	1.00	0.37	0.11	0.00
		EnvEU4	16.000	12.000	15.000	13.000	16.000	18.000	18.000	12.000	0.67	0.00	0.50	0.17	0.67	1.00

			Originals						MAX	MIN	Normalized					
	Indicator \ Year		1997	1998	1999	2000	2001	2002			1997	1998	1999	2000	2001	2002
ITALY	Economic	EcEU1	0.017	0.003	-0.004	0.030	-0.009	-0.013	0.030	-0.013	0.69	0.37	0.20	1.00	0.08	0.00
		EcEU2	0.698	0.630	0.658	0.659	0.686	0.690	0.698	0.630	1.00	0.00	0.40	0.42	0.82	0.88
		EcEU3	0.071	0.069	0.063	0.060	0.054	0.048	0.071	0.048	1.00	0.95	0.66	0.51	0.23	0.00
		EcEU4	0.146	0.157	0.151	0.122	0.106	0.098	0.157	0.098	0.82	1.00	0.90	0.41	0.14	0.00
		EcEU5	1.085	1.085	1.050	1.011	1.029	1.008	1.085	1.008	1.00	1.00	0.55	0.04	0.28	0.00
	Social	SocEU1	3.000	0.400	0.800	-1.200	1.500	0.500	3.000	-1.200	1.00	0.38	0.48	0.00	0.64	0.40
		SocEU2	5,321	5,006	4,889	4,930	4,698	4,105	5,321	4,105	0.00	0.26	0.36	0.32	0.51	1.00
		SocEU3	-0.005	0.017	0.001	-0.002	-0.002	0.011	0.017	-0.005	0.00	1.00	0.29	0.13	0.12	0.74
		SocEU4	0.305	0.305	0.302	0.305	0.307	0.304	0.307	0.302	0.59	0.55	0.00	0.62	1.00	0.42
		SocEU5	0.005	0.311	0.046	0.024	-0.078	0.114	0.311	-0.078	0.79	0.00	0.68	0.74	1.00	0.51
		SocEU6	703.600	304.400	585.400	310.600	607.400	425.700	703.600	304.400	0.00	1.00	0.30	0.98	0.24	0.70
	Environmental	EnvEU1	0.566	0.537	0.566	0.572	0.559	0.538	0.572	0.537	0.15	1.00	0.15	0.00	0.35	0.96
		EnvEU2	6.1E-05	5.0E-05	4.8E-05	4.2E-05	4.4E-05	4.5E-05	6.1E-05	4.2E-05	0.00	0.58	0.70	1.00	0.88	0.85
		EnvEU3	0.172	0.168	0.179	0.178	0.178	0.178	0.179	0.168	0.63	1.00	0.00	0.07	0.12	0.08
		EnvEU4	14.000	14.000	10.000	14.000	10.000	11.000	14.000	10.000	1.00	1.00	0.00	1.00	0.00	0.25

Germany

An outstanding aspect in the German case (figure 3) is the gradual decrease of the aids granted to the manufacturing industry in the studied period. Thus 1997 is the peak of the aid allocation and 2002 - its lowest point.

As far as the economic variables are concerned, it could be affirmed that the decrease in aid allocation to the industry is parallel to the decline of economic results. The R&D- related indicator "Research and Development Intensity" (EcEU2) is the only one to heighten its value after the EU SDS launch.

Results are promising in environmental terms. The "Emission of greenhouse gases", "Emission of acidifying pollutants" and "Final energy consumption" indicators maintain a decreasing tendency of their levels, thus being positive in sustainability terms. In the same way an increase of the EnvEU4 "Percentage of Investment related to pollution control" indicator is observed despite the aid allocation reduction. However, Germany stands out as the country most committed to environmentally oriented aids (Rivera and Muñoz, 2007).

The social parameters of the variables show an evolution akin to the financial effort of the administration. Thus 2002 is the period of least aids granted with the consequent lowest results in the "Employment Growth" (SocEU3), "Female Employment" (SocEU4) and "Industrial Disputes, Strikes and Lockouts" (SocEU6) indicators.

France

The global evolution of the indicators (figure 4) in the French environment resembles the German case. The only differences perceived refer to the EcEU5 "Operative Efficiency" indicator, which despite its stagnation does not reach the low speed observed in Germany. The social tendencies are similar to the ones in Germany with the exception of the increase of the "Standardised Incidence Rate of Accidents at Work" (SocEU1) and the subsidence of the "Industrial Disputes, Strikes and Lockouts" one (SocEu6).

Italy

The abovementioned evolution of the German and French cases is similar to the Italian scene (figure 5) as well, with a slight increase of the aids granted by the administration to the industry. These similarities are especially eminent in economic and environmental terms, yet in the latter the EnvEU3 y EnvEU4 indicators, i.e. energy consumption and "Percentage of Investment related to pollution control" ones display worse levels.

As far as the social indicators are concerned, it is difficult to draw conclusions that would characterise the evolution of these variables over the analysed period. Nevertheless, the improvement of the accidents at work ratio (SocEU2) and the decrease of the work conflicts (SocEU6) in the final period should be underscored.

Generally speaking, the analysis of the graphics profile reveals that the level of the aids allocated is not linked to the evolution of the environmental indicators, but seems to present closer relation to the social and economic ones. A possible explanation may be the increment of environmental laws over the studied period, the high social protection level in countries such as Germany, France or Italy and the differences in State aids allocation among countries.

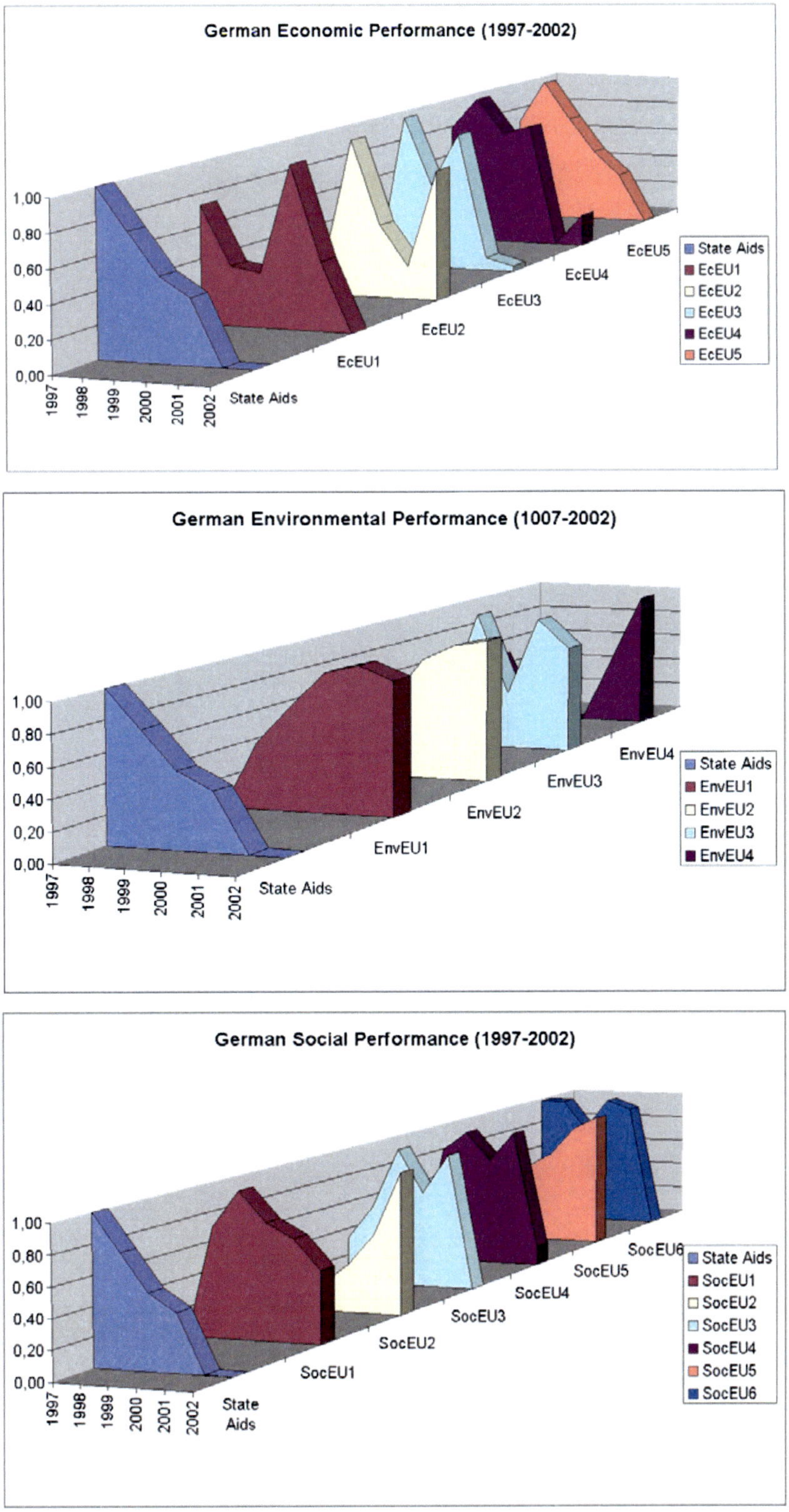

Figure 3. German Sustanible Results.

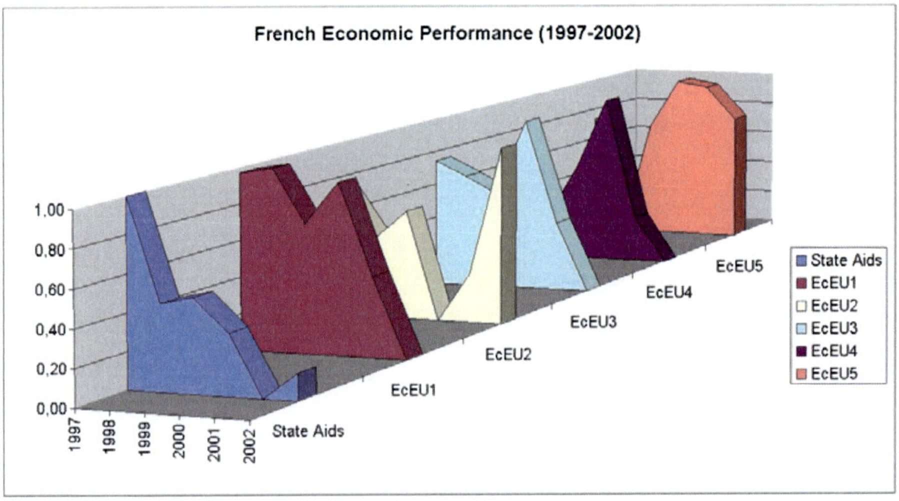

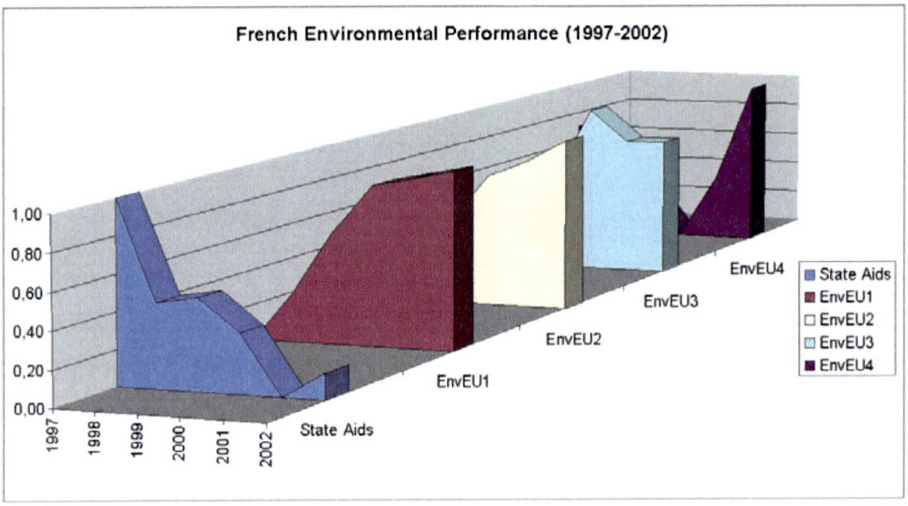

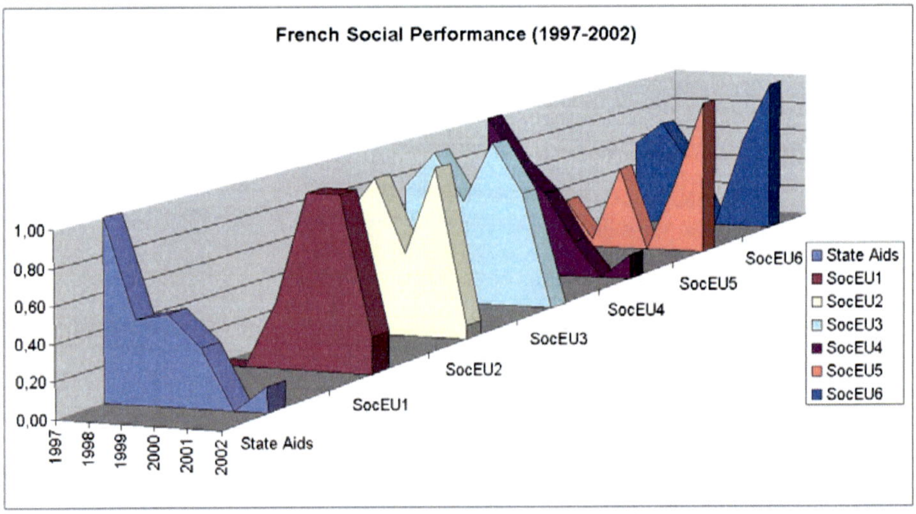

Figure 4. French Sustanible Results.

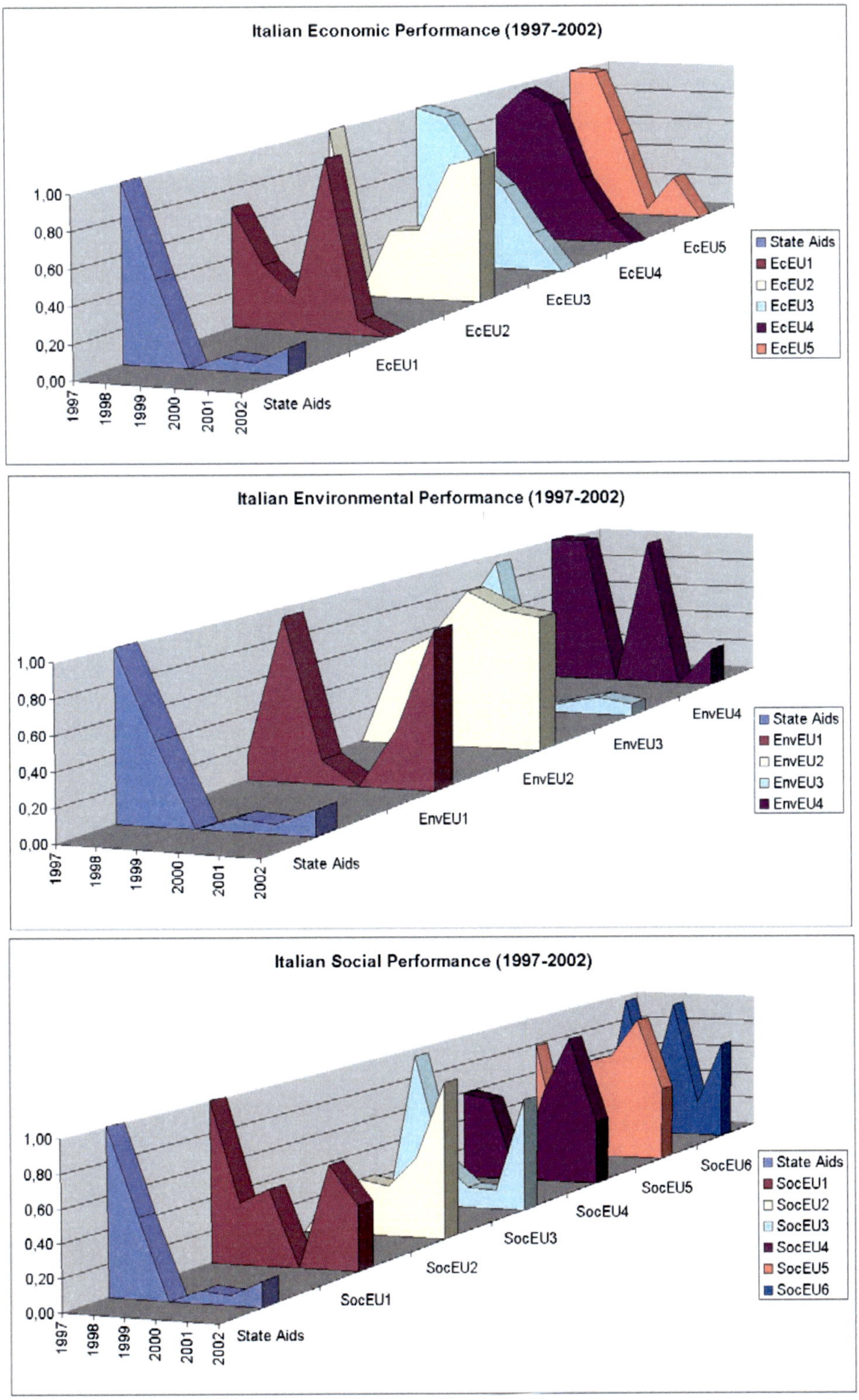

Figure 5. Italian Sustanible Results.

3.2. Results from the Spanish Sector Analysis

The results obtained from the analysis are shown in table 8 (hypothesis H1), table 9 (hypothesis H2), and table 10 (hypothesis H3). They enable us to tentatively state that capital subsidies received by industrial enterprises have a positive or negative effect on business performance, this being measured in economic, environmental and social terms.

Table 8 shows the results obtained when testing hypothesis H1. According to the results, more heavily subsidised sectors only show better indicators than less subsidised sectors in market share, percentage of enterprises that carry out R&D activities, productive efficiency, (but only when efficiency is related to personnel costs), and in investor effort. The less subsidised sectors present better results in export activity, operating expenses, profitability, R&D expenditure, number of patents and productive efficiency related to volume of assets. The remaining variables do not show significant differences. The financial risk of subsidised sectors (debt repayment ability) does not improve. In this case, financial risk deterioration does not imply an increase in profitability. In contrast, the less subsidised sectors show greater profitability than the more heavily subsidised sectors. In this respect, capital subsidies do not explicitly appear to be economically or financially efficient.

As far as the environmental variables are concerned, we consider that the differences between the nature of the activity of each sector may have had an important influence on the results. Notwithstanding, results show that the more heavily subsidised sectors have worse emissions indicators than the less subsidised ones in all cases (table 9), which would suggest environmental inefficiencies in capital subsidies to industry. Nevertheless, we should emphasise the need for an in-depth study to establish more accurate conclusions.

With regard to the social efficiency, where socio-labour indexes are used, capital subsidies also appear to be inefficient (table 10). The more heavily subsidised sectors only show a greater indicator in terms of the number of employees, but it should be highlighted that they have worse quality employment due to their greater percentage of temporary employment. Furthermore, these sectors do not seem to present a greater rate of employment creation, remunerations or extra social contributions. In addition, the percentage of enterprises with steady employment reduction reveals no significant differences between the two samples. On the other hand, the IRA indicator, concerning safety at work, and the FemER ratio, which represents equality of opportunities, show better results in the less subsidised sectors.

Table 8. Spanish Industry Financial-economic performance

GRI	Variable	Sample	Mean	Median	K-S (Sig)		Levene St. (Sig)	K-W (Sig)	ANOVA Sig.	Sub effect
EC1	MS	(-) Sub	28.866	28.200	*0.000	(a)	*0.000	*0.000	*0.002	+
		(+) Sub	**30.225**	**29.700**	*0.000	(b)	*0.007			
EC2	FS/NATOI	(-) Sub	**0.252**	**0.238**	*0.000	(a)	0.436	*0.000	*0.000	-
		(+) Sub	0.202	0.179	*0.000	(b)	0.574			
	ExEn.	(-) Sub	**74.061**	**72.700**	*0.000	(a)	0.165	*0.002	*0.007	-
		(+) Sub	69.966	75.000	*0.000	(b)	0.302			
EC3	OE/NATOI	(-) Sub	0.707	0.704	0.200	(a)	*0.009	*0.002	*0.007	-
		(+) Sub	**0.724**	**0.726**	0.200	(b)	*0.009			
EC5	Re	(-) Sub	26,714	25,773	*0.002	(a)	0.157	0.271	0.264	NULL
		(+) Sub	25,853	24,304	*0.000	(b)	0.126			
EC6	ORE	(-) Sub	**14.245**	**15.500**	*0.000	(a)	0.146	*0.000	*0.005	-
		(+) Sub	11.229	12.900	*0.000	(b)	0.130			
	DClt	(-) Sub	**8.011**	6.600	0.000	(a)	0.462	0.957	0.818	NULL
		(+) Sub	7.887	**6.900**	0.000	(b)	0.564			
	DCst	(-) Sub	7.592	6.000	0.000	(a)	0.700	0.864	0.944	NULL
		(+) Sub	**7.694**	**6.200**	0.000	(b)	0.700			
	DRA	(-) Sub	0.170	0.166	*0.002	(a)	0.344	0.349	0.300	NULL
		(+) Sub	0.162	0.161	*0.002	(b)	0.359			
EC13	No R&D	(-) Sub	50.598	**55.300**	*0.000	(a)	*0.003	*0.002	*0.004	+
		(+) Sub	**55.534**	51.900	*0.000	(b)	*0.009			
	R&D/TS	(-) Sub	1.915	**1.800**	*0.000	(a)	**0.052	*0.000	0.548	-
		(+) Sub	**2.661**	0.900	*0.000	(b)	0.263			
	RP	(-) Sub	**0.966**	**0.100**	*0.000	(a)	*0.000	*0.000	*0.002	-
		(+) Sub	0.160	0.100	*0.000	(b)	*0.007			
Others	NATOI/TA	(-) Sub	**1.191**	**1.202**	0.200	(a)	*0.000	*0.008	*0.002	-
		(+) Sub	1.105	1.144	*0.002	(b)	*0.000			
	NATOI/PC	(-) Sub	5.325	5.105	*0.047	(a)	*0.000	*0.000	*0.000	+
		(+) Sub	**6.643**	**6.107**	*0.000	(b)	*0.000			
	GVAfc/PC	(-) Sub	1.558	1.545	*0.031	(a)	*0.000	*0.000	*0.000	+
		(+) Sub	**1.711**	**1.680**	**0.081	(b)	*0.000			
	ORNA	(-) Sub	**13.102**	**12.900**	*0.000	(a)	**0.084	**0.062	*0.000	-
		(+) Sub	10.554	11.500	*0.000	(b)	**0.062			
	IE	(-) Sub	4.792	3.600	*0.000	(a)	*0.047	*0.026	0.113	+
		(+) Sub	**6.754**	**4.300**	*0.000	(b)	0.164			

(a) Based on Mean, (b) Based on Median.

* Significant at 5% **Significant at 10%.

(+) The more heavily subsidised sector indexes are significantly better than the less subsidised sector indexes.

(-) The less subsidised sector indexes are significantly better than the more heavily subsidised sector indexes.

NULL: There is no effect.

Table 9. Spanish Industry Environmental performance

GRI	Variable	Sample	Mean	Median	K-S (Sig)	Levene St. (Sig)		K-W (Sig)	ANOVA Sig.	Sub effect
EN8	Sox	(-) Sub	9.66E-04	1.67E-04	*0.000	(a)	*0.000	*0.005	*0.003	-
EN10		(+) Sub	**2.91E-03**	**3.41E-04**	*0.000	(b)	*0.003			
	Nox	(-) Sub	5.05E-04	1.61E-04	*0.000	(a)	*0.000	*0.000	*0.000	-
		(+) Sub	**2.65E-03**	**1.75E-03**	*0.000	(b)	*0.000			
	NMVOC	(-) Sub	1.32E-03	4.12E-04	*0.000	(a)	*0.014	0.299	0.715	NULL
		(+) Sub	**1.45E-03**	**1.60E-03**	*0.001	(b)	0.528			
	CH4	(-) Sub	**2.78E-04**	5.66E-06	*0.000	(a)	*0.000	*0.047	0.130	-
		(+) Sub	1.11E-04	**7.33E-05**	*0.000	(b)	**0.097			
	CO	(-) Sub	7.41E-04	3.80E-04	*0.000	(a)	*0.000	*0.000	*0.000	-
		(+) Sub	**7.44E-03**	**4.88E-03**	*0.000	(b)	*0.000			
	CO2	(-) Sub	1.70E-04	2.92E-05	*0.000	(a)	*0.000	*0.000	*0.000	-
		(+) Sub	**9.13E-04**	**2.64E-04**	*0.000	(b)	*0.000			
	N2O	(-) Sub	**7.67E-05**	2.72E-06	*0.000	(a)	0.125	*0.001	0.854	-
		(+) Sub	7.03E-05	**1.38E-05**	*0.000	(b)	0.793			

(a) Based on Mean, (b) Based on Median.

* Significant at 5%. **Significant at 10%.

(+) The more subsidised sectors indexes are significantly better than the less subsidised sectors indexes.

(-) The less subsidised sectors indexes are significantly better than the more subsidised sectors indexes.

NULL: There is no effect.

Table 10. Spanish Industry Social performance

GRI	Variable	Sample	Mean	Median	K-S (Sig)	Levene St. (Sig)		K-W (Sig)	ANOVA Sig.	Sub effect
LA1	NE	(-) Sub	146.39	147.57	*0.038	(a)	*0.000	*0.000	*0.000	+
		(+) Sub	**227.29**	**252.50**	0.161	(b)	*0.000			
	TE	(-) Sub	16.994	16.600	*0.005	(a)	0.485	*0.000	*0.000	-
		(+) Sub	**20.269**	**20.500**	0.200	(b)	0.477			
LA2	EC	(-) Sub	0.007	0.005	0.151	(a)	0.638	0.570	0.553	NULL
		(+) Sub	**0.014**	**0.012**	0.200	(b)	0.637			
LA12	ExCon	(-) Sub	**2,728**	**2,577**	*0.003	(a)	0.642	0.452	0.388	NULL
		(+) Sub	2,568	2,178	*0.000	(b)	0.791			
LA4	EPER	(-) Sub	12.839	9.400	*0.000	(a)	*0.000	0.676	0.155	NULL
		(+) Sub	**15.348**	**9.800**	*0.000	(b)	*0.012			
LA5	IRA	(-) Sub	6,929.5	5,816.0	*0.000	(a)	0.215	*0.000	*0.000	-
		(+) Sub	**13,468.0**	**13,265.3**	0.200	(b)	0.116			
LA11	FemER	(-) Sub	**0.290**	**0.250**	*0.000	(a)	*0.000	*0.000	*0.000	-
		(+) Sub	0.144	0.114	*0.000	(b)	*0.002			

(a) Based on Mean, (b) Based on Median.

* Significant at 5% . **Significant at 10%.

(+) The more heavily subsidised sector indexes are significantly better than the less subsidised sector indexes.

(-) The less subsidised sector indexes are significantly better than the more heavily subsidised sector indexes.

NULL: There is no effect.

4. CONCLUSION

The manufacturing sector has traditionally benefited more than others from the EU State aid. Since its origins, the EU has incorporated aspects of economic, social and environmental protection into its objectives. According to them, the end target of the aids goes beyond the economic goals and focuses on a more sustainable framework. Economic development, social cohesion, and environmental protection are present not only in several EU Treaties, but also in public policies. At the Gothenburg European Council (2001), the EU specified a Sustainable Development Strategy, adding an environmental dimension to the Lisbon strategy (which until that date had only covered social and economic dimensions), and establishing the principle of a coordinated examination of the economic, social and environmental effects of all policies as the basis for the Union's Sustainable Development Strategy.

To our knowledge, the empirical literature on the evaluation of public policies supporting enterprise financing generally focuses on economic or financial impacts. In the same line as the aforementioned sustainable development strategy, our research centres on the development of a comprehensive effectiveness assessment of the public financial instruments designed for the manufacturing industry. Effectiveness in this case is understood not only as economic, but also as social and environmental one. To achieve the research objective we present a descriptive analysis based upon an array of company sustainable performance indicators, i.e. economic, social and environmental of a number of European Union countries and the evolution of the State aids transferred to industry.

In order to go in greater depth in the impact analysis of these financial instruments we analyse their social and environmental effectiveness by means of a sector study in the context of the Spanish industry results.

In the first place, the survey shows the existing limitations of the quality and availability of public information concerning the economic, social and environmental performance of the studied enterprise sectors.

The effectiveness of the State aids received by the manufacturing industries of different European Union countries has been analysed according to the evolution of a set of core indicators of Sustainable Development that has been generated by that sector and the volume of the public aids it has received.

The analysis has been limited by the impossibility to compare the different countries thus creating contextually dependent results inherent to each country and time period. In absolute terms, Germany, France and Italy are the prime aid recipients, although they are the ones with highest GDP volume.

The analysis of the graphics profile reveals that the level of the aids allocated is not linked to the evolution of the environmental indicators, but seems to present closer relation to the social and economic ones. A possible explanation may be the increment of environmental laws over the studied period, the high social protection level in countries such as Germany, France or Italy and the differences in State aids allocation among countries.

In any case and regarding the study contour, the EU Strategy for Sustainable Development approved in 2001 seems neither to have introduced any important changes leading to socially responsible results and therefore favourable for the sustainable development generated by the European manufacturing industry, nor to have increased the effectiveness of the State aids.

Nevertheless, the presented results do not demonstrate that the abolition of aids will be favourable for the sustainable development, since in countries like Italy and France present good results in years with high relative volume of State aids received.

This research also presents a sector study of the economic, social and environmental effectiveness of these financial instruments through an analysis of the Spanish industry. We have attempted to determine to what extent the most heavily subsidised sectors achieve better performance in economic, financial, social and environmental terms than less subsidised ones.

The results obtained suggest that capital subsidies do not seem to be effective in terms of sustainability. With regard to economic-financial effectiveness, the results only show a certain positive impact when we refer to productive effectiveness, market share, number of enterprises that undertake R&D activities or investor effort. In the remaining variables, the more heavily subsidised sectors do not show any improved economic or financial performance.

In relation to the environmental effectiveness of capital subsidies, results show that, in all cases, the more heavily subsidised sectors have worse emissions indicators than less subsidised ones. This fact would suggest low environmental effectiveness of capital subsidies to industry; nevertheless, we should highlight the need for an exhaustive study to establish more accurate conclusions, in light of the differences between the nature of each sector activity.

In terms of social effectiveness, the more heavily subsidised sectors only show better results than less subsidised sectors with regard to the number of employees. We can therefore conclude that capital subsidies do not seem effective in social terms.

5. References

AECA (1998). *Indicadores para la gestión empresarial.* Madrid: Spanish Accounting and Company Administration Association.

Albi, E. (2000). *Público y Privado. Un acuerdo necesario.* Barcelona: Ariel Ed.

Azapagic, A. (2004). Developing a framework for sustainable development indicators for the mining and minerals industry. *Journal of Cleaner Production,* 12(6), 639-662.

Becchetti, L., & Trovato, G. (2002). The determinants of growth for SMES. The role of the availability of external finance. *Small Business Economics,* 19(4), 291-306.

Bell, D.V., & Grinstein, M. (2002). *The role of Government in advancing corporate sustainability.* http://www.g7.utoronto.ca/scholar/2002/bell11062002.pdf

Bergström, F. (2000). Capital subsidies and the performance of firms. *Small Business Economics,* 14(3), 183-193.

Bragdon, J. H. Jr., & Karash, R. (2002). Living-asset stewardship: How organizational learning leads to exceptional market returns. *Reflections*, 4(1), 55-65.

Bronzini, R., & de Blasio, G. (2006). Evaluating the impact of investment incentives: The case of Italy's Law 488/1992. *Journal of Urban Economics,* 60(2), 327-349.

Calomiris, C., & Himmelberg, C.W. (1995). Government credit policy and industrial performance. Japanese machine tool producers, 1963-1991. *Policy Research Working Paper* 1.434. The World Bank.

Calvo-Flores, A., García, D., & Madrid, A. (2004). Efectos Económicos y Financieros de las Subvenciones a la Inversión en la Pyme. Un Estudio Empírico. *Revista Española de Financiación y Contabilidad,* 33(123), 899-933.

Carroll, A.B. (1979). A three Dimensional Conceptual Model of Corporate Performance. *Academy of Management Review,* 4(4), 497-505.

Christmann, P. (2000). Effects of best practices of environmental management on cost advantage: The role of complementary assets. *Academy of Management Journal,* 43(4), 663-680.

Clinch, J.P., & Dunne, L. (2006). Environmental tax reform: an assessment of social responses in Ireland. *Energy Policy,* 34(8), 950-959.

CODED (2006). *The Eurostat Concepts and Definitions Database.* http://forum.europa.eu.int/irc/dsis/coded/info/data/coded/en.htm

Czarnitzki, D. (2006). Research and Development in Small and Medium-Sized Enterprises: the Role of Financial Constraints and Public Funding. *Scottish Journal of Political Economy,* 53(3), 335-357.

David, P.A., Hall, B.H., & Toole, A.A. (2000). Is public R&D a complement or substitute for private R&D? A review of the econometric evidence. *Research Policy,* 29 (4/5), 497-530.

De la Cuesta-González, M., & Valor-Martínez, C. (2004). Fostering Corporate Social Responsibility Through Public Initiative: From the EU to the Spanish Case. *Journal of Business Ethics,* 55(3), 275-293.

De la Cuesta-González, M., Muñoz-Torres, M.J., & Fernández-Izquierdo, M.A. (2006). Analysis of Social Performance in the Spanish Financial Industry Through Public Data. A Proposal. *Journal of Business Ethics,* 69(3), 289-304.

Elkington, J. (1997). *Cannibals with Forks: The Triple Bottom Line of 21st Century Business.* Oxford: Capstone Publishing.

European Commission (2001). *Green Paper: Promoting an European framework for Corporate Social Responsibility.* http://ec.europa.eu/employment_social/ soc-dial/csr/greenpaper.htm

European Commission (2002a). *State aid scoreboard. COM(2002) 242 final.* http://eur-lex.europa.eu/LexUriServ/site/en/com/2002/com2002_0242en01.pdf

European Commission (2002b). *Communication from the Commission, concerning Corporate Social Responsibility: A business contribution to Sustainable Development.* http://ec.europa.eu/employment_social/soc-dial/csr/csr2002_en.pdf

European Commission (2003a). *Mapping Instruments for Corporate Social Responsibility.* http://ec.europa.eu/employment_social/soc-dial/csr/mapping_ final.pdf

European Commission (2003b). *State Aid Scoreboard, Spring. COM(2003)225 final.* http://ec.europa.eu/comm/competition/state_aid/studies_reports/archive/2003_en.pdf

European Commission (2004). *Corporate Social Responsibility. National public policies in the European Union.* http://ec.europa.eu/employment_social/ publications/2004/ke 1103005_en.pdf

Eurostat (2006). *Statistical Office of the European Communities.* Available at: http://epp.eurostat.ec.europa.eu/portal/page?_pageid=1090,30070682,1090_33076576&_dad=portal&_schema=PORTAL

Figge, F., & Hahn, T. (2004). Sustainable value added- measuring corporate contributions to sustainable beyond eco-efficiency. *Ecological Economics,* 48(2), 173-187.

Fox, T., Ward, H., & Howard, B. (2002). *Public sector roles in strengthening corporate social responsibility: a baseline study.* Washington: Corporate Social Responsibility Practice, The World Bank.

Freeman, R.E. (1984). *Strategic Management: A Stakeholder Approach.* Marshfield: Pitman Publishing Inc.

Fuest, C., & Tillessen, P. (2005). Why do governments use closed ended subsidies to support entrepreneurial investment? *Economics Letters,* 89(1), 24-30.

Gabe, T. M., & Kraybill, D.S. (2002). The effect of state economic development incentives on employment growth of establishments. *Journal of Regional Science,* 42(4), 703-730.

García-Quevedo, J. (2004). Do public subsidies complement business R&D? A meta-analysis of the econometric evidence. *Kyklos,* 57(1), 87-102.

Girma, S., Görg, H., & Strobl, L. (2003). *Government Grants, Plant Survival and Employment Growth: A Micro-Econometric Analysis.* Discussion Paper No. 838. Bonn: Institute for the Study of Labor (IZA).

Glazyrina, I., Glazyrinb, V., & Vinnichenkoa, S. (2006). The polluter pays principle and potential conflicts in society. *Ecological Economics,* 59(3), 324-330.

Görg, H., & Strobl, E. (2006). Do Government Subsidies Stimulate Training Expenditure? Microeconometric Evidence from Plant-Level Data. *Southern Economic Journal,* 72(4), 860-876.

GRI (2002). *Sustainability Reporting Guidelines.* Boston: Global Reporting Initiative.

GRI (2006). *Sustainability Reporting Guidelines, G3. Global Reporting Initiative* http://www.globalreporting.org/ReportingFramework/G3Online/

Hujer, R., & Radic, D. (2005). Evaluating the impacts of subsidies on innovation activities in Germany. *Scottish Journal of Political Economy,* 52(4), 565-586.

Hyytinen, A., & Toivanen, O. (2005). Do financial constraints hold back innovation and growth?: Evidence on the role of public policy. *Research Policy,* 34(9), 1385-1403.

Harris, R., & Robinson, C. (2005). Industrial policy in Great Britain and its effect on total factor productivity in manufacturing plants, 1990-1998. *Scottish Journal of Political Economy,* 51(4), 528-543.

Klassen, R.D., & Whybark, D.C. (1999). The impact of environmental technologies on manufacturing performance. *Academy of Management Journal,* 42(6), 599-615.

Koga, T. (2005). R&D Subsidy and Self-Financed R&D: The Case of Japanese High-Technology Start-Up. *Small Business Economics,* 24(1), 53-62.

Konrad, A., Steurer, R., Langer, M.E., & Martinuzzi, A. (2006). Empirical Findings on Business-Society Relations in Europe. *Journal of Business Ethics,* 63(1), 89-105.

Krajnc, D., & Glavič, P. (2005a). A model for integrated assessment of sustainable development. *Resources, Conservation and Recycling,* 43(2), 189-208.

Krajnc, D., & Glavič, P. (2005b). How to compare companies on relevant dimensions of sustainability. *Ecological Economics,* 55(4), 551-563.

Margolis, J., & Walsh, J. (2003). Misery Loves Companies: Rethinking Social Initiatives by Business. *Administrative Science Quarterly,* 48(2), 268-305

Moneva, J.M., Rivera-Lirio, J.M., & Muñoz-Torres, M.J. (2007). The corporate stakeholder commitment and social and financial performance. *Industrial Management & Data Systems,* 107(1), 84-102.

Morgan, R., & Strong, C. (2003). Business performance and dimensions of strategic orientation. *Journal of Business Research,* 56(3), 163-176

Muñoz-Torres, M.J., Rivera-Lirio, J.M. & Moneva, J.M. (2007). The sustainability approach of organisations. A fuzzy-logic-based measurement. *Paper presented at the MIC'07 – 8th Management International Conference,* Portorož, Slovenia, November.

OECD (2006). STAN Indicators Database. Organisation for Economic Co-operation and Development http://www.oecd.org

Ohashi, H. (2005). Learning by doing, export subsidies, and industry growth: Japanese steel in the 1950s and 1960s. *Journal of International Economics,* 66(2), 297-323.

Orlitzky, M., Schmidt, F.L., & Rynes, S. (2003). Corporate Social and Financial Performance: A Meta-analysis. *Organization Studies,* 24 (3), 403-441.

Pablo Marti, F. (2004). Promoting the Entry of New Firms. *Small Business Economics* 22(3-4), 209-221.

Popp, D. (2006). R&D subsidies and climate policy: Is there a "free lunch"? *Climatic Change,* 77(3-4), 311-341.

Rivera-Lirio, J.M. & Muñoz-Torres, M.J. (2007). Public Policies, European Industry and Sustainable Development. A Fuzzy Logic Based Study. Paper presented at the XIV Congress of International Association for Fuzzy-Set Management and Economy. *Computational Intelligence Applied to New Digital Economy and Business Ecosystems,* Poiana Brasov – Romania, November.

Samaniego, R.M. (2006). Industrial subsidies and technology adoption in general equilibrium. *Journal of Economic Dynamics & Control,* 30 (9-10), 1589-1614.

Sakano, R., Obeng, K., & Azam, G. (1997). Subsidies and inefficiency: stochastic frontier approach. *Contemporary Economic Policy,* 15(3), 113-127.

State Aid Scoreboard (2006). *Statistical tables, Country-specific tables.* http://ec.europa.eu/comm/competition/state_aid/scoreboard/stat_tables.html

Trovato, G., & Alfó, M. (2006). Credit rationing and the financial structure of Italian small and medium enterprises. *Journal of Applied Economics,* 9(1), 167-184.

Wagner, T. (2005). Environmental policy and the equilibrium rate of unemployment. *Journal of Environmental Economics and Management,* 49(1), 132-156.

World Commission on Environment and Development (1987). *Our Common Future.* Oxford: Oxford University Press.

Zhu, P., Xu, W., & Lundin, N. (2006). The impact of government's fundings and tax incentives on industrial R&D investments-Empirical evidences from industrial sectors in Shanghai. *China Economic Review,* 17(1), 51-69.

In: Corporate Social Responsibility
Editor: Adam R. Timpere
ISBN: 978-1-60456-284-2

Chapter 2

CORPORATE SOCIAL RESPONSIBILITY: FROM SIDELINE SPECIALIST TO MAINSTREAM ACTIVITY

Graham Hubbard
School of Business, The University of Adelaide, Australia

ABSTRACT

To date, corporate social responsibility (CSR) activities have been the responsibility of specialists in organizations. 'CSR' has been seen as a specialist activity, an add-on to the mainstream business, something nice to be 'seen' to be doing. Global events in 2006 changed the paradigm for organizations, for individuals and for countries. CSR has developed a momentum that is destined to lead to it being a mainstream business activity attitude and influence on organization decisions. The paper outlines the changes that are likely to be made within organizations as a result, in terms of three aspects – the organization/business strategy, operational changes and changes in measuring and reporting organizational performance. Through making these changes, CSR will become a part of the mainstream way of organizational thinking and behaving and organizations will think and act differently as a result.

To date, corporate social responsibility (CSR) activities have been the responsibility of specialists in organizations. 'CSR' has been seen as a specialist activity, an add-on to the mainstream business, something nice to be 'seen' to be doing. It has been located in marketing, operations or corporate services functions of the organization. Global events in 2006 changed the paradigm for organizations, and for individuals and countries. CSR has developed a momentum that is destined to lead to it being a mainstream business activity attitude and influence on organization decisions. This paper first outlines the current position which CSR has occupied as a specialist sideline. The key events of 2006 are then outlined, followed by the responses which have occurred, at individual, non-government (NGO), community, organization and government levels. The paper outlines the changes that are likely to be made within organizations as a result in terms of three aspects – the organization/business strategy, operational changes and changes in measuring and reporting organizational performance. Through making these changes, CSR will become a part of the mainstream way of organizational thinking and behaving.

CSR has many definitions. We model our definition of

> 'operating the organisation in such a way that considers the needs of all its stakeholders and the natural environment'

on Waddock and Bodwell (2004). CSR has two dimensions to be concerned with, apart from the normal economic considerations required to operate an organization. They are the social dimension, considered to include customer, employee, supplier, community and government stakeholders, and the environmental dimension, both within the organisation's operations and outside it (see Figure 1). Of course environment issues are also part of the 'social' aspect of the organisation's responsibility but, due to its particular and growing short-term importance, it is increasingly singled out as a unique element.

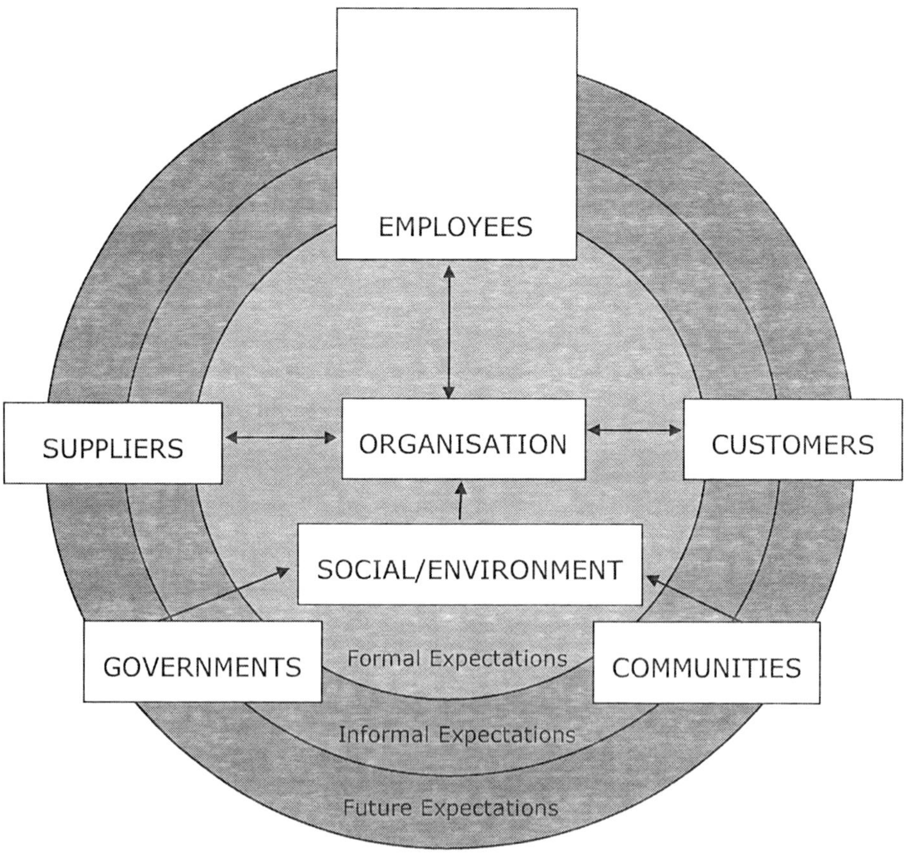

Figure 1. A CSR Framework of Responsibilities for Organisations.

Aguilera et al (2007) proposed a model of CSR that recognizes the wide variety of different motivations which the stakeholder groups affected by the organization have in seeking 'CSR' themselves from the organisation. They conclude that the actual CSR that results in any organization will depend on the interplay of these different motivations, the strength and power of the particular stakeholder groups and the institutional context in which the organization finds itself. Figure 2 outlines an adapted version of Aguilera et al's model.

Stakeholder	Motivations	Mechanisms for achieving 'CSR' from own perspective
Employees	Salary Good working conditions Health and safety Job security Equitable treatment Involvement Development opportunities	Contractual employment agreement Employment laws Involvement Seek help from outside stakeholders
Managers	As above except 'power' instead of 'involvement'	As above, except 'decisionmaking ability' instead of 'involvement'
Customers	Good products Fair prices Fair treatment No safety problems from products	Complaints, advice Returns Not buying Legal action Media action Involve other stakeholders
Suppliers	Continued business Growth Fair prices Fair treatment	Complaints, advice Not selling Legal action Media action Involve other stakeholders
NGOs	Protect special interest group(s)	Complaints, advice Media action Legal action Involve other stakeholders
Communities	Economic impact Growth Ethical employer Good relationship Minimum negative environmental impacts	Complaints, advice Media action Legal action Regulations
Governments	Taxes Growth No political problems Minimum negative environmental impacts	Complaints, advice Media action Legal action New laws, regulations

Figure 2. Stakeholders, Motivations and Mechanisms for achieving CSR outcomes.

This helps to explain why particular organizations have reacted quite differently to the concept of CSR to date. For instance, mining organizations have been under great CSR pressure for some time, due to the enormity of the upheaval and impact of their operations on the environment and on the often small local communities in which they operate. The external attention to the impacts of their emissions, and a continual series of catastrophic events in mining (eg mine collapses, land and water contamination, social exploitation and local community social impacts) have led to miners being one of the first industries to address these CSR issues. On the other hand, many tertiary industries such as financial services, education, retailing, have been late comers to CSR, seeing themselves as having limited impact on both the human communities and their environment and having faced limited external pressure from their stakeholders.

Organizations are now seen as having to measure performance on three dimensions – economic, social and environmental – and to do well on all three to be considered to be performing 'well'. This new, wider and more demanding perspective on the organisation's responsibilities has occurred over time as the importance of the impact of the organisation's activities on its various stakeholder groups, and on the natural environment, have been recognized as increasingly important. Another key driver has been the increasing recognition that the world faces resource constraints and usage consequences so that humans in total cannot continue to operate as they have.

CSR as Specialist Activity

This view of CSR is quite different from recently-held perspectives (which are still held in many organizations), which focus mainly on corporate marketing and philanthropy. In this view of CSR, by making payments and contributing time to community-based organizations and charities, such as the arts, health, welfare, education or other not-for-profit groups, the organization could be seen to be a 'good citizen' through the amount of support given to such groups.

This increasingly outdated view sees CSR as being a sub-function of functions of the organization, such as marketing, operations or corporate services. Those organisations placing CSR activities within the marketing function see it as an indirect way of promoting the organization, of creating 'feel good' images of it. While these perceptions might subsequently have a positive influence purchase behaviour, this is often seen as desirable, but not necessary. Alternatively, in cases of unsocial products or services, it is seen as a way to offset negative perceptions about the organization or its products. For instance, tobacco, alcohol, fast food and confectionery manufacturers have consistently been major sponsors of community events, making it more difficult for the community to criticize them, in case the benefits from CSR activities are withdrawn as a result.

Those placing CSR in operations similarly do this to offset negative aspects of the operations, such as large scale change to the environment from mining, agriculture or forestry operations. Those placing CSR in corporate services see it as a financial activity, with the amounts to be distributed often based on personal corporate whims or interests, rather than any business relationships. For instance, sporting sponsorships are often related to the personal interests of the CEO or top management team.

This older view of CSR means it is not seen an organization-wide issue, but a functional issue. Hence it is seen to be of lower importance. Indeed, hostility to CSR exists in many organizations, where it is seen as a cost that decreases shareholder (economic) value, with no clear benefits coming from the activity.

A Paradigm Change: The Events of 2006

In 2006, several unrelated events occurred which changed the views of so many people around the world that the importance of CSR increased dramatically. One event was the release of a documentary film, *An Inconvenient Truth*, narrated by Al Gore, former US Vice President and narrowly failed presidential candidate in 2000. Not noted for his oratory skills as a politician, coming from a country not noted for its environmental concerns and using a normally non-entertaining documentary style, Gore's film, with its powerful images of cataclysmic environmental changes, became a landmark mass entertainment film which left most who saw it significantly changed in their attitudes to the state of their world. Many signed up to become 'ambassadors' to take the message to their organizations and community groups. Many convinced their organizations to show the film to their employees, thus expanding the influence of the film significantly. In October 2007, Gore was given the Nobel Peace prize for his work in influencing so many people to change their views. Strangely, he remains a prophet without great honour in his own country, which leads the way in unsustainable environmental practices.

Disturbing as the images from *An Inconvenient Truth* were, many people and most organizations were concerned that the changes required to be made would have such significant economic costs and would cause such economic dislocation that they felt unable to support them. What would be the point of adding pollution controls, or increasing the costs of products if we could no longer afford to buy them or they could no longer be sold on open international markets when other countries did not similarly care about environmental costs?

In September 2006, shortly after *An Inconvenient Truth* was shown, the Stern Report, a report commissioned by the UK government into the economic effects of climate change, was released. Stern, a widely respected economist, confirmed that climate change was a reality and that it must be addressed immediately from both an economic and a scientific perspective. Most importantly, the report concluded that the required changes could be made to the global economy at a cost of only around 1% of Gross Domestic Product (GDP). This is the equivalent of less than a third of one year's GDP and is less than the impact of a one year recession.

Stern was a fiscal conservative, an economist and not a 'greenie' with an axe to grind. The UK government similarly was viewed as economically credible. Therefore, Stern's report, which suggested for the first time that the task of economically adapting to climate change – increasingly being seen as the key part of CSR in the short term – was feasible, was embraced. More than that, Stern's warning to begin national and organizational action immediately added fuel to Gore's populist message. Now people, governments and business could see a feasible economic outcome from undertaking climate change.

In May 2006, the Intergovernmental Panel on Climate Change made its report on the ecological state of the world. While its earlier reports (1997 and 2002) had strongly hinted at the deteriorating environment and particularly at the role mankind in increasing world temperatures, this report was unequivocal. It concluded that the temperatures of the world were changing significantly and were increasing overall. The cause of the changes were man-made, particularly through greenhouse gas (GHG) emissions, specifically CO2, which had reached 430 parts per million. Immediate action was needed to change organizational and community practices to stop further increases. The IPCC was also awarded the Nobel Peace Prize in 2007 for its contribution to bringing this critical global issue to world attention.

The main causes of environmental problems in these reports were seen to be the use of fossil fuels, the loss of carbon-absorbing forests, the volumes of activity and the use of inefficient and harmful technologies. Actions recommended included seeking greater energy efficiency, switching from coal for power generation, using more efficient vehicles and more public transport, making buildings, industry and agriculture more efficient, regrowing and protecting forests, and changing waste management practices.

Even if action were taken immediately, due to the delays in those actions taking effect, GHG emissions would continue to rise, such that further temperature rises of 1-5C were likely to occur. 0.7C has occurred to date, so the likely future changes are already much greater than have been experienced, changes which have themselves been noted by many people and which were highlighted in *An Inconvenient Truth*. The world would have to not just stop increasing emissions, but would have to significantly decrease emissions from current levels. Given increasing global population, expectations of increased standards of living for everyone, this is an extraordinarily challenging prospect.

After these three reports/events, even the US and Australian governments – the only two nations of significance not to sign the Kyoto Protocol, whereby countries promised only to increase their GHG emissions by small percentages on their 1990 levels – finally admitted that climate change was a reality and that national and international action was required to influence organization and individual behavior.

These three major events were supplemented by an observed pattern of increasing natural disasters around the world. At the end of 2006, 11 of the hottest 12 years ever had occurred in a row. Major bush fires occurred in many countries, often earlier in the season than ever before. In Australia, at the start of the summer season in November 2006, governments were forced to impose massive water restrictions across virtually the whole of the continent for the first time ever, as the long running drought failed to break. The forecast for 2007-08 was that no water at all would be available for irrigators on the country's major Murray-Murrumbidgee river system, with significant negative GDP effects expected. Climatologists saw these events not only as typical of future forecasts. Worse, they saw these events as likely to be outdone by future events. For instance, in 2007 it is clear that global temperatures are actually at the upper end of the 1-5C global warming scenario and it is predicted that the complete Arctic ice shelf will disappear within just 6 more years – in 2013!!

Earlier Warnings Ignored

Many years ago, similar cataclysmic warnings had been issued about man's effect on the state of the natural environment. Meadows et al (1972) produced a famous model of the world for 'The Club of Rome', a group of 30 eminent non-government, independent, international thinkers, using a Massachussets Institute of Technology international project team. Entitled *The Limits to Growth*, the model had four interdependent components – economic, political, natural and social systems. The study concluded (p 23-24):

> If the present growth trends in world population, industrialization, pollution, food production and resource depletion continue unchanged, the limits to growth on this planet will be reached sometime within the next one hundred years...It is possible to alter these growth trends and to establish a condition of ecological and economic stability that is sustainable...If the world's people decide to strive for this second out come rather than the first, the sooner they begin working to attain it, the greater will be their chances.

It saw that any one of the five major variables – world population, industrialization, pollution, food production and resource depletion – could independently cause the collapse of the system and the combination certainly would. Management and control of all five were required for future survival. Since that time, specific issues which they identified – DDT, food production, land productivity, mercury consumption, metal consumption per person – have been addressed and others which they did not explicitly raise – eg CFCs, the ozone layer – have also. China's one-child policy has had a significant impact on its population growth, as has education in developed countries, where population growth is below replacement levels. Interestingly, the study predicted a CO2 level of 380 parts per million in 2000, the issue which is currently 'suddenly' being seen as a key issue... In this respect, these predictions have been very accurate and gave the world plenty of time to address the issues, but relatively little action has been taken.

Similarly, Australia's 2007 Man of the Year, Professor Tim Flannery, produced a book in 2005, *The Weather Makers: the history and future impact of climate change*, which raised all the issues that converged in 2006, but, powerful and well written though this book is and was, it did not have the impact the 2006 events did. However, Flannery's role as Australian of the Year in 2007 has enabled him to spread his message much more widely now and receives much more public attention.

Corporate and Social Responses to the Events of 2006

As a result of the collective impact of these events, in 2006 a massive wave of environmental and social change has been released across all ranges of communities. Individuals, NGOs, communities, businesses and governments have responded in a wide variety of ways.

Many individuals have long known of these environmental effects, but have been effectively sidelined during the 1990s and 2000s. Following the significant sharemarket and property recessions that occurred in most countries in the early 1990s, the Asian foreign exchange collapses and realignments in the mid-1990s and the Internet bubble bursts and Y2K fizzles of 2000-01, economic values dominated organization thinking. The increasing deregulation of international trade has also led to a focus on economic issues, in the face of increasingly cheap imports, particularly from China.

Generation Ys, now represented in the workforce in significant numbers, have widely differing attitudes to their predecessors. They expect that organizations will be 'cool' places to work (fuelled by Internet dotcom employment practices also, which encouraged the development of social communities and networks within the workplace) that will be environmentally-oriented. Gen Ys have been known to quiz CEOs about the organisation's values and practices and, if not satisfied that they are desirable, not to take the job. Many older workers have embraced the concepts themselves attitudinally and in their home lives.

In terms of the environment, BP research shows that younger people (18-29) want to be seen to be doing the right thing, but are less likely to do much apart from recycling. The 30-44 year olds are less aware of green issues, but feel more guilty and are often prompted by their children. Older age groups (45-54) are more scared and worried but feel unable to affect change. The biggest changes seen were take up of 'green' electricity, installing solar energy, buying low energy whitegoods and switching to energy friendly detergents (Gettler, 2007). Thus, individuals in organizations have been ready and willing to make changes in their organizations, but those changes have only been made if the powerful management group has agreed to do so.

The focus of individuals, NGOs and communities also depends on local environments, consistent with Aguilera et al's (2007) model. Some communities and countries are more advanced than others, so what is 'new' or 'current' in one location is standard in another, or inconceivable elsewhere. For instance, the community of Vaxjo, Sweden, a town of around 85,000, decided in 1996 to cut out fossil fuels. It replaced coal with wood chips, sawdust and other wood waste to generate its power and also to simultaneously provide hot water to the city. It has replaced petrol with biogas buses and encourages people to take the bus or walk. Housing has been redesigned and high density living has been encouraged in place of urban sprawl. The Vaxjo model is being replicated in other Swedish towns, Sweden's annual GHG emissions per capita are 3.5 tonnes and falling, compared with over 20 for the US and Australia (Williams, 2007).

Non-government organizations (NGOs) have become powerful lobby groups during the last few years for CSR. For instance, the World Wildlife Fund argues for species diversity and preservation, the Wilderness Society and Conservation Foundations lobby for protection of natural environments, Greenpeace campaigns against what it sees as unsavoury or unsustainable business practices, Save the Children works for the rights of children and against child labour.

The business reaction has been more muted, though business people as individuals have also felt the need for much greater business response. For instance, a 2006 McKinsey survey of business executives found that only 3% thought that their company was doing a good job in handling social issues, with 70% seeing room for improvement, mostly substantial. Notably only 8% felt that organizations were genuinely concerned about CSR issues with almost 90% feeling that responses were motivated by PR or business interests. This is clearly old-perspective thinking about CSR. Nevertheless, environmental issues ranked third in expected effects on shareholder value over the next 5 years (Bonini et al, 2006). Again, however, the expected effect is negative, which means business executives are rarely in favour of such action, especially if it impacts their own incentive payments, which are usually based on financial performance, so directly.

However, times are changing. In 2006 however, significant groups of businesses began to stand up and be counted. While BP's John Browne is credited as being the first CEO of a multinational corporation to formally recognize and say his organization would respond to global warming in 1997, organisations such as the UK Corporate Leaders Group on Climate Change and the US Climate Action Partnership have recently been formed to formally lobby for businesses and governments to address wider CSR issues. Australia's Business Roundtable on Climate Change, a small group of concerned major businesses, have positively and publically addressed the need for business to address environmental issues, taking a different view from the major Business Council of Australia's perspective at the time (in 2007, this has now changed). They argued that a 60% reduction in GHG emissions was necessary by 2050 and that the economic effects on business were much more limited than had previously been imagined.

Tomorrow's Company, a UK research-based, pro-business NGO, published its enquiry on the global corporation of the future in 2007. It concluded that (p 4):

> The survival and success of tomorrow's global company is bound up with the health of a complex global system made up of three interdependent sub-systems – the natural environment, the social and political system and the global economy. ...the purpose of tomorrow's global company is 'to provide ever better goods and services in a way that is profitable, ethical and respects the environment, individuals and the communities in which it operates'...should expand its view of success and redefine it in terms of lasting positive impacts for business, society and the environment.

A Business Council of Australia survey found that only 7% of major companies did not require a business case for their philanthropic contributions in 2007 (Potter and Symonds, 2007). This specifically overcomes the objection that philanthropy is not in the interests of shareholders. Consistent with this, a survey of Australian directors indicated that only 40% ranked shareholders first amongst groups that were to be addressed by directors, compared with 80% in the US (Durkin 2007). Thus we can see that businesses too are slowly changing to embrace the need for a wider perspective on business and business success.

During the course of 2006 and 2007, many businesses began to declare that they would become 'carbon neutral'. This meant they intended to either reduce their CO_2 emissions to zero or, where this was not possible, pay other organizations to offset their carbon emissions, for instance, by planting trees to absorb the equivalent amount of carbon generated by the business's operations. For instance, BSkyB, the UK pay-TV company, went 'carbon neutral' in 2006. In 2007, its parent organization, the giant media and entertainment company News Corporation, announced that it too would become carbon neutral by 2008. Further, News announced that climate change needed to be repositioned as 'exciting' and it would use its publications to promote such a campaign. For instance, the *Adelaide Advertiser* now has a '1C' (one degree Celsius) campaign, with daily tips and articles about how individuals can contribute to a wide variety of activities that contribute towards global warming. This was rather remarkable, as News Corporation papers had until that time been known for being skeptical and negative about climate change. The change of view of the key owner, Rupert Murdoch, caused a wholesale change in editorial attitudes to occur within the corporation.

Notably missing from major action have been governments. While most governments signed the Kyoto Protocol, few countries seem to have made much real change as a result of this process and few are expected to meet their Kyoto Protocol commitments to decrease carbon emissions by 2011. However, recognizing this, in 2005, the European Union began a carbon trading rights scheme for a major part of industry responsible for a major part of the EU emissions. Under the scheme, organizations have to pay for any carbon emissions beyond those for which they have been given permits. While the scheme has had major problems (primarily due to generous handing out of permits at the start, so that carbon rights have traded at relatively low prices), the psychological impact of having to consider paying for this emission, the actual payments and the clear prospect of higher future payments is driving innovation and change in the EU. The learning benefits to the whole world are also extremely valuable. By 2007, a number of governments had agreed to set specific CO2 target reductions, in both the short and long term (see Figure 3).

Country	Target
European Union	20% by 2020; no longer term target
UK	20% by 2020; 60% by 2050 (Opposition party: 25% by 2020; 80% by 2050)
Germany	50% by 2050
US	No target
California	1990 levels/25% by 2020; 80% by 2050
Japan	50% cut – no time frame
China	20% reduction in 'energy use per unit of GDP' by 2010
Australia	30% renewables by 2020 (Opposition party: no short term target; 60% by 2050)
New Zealand	Capped emissions by 2010

Figure 3. Government GHG Emission Targets in 2007.

Overall, there are fundamental similarities that need to be addressed in most countries and communities in the long run. Environmentally, the meta-issues of:

- what resources are used
- efficient resource use
- limiting emissions of all types, particularly toxic emissions
- recycling as much as possible of whatever wastes are produced

are the key concepts. What an organization uses, how efficiently it uses those resources, what products and waste emissions it produces and what happens to those products at the end of their lives are common issues that many organizations have to address for the good – and the survival – of the planet.

This has led to a common focus on:

- Resource use, particularly of non-renewables, resources with limited supply or those with dangerous emissions or by-products (eg oil, coal, chemicals)
- Water use (since clean water is fundamental to life and so many communities either do not have this or their supplies are reducing or are insecure)
- Energy use (since this is a key to GHG generation, particularly via oil and coal usage)
- GHG emissions (though in reality CO2 is focused on almost exclusively in public forums, to the exclusion of all other emissions)
- Recycling (since the less waste required, the more efficient the system is seen to be and the less resources have to be used for a particular quantity of production)

Socially, there is an increasingly common focus on the supply chain activities, including:

- employee treatment
- customer perceptions
- supplier treatment
- community relations

However, with the extraordinary focus on environmental issues at the moment – a situation which seems likely to be exacerbated over the next 5 years – strictly 'social' issues seem likely to remain poor cousins over this time period.

MEASURING ORGANIZATION PERFORMANCE

As the definition of organizational responsibility has changed from economic value creation alone to a wider view, a variety of performance measurement systems have begun to be developed to take a wider account of organizational performance, than simply economic, financial or shareholder value. The balanced scorecard (Kaplan and Norton 1992) measures financial, customer/market, short-term efficiency and long term growth and development performance of the organization. It therefore includes a 'social' measure of customer or market performance (eg customer satisfaction, customer complaints, market share are common measures) and can often include employee measures (eg employee morale, organizational climate, employee turnover) – another aspect of social performance. Indeed it can include whatever the organization wishes to include but, with the exception of customers, the sections are normally largely internally focused, so 'performacne' for most other external stakeholders is not likely to be considered in a balanced scorecard measurement system.

More recently, triple bottom line (economic, social, environmental - Elkington, 1997) reporting and a sustainable balanced scorecard (Hubbard, 2006) have been suggested as conceptual ways to expand the variety of stakeholders and issues considered in organisational performance measurement. However, these remain at the concept stage and have not been implemented in any significant way.

In 2002, the Global Reporting Initiative (GRI), a joint venture of the United Nations and many global businesses, developed a complex set of economic, social and environmental measures which organizations might assess themselves on. In 2006, the GRI produced the third version of their framework (see Figure 4 for a summary of the measures). The GRI framework seems to be developing as a standard worldwide, with now over 15,000 reports having been submitted to the corporateregister.com website since the GRI began. Nevertheless, there are many problems with the GRI framework (and all of the other multidimensional frameworks that have been developed), including:

Social Measures	Environment Measures
Suppliers	Materials used
Products and services	Energy used
Compliance	Water use
Transport	Biodiversity
Employment	Emissions, effluents and waste
Labour/management relations	
Health and safety	
Training and education	
Employment diversity and opportunity	
Employment non-discrimination	
Freedom of association and collective bargaining	
Child labour	
Disciplinary practices	
Security practices	
Indigenous rights	
Community impact	
Bribery and corruption	
Political contributions	
Competition and pricing	
Customer health and safety	
Product and services	
Advertising	
Respect for privacy	

Figure 4. The Global Reporting Initiative Reporting Framework.

- *Not all the measures are relevant for all organizations.* Financial reporting is increasingly globally standardized so that reports from one organization contain the same headings and information as reports from others, enabling comparison and benchmarking. This is not the case for the GRI framework. For instance, child labour may be an issue for retailers sourcing product from developing countries, but is unlikely to be an issue for financial service providers.
- *The measures are generally not certified.* Currently, reporting is largely self-assessed and self-reported. Some evidence suggests that organizations are reporting mainly the good aspects of their performance, rather than covering all aspects (Jones et al, 2005; O'Dwyer and Owen, 2005). While auditing systems are being developed (eg ISO 14064) and an auditing 'profession' is developing, a close reading of even those reports which profess to be externally verified indicates that the verification only applies to certain components of the particular report.
- *There are no benchmarks for performance.* Whilst we understand benchmarks in financial reports, where we can compare a return on equity of 15% pa or a sales growth rate of 10% pa across organizations, this is not well understood for social and environmental measures. For instance, if water usage is 2 kl/litre of production, is this good or bad? Without some sense of 'good' or 'standard' performance, actual performance can only be assessed as trend information at best (ie the organization is getting better or worse on a particular measure). What does a GHG emission of 2 tonnes mean? Can we compare this within an industry or across industries? What does a philanthropic contribution of $15m for the year mean? Can it be compared to

a competitor who contributes $30m when the contributions go to widely differing organizations and causes?

- *The current focus is largely on environmental measures alone.* Little attention is being given to social measure development. While customer satisfaction and employee morale are well developedconceptually, there is little agreement on what or how to measure social performance.
- *There is no way to 'add' the extremely complex set of measures.* The system includes almost 30 major categories of measures.For instance how do you add emissions volume and recycling percentages? Does one 'good' performance balance out a 'bad' result? This makes the final assessment of how an organization – as a whole – is doing on either environmental or social measures virtually impossible to do on an objective basis. Indeed, this complexity is likely to prove the biggest hurdle in the long term.
- *The lack of integration of CSR reporting with standard financial reporting.* While CSR and 'sustainability' or similarly named reports are being developed, they are currently separate from the mainstream financial reporting systems. Consequently, they are not being treated as equivalent or part of the 'main' report and assessment of an organization. For instance, GRI reports include economic assessments, but people naturally look to existing financial reports for economic information.

The measurement of organizational performance including all CSR components is extremely underdeveloped at this time. Some organizations are reporting some of what they are doing. Reporting is voluntary and is generally not audited. There are no clear benchmarks. Reports are very complex and difficult to assess.

From Sideline Specialist to Mainstream Activity

What we have demonstrated is that there has been a sudden and rapid change in the role of CSR in organizations and in the general community. CSR has gone, prior to 2006, from a sub-functional, somewhat discretionary, activity, based on the specific needs and whims of each organization towards what will eventually be a mainstream activity. Chief Sustainability Officer (CSO) positions are now being developed, similar to CFO and CIO positions, indicating that CSR can now rise into the top level of organizations and be seen as organization-wide activities. Indeed, many people believe that environmental sustainability issues – perhaps the core of the new CSR – will be fundamental to an organisation's 'licence to operate' in future.

CSR will be a required activity (as legal requirements for organizations change) and will eventually become an attitude, individual skill and organizational capability required throughout the organization. Hart (1995) argued that attitudes towards CSR will change from seeing it as something required by law which has to be accepted, begrudgingly, to an attitude of embracing the principles and incorporating them in present product design. Eventually, he argued that organizations would then take a wider view – that CSR should apply not just to activities inside the organization, but also to the whole system in which the organization operates, including suppliers, customers and other stakeholders. This is exactly how the importance of 'total quality management' occurred during the 1990s, in response to the Japanese advances and leadership in this area. No longer do we have 'quality' officers. Yet quality is taken for granted in most organizations. We expect quality. We assume that organizational systems are robust, consistent and deliver 'quality' outcomes, with 'quality' levels decided by the organization.

But how will that occur for CSR principles? To do this, CSR will impact three specific aspects of the organization – the organization/business strategy, its operations and its measurement and reporting systems. Consistent with the model outlined in Figure 1 earlier, key influences and influencers of each organisation's development of CSR will be government and industry laws, rules and regulations and the views and pressures of external stakeholders, such as NGOs and communities. We now consider each of these three aspects to see how they are likely to change as CSR becomes a mainstream activity and way of thinking.

1. Organisation/Business Strategy Changes

The strategy of the organization reflects what it plans to do, how it plans to compete and where it wants to get to as a result of its strategy. There are many ways to conceive of organization/business strategy eg through vision, mission, strategic intent, core purpose and other named and unnamed statements. Hubbard (2004) proposes five key questions (5Qs) which aim to get at the strategy of the organization, regardless of how it is currently expressed. By addressing these 5Qs, we can see how CSR may change the strategy options open to organizations.

Q1. Does the Organization Intend to Grow (Profitably)?

Most organizations (and governments and individuals) have an implicit expectation of growth. Everyone wants to have more, to be better off materially. However, we noted that growth was seen by the Club of Rome as one of the key drivers of world destruction. The faster the number of people grows, the more resources are used, the more pollution, the less land is available per person etc. If we could hold the population of the world steady, then organizations could only sell to more people by winning customers from their competitors ie it would be a win/lose no growth game. If individuals could be content with their current levels of tangible and intangible goods and services, the world may well be sustainable in terms of resource depletion and pollution emissions at the current level. If richer countries (and individuals) gave up some wealth to poorer countries (and individuals), the current global position would hold and environmental sustainability might be achievable with little other change

All of these are 'no growth' options. This seems unlikely in practice. However, education, laws and social pressures may change (reduce) expected future growth rates. Having a stronger educational understanding of the resource constraints that exist and the implications for overloading or overusing them, may well lead to lower growth rates occurring. If governments make laws, such as making it an offence to use resources or materials for certain purposes, usage will drop. If NGOs and communities take it into their own hands to campaign for or against certain practices, again usage of resources may be reduced. For instance, if people use less water, less energy, less carbon and less materials through either changing expectations or productivity improvements, then organizations in those industries will grow more slowly...or even decline in sales unit terms (sales dollars may rise if prices/unit rises, as seems likely).

This seems entirely feasible. Governments are developing such targets, so we can expect per person usage to decline and, hence, at minimum slowing down unit usage. Growth may not be lauded for all organizations (and countries and individuals) as it currently is. By focusing on quality of living rather than economic quantity of living, people may be encouraged to reduce their (economic) growth expectations. Thus, in some industries, 'growth' may actually be targeted as a lower unit number.

Q2. What Products and Services will the Organization Offer Its Customers?

Much of the emotional focus is on products for which demand can be expected to decline. For instance, it seems certain that coal and oil will be used much less in future as a consequence of targets to reduce GHG emissions. Coal and oil are forecast to fall from 65% of world energy to 30% by 2030 (Enkvist et al, 2007). Reforestation rather than deforestation is another expected major change. However, while coal mining, logging and wood user industries may decline in activity, industries and technologies with much lower GHG and other emission issues will rise to replace them. The industries of the future will include renewable energy sources (wind, solar, hydro, geothermal, nuclear), recycling of all products and emission controls, to name a few.

This is the natural way of industry evolutions. Some industries rise and others fall. Where governments (on behalf of their societies) take deliberate actions to reduce the size of an industry or organization, there is likely to be and a need for compensation and retraining. These will be difficult government and social decisions, but we should not fail to undertake these critical and large industry changes just because an industry currently exists.

Q3. What Customers and Markets Will the Organization Serve?

Major changes do not seem likely here from the rise of CSR, but the deregulation of trade means that organizations who develop successful products can now sell them throughout the world, while slow adapters can expect to be beaten to markets by international companies. For instance, India's Tata Group is now operating outsourcing activities for US companies not in India but also in the US, proving able to provide the service even more effectively with locals than local Americans can do!

However, new definitions of 'value' will emerge. Currently 'value' is only based on economic principles – what people will pay for a particular good or service. It seems likely that future definitions of value – on which basis decisions about customers and markets served will be made – will include environmental value, impact on organizational reputation and other environmental or social measures. Thus what is produced, and for whom, may significantly change when 'value' is defined differently. For instance, the rapid growth of organic food and the growth of locally produced foods (reflecting the value of buying local rather than buying cheapest) are examples of new customer and market categories emerging.

Q4. What Generic Strategy Will the Organization Use to Develop a Sustainable Competitive Advantage over Its Competitors?

The standard options here include focusing, differentiating – both in any number of unique ways – and being the low cost competitor in the industry. Again fundamentally new options ar unlikely to occur here. But more creative ways of thinking about business models will emerge. For instance, governments will impose rules requiring life cycle product stewardship. This will require companies to take back their products at the end of their lives, thus making the disposal of the product an expense to the company. Tighter rules on disposal will be developed, thus forcing companies to reuse products and materials that previously they have thrown away. Therefore, major changes in organizational business models are more likely as cost structures change. For instance, when the disposal value of electrical appliances is costed in, it may be that longer lasting, repairable electrical appliances will again prove to be 'economical' from a social perspective.

Q5. What Position in the Industry Does the Organization Expect to Achieve?

Typical answers here have been growth oriented (eg 'double our size in 5 years'), market position oriented (eg 'be no. 1 in the industry') or profitability oriented (eg 'maximise shareholder value' or 'be the most profitable organization in the industry'). In future a range of different 'positions' will arise. For instance being 'the most environmentally friendly firm', being the 'employer of choice', being the 'most innovative', or being 'the best stakeholder partner' are just a few of the positions that might be expected to be highly attractive as organizations take a wider view of the relative importance of their various stakeholder groups and the values which each group has, as well as the changing value of social and environmental issues for the society as a whole.

Phase	Focus
1. Pollution prevention	Emissions control Product meets stated quality and legal requirements Operating regulations met; no OH&S issues
2. Product stewardship	Product design to avoid emissions, waste creation Product costs to consider total product costs, including waste and emissions. Production processes to avoid emissions, waste
3. Sustainable development	Ensuring suppliers apply similar principles, processes in own activities that feed into organization Considering community perspectives on organization activities Applying life cycle costing

Figure 5. Changing Perspectives on CSR Issues over Time.

Another way of thinking about changes in strategic options comes from Hart (1995). He proposed three interlinking strategies for his 'natural resource-based view of the firm'. He argued that organizations began their environmental thinking via considering preventing pollution, as an emissions-based, or 'end of pipe' approach ot the issue. They would then move to the idea of better design and costing of products, through product stewardship and life cycle costing, to stop pollution and waste at source. As organizations embraced this notion, they would eventually move to a wider view of sustainable development, under which they would consider the impact of their strategies and actions not just on the current period but on the future as well, leading them to embrace lower impact technologies (see Figure 5).

Similarly, Lash and Wellington (2007) argued that organizations had to deal with six different types of risks in their strategies in relation to environmental actions or inactions. These were regulatory risk, supply chain risk, product and technology risk, litigation risk, reputation risk and physical risk from the climate itself. They argued that organizations needed to not only consider the threats posed by such risks to their individual contexts, but that there were significant opportunities for fast-moving organizations which took proactive views of these risks and positioned themselves positively in respect of each area. For instance the development of carbon trading markets, BP's positioning of itself as 'beyond petroleum' and the development of 'green buildings' are some examples of positive strategies to address these risks.

2. Operational Changes

The second aspect, and the one in which most people are likely to see clear changes from current practice, is in the area of operations. Here, there are many changes that can be expected. Lovins et al (2007) argued that four possible ways to make positive changes to influence environmental practices were:

- *Increase the efficiency of use.* As much as 40% of total energy use/GHG emissions come from existing buildings (and houses), so concentrating on making existing buildings more efficient can have a major effect on the overall energy needs of the organization, and the country. This can be done by designing the system using holistic system thinking rather than partial thinking and by minimizing waste of energy, water and materials used. For instance, using lighting levels that automatically adjust to the natural light level (rather than the fixed levels currently used) and by automatically dimming lights when they are not being used can substantially reduce the total electricity usage of the organization. Using chilled beam cooling rather than electrically cooled air is cheaper and more healthy for employees. Recycling materials is often cheaper in terms of total costs than using virgin materials (with their associated energy, transport and emission costs). Changing standards on paper to use 100% recycled paper, printing double-sided and turning off printers when not in use have been shown to have major cost savings, with no loss of organizational efficiency or output.
- *Shift to biologically inspired production models* ie use different business models that eliminate waste by using closed loop production systems that take account of nature's ecosystems. This is based on the principle that 'waste equals food' for some (other) production process. For instance, rather than disposing into landfill, plastic can be remoulded into public seating. Rather than dumping in the ocean, sewage can be treated to create non-drinking water for industrial or household uses or even clean and drinkable water, even within ordinary office buildings.

- *Move to a solutions-based business model* ie change the definition of 'value' (and of 'cost'). For instance, in terms of 'value', Interface has moved from being a carpet seller to a floor solutions leasing company (Lovins et al 2007). Instead of selling the carpet to customers, Interface leases it and services and maintains it during its life, which is what customers really value. Since most of the wear occurs in small areas, rather than replace the whole carpet – as the customer would have done – Interface replaces the worn pieces (generally less than 20%), thus making massive savings on material use, prolonging carpet life and providing a better service to the customer. In terms of 'cost', we can expect pressure to focus on 'life cycle costing' rather than short term current measures of 'cost', which ignore externalities (pollution, emission and waste costs incurred by other organizations during the process) and also ignore the disposal costs incurred at the end of the product's life. This is likely to fundamentally change our views of what many products 'cost'. For instance, costs to society of alcohol abuse are so great that, if it were costed to account for the social costs incurred (as tobacco has increasingly been), it could dramatically decrease alcohol consumption.
- *Reinvest in natural capital.* For instance, either by using more natural products or by investing in offsets, such as carbon offsets, mine restoration or taking responsibility for product disposal to neutralize the effects of its production activities, an organization can protect its reputation as a socially responsible company and reduces its risk of being attacked by NGO pressure groups.

In arguing about how GHGs specifically could be reduced, Stern (2007) added three other ways of thinking about operational changes that are likely to have wider use and impact. These come from government actions, not organization actions. They are:

- *Decrease demand for the end product.* This can be done externally by governments or regulators, by regulation, taxes or subsidizing competing products. For instance, governments are increasingly coming to the view that carbon emissions should be taxed, either directly or via cap and trade market licensing and pricing mechanisms. Some airports, cities and transport companies charge environmental levies, congestion levies and pollution levies. As the taxes increase consumers' costs, they have a bigger incentive to decrease demand. The taxes can be manipulated to achieve the demand desired. For instance, Sweden, which introduced carbon taxes in 1991, taxes GHG emissions at $US50-150/tonne, whereas the EU uses a market based system whereby the price has fluctuated between $US8-40/tonne while the US has yet to begin such a system to influence demand to decline.
- *Use new technologies.* Replacement technologies to address GHG problems are already available, but are not yet well used. For instance, some governments are now regulating that electricity producers have to produce a minimum percentage of renewable energy within their mix. This has forced generators to invest in renewables, increasing the demand for them, increasing the experience with them and providing companies with incentives to reduce the costs of renewables, all of which makes renewables more desirable and decreases the GHG emissions as a direct result.

- *Regulate emissions.* At the moment, the focus is only on GHG emissions and only then for large emitters. Farming, building, manufacturing are not included in systems, even for GHGs. Regulation of other emissions and of other producers of emissions will clearly occur.

Hargroves and Smith (2005) offered many ways in which efficiencies and innovation in environmental thinking could result in process and product benefits. These included material savings from whole system design, increased process yields and reduced downtime, byproducts and waste convertible into valuable forms, lower packaging costs, greater resource productivity of inputs and reduced material storage costs.

One of the major, but underfocussed on, areas for CSR changes relate to office buildings. Buildings account for up to 40% of total energy use, 25% of GHG emissions and 12% of water consumption. Other major GHG users are power stations (24%), transport (12%) and deforestation (18%). Even old buildings can improve their efficiency by 35% using existing technologies and efficiencies. Star-rating efficiency systems for buildings have been developed by national Green Building Councils, with 6 star ratings being awarded for world-leading buildings. In 2007 these included the Royal Bank of Scotland building (Edinburgh), ING headquarters (Amsterdam), Bank of America building (New York), Melbourne City Council building CH2, Lend Lease building and the ANZ Bank building (all in Melbourne). These world-leading buildings produce significant electricity, water and waste savings through better insulation, lighting, heating, cooling, toilet systems, internal and external design and use of innovative materials and finishings. Further, improvements in buildings lead to improved employee morale and lower absenteeism, providing further CSR benefits.

Operational Changes	Examples
Solutions-based business model	From owning to renting; from product/service to bundling; better understanding true customer needs/customer design
Decrease demand for end product	Tax product/process; education; change laws
Biological production model	Process design; use of natural resources with biodegradable emissions; recycle waste
New technology	Use solar, wind, hydro and other renewables; seek technology with minimum GHG emissions
Increase efficiency of use	Building design; recycling; energy, water, materials usage actions
Regulate emissions	Tax emissions; change laws; penalties for breaking laws

Figure 6. Operational Change Concepts.

In terms of activities within buildings once built, the top ways in which employees believe their offices can be more environmentally friendly include getting rid of disposable coffee cups, using recycled paper and double-sided printing, unplugging phone chargers, using reusable lunch containers, receiving communications electronically and raising the thermostat temperature (Durkin, 2207b).

McKinsey studies have estimated that existing technologies in buildings alone, such as building insulation, fuel efficiency, lighting, airconditioning, water heating, biofuel, electrical standby losses and CO2 replacements can abate around 20% of the total carbon reduction target for the world (Enkvist et al, 2007). They further argued that nuclear power, forestation, clean coal/carbon capture and storage, wind power, biomass, gas, waste and biodiesel could abate the other 80% at a cost of no more than 40 euros per tonne. (By comparison, the European Union Emission Trading Scheme has been trading lower than this price over most of its history, while the Intergovernmental Panel on Climate Change recommended a price of $US100/tonne and Sweden currently charges $US 50-150/tonne.)

Figure 6 combines these ways of thinking. The many examples discussed above indicate the wide range of ways in which operations are likely to be changed in the near future in most organizations.

In summary, the operational solutions required for environmental change are technically feasible already. But are governments and organizations willing to engage and lead?

In terms of social issues, there is currently much less focus on what changes are required. Conceptually, however, applying value chain or business system approaches, the following areas are likely to be focused on:

- *Supplier practices.* Likely issues to arise here include concerns over production sourcing (eg whether 'fairtrade' practices are being applied, particularly in underdeveloped countries) and production processes (eg if production is outsourced to other countries, are emission problems simply being transferred from one part of the globe to another, with no net saving?)
- *Employee practices.* While much attention has been paid to this, the development of increasingly unequal remuneration between people at the top and the bottom of organizations is likely to raise questions of equity and fairness. It also seems that organizations with clear and practiced sets of values are associated with satisfied employees, so more focus may be expected around the issues required to satisfy employees, particularly in times of global labour shortages.
- *Customer satisfaction.* Considerable attention has also been placed on this aspect in the past, due heavily to the developments of the total quality management movement. Of all the social areas, this is perhaps the best developed in terms of available existing practices and is likely to see the least change. However, involving customers in product design is a recent innovation consistent with an open and transparent organization seeking to deliver customer value and this trend may take off.
- *Community connections.* Increasingly, organizations are expected to be actively engaged in their communities. Given organisations' increasing impact on communities, this pressure is likely to increase. Being open and transparent (eg providing information on its activities), assisting communities with needs which are within the organisation's capabilities and resources (eg providing managerial input into not-for-profit organizations), and acting ethically (eg clearly stating the values of the organization and ensuring practices match values) are likely to be major issues for many organizations used to being rather private in their dealings.

3. Measuring and Reporting System Changes

The third aspect where change will occur is in measuring and reporting organizational performance. Lovins et al (2007) noted that current (financially-oriented) organizational performance systems are like broken compasses. They are not giving good directions for organizational decisionmaking because:

- *Costing decisions are based only on initial cost and not lifetime costs.* Life cycle costing includes the maintenance costs and disposal costs of items. While an item may be cheap to purchase, if its operating costs are high or it lasts a much shorter period than competing products with higher initial costs, incorrect financial decisions will be made.
- *Short terms are used to assess long term financial decisions.* For instance, when investment lasts 10 or more years, using a payback period of 2-3 years, or even using a discounted cash flow technique over a 5 year period, can lead to decisions which favour short term returns rather than correct financial returns. For instance, Google has installed a solar energy generation system at its headquarters which is large enough to power 1,000 homes. Google believes that the system will pay for itself economically in 7-8 years and expects to generate 'free' electricity for years beyond this. Google also wants to be know as being environmentally friendly because this is healthier for its employees (Cain, 2007).
- *There is little focus on resource and energy use in many organisations since they form only a small part of the total costs of the product or service.* For instance, energy use is often only 2-3% of total costs. Raw materials for service organizations may be only 5-10% of costs. Why worry about them? Yet if these costs could be halved through efficient use of different practices, the need for more power stations – a prime cause of GHG emissions – and the depletion of resources – particularly minerals and forests, which are also prime causes of GHG emissions – could be dramatically impacted. Again this is another example of partial thinking rather than holistic systems thinking.
- *Executive incentive systems encourage short-term behaviour.* Executives – and sometimes everyone in the organization – are increasingly receiving part of their compensation for meeting or beating key performance indicators. To the extent that those indicators are based on a single year's performance, and on financial measures, there is a great incentive for individual managers to seek solutions that maximize short-term financial outcomes. For instance, Reducing R&D can increase short term profits at the expense of reduced long term innovation. Firing employees and hiring lower paid contractors can be rewarded if the KPI for a manager is 'salaries/sales' or 'total salaries bill' (when contractor costs can be reported as 'consultants' or 'supplies'. Therefore executive incentive systems need to be redesigned to match the long term best interests, not only of the organization, but of the whole community if possible.
- *Tax laws and regulators encourage inappropriate behaviour.* For instance, tax laws give immediate tax reductions for expenses, but only partial short term tax reductions for investments. While this is logical in accounting terms, it provides a tax incentive

for expenses over investments – just the wrong signal when we are considering life cycle costs. Similarly, governments periodically encourage or discourage business activity via tax regulations. For instance, if investors can get an immediate tax write-off for one type of investment (eg films and art investments) but not for other types (eg developing more efficient energy systems), then investment will be artificially attracted to those favoured areas. While there may be good political or national reasons for encouraging particular types of investments, they will undoubtedly skew the investment decisionmaking in ways that are unlikely to be economically, objectively or even socially sensible.

- *Government regulations favour inappropriate organizational decisions.* For instance, until recently it was an offence to install a rainwater tank on a home property in some parts of Australia. The use of solar panels on houses and buildings remains unsupported and not required for new buildings, thereby missing a huge opportunity for capturing free renewable power. Not until the calamity of the long and continuing drought has this changed. Buildings are now being encouraged to not only collect rainwater, but also to reuse grey water and even consider black water (sewage) recycling in 6-star buildings, which is now considered world best practice in building design!

Pressures from external stakeholders, including NGOs, local pressure groups and communities, have led to new ways of reporting organization performance. Earlier we noted that the Global Reporting Initiative (GRI) system of measurement has gained considerable traction across major international organisations. Coupled with its use by many major organizations worldwide, its non-proprietary nature and involvement of users in its development, the development of a global database of 14,000 GRI-based reports from over 3,500 organisations in over 80 countries by Corporate Register and its incorporation in some investment organisations' assessment systems, it seems likely that it may provide the basis for a future CSR 'standard'.

The pressure for wider performance reporting has also begun to have a significant impact in the investment community. Ozlitsky et al (2003) conducted a meta-analysis of the CSR literature and found a significant positive link between social and environmental performance and financial results. Aguilera et al (2007) argued that it is no longer whether or not CSR is useful, but how organizations tackle and implement it. Whether there is a link between financial and non-financial performance or not, a wider and balanced view of organizational performance would suggest that an organization which did exceedingly well in the CSR areas and adequately in the financial area ought to be rated similarly or better by the wider community than an organization with high financial performance but low CSR performance. These are different aspects of total performance measurement, not necessarily aspects which are correlated directly.

In the investment community, the concept of 'socially responsible investment' (SRI) has been developed to cater for those investors wishing to support their social and environmental principles. It has become so attractive to investors that in 2005, almost 10% of managed funds were invested in the US in this way, with Europe also reporting significant investment (Tomorrows Company, 2007). The Dow Jones has developed its Global Sustainability Index to provide investors with an index to invest in of leading organizations by industry which are perceived to be socially responsible. In 2006, the United Nations developed its Principles for

Responsible Investment (PRI) to provide an environmental, social and governance framework to guide investors seeking organizations with strong CSR philosophies and practices to invest in. By 2007, after one year, it had 180 institutional supporters, representing $US8 trillion of funds under management.

Various organisations have also developed voluntary or compulsory assessment systems or reports on organizations – mainly listed ones – which provide investors with information about social responsibility, under a variety of different frameworks.

At the individual level, Generation Y employees are increasingly demanding to work for organizations with perceived good social and environmental policies, practices and records and many organisations now have a host of CSR information on their websites, for investors, customers, employees, potential employees, NGOs and others to use to make judgements about the organisation.

For all these reasons, we are seeing great changes in the ways in which organizations measure and report their performance. What can we expect in the future? The key developments are likely to be:

- development of standardized frameworks for reporting CSR performance
- certification of such frameworks
- the integration of these frameworks with economic reporting standards and frameworks
- focusing of these frameworks on a smaller number of the most important measures
- development of benchmarks for those measures
- treatment of CSR reporting as of similar levels of importance to the financial results

In this way, CSR reporting will become standardized, reliable, be benchmarked and treated as of similar quality, standard and relevance to financial information, thus enabling a proper stakeholder evaluation of organizational performance to be made.

Summary and Conclusions

We have outlined how the position of CSR within organizations pre-2006 as a specialist sub-function is rapidly changing to CSR as a mainstream organizational philosophy, with new, organization-wide sets of practices being developed to address the wide range of issues that are emerging. Changes occurred in 2006 which mobilized a wide range of stakeholders, from individuals, communities, NGOs, businesses and governments, providing the impetus for the widescale and widespread changes that are now under way in many countries. These changes provide CSR with the opportunity to reposition itself from being a sideline discretionary activity to being a mainstream way of thinking, just as total quality management did during the 1990s.

The current focus within CSR has shifted dramatically to the environmental aspects, due to the perceived environmental crisis which the world, its organizations and its people are facing around the general issue of climate change. Everyone and every organization worldwide will be affected by these issues. Nevertheless, the social issues are also of great importance and will not be forgotten. Indeed, in a global world of labour shortages, paying attention to social issues within the organization will be key to attracting the right people to be able to survive and address the environmental changes that need to be made.

The changes that are expected to result are widespread and have begun, but we have only seen the start of what will be fundamental and major changes for most organizations. These changes will include changes of strategic thinking and conceptualization, changes of operational practice and changes of organizational reporting of performance. Based on the analysis above, as CSR moves to become mainstream both in activities and in thinking, the organization of the future is likely to have the following features:

- Its corporate/business strategy will be aligned with environmental requirements imposed by governments, industries and external stakeholder pressures, which will vary by organization, industry and location.
- It will seek only sustainable growth, considering stakeholder expectations,not just shareholder ones.
- Its operations will have environmental thinking incorporated in every aspect of its operations, including manufacturing, servicing, head office functions, local and international activities.
- Compared with current practices, it will be heavily focused on efficient material use, minimal non-renewable energy use, minimal carbon and other harmful emissions and waste, recycling whatever and wherever possible.
- It will use life cycle costing to make best decisions over materials used, processes used and products and services produced.
- It will be a values-driven organization, aligning its actual behaviour with stated values.
- It will seek to align its suppliers and customers to its own practices and values, having other stakeholders aware of them.
- It will seek only sustainable economic growth and will apply a balanced perspective to assessing its performance in all aspects.
- It will report financial, social and environmental information within one report, with social and environmental information subject to similar audit and certification processes as financial information currently uses.
- Standardisation of social and environmental information will exist, focusing on a small number of key performance indicators that emerge from global standard setting systems.

These changes will occur differently in different organisations, industries and countries, but the critical and global nature of the issues will mean the issues must be tackled head on immediately. We can expect major changes in all areas within five years if the world is to meet even a single target of a 30% reduction in GHG emissions by 2020, let alone all the other changes that are being sought.

References

Aguilera, R., Rupp, D., Williams, C. and Ganapathi, J. (2007) 'Putting the S back in corporate social responsibility: a multilevel theory of social change in organisations', *The Academy of Management Review*, Vol 32, No 3, July pp 836-863.

Bonini, S., Mendonca, L. and Oppenheim, J. (2006) 'When social issues become strategic', *McKinseyQuarterly,* Vol 2: 20-39.

Buffini, F. (2006) 'Super funds demonstrate their social conscience', *The Australian Financial Review*, October 16: 3.

Cain, A. (2007) 'Power search is key to Google's place in the sun', *The Australian Financial Review: Special Report Green Buildings*, October 3: 14.

Durkin, P. (2007a) 'Directors show sense of balance' *The Australian Financial Review*, September 12.

Durkin, P. (2007b) 'Gen Y push for greener offices', *The Australian Financial Review'*, August 29.

Elkington, J. (1997) *Cannibals with forks: the triple bottom line of 21st century business,* Capstone.

Enkvist, P-A., Naucler, T. and Rosander, J. (2007) 'A cost curve for greenhouse gas reduction', *McKinsey Quarterly, (1) 35-45.*

Flannery, T. (2005) *The weather makers: the history and future impact of climate change*, Text.

Gettler, L. (2007) '"Green" awareness can depend on life factors', *The Age*, August 30. See also www.bp.com.au for more detailed survey results.

Hargroves, K. and Smith, M. (2005) *The Natural Advantage of Nations*, Earthscan.

Hart, S. (1995) 'The natural resource-based view of the firm', *Academy of Management Review*, 20 (4): 986-1014.

Hubbard, G. (2006) 'Measuring organizational performance: beyond the triple bottom line', *Business Strategy and the Environment*, Wiley InterScience online, December.

Hubbard, G. (2004) *Strategic management: thinking, analysis and action*, (2nd ed), Pearson.

Intergovernmental Panel on Climate Change: United Nations Framework Convention on Climate Change (2007) www.ipcc.ch .

Jones, S., Frost, G., Loftus, J. and van der Laan, S. (2005) *Sustainability reporting: practices, performance and potential*, The Australian Society of Certified Practising Accountants.

Kaplan, R and Norton, D. (1992) *The balanced scorecard*, Harvard Business School.

Lash, J. and Wellington, F. (2007) 'Competitive advantage on a warming planet' *Harvard Business Review*, March, 94-103.

Lovins, A. Lovins, H. and Hawken, P. (2007) 'A road map for natural capitalism', *Harvard Business Review*, July-August, 172-183.

Meadows, D. H., Meadows, D. L., Randers, J. and Behrens, W. (1972) *The limits to growth*, Earth Island.

O'Dwyer, B. and Owen, D. (2005) 'Assurance statement practice in environmental, social and sustainability reporting: a critical evaluation, *British Accounting Review*, 37: 205-229.

Orlitzsky, M., Schmidt, F. and Rynes, S. (2003) 'Corporate social and financial performance: a meta-analysis, *Organisation Studies,* 24: 403-441.

Potter, B. and Symonds, A. (2007) 'The business of philanthropy', *The Australian Financial Review,* June 14: 11.

Stern, N. (2006) *The stern report*, www.sternreview.org.uk

Stern, N. (2007) 'The economics of climate change and the need for business leadership to tackle the problem', *Business Leaders Forum on Climate Change*, March 28, Canberra, 7-13.

Tomorrow's Company (2007) *Tomorrow's global company: challenges and choices*, Tomorrow's Company.

Waddock, S. and Bodwell, C. (2004) 'Managing responsibility: what can be learned from the quality movement', *California Management Review* 47(1): 25-38.

Williams, L. (2007) 'Emission possible', *The Age*, June 18: 7.

In: Corporate Social Responsibility
Editor: Adam R. Timpere
ISBN: 978-1-60456-284-2

Chapter 3

CORPORATE SOCIAL RESPONSIBILITY AND BUSINESS DECISIONS - SYNERGY OR CYNICISM?

Lorice Stainer[*]
University of Hertfordshire Business School
De Havilland Campus, Hatfield, Hertfordshire AL10 9AB, UK

Conducting business has become exponentially more complex because of the many rapid changes that have occurred over the last few decades. The contemporary customer or consumer is demanding high quality, swiftness and reliability in the delivery of products or services, all reflected in low pricing, good value and innovation. As organisations are now progressively performing in a global market, they need to be even more alert and competitive. Therefore, management in the twenty-first century needs to meet such challenges by ensuring to embrace the necessary tools and principles as well as integrate all business functions for long-term success. It also has to deal increasingly with diverse pressures, ranging from the more traditional productivity and efficiency dimensions to the more recent elements regarding societal responsibility and public image, as well as the whole 'package' of business risks.

As such, corporate strategy has considerably matured. According to Towells (2003), it has gone through the classical, evolutionary, processual and systemic approaches to today's more common known stage of resources and capabilities. Atkinson (2004) suggests that too many organisations have failed to create a strong business strategy to outwit their competitors, dominate market intelligence, retain existing customers and market share whilst, at the same time, attracting the loyalty of new customers. O'Regan & Ghobadian (2005) support this view by noting that, in the present turbulent business environment, managers increasingly need reliable navigational tools to achieve such a competitive advantage. Thus, when corporate objectives have been identified, it is necessary to develop viable strategies for

[*] E-mail for correspondence: L.Stainer@herts.ac.uk

Dr. Lorice Stainer is Principal Research Fellow in Business Ethics at the University of Hertfordshire Business School. She is a Fellow of the Institute of Management Services and the European Institute of Industrial Engineers as well as Member of the Institute of Business Ethics and Transparency International (UK). She has had many years work experience in commerce and industry as well as in teaching and implementation in a socially responsible manner. Management decision-making should not only focus on the outputs of the business process but should review, rethink its managerial practices and corporate structure and look further downstream to the outcomes of that process which relate to quality of life factors. Such a transformation in strategy should be performed effectively as well as efficiently in the pursuit of increased productivity and ameliorated reputation.

As Peters (2000) proclaims, excellent firms do not believe in excellence – only in constant improvement and constant change. This is because the road is neither straight nor flat in relation to strategic change and is full of trials and tribulations. Especially concerning ethical dilemmas, Mullins (2005) argues that when a decision is made with a degree of urgency that overrides the normal democratic process, there *is* crisis – a neurotic aspect that management should avoid. As Alan Roberts (2004), Chair of the UK Ethical Trading Initiatives, states, the market place is still hugely demanding and the drive to achieve even lower prices continues unabated with this trend presenting the greatest challenge to ethical code implementation. Petersen (2002) strongly suggests that organisations should strive for spirited and value-based leadership, acknowledging that there must be a shift from the 'look-away' society as well as from the publicly perceived erosion of responsibility. Thus, when making decisions, explicit self-diagnosis and ethical initiatives must be forceful enough to put principles, whether economic or moral, into practice and be weaved into the fabric of performance excellence. To operate in its own best interests, an organisation should show enthusiasm in accepting full responsibility for its actions and, in this way, build and nurture a good and sustainable image. In the words of Matsushita (2000), "Profits should be a reflection not of corporate greed but a vote of confidence from society that what is offered by the firm is valued". As such, inter-connectedness with the wider communities is paramount for mutual understanding in order to create empathy and kinship. It is firmly felt that there must be a bedrock of good ethical behaviour which is seen, not as an 'add-on phenomenon', but as a key determinant of the very essence of an inclusive and civilised conduct of business for survival and long-term performance.

Philippa Foster Back (2007), Director of the UK Institute of Business Ethics, neatly distinguishes between ethics and corporate social responsibility [CSR], advocating that the former relates to 'doing things ethically' and the latter 'doing ethical things'. However, Boehm (2002) believes that there is disparity between what CSR is supposed to mean to what the academic community and business practitioners expound. Much unfair cynicism and scepticism has emanated about its credibility and worthiness in the pursuit of performance goals. As such, management needs to master the moral decision-making maze by taking ordered steps of asking questions and providing answers that can readily be applied to solving problems and dilemmas in business, especially in strategic terms. The fundamental motive of CSR must be to show that ethical principles, from wherever derived, can improve reasoning and harmonise decisions to enhance performance. It could be viewed as a 'balance sheet' which deliberately prevents chaotic thinking in the pursuit of improved stakeholder relationships as well as the triple bottom line. By building social issues into its thinking, every business, as advocated by Davis (2005), can recast the debate about its role and examples abound of the long-term business impact on the fast-growing social issues. In his view, the

researching in the areas of business ethics, corporate social responsibility and environmental management. She is also currently a consultant with Ethical Dimensions.

CEOs of today's big corporations should take the opportunity to restate and reinforce their own social contracts in order to help secure the invested billions of their shareholders. Indeed, management at all levels must not just sit tight, with fingers crossed, 'dreaming and hoping' that moral dilemmas will be self-resolving. After all, it is those principles of moral conduct and matters of conscience that apply to people which are an unknown and individual 'quantity' and must, thus, be nurtured.

Organisations ought to aid and play their role as citizens in developing social capital which, as Andriof & Waddock (2002) profess, is the necessary glue that keeps pro-active stakeholder relationships together. They do so by providing the basis for trust, cooperation and collective action, within and outside the workplace, through the establishment of sound ethical values. These attributes are the vital components of long-term thinking and performance excellence. It is, therefore, crucial to inculcate 'efficient' behaviour, that is to 'think before you act', and ask inherently and continuously the key questions of what, when, who, why, where and how? This is because the consequent impact in relation to the organisation's stated values - whether beneficial or adverse, internal or external, local or global - has to be regularly monitored and assessed. In fact, one of the first challenges which an organisation has to face in setting strategy and making decisions is to accept that it is not just a 'money' motivated purposive entity. It needs to identify the main stages of its growth and understand how its structure may change as it develops with a different life-cycle of increasing pressures on the formulating, implementing and monitoring strategic policies. The contemporary demands arise from such issues as globalisation, sustainability, demographic and technological change as well as social responsibility. In this regard, management requires time to, not only ponder, but also deliberate and conceptualise; unfortunately, all too often, logic is sacrificed for rapidity.

A responsible decision-making culture has to be built brick by brick, seen as clear and transparent as well as maintained through effective communication, thus monitoring its ethical temperature. Bishop (2005) states that, "in this post-modernist age, if we demand respect for our decisions, then they have to be seen, not as arbitrary, but as based on a clear process of ethical prescriptions". Therefore, it is imperative to have a vision and mission as well as be able to connect with stakeholders who, of course, do not come in 'neat' packages. Be they individual or organised groups, they certainly have influence on the form and substance of business activities. Indeed, the pathway is to progress in a sustainable and ethical manner.

Corporate Social Responsibility – The State of the Art

What is responsibility? The connotations are infinite and wide and can include being liable, answerable, accountable, reliable and also trustworthy. Pinning down its meaning, according to Cowe (2002), is often difficult, particularly for the business world; since the whole concept concerns action that is prescribed in laws or regulation, there seems to be no clear formal definition. Carroll (1997) claims that social responsibility has a four-part perspective which expounds that business should fulfil its economic, legal and ethical, as well as discretionary or philanthropic responsibility to society. In his view, it is normative, in that it proposes what business 'ought to do', and descriptive, in that it captures the essence of what a socially responsible business 'does'. Crowther & Rayman-Bacchus (2004) believe that the term CSR is currently in vogue but, as a concept, it is *vague* and means different things to different people, arousing a heated debate especially in such a globalised economy. It is felt that the best resumé of what CSR is about is neatly provided by the World Business Council for Sustainable Development (2003). It proclaims that CSR relates to commitment by business to contribute to sustainable economic development working with employees, their families, the local community and society at large in order to improve their quality of life. Simply, CSR can be interpreted as how responsible companies should interact with those other than their owners or shareholders, with the aim to minimise the risks of conflicts of interest.

An important and difficult implication is the notion that what may have been perceived as responsible, reasonable or acceptable in one decade may not be so in another. Therefore, the contemporary organisations are expected to understand what their changing impacts are on society and should constantly work towards improving those impacts; in order words, they should not just be 'CSR aware' but 'CSR active' by fundamentally behave ethically. As Warnock (2006) emphatically states, no set of laws or principles can cause people to be good and it is this preference for good rather than evil that stems all morality, whether theoretical or practical. The difficulties in moving towards CSR often raise the inevitable question of how environmental and social dimensions can be integrated with economic business goals. What is salient is that it is not a 'magic' potion that will ensure better results but it deserves to be adopted as a core management practice, like any other in the business arena. However, it should not to be considered solely for reasons of public image.

Is there a link between business performance, competitiveness, social responsibility and economic success? The answer must be emphatically 'yes' because, as Stainer (2004) asserts, today's bottom line is changing by increasing the emphasis on corporate responsibility and sustainable development where organisations need to show enthusiasm in being accountable. The synergy and inter-relationship between performance and CSR would inevitably signal the dawn of a new inclusive era of enlightened business strategic thinking that is clearly appropriate for this century. The instrumental motive of CSR is to underline the fact that ethical principles can advance reasoning and decision-making to improve the overall effectiveness and quality of performance. The thrust should aim to permeate and embed values into the whole organisation and, as Zadek (2001) proclaims, the corporate intention should be to move towards a more civil society and become a 'civil corporation'. Moral decision-making can be genuinely aided and energised through:

- Analysing oneself in relation to integrity and objectivity
- Listening to intuition
- Leading with compassion
- Having concern for others
- Adding stakeholder value

The CSR concept must be founded on the moral soul of the organisation and inculcated into the hierarchy, with the understanding that every business does not operate in a vacuum. The fundamental dilemma is to find ways to entwine objectives, decision variables and quality-of-life ingredients entwined with desirable values. Since the late 1970s, Lewis (2003) reports that public perception on the role of companies in society has changed significantly and, in general, for the better. This is confirmed by Webley & Dryden (2005) who proclaim that, in a survey carried in the United Kingdom by the Institute of Business Ethics, much was learned about attitudes to ethics at work. Amongst the findings, two major outcomes plainly surface: [i] 80% of employees feel positive about the ethical practices and standards in their workplace and that business is conducted honestly and [ii] 67% think that the organisation lives up to its stated policies on corporate responsibility.

Schwartz & Carroll (2003) affirm that CSR is composed by over-lapping the three domains of economic, ethical and legal. But, what is new and manifest is that managers are trying to contribute to this all important issue. Indeed, there is a wide acceptance of the challenges ahead with many pathways burgeoning and growing. The approach taken by Stainer *et al* (1999) is a value-based one, where each business is actually able to identify its own set of values which, concurrently, supports operations and is shared by its major stakeholders. They have devised the *Value to Stakeholders Index* which provides a powerful inclusive measure of value for business excellence. In truth, whatever the methodology, there should be an appreciation of the moral 'minefield' of the business environment in which values are utilised, understood and appreciated. What must not be forgotten is that the world is not naturally orderly and, thus, to make ethical decisions can be extremely difficult. However, in the end, it is the individual responsibility and judgement by all parties alike that remains at the core of 'good' business and this, surely, must be the 'right' standpoint to take.

Mestre *et al* (2005) purport that business must strive to be a leading player in the moral community; it should, at the same time, pursue the triple bottom line philosophy. However, few have the inclination or vision to begin the long and arduous journey of CSR as it is generally perceived as a marathon, a process with no ending. Zadek & Tuppen (2004) propound that perhaps the time is coming when companies should cease compartmentalising the economic, social and environmental issues in favour of new and innovative ways of reporting their 'joined-up' contributions to a more sustainable society. Certainly, in the words of Tyger (2001), "vital to every operation is cooperation". After all, businesses are comprised of individuals, be they rogues, angels or 'in-between' and, as such, possess natural differences in beliefs, values and moral principles. Whether individually or collectively, they set the moral standards and embody the social parameters regarding such controversial notions as fairness and honesty. Indeed, it is important to realise that there will always be a conflict between personal and corporate values as well as short-term and long-term values - these cannot be easily measured! Often, the perception is not so much to 'have' principles but to 'know how' to use them.

Fundamentals of CSR relate to comporting with professionalism and trust, the latter to be built with confidence and consideration, thus avoiding deception and suspicion. With regard to compliance with the law or, indeed, the spirit of the law, there must be no weak justification for breaking it because of the notion that 'everybody else does it'. In this vein, respect for the well-being of others, through observing basic rights, is to be adopted when acting in good faith in a fair, factual and honest manner. The concerns are not just about deciphering between 'right or wrong', 'ought or ought not', 'good or bad' but to act with a pro-active level of responsibility. A tenet that could generally be adopted is that if an action is hateful or distasteful to oneself, the ensuing personal behaviour would be not to act in this manner towards others.

Every organisation would enhance greatly its image and reputation, as well as its economic viability, in clarifying its corporate values and looking inwardly at its behaviour. Such a value-based strategy would embrace the desires and galvanise the moral principles and practices of both internal and external stakeholders. As far as Blanchard & O'Connor (1997) are concerned, the foundations of managing by values should evolve as: *Be Ethical, Be Responsive and Be Profitable*. In properly effected management, these three attitudes would endorse the view that there is only one boss: the company's values. Such a stance would enhance loyalty towards the organisation, breed self-respect and appreciation from peers as well encourage creativity and self-development. In short, in order to deliver reduced risk of 'unacceptable' decisions, the organisation should identify, articulate, modify as well as understand three significant facets:

[i] its overall operational requirements
[ii] where and why differences may occur
[iii] whether its values are established within its 'local' moral framework

Cascaded down, as Marr (2006) propounds, value must be underpinned by a shared understanding of the strategy which, in turn, would help create a common purpose, a shared identity and a sense of community. To become world class, such an inter-play is sure to provide true cross-fertilisation throughout.

There are no ifs or buts in the sentiment that organisations should add 'value', in economic and reputational terms, the latter being the intangible asset that can make or break a business. Though the word relates different things to different people and is often abused in relation to its use and meaning, it can also be interpreted as a belief or moral principle that lies behind a company's culture. It is through such a corporate culture that the values of managers and employees alike are shaped and pointed in a common direction. Sustained values should be basic truths that are virtually impossible to refute and need to be identified and stated simply so that they can be easily understood and employed. In this regard, two salient examples come to the fore: [1] the chemicals company Eastman articulates its values as, almost, single words: honesty and integrity, fairness, trust, teamwork, diversity, employee well-being, citizenship and, lastly, winning attitude; [2] United Biscuits, in the introduction to the Company's Statement on Ethics and Operating Principles, quite clearly articulate that "Beliefs and values must always come before policies, practices and goals; the latter must be altered if they violate fundamental beliefs". The concepts of 'core value' and 'shared value' underpin the approach to business success. Concurring with Sadler (2002), there are two issues that are clear: [a] the choice of a purpose reflects the organisation's values and [b] an exclusive focus on the bottom line 'shareholder value' sadly reflects materialistic and economic criteria. Stainer & Stainer (2003a) avow that it is the way in which values are, firstly, utilised in the overall corporate strategy and, secondly, accepted by society. Stainer (2006) proposes a basic schema, representing the CSR cycle in relation to its cardinal components [Figure 1]:

As can be seen, it is founded on the mission of values of the organisation. The loop consists of *communication* where the challenge faced, according to Mestre *et al* (2007), is compounded by the fact that individuals are required to communicate vertically with superiors and subordinates as well as horizontally with peers. *Decisions* and their *implementation* may appear simplistic but are often clouded by ambiguity, multiple points of view and conflicting responsibilities. Those who experience *managerial support* would inevitably demonstrate higher *commitment* leading to improved *outcomes* which are the ultimate result of the productive process. Indeed, *assessment and monitoring*, seriously conducted, would reveal how CSR is manifested within the organisation. This is especially when carrying out a *strategic review* to ascertain, as articulated by Stainer & Stainer (2003b), whether values have been nurtured to balance at least major stakeholder expectations. The concept of the CSR cycle assists management to effectively focus on the drivers of exemplary operations.

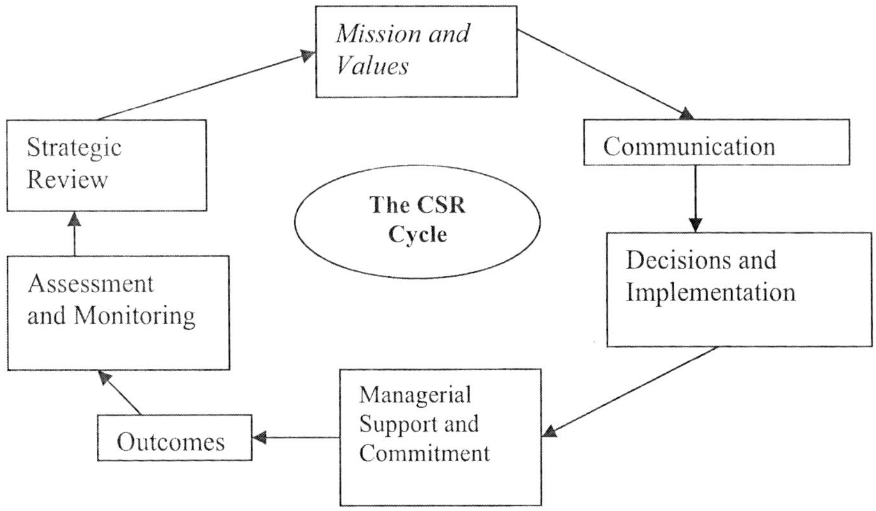

Figure 1. The CSR Cycle and Its Components.

Like beauty and quality, Stainer *et al* (1999) claim that morality is in the eyes of the beholder and most difficult to assess - this can certainly be further compounded by such factors as strategic change, behaviour of others and information availability. The business ethical stance in day-to-day activities can be well enhanced through an all-embracing and inclusive approach. Stainer (2006) believes that this ought to acknowledge the *four* pivotal dimensions of ethical thinking which, in turn, would foster an inherent culture of respect, responsibility and trust:

(a) *ethical awareness* - Kidder & Bloom (2001) define it as a sensitivity to emerging ethical issues and a willingness to see their broad implications; they stress that such awareness helps create conditions of trust enabling people to deal with issues and to read the moral barometer astutely and accurately. Management should be alert to potential ethical problems and dilemmas.

(b) *moral intent* - As espoused by LaFollette (2000), genuine intentions are themselves habits acquired, developed and enhanced over time. When facing difficult decisions, managers often experience a 'gut' feeling of what is 'right' or 'wrong'. Thus, it is inevitable that managerial assumptions and behavioural issues can encourage or impede on actual ethical conduct within the workplace.

(c) *principled judgement* - Among their features of moral pronouncement, Kaptein & Wempe (2002) state that moral judgements are key because they evoke feelings of shame or pride and are concerned with actions and attitudes. There is often a call for help and guidance to interpret the significance of the information and to consider implications for policy and practice, thus enhancing moral judgement.

(d) *responsible action* – It is assumed that those with strong moral values would reinforce moral action and practice, as highlighted by Foster Back (2005). She underlines that ethical acumen is a key competence for business leadership because the ethical leader's attributes ought to include moral courage, openness, fair-mindedness, honesty and the ability to listen to stakeholders. This action is the climax of bonding together awareness, intent and judgement – the foundations of *corporate social responsibility*.

The ethical framework used by Lantos (2001) examines CSR as altruistic and strategic; the former relates to minimum expectations whilst the latter is when an organisation undertakes certain 'caring corporate community service activities' that accomplish strategic business goals. In other words, what is good for business appears to be good for society but what must not be forgotten, in the rush to just blame business for society's ills, is that there must be personal responsibility by everyone.

Responsible Business Decision-Making

Whatever scenario, Webley (2006) purports that there is a gap in many organisations between having an ethics policy and its effect on the business decisions and behaviour of employees. It is often a strenuous journey for companies to invest resources in demonstrable ethics programmes which would, ultimately, enhance their reputation and leave them better prepared for a sustainable future. Over time, it is religions and philosophical theories that had a role to play in making decisions as they form a basis for beliefs, values and morality. However, it must be understood, as Stainer (2004) intimates, that there can be disagreement and conflict between them, often leading the decision-maker to despair when resolving ethical issues or concluding that one resolution is as good as, or better than, another. Indeed, double standards must not be tolerated and rational tools must be used. Miller *et al* (1997) underline the need to concentrate on those matters related to the larger and consequential ones which, firstly, govern the actions that take place, secondly, shape the future direction of the organisation and, thirdly, affect the lives of the people within it. Consequences of actions may be considered through the Jewish *Mishnah* Ethics of the Fathers 4:2 – "for one positive act leads to another positive act and one transgression leads to another transgression".

What is most salient, in practical business situations, is the underlying knowledge that enriches and improves the thought process. The best vehicle is to, not only analyse to the full each issue for its own merit, but also develop thorough and powerful arguments for what is to be considered as the 'correct' judgement. This is where values, objectives and decision variables ought to be interlaced. In practical terms, Gully *et* al (2006) reveal a comprehensive, adroit and logical decision-making process to assist managers in their operational and strategic deliberations, whatever the time scale [Figure 2]:

The illustration shows that the traditional course of making a decision regarding a situation, dilemma or problem ought to be re-visited through a moral 'double check' in order to reach the final decision, making the necessary changes. This rationale is because ethics have a significant place in the business decision-making world. The ethical process of rationality ought also relate to:

a. identifying or analysing a situation/problem
b. ensuring up-to-date information is at hand
c. exploring the alternatives
d. selecting one through a weighting method
e. implementing it and evaluating the results with the best of intentions

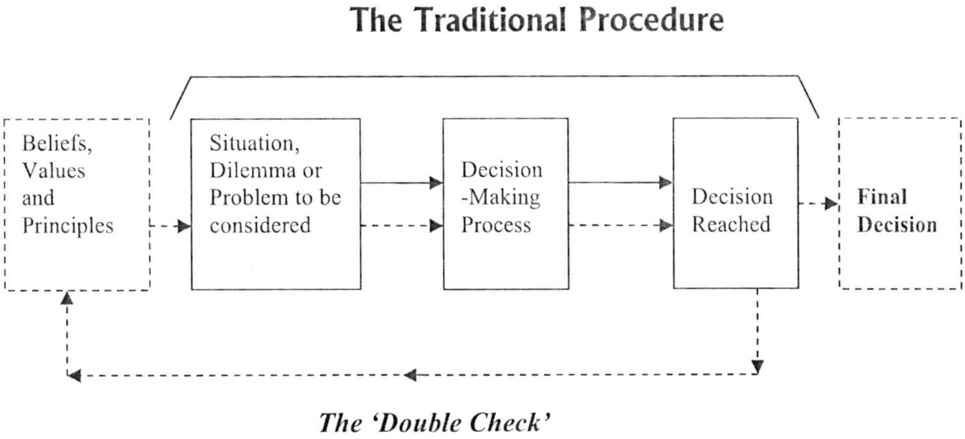

Figure 2. Management Decision-Making Reviewed.

This managerial challenge has no one route and, often, there is no one single starting point. Over two decades ago, Rest (1986) suggested a distinct four-part model, where success is to be achieved at each stage of the decision-making process:

Stage 1: recognition of the moral issue(s) involved
Stage 2: capability of moral judgement by the decision-maker
Stage 3: intent where the decision-maker must have resolve to behave morally
Stage 4: action on the moral concerns

À la Rest, Kidder & Bloom (2001), when discussing ethical fitness, also propose a four-step workout of moral awareness, values definition, ethical analysis and dilemma resolution. Still, ethical decisions may be easy when the facts are clear and choices are perceived as 'right' or 'wrong'; however, it is a different story when the situation is controversial and complex, such as being clouded by ambiguity, multiple points of view and conflicting responsibilities. Thus, the process of moral decision-making, as stated by Monks & Minow (2001), requires, at minimum, the capacity to, firstly, use moral reasoning and, secondly, control not only overt corporate acts but also the structure of policies and rules. Being aware of judgemental heuristics which are generally inherent in individual behaviour, with their potential biases, can assist decision-making competence. Yet, managers are rarely alert to the fact that they naturally utilise such mechanisms in their thought processes and they need to 'consciously' employ them in their decision-making because every process relies on the experience, intelligence and integrity of the decision-maker. Yet, problems do arise because of the subjectivity and definition of what is perceived to be acceptable or unacceptable. In the main, high business responsibility must match societal expectations. Certainly, every manager ought to have the moral courage to understand that it is imperative to go down the route of ethical thinking. As President Lyndon Johnson once stated: "Doing the right thing is easy, it's knowing what the right thing is that is the difficult part".

As businesses do not operate in isolation, how to be commercially successful in a highly competitive international arena, while at the same time balancing the concern for people, profits and ecology is a fundamental issue facing contemporary management. Thus there is a definite urgency for them to find appropriate ways of improving their decision-making, an activity which lies at the heart of management. This should be underpinned through frameworks and procedures that allow logical and relevant measurement and analysis. As Creelman (1996) propounds, the key is to discover how human, organisational and customer intellectual assets can be balanced so that they can combine to create value. Developing a family of metrics, it is believed that 'qualitative' facets, welded to 'quantitative' ones, offer findings and opinions that may influence not only policies but also behaviour and attitude in the work environment for the better. These should be a combination of traditional measures, such as productivity, quality and customer satisfaction, to be allied to those more *avant-garde*, such as societal, ethical and environmental dimensions. Undeniably, all the actions of any organisation are, explicitly or implicitly, the result of decisions. Though decisions give the perception of being decisive, they are often taken under constraints with disregard to consequent impacts on the stakeholder community. With good intentions aside, today's problems often emanate from yesterday's solutions and, thus, it is important to be conscious of that prevention is better than cure.

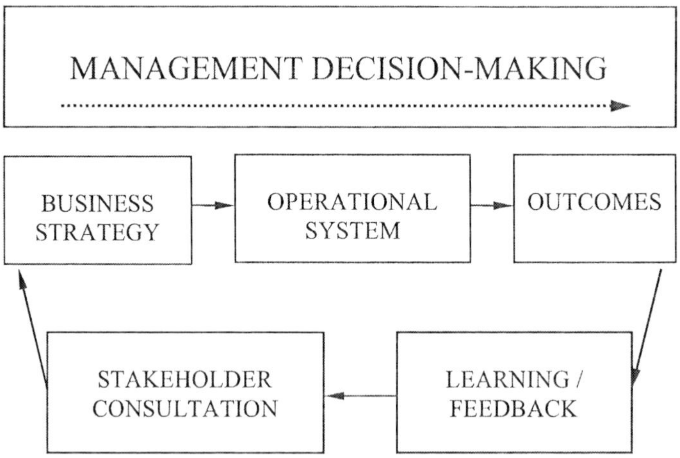

Figure 3. Management Decision-Making Cycle.

In general, the business *modus operandi* can be translated into a basic schema representing the operational system of Inputs, to Process through to Outputs. Yet, the management decision-making process, illustrated by Stainer (2004), must be perceived to span from the initial business strategy, through the whole operational system to the long-term impact of the business on stakeholders as outcomes [Figure 3]. It is these outcomes which ought to be concentrated upon as these are pertinent in relation to the ensuing effects. The lessons learnt need to be monitored as well as fed back, with stakeholder consultation, in the pursuit of excellence.

Management ethics are the moral premise on which executive decisions are made and should not be seen as a 'veneer' because the duty of any organisation is to behave honestly and with integrity as well as link morality and responsibility in the management decision-making processes. These actions should be underpinned with metrics that can provide a strategic focus so that everyone in the organisation can understand and work towards the same objectives and goals. Properly used, such indicators could formulate performance direction and, hence, new approaches and solutions could be introduced to either remedy or improve situations. It is important to realise that, whether a framework is to be employed or a measurement to be carried out, no methodology is perfect because they are only a thermometer, not a panacea, but furnish the analytical basis of decision-making. This is especially true in such volatile and controversial facets of the conduct of business within a multi-cultural global environment. Needless to say, each organisation should adapt according to its own stakeholder demands, strategic needs as well as its individual business environment.

As Lord Thurlow (1731-1806) proclaimed, corporations have neither bodies to be punished nor souls to be condemned; they therefore do as they like. In this vein, successful strategic thinking needs to take into account the welfare and better quality of life for those working within the organisation and the wider society. Much time, commitment and effort need to be invested in the moral minefield of business decision-making because of the continual cultural shift in social attitudes and values. Though organisations, be they small, medium or large, are creators of wealth and jobs, they must also anticipate and recognise their impact, whether beneficial or adverse, internal or external, local or global.

CSR and Decision Making

According to O'Regan & Ghobadian (2005), there is close relationship between well-developed strategic plans and superior performance. Yet, Warren (2003) moans that strategic management is in a bad way but stresses that the problem can and must be fixed through the notion of 'professionalisation'. This concept points to a number of features which could generate confidence in decision-making whereby, firstly, management knows what it is doing and, secondly, will recommend and carry out sound courses of action. On a gloomy side, it is felt that most strategic initiatives taken by the majority of organisations carry a very high risk of failure and that the price of relying on gifted 'amateurs', advised by those with vested interests, is enormous. Indeed, there often seems to be a chasm between strategic intent and its execution, be it wide or narrow, and that is why strategy itself ought to be holistic across the entire business, cutting right through all levels of the hierarchy. It also ought to become an integral part of each managerial function – all in a commendable climate of CSR.

No decision-making methodology is perfect, especially in such volatile and controversial facets of the conduct of business within a global environment. But, what is encouraging is that greater consciousness is intensifying. In this regard, the high-performing socially responsible organisation would need to focus on four core features, as shown by Stainer & Stainer (2003b), that should be welded and not confined within their own silos [Figure 4]:

The ethical decision-making process should take into account the question of inclusive value, coupled with a stakeholder approach of dialogue and sensitivity. As such, this proposal should be linked to performance criteria as well as strategic goals. It is this synergetic interactivity and mutuality of such interrelationships that make it clear that organisations and stakeholders share the power and responsibility. This phenomenon would influence the economic potential for the business which, in turn, would benefit society as a whole. The weaving together of these elements would provide management with an umbrella perspective as organisations do work within a societal framework. Given the uncertainty that usually comes with such a scenario, organisations should demonstrate their ability in decision-making to cope with the 'feasible' rather than the 'desirable', acknowledging what could be interpreted as corporate 'political' implications.

Organisations have significantly altered in recent years in that they have become more dynamic and have to face constant challenges. Indeed, there has been a giant moral leap since the rudimentary ethics policies of yesteryear. The socially-responsive organisation should consider in its decision-making various strategies and carefully plan for the effects and impacts. It must aim to permeate values, be they openness, transparency, accountability or tolerance, through such implements as statements of company philosophy or codes of integrity. This *travail* should be interpreted into practical guidelines and codes of good conduct and best practice. It is with foresight, rather than hindsight, that the wise manager should take on board the pros and cons of the situation before proceeding with a final decision, ensuring that there is an agreed-upon and formalised process to consider each decision for its own merit, laying out the facts, alternatives and obligations.

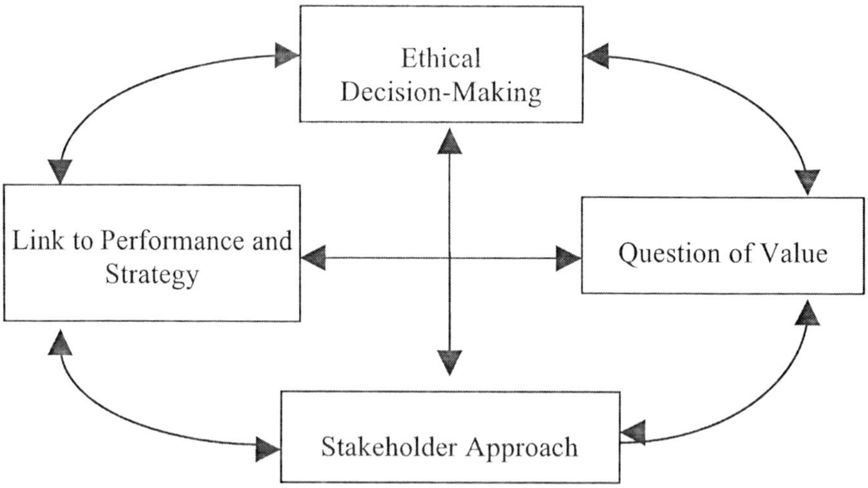

Figure 4. Core Features and Their Interrelationships.

Whether the reasons are based on risk avoidance or increased flexibility, it is important, as expounded by Henriques (2004), to foster an inclusive communication system in order to be sensitive to CSR, sustainability and the triple bottom line. From the outset, listening to and working with stakeholders are essential rudiments in decision-making. This is to be carried out in a logical, straightforward and open manner because it would add value and stimulate organisational performance. In the modern competitive arena, organisations should be focusing on the twin levels of business performance attainment and ethical decision-making [Figure 5]. It can be appreciated that, should high levels of both these two components be achieved, their culmination would strategically propel the organisation towards attaining world-class status. In the end, according to Fort (2003), there are ethical choices that every company makes about what kind of a company it wants to be and, in the long run, those choices make all the differences in the world.

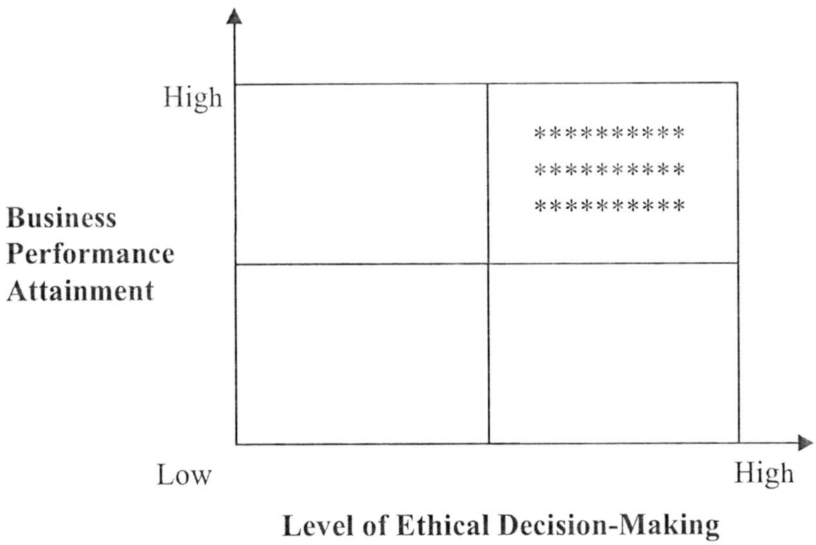

Figure 5. The Relationship Between Business Performance Attainment and the Level of Ethical Decision Making.

Responsible business decisions must be based on sound moral values, which are implicitly related to standards of ethical behaviour. Executing this agenda, the forward-looking organisation would have the aspiration to achieve betterment for its stakeholders - an added-value purpose and an inclusive kinship to strive toward. Thus, an ethical culture can be nurtured through the instigation and use of value-based management techniques, the main benefits of which will be an improved corporate image and a better physical and moral environment, both in and out of the workplace. Stainer (2006) puts forward an example of the inter-twining of strategy with performance and CSR [Figure 6]. As can be seen, improved performance must be perceived as a continuum in terms of the ability to meet employee and customer satisfaction, concurrently augmenting reputation and generating increased demand and market share. In this way, profits or added value potential, through greater freedom in cost/price policies, could be well achieved. In the words of Fountain (2001), "if a person [or organisation] is responsible, most other virtues follow". The synergy and interrelationship between performance and its management with CSR would inevitably signal the dawn of new era of enlightened business strategic thinking.

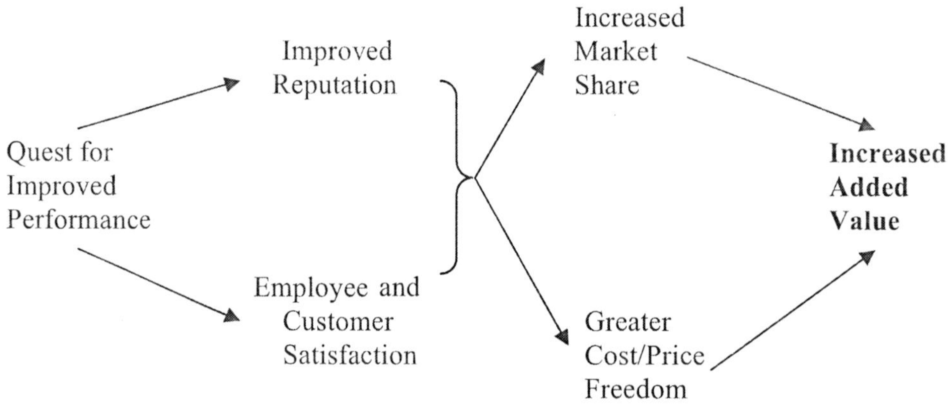

Figure 6. Increased Added Value from Improved Performance.

The difficulty is to determine, understand as well as seek to resolve the complexity of making managerial decisions in an ethical manner. The real driving force is the way in which stakeholder values and expectations are gleaned, communicated and utilised in corporate strategy as well as accepted by the wider society. In the contemporary business environment, as Marchica (2004) states, what is needed is an accountable organisation that reclaims integrity and restores trust. In the 'new' economy, Hagan & Moon (2001) also stress that business models must incorporate accountability which would involve a broader ethical dimension with which businesses must grapple. This view must be embraced because, as Stainer (2004) indicates, the consequent impact could be a greater risk of ethical conflict that can damage an organisation. Indeed, the bottom line is changing through increasing the emphasis on sustainable development and CSR, based on 'unambiguous' ethics. In the contemporary environment, every business should:

1. meet society's expectations
2. build knowledge and CSR skills
3. question 'business as usual' syndrome
4. strengthen stakeholder relations
5. take a long-term view

In a similar vein on an international level, McIntosh *et al* (2003) purport that the United Nations Global Compact seeks to align businesses on the road to perceive capitalism 'with a human face'. However, Hopkins (2007) feels that the United Nations show excellent intent in this direction but, sadly, do not have the power or the reach of the multi-national enterprises to be particularly effective. Yet, to be financially successful in a highly competitive 'battlefield' is being acutely magnified through:

- the globalisation syndrome
- the rise in corporate scandals
- societal perception of unethical behaviour by organisations
- growing public distrust of corporate activity
- technological advancement

Yet, it must be remembered that ethical problems in business are as old as business itself. Holden *et al* (2001) propose that, if society gives a business the licence to operate, then reputation and its management are all about ensuring that such a licence will be renewed. With discreet moral leadership, business ought to provide a system by which to disseminate an inherent ethical culture. Both individual characteristics and organisational contexts are vital keys for the understanding of ethics-related attitudes and behaviours. Practical approaches can assist the decision-maker to get to grips with complexity and give access to unexpected questions and means of changing situations through the capacity of using moral deduction. This is especially true when outcomes affect society at large. Exemplary corporate conduct can certainly be guided and achieved, at all levels, through commitment, flexibility, dialogue and communication, as well as linking performance to responsibility.

Whenever questions arise, such as ‘is it fair?’ or ‘is it right?’, the decision-maker is entering a minefield of ethical dilemmas. As Ruskin (2000) affirms: "what we think or what we believe is, in the end, of little consequence. The only thing of consequence is what we do". This reasoning confirms that management decisions and consequent actions, structured on stakeholder values, efficaciously designed, measured and monitored, are the cardinal ingredients to performance advances. Not only has a shift in ethics occurred and value-based management become essential, there is also a definite synergy between business excellence and good ethical practice, driven by integrity and trust. Yet, one must ask the question: where does responsibility end? In response, Simms (2004) underlines that individual responsibility, whether that of the manager or consumer, must not be forgotten in the rush to blame big businesses for society’s ills. According to Stainer (1999), it should be apparent that if an organisation’s accountability is to the wide society then, surely, society’s responsibility must be to morality. Businesses that wish to thrive in the next decade and beyond must look for new perspectives in this arena and keep their minds open, or at least ajar.

Aiding and developing moral awareness and judgement within the organisation should be a main ingredient of its long-term strategy. Cramer (2005) analyses the learning experiences of companies in the Netherlands trying to implement corporate social responsibility in their business practices. She concludes and reiterates that most of the learning accrued at the individual and organisational levels does not seem to be successful without CSR being embedded in the business culture. Research findings by Whitehouse (2006) in the UK suggest that CSR reveals itself among large companies not as a uniform concept but as a variety of conceptions. As such, based on the CSR stakeholder model by De Colle (2005), an efficacious plan is presented and can be seen as a ‘meta-process’ for improved organisational decision-making:

- Identify and map all stakeholders and ensure continuous engagement
- Assess issues at stake
- Recognise corporate values and existing commitments
- Prioritise issues
- Develop appropriate policies
- Set objectives
- Measure performance
- Report and communicate and review

Needless to say, there are so many different directions in which CSR is developing. The question is very much related to the long-term to see not what the corporation stands for but what it could be in the coming years. For visionaries, CSR ought to bear the seeds of a future where an organisation is so up-to-date that it really is part of a human and democratic world. Just as good parents have the responsibility to help their children develop moral values and judgement in making decisions, so too has business to show the lead to its stakeholders. A value-based mission ought not lower its standards and management should act with human dignity and respect. The conviction that transcends is that every organisation should judge it necessary to incorporate morality and responsibility in its decision-making.

Conclusion

The overall impression is that CSR is on the 'hot list' of emerging social phenomena, with much debate and discussion emanating from its agenda. It might annoy and aggravate many in the business world but, emphatically, it strikes a chord with the general public. Kitchin (2002) states that "one moment, CSR seems to mean the engagement of non-governmental organizations; the next it is all about charitable donations; five minutes later it seems to mean the ethical treatment of employees – one minute the NGOs are calling the shots, the next the accountants are in on the act selling reputation assurance". Jones (2003) truly argues that it is quite problematic for CSR to be exercised with the aim of obtaining calculative advantage or strategic competitive edge. In his opinion, if being socially responsible means 'giving back' to society, then as soon as an organisation starts to calculate the returns from being socially responsible, or as soon as it starts to strategise being ethical, it is actually not committing the act of giving. It seems that confusion continues in the nature and purpose of CSR.

An ethical decision is meant to relate to a judgement about right and wrong but, as Morris (2004) point outs, by using this language, the situation has instantly been identified as moral in nature. The correct stance is to embark on this passage *before* situations are examined and considered. As far as CSR is concerned, the socially responsible aspects should be inculcated into the organisational policies and processes and not used solely as management instruments for strategic competitive advantage. Hopkins (2007) vehemently believes that, in the future, CSR will be embedded in organisational culture and profile to such an extent that it will not be explicitly noticed anymore and will probably disappear. Yet, the sentiments behind it will be in place and the organisation, whatever its size or perceived 'power', will certainly change its form and CSR will just become part and parcel of normal business practice. Bendell (2005) states that, understanding power and its responsible use is probably the bedrock question underlying much work on corporate citizenship. Crowther & Rayman-Bacchus (2004) suggest that the concern with CSR is part of a wider social movement in which citizens are seeking to wrest power back from the global corporate world and demand a share in the benefits of civilisation. They present a full range of meaning to the notion of responsibility; the arguments appertain to:

(a) *retrospective* responsibility which seeks to allocate blame and reasons for the state of relations between corporation and stakeholders, and
(b) *prospective* responsibility where corporations and governments have obligations and duties to exercise

Cynically, *The Economist* (2005) points out that businesses should not, or be asked to, do the work of governments. Social justice and public good do not come under their direct province but, yet, it is imperative for them to consider and listen to their stakeholders. The point that critics should be making, as far as Brittan (1996) is concerned, is that the CSR movement lacks the legitimacy of either the market or the political process. He feels it is "an attempt to achieve public policy objectives on the cheap and on the side". Young (2005) expresses disappointment with British businesses; they do no not seem to quite get the thrust of what CSR is about. In his view, they stop acting like businesses and get all charitable; what they should do is act like a business but keep a CSR hat on. Stern (2004), contemplating the perils of CSR, states that when companies sign up publicly to something called 'CSR', they open a can of worms because every business decision or action would be subjected to the CSR test and its implications on stakeholders. He affirms vigorously that CSR is bound to fail in companies where it is adopted simply for reasons of public relations – that is not only dishonest, it is misguided. Unfortunately, CSR can potentially be perceived as a dangerous mix of power and unaccountability as well as a waste of resources; thus, is it best to just stick to legislation and regulation?

Historically, Aristotle and John Stuart Mill could not resolve ethical dilemmas once and for all. So how is it likely that today's business leaders can solve them with ethical jargon? And, indeed, Waddock & Bodwell (2007) ask the question: why bother? The answer is quite simple in that never has it been easier for employees, activists, investors, community members, the media and other critical observers to find fault with companies. The problem encountered by every business is that, on one hand, the domain of responsibility defines the parameters of decision-making performance that are relevant and, on the other, that performance defines a domain of responsibility. This catch-22 situation is to be firmly dealt with by management to ascertain the appropriate starting point. Thus, it is felt that every organisation has to be *au courant* because the stakeholding keys will be responsible for the harvesting of economic and societal rewards as well as long-term prosperity. De Geus (1997) asserts that companies often die because their managers focus on the economic activity of producing goods and services and they forget that their organisation's true nature is that of a community of humans. They opt to 'plaster over the cracks' and are reluctant to talk about ethical values rather than fundamentally establish a corporate behavioural culture change. Smith (2003) focuses mainly on 'how' companies can be socially responsible: they ought to expect little from their CSR activities and become socially responsible as "that is the noble way for corporations to behave". In the words of industrialist Charles Wang, "Ultimately, it is not about the money we make; it is about the journey we take".

The frameworks and practical approaches discussed assess, review and re-balance the different techniques for any business to achieve intended outcomes through the notion of the triple bottom line. An integrated CSR management philosophy will enable organisations to achieve the benefits of the social and ethical alchemy. Peters (2004) suggests that there is no harm in using some of the lessons from the quality assurance movement, with CSR being played out against a capitalist imperative with its messages heard using the language of capital. In tangent, William Kendall (2004), Chief Executive of Green and Blacks in the UK, believes that "in the same way top boards became more aware of environmental matters, they are becoming more aware of ethics as an issue in business – they have to do it because it is part of the product and the cost of being in business".

In order to be effective and efficient, business decision-making, conducted responsibly and synergetically, must be robust and would require an enlightened avenue of effective strategies which embrace integrity and commitment, welded to inclusive values. This is because, if reality and high principled rhetoric do not match, there is a heavy price to be paid. At the crux, decision-making in the business environment must be an activity accomplished with timeless values in mind. With vision, those that wish to thrive and be sustainable in the future must look for new perspectives and rise above cynicism where the terms 'business' and 'ethics' provide an oxymoron. It is undeniable that the economic and moral link must be galvanised in the quest for responsible corporate performance success.

References

Andriof, J. & Waddock, S. (2002) 'Unfolding stakeholder engagement' in *Unfolding Stakeholder Thinking – Theory, Responsibility and Engagement*, J. Andriof, S. Waddock, B. Husted & S. Sutherland Rahman (eds), Sheffield, Greenleaf Publishing.

Atkinson, P. (2004) 'Strategy – failing to plan is planning to fail', *Management Services*, Vol.48, No.1, pp.14-18.

Bendell, J. (2005) *Lifeworth Annual Review of Corporate Responsibility*, http://www.lifeworth.net

Bishop, A. (2005) 'Moral principles defined: a decision-making perspective', *International Journal of Management and Decision Making*, Vol.6, Nos.3/4, pp.326-333.

Blanchard, K. & O'Connor, M. (1997) *Managing By Values*, San Francisco, Berrett-Koehler.

Boehm, A. (2002) 'Corporate social responsibility: a complementary perspective of community and corporate leaders', *Business and Society Review*, Vol.107, No.2, pp.171-194.

Brittan, S. (1996) *Capitalism with a Human Face*, London, Fontana Press.

Carroll, A.B. (1997) 'Social responsibility', in *The Blackwell Encyclopedic Dictionary of Business Ethics*, P.H. Werhane & R.E. Freeman (eds), Malden, Mass, Blackwell Publishers.

Cowe, R. (2002) 'Winning board games', in *Business Sustainability – CBI-KPMG Business Guide*, R. Cowe, London, Caspian Publishing.

Cramer, J. (2005) 'Company learning about corporate social responsibility', *Business Strategy and the Environment*, Vol.14, No.4, pp.255-266.

Creelman, J. (1996) 'Why money's only part of the score', *Financial Director*, April, pp.39-44.

Crowther, D. & Rayman-Bacchus, L. (2004) *Perspectives on Corporate Social Responsibility*, Aldershot, Ashgate Publishing.

Davis, I. (2005) 'The biggest contract', *The Economist*, Vo.375, No.8428, 28 May, pp.87-89

De Colle, S. (2005) 'A stakeholder management model for ethical decision making', *International Journal of Management and Decision Making*, Vol.6, Nos.3/4, pp.299-314

De Geus, A. (1997) *The Living Company*, London, Nicholas Brearley.

Fort, T. (2003) 'The best ethical choices come when long-term impact rules', in *The Ethical Challenge – How to Lead with Unyielding Integrity*, N.M. Tichy & A.R. McGill (eds), San Francisco, Jossey-Bass.

Foster Back, P. (2005) *Setting the Tone – Ethical Business Leadership*, London, Institute of Business Ethics.

Foster Back, P. (2007) 'Ethics in business: the key things you need to know', Paper presented at Middlesex University Business School, London, 21 March 2007.

Fountain, D. (2001) 'Common sense talk', *Asian Productivity Organization News*, Vol.31, No.11, p.4.

Gully, A. Stainer, L. & Stainer, A. (2006) 'Responsible business decisions: an over-arching framework', *Journal of Public Affairs*, August-November, Vol.6, Nos.3/4, pp.185-196.

Hagan, J. & Moon, C. (2001) 'New economy, new ethics' in *Business Ethics – Facing Up to the Issues*, C. Moon & C. Bonny (eds), London, Profile Books.

Henriques, A. (2004) 'CSR, sustainability and the triple bottom line', in *The Triple Bottom Line – Does It All Add Up?*, A. Henriques & J. Richardson (eds), London, Earthscan.

Holden, T., Adnan, T., Browne, J. & Willhelmij, P. (2001) 'Licence renewed – who's in charge of corporate reputation?', *RSA Journal*, Vol.CXLVIII, No.5499, pp.20-21.

Hopkins, M. (2007) *Corporate Social Responsibility and International Development – Is Business the Solution?*, London, Earthscan.

Jones, C. (2003) 'As if business ethics were possible: 'within such limits ....', *Organization*, Vol.10, No.2, pp.223-248.

Kaptein, M. & Wempe, J. (2002) *The Balanced Company – A Theory of Corporate Integrity*, Oxford, Oxford University Press.

Kendall, W. (2004) 'Cover story on William Kendall', *Director*, Vol.57, No.8, pp.56-61.

Kidder, R. & Bloom, S. (2001) 'Ethical fitness in today's business environment', in *Business Ethics – Facing up to the Issues*, C. Moon & C. Bonny (eds), London, Profile Books Ltd.

Kitchen, T. (2002) 'Corporate social responsibility – a brand explanation', *Brand Management*, Vol.10, Nos.4/5, pp.312-326.

LaFollette, H. (2000) 'Pragmatic ethics', in *The Blackwell Guide to Ethical Theory*, H. LaFollette (ed), Malden, Blackwell Publishers.

Lantos, G.P. (2001) 'The boundaries of strategic corporate social responsibility', *Journal of Consumer Marketing*, Vol.18, No.2, pp.595-630.

Lewis, S. (2003) 'Reputation and corporate responsibility', *Journal of Communication Management*, Vol.7, No.4, pp.356-394.

Marchica, J. (2004) *The Accountable Organization –Reclaiming Integrity, Restoring Trust*, London, Davies-Black Publishing.

Marr, B. (2006) *Strategic Performance Management – Leveraging and Measuring Your Intangible Value Drivers*, Oxford, Butterworth-Heinemann.

Matsushita, K. (2000) 'Common sense talk', *Asian Productivity Organization News*, Vol.30, No.8, p.4.

McIntosh, M., Thomas, R., Leipziger, D. & Coleman, G. (2003) *Living Corporate Citizenship – Strategic Routes to Socially Responsible Business*, London, FT/Prentice Hall.

Mestre, M., Stainer, A. & Stainer, L. (2005) 'Making situations visible: ethics, truth and decisions', *International Journal of Management and Decision Making*, Vol.6, Nos.3/4, pp.315-325.

Mestre, M., Stainer, L. & Stainer, A. (2007) 'First-line management – the operational and ethical challenges', *International Journal of Human Resources Development and Management*, Vol.7, No.2, pp.105-118.

Miller, S.J., Hickson, D.J. & Wilson D.C. (1997) 'Decision-making in organizations', in *Handbook of Organization Studies*, S.R. Clegg, C. Hardy & W.R. Nord (eds), London, Sage.

Monks, R.A.G. & Minow, N. (2001) *Corporate Governance*, Oxford, Blackwell Publishing

Morris, D. (2004) 'Defining a moral problem in business ethics', *Journal of Business Ethics*, Iss.49, pp-347-357.

Mullins, S. (2005) 'Ethical crisis management?', *International Journal of Management and Decision Making*, Vol.6, Nos.3/4, pp.372-381.

O'Regan, N. & Ghobadian, A. (2005) 'The strategic planning process: a navigational tool for competitive advantage', *International Journal of Process Management and Benchmarking*, Vol.1, No.1, pp.63-81.

Peters, J. (2004) 'Social responsibility is free – how good capitalism can co-exist with corporate social responsibility', in *Perspectives on Corporate Social Responsibility*, D. Crowther & L. Rayman-Bacchus (eds), Aldershot, Ashgate Publishing.

Peters, T. (2000) 'Common sense talk', *Asian Productivity Organization News*, Vol.30, No.11, p.4.

Petersen, V.C. (2002) *Beyond Rules in Society and Business*, Cheltenham, Edward Elgar Publishing.

Rest, J.R. (1986) *Moral Development: Advances in Research and Theory*, New York, Praeger

Roberts, A. (2004) Foreword to *Taking the Temperature – Ethical Supply Chain Management*, L. Jamison & H. Murdoch (eds), London, Institute of Business Ethics.

Ruskin, J. (2000) 'Common sense talk', *Asian Productivity Organization News*, Vol.30, No.8, p.4.

Sadler, P. (2002) *Building Tomorrow's Company – A Guide to Sustainable Business Success*, London, Kogan Page.

Schwartz, M.S. & Carroll, A.B. (2003) 'Corporate social responsibility – a three-domain approach', *Business Ethics Quarterly*, Vol.13, No.4, pp.503-530.

Simms, J. (2004) 'Buyer beware', *Director*, Vol.57, No.10, p.27.

Smith, N.C. (2003) 'Corporate social responsibility: whether or how?', *California Management Review*, Vol.45, No.4, pp.52-76.

Stainer, A. (1999) 'Productivity, performance and paradise', *Management Services*, Vol.43, No.6, pp.8-11.

Stainer, A. & Stainer, L. (2003a) 'Total productivity: a stakeholder perspective', *International Journal of Business Performance Management*, Vol.5, Nos.2/3, pp.166-173.

Stainer, A. & Stainer, L. (2003b) 'Management decision-making – an ethical perspective', *Municipal Engineer*, December, Vol.156, Iss.ME4, pp.223-227.

Stainer, L. (2004) 'Ethical dimensions of management decision-making', *Strategic Change*, September-October, Vol.13, No.6, pp.333-342.

Stainer, L. (2006) 'Performance management and corporate social responsibility: the strategic connection', *Strategic Change*, August, Vol.15, No.5, pp.253-264.

Stainer, L., Stainer, A. & Gully, A. (1999) 'Ethics and performance management', *International Journal of Technology Management*, Vol.17, Nos.7/8, pp.776-785.

Stern, S. (2004) 'The Perils of CSR', *RSA Journal*, Vol.CLI, No.5510, pp.32-35.

The Economist (2005) 'The good company – a survey of corporate social responsibility', *The Economist*, 22 January.

Towells, S. (2003) 'From planning to strategic intent', *Strategy Magazine*, No.1, pp.20-24.

Tyger, F. (2001) 'Common sense talk', *Asian Productivity Organization News*, Vol.31, No.7, p.4.

Waddock, S. & Bodwell, C. (2007) *Total Responsibility Management: The Manual*, Sheffield, Greenleaf Publishing.

Warnock, B.M. (2006) 'The foundations of global morality', *RSA Journal*, Vol.CLIII, No.5522, pp.24-31.

Warren, K. (2003) 'Professionalizing strategic management', *Strategy Magazine*, Iss.1, pp.3-6

Webley, S. (2006) *Making Business Ethics Work – The Foundations of Effective Embedding*, London, Institute of Business Ethics.

Webley, S. & Dryden, P. (2005) *Ethics at Work – A National Survey*, London, Institute of Business Ethics.

Whitehouse, L. (2006) 'Corporate social responsibility: views from the frontline', *Journal of Business Ethics*, Iss.63, pp.279-296.

World Business Council for Sustainable Development (2003), http://www.wbcsd.org

Young, M. (2005) 'From the top – director of the month', *Director*, Vol.58, No.12, p.17.

Zadek, S. (2001) *The Civil Corporation – The New Economy of Corporate Citizenship*, London, Earthscan.

Zadek, S. & Tuppen, C. (2004) 'Adding values: the economics of sustainable business', in *Tomorrow's History*, S. Zadek & P. Raynard (eds), Sheffield, Greenleaf Publishing.

In: Corporate Social Responsibility
Editor: Adam R. Timpere

ISBN: 978-1-60456-284-2

Chapter 4

SHIFTING LOCUS OF INFLUENCE IN THE LABOR UNION MOVEMENT: NEGOTIATIONS IN INTERNATIONAL FRAMEWORK AGREEMENTS

Niklas Egels-Zandén*

Centre for Business in Society, School of Business, Economics and Law at Göteborg University, Box 600, SE – 405 30 Göteborg, Sweden

ABSTRACT

In the ongoing globalization of business, *transnational* industrial relations systems are emerging as complements to traditional *national* systems. Integral to the emergent transnational systems are international framework agreements (IFAs). This chapter shows that a previously unrecognised key aspect of IFAs is that they shift the locus of influence in the union movement from national unions to either global union federations or enterprise level unions. Based on a study of an IFA signing process, this chapter shows how this tension between different levels of the union movement affected both the IFA signing process and the IFA content. The outcome in the studied case was that the locus of influence was decentralized to the enterprise level union. This result challenges the prevalent argument that IFAs centralize influence to global union federations. Instead, this chapter proposes that the locus of influence will be decentralized to the enterprise level when: i) there is a trustful corporate-enterprise level union relation, ii) there is a distrustful corporate-global level union relation, and iii) the corporate driver for adopting an IFA is to foster its relations with its enterprise level union. On the other hand, the locus of influence will be centralized to the global level when: i) there is a distrustful corporate-enterprise level union relation, ii) there is a trustful corporate-global level union relation, and iii) the corporate driver for adopting an IFA is to improve its external legitimacy.

* Niklas.Egels-Zanden@handels.gu.se +46-31-7862729 (telephone)

INTRODUCTION

A process of globalisation is ongoing, marking profound shifts in economic structures, institutional arrangements and the organisation of work (e.g., Stiglitz, 2003; Bhagwati, 2005; Cohen, 2006). Evidence of this development includes increasing competitive pressure, global outsourcing, communications technology evolution, and a homogenisation of consumer tastes and branding (e.g., Klein, 2000). Importantly, the ongoing globalisation is challenging the national organisation of work by introducing a transnational logic of organisation. The transnational organisation of production became prevalent during the 1980s and 1990s as European and US-based TNCs started to offshore much of their production to developing countries (e.g., Jones, 2005; Taylor, 2005). This trend was particularly evident in low-skill industries – such as the garment, footwear and toy industries – in which TNCs to a large extent pursue low-cost strategies (e.g., Christerson and Appelbaum, 1995; Hathcote and Nam, 1999).

The transnational organisation of work is problematic for labour unions that mainly base their activities on national organisations. There are two potential union strategies in response to this challenge. First, unions could redirect focus and influence from the national union level to the enterprise level union, i.e. they could *decentralise* their work to individual TNC enterprise level unions. Second, unions could redirect focus and influence from the national union level to the global union level, i.e. they could *centralise* their work to global union federations (GUFs). At the core of this centralization vs. decentralization tension is the key issue of who should have the right to represent individuals in democratic structures, i.e. where should negotiation power be located within a representative democratic structure such as the labour union movement? Phrased differently, how far from the voters and financers (i.e. individual workers at specific companies) should negotiation power be located? The purpose of this chapter is to study this tension and shifting of locus of dominance in the labour union movement as it is manifested in the negotiations of international framework agreements.

International framework agreements (IFAs) are one of the labour union movement's main responses to the ongoing transnationalisation of work. Unions promote IFAs as an alternative to the currently commonplace voluntary non-binding codes of conduct approach. While codes of conduct and IFAs share the same objective, i.e., to increase the responsibility of TNCs for workers' rights (cf. Braun and Gearhart, 2004; Compa, 2004; Roman, 2004), codes of conduct are unilaterally adopted by corporations and IFAs are negotiated agreements between corporations and labor unions. Today, most TNCs have adopted codes of conduct (e.g., Schlegelmilch and Houston, 1989; Sethi, 1999; Guillén et al., 2002; Nijhof et al., 2003; Kaptein, 2004), whereas only a handful have adopted IFAs (Hammer, 2005; Riisgaard, 2005). However, the number of signed IFAs are steadily increasing (Hammer, 2005; Riisgaard, 2005), making IFAs increasingly important to study.

So far, academic research has almost solely been devoted to codes of conduct and largely neglected IFAs (cf. Egels-Zandén and Hyllman, 2007). Recently, a handful of empirical studies have started to fill the IFA research void (Wills, 2002; Miller, 2004; Fairbrother and Hammer, 2005; Hammer, 2005; Riisgaard, 2005; Anner et al., 2006; Egels-Zandén and Hyllman, 2007). However, while making important contributions, this previous research has neglected some critical aspects of IFAs. In particular, previous research has neglected the centralization vs. decentralization tension *within* the union movement. The purpose of this chapter is to address this gap based on a study of the negotiations leading to the signing of a recent IFA between labor unions and a European TNC.

Previous Research into International Framework Agreements

As noted above, there are two main types of materializations of the emerging transnational industrial relations system: codes of conduct and international framework agreements (IFAs). The main difference between codes of conduct and IFAs are that codes are unilaterally adopted by corporations and IFAs negotiated agreements between corporations and labor unions. Today, the code of conduct approach dominates transnational industrial relations systems, but the importance of IFAs in transnational relations are steadily increasing (Hammer, 2005; Riisgaard, 2005).

Similarly to the dominance of codes of conduct among practitioners, researchers have almost exclusively been interested in codes of conduct as compared to IFAs. While there is ample research into different aspects of codes of conduct (e.g., Cowton and Thompson, 2000; Frenkel, 2001; van Tulder and Kolk, 2001; Nijhof et al., 2003; Egels-Zandén, 2007), it is only recently that a handful of studies have started to analyse IFAs. First, several authors note that IFAs are becoming an increasingly important part of labour unions' agenda (e.g., Gallin, 2000; Muller-Camen et al., 2001; Wills, 2001; Connor, 2004; Spooner, 2004; Chang and Wong, 2005; Royle, 2005; Andersen, 2006; Turnbull, 2006; Waddington, 2006; Doellgast and Greer, 2007). However, these studies do little more than notice that more research is needed into IFAs.

Second, there are some studies that have focused on analysing the content of IFAs, showing that most IFAs have been signed during the last years, build on ILO and UN Conventions, cover both company's own and their suppliers' operations, and involve labour unions in the negotiation processes (Hammer, 2005). Egels-Zandén and Hyllman (2007) also shows that IFAs include more processual aspects of worker representation than do codes of conduct, and Anner et al. (2006) provides comparisons between IFAs and other transnational union strategies.

Third, some studies have focused on the motives for adopting IFAs. Miller (2004) studied the motives by analysing global union federations' strategies for pressuring TNCs to sign IFAs. Miller (2004) found that despite extensive efforts to sign IFAs, global union federations have so-far had only limited success. Riisgaard (2005) also studied the motives concluding that external NGO and union pressure threatening TNCs' legitimacy was important for the signing of IFAs.

Finally, there are a handful of recent empirical studies into the actual implementation of IFAs. Wills (2002) studied the Accor-IUF agreement in developed countries such as USA and Canada and found that IFAs: i) secure access for local unions to workplaces, ii) develop the international dimension of daily union work, iii) provide international support to local union organizing and local negotiations and disputes, and iv) foster internationalism among the workforce. Riisgaard (2005) complemented this picture by studying the Chiquita-COLSIBA IFA in developing countries and showing that it was not fully implemented and that workers were uninformed about the IFA. A recent International Metalworkers' Federation (IMF) commissioned study of 27 foreign-owned IMF related factories has also supported Riisgaard's (2005) findings (AMRC, 2007).

While all of this previous research provides valuable insights into IFAs and the emerging transnational industrial relations system, they neglect the fact that IFAs are leading to a shifting locus of influence in the union movement from a traditional national to a transnational level. The purpose of this chapter is to address this gap in previous research and by doing this provide insights into both the ongoing changes in the union movement and the processes of signing IFAs. As will be shown in this chapter, the tension within the union movement is not simply an abstract theoretical tension. On the contrary, it is manifested in the ongoing negotiations of IFAs and, hence, important to analyse in order to understand IFAs.

The lack of research into the centralization-decentralization tension in the union movement as manifested in the process of signing IFAs is likely related to two factors. First, the role of labour unions is largely neglected in CSR and business ethics literature (Michalos, 1997; Leahy, 2001; Riisgaard, 2005; Provis, 2006), i.e. business ethics researchers have likely ignored IFAs due to their close link to union issues. At the same time, industrial relation researchers have interpreted IFAs as part of the CSR trend (e.g., Miller, 2004; Riisgaard, 2005; Shanahan and Khagram, 2006; Waddington, 2006); a trend that only sparsely has been studied in industrial relations literature (Egels-Zandén and Hyllman, 2007). Hence, IFAs have ended up in a vacuum between two research streams. Second, previous research into tensions between actors in transnational industrial relations has almost exclusively focused on tensions *between* groups of actors. For example, the tension between labour unions and NGOs in transnational industrial relations have received increasing attention recently (e.g., Justice, 2003; Braun and Gearhart, 2004; Roman, 2004; Spooner, 2004; Egels-Zandén and Hyllman, 2006). However, tensions *within* a group of actors – be it NGOs, TNCs, or unions – have largely been left unanalysed. Hence, among the sparse existing research that has focused on IFAs, the focus has been on tensions *between* rather than *within* groups of actors and this has led to a gap in research into the role of tensions within the union movement in the signing of IFAs.

From National to Transnational Industrial Relations

To fully understand the significance of codes of conduct and international framework agreements for industrial relations, a short background is needed regarding recent trends in industrial relations. Traditionally, industrial relations have been handled through collective bargaining and industrial agreements between firms, labour unions, and governments (e.g., Dunlop, 1958; Emery and Thorsrud, 1969; Hedlund and Otterbeck, 1977; Bamber and Lansbury, 1998). These bargaining and industrial agreements have predominantly been based on national legislation and thus been characterised by a high degree of national path-dependence (e.g., IDE, 1981; Piazza, 2002). Hence, industrial relations systems has historically been embedded in a context of national, tripartite arrangements negotiated by actors engaged in ongoing relationships with each other.

However, these national and tripartite industrial relations systems have been challenged by the ongoing globalisation with production moving geographically from a European and US setting to a predominantly Asian setting (cf. Frenkel, 2001; Schrage, 2004). In this process, the European and US national arenas where workers' rights issues traditionally have been negotiated become less relevant and, consequently, the dominant actors in these setting such as national European and US governments loose influence. In contrast, the national settings of developing countries (mainly in Asia) increase in importance. Many Asian countries have fairly stringent labour laws similar to those in Europe and US with countries such as China and Vietnam recently making profound changes in their labour laws (Warner, 1996; Chan, 1998; Ding and Warner, 1999; Cooney et al., 2002). However, there are large gaps between the labour law and practice in these countries – especially in the countries with recently changed laws (Zhu and Fahey, 1999; Lau, 2001; Liew, 2001; Cooney et al., 2002; Chen, 2003; Cooke, 2004; Frenkel and Kim, 2004).

In practice, this means that TNCs that are offshoring production to Asian countries are entering national settings with little labour law enforcement. Since transnational institutions for workers' rights have not yet developed to balance the offshoring trend and the weak enforcement of Asian labour laws, there are industrial relations governance gaps that are starting to be filled by TNCs, unions, and NGOs (Beck, 1992; Rosenau and Czempiel, 1992; Strange, 1996; Christmann and Taylor, 2002; Frenkel and Scott, 2002; Sullivan, 2003; Frenkel and Kim, 2004; Prieto and Quinteros, 2004). These gaps have been filled by the introduction of transnational "soft law" in the form of codes of conduct and/or international framework agreements (Emmelhainz and Adams, 1999; Kolk and van Tulder, 2002; Sethi, 2002; Radin, 2004; Bartley, 2005).

Hence, codes of conduct and international framework agreements comprise *transnational* industrial relations systems that operates in parallel with traditional *national* industrial relations systems. The purpose of this chapter is not to discuss the intricate relations between these national and transnational systems (for an overview of these issues see for example Bartley (2005)). For the purpose of this chapter, it is enough to notice that the emergence of a complementary *transnational* industrial relations system challenges the traditional *national* level of dominance in the labour union movement.

The above described emergence of a transnational industrial relations system in the form of codes of conduct and/or international framework agreements means that negotiations of certain fundament workers' rights issues move from a national (mainly Asian) setting to a transnational (mainly Western) setting. Hence, the transnational industrial relations system *centralise* negotiations of certain fundamental workers' rights. Thörnqvist (1999) argues that decentralisation of workers' rights is partly done to widen wage differentials and stimulate flexibility. Consequently, centralisation of negotiations of fundamental workers' rights could be seen as an attempt to achieve the opposite, i.e. to introduce less wage differentials and limit flexibility. These arguments are also closely linked to those presented by proponents of codes of conduct and/or international framework agreements.

The question of interest in this chapter is where this centralisation of negotiations ends up in the labour union movement hierarchy, i.e. where is the locus of influence shifted to? There are two main potential answers to this question. First, dominance could be shifted from national unions to global union federations, implying a *centralisation* of influence in the union movement. Second, dominance could be shifted from national unions to corporate level unions, implying a *decentralisation* of influence in the union movement.

Fundamentally, this centralization vs. decentralization debate is about the central and general issue of who should have the right to represent individuals in democratic structures, i.e. where should negotiation power be located within the representative democratic structures of the labour union movement. More specifically, what hierarchical level within the union movement is the legitimate spokesperson in transnational industrial relations issues? Should the union movement's transnational industrial relation strategies be mainly bottom-up driven (the effect of decentralization to enterprise level unions) or should strategies be mainly top-down driven (the effect of centralization to global level unions)? Phrased differently, how far from the voters and financers (i.e. individual workers at specific companies) should negotiation power be located?

Method

To explore how the centralization-decentralization tension within the union movement is manifested in and affect the signing of IFAs, I make use of material from an explorative study of the IFA signing process in a European TNC – hereafter referred to as "EuroCorp"[1]. Given the limited understandings of IFAs, the reliance on a qualitative study is in line with previously proposed methods (e.g., Marshall and Rossman, 1995; Lee, 1999; Maguire et al., 2004). EuroCorp was chosen since it is ranked as one of the best European CSR firms and it is also one of the few TNCs that has signed an international framework agreement.

The study of the centralization-decentralization tension in the signing of an IFA is part of a larger study of EuroCorp CSR practices in both Europe and Asia. Data for this larger study was gathered from interviews, written documentation and observations. Between 2005 and 2007, over 100 actors that had links to EuroCorp's CSR practices were interviewed. This included EuroCorp top and middle management, EuroCorp's CSR department, EuroCorp workers, international and local EuroCorp union representatives as well as local and international stakeholders. For the sub-study of the signing of EuroCorp's IFA, I mainly relied on semi-structured interviews with the key actors involved in the process. This included corporate representatives, and enterprise, national and global level union representatives. The interviews lasted on average one hour. In addition to interview data, analysis of documents (mainly different versions of the emergent international framework agreement) was used as background for the interviews and as a complement to the verbal sources.

The collected data were used to construct a chronological representation of EuroCorp's process of signing an IFA focusing on key decision points and conflicts. This chronological representation was then condensed into a short description of the signing process and a more extensive section on how the tension within the union movement affected the process. This empirical description was then sent to the interviewed representatives to validate the description of the definition process. Finally, the interviewees' suggested changes were incorporated into the final description of the definition process.

[1] "EuroCorp" is a anonymized name that has no reference to either the studied TNC's name or any potential firm and/or organization actually named "EuroCorp".

The Process of Developing an International Framework Agreement

Background: International Workers' Rights Turbulence

The focus on corporate social responsibility in relation to developing countries started in late 1980s and early 1990s with activist campaigning uncovering the working conditions in TNCs' and their suppliers' operations (e.g., van Tulder and Kolk, 2001; Roberts, 2003; Frenkel and Kim, 2004; Bartley, 2007). Issues such as child labour and sweatshops were readily debated in mass media putting extensive pressure on TNCs to justify their operations. In the early 1990s, TNCs such as Levi's, GAP, Nike, and Reebok responded to this criticism and embraced and extended responsibility for workers' rights (e.g., Braun and Gearhart, 2004). This extended responsibility was mainly operationalised through corporate adoption of codes of conduct (e.g., Schlegelmilch and Houston, 1989; Sethi, 1999; van Tulder and Kolk, 2001; Guillén et al., 2002; Nijhof et al., 2003). In turn, this led to a growing number of organizations focused on monitoring these codes of conduct and the establishment of organisations such as Fair Labor Association (FLA) and Social Accountability International (SAI) (e.g., O'Rourke, 2003; Esbenshade, 2004; Bartley, 2007).

In parallel with the NGO driven emergence of codes of conduct as a way to operationalise corporate responsibility, labour unions started to develop an alternative way to operationalise corporate responsibility: international framework agreements. Already in the mid 1980s Danone and IUF had signed an IFA, and in the mid 1990s Accor, Statoil, IKEA and other companies started to sign IFAs (Fairbrother and Hammer, 2005; Hammer, 2005). In this way, two competing (or complementary) ways of operationalising corporate responsibility emerged with NGOs and companies mainly promoting codes of conduct and labour unions mainly promoting IFAs (Gallin, 2000; Connor, 2004; Hammer, 2005; Riisgaard, 2005; Egels-Zandén and Hyllman, 2006). The unions' critique of codes of conduct was to a large extent rooted in them being sceptical of unilaterally 'given rights' (cf. Justice, 2003; Roman, 2004; Lipschutz, 2004). Instead, the union movement opted for signed corporate-union agreements to regulate workers' rights. Hence, the union movement attempted to base the emerging *transnational* industrial relations system on a similar "bargaining logic" as that dominating *national* industrial relations in mainly Europe and US.[2]

Process Initiation: The Global Union Federation Proposes an IFA

It was in this turbulent setting of the mid 1990s that the idea of a EuroCorp IFA emerged. The EuroCorp international framework agreement idea was instigated by the global union federation responsible for EuroCorp. The GUF had at that time recently that had taken a policy decision to prioritize and promote IFAs, and as a step in the implementation of this strategy GUF representatives raised the issue of an IFA at one of the EuroCorp World Works Council meetings.

---

[2] For a discussion on the main characteristics of national industrial relations systems in Europe and US see for example Dunlop (1958), Emery and Thorsrud (1969), Bamber and Lansbury (1998), and Huzzard et al. (2004).

During the World Works Council meeting, the GUF representatives and enterprise level union representatives also had the opportunity to discuss how to move forward with a EuroCorp IFA. As one of the EuroCorp enterprise level union representatives noted, the timing of this GUF initiative was favourable since the enterprise level union was looking for a way to handle issues of workers' rights globally in EuroCorp.

> "It all started in mid 1990s. The reason was that at that time EuroCorp was being questioned regarding how EuroCorp handled issues mainly related to child labour, working environment, salaries, etc., in different countries. We [i.e., the enterprise level union] wanted to have a general EuroCorp view of how to treat employees regardless of where production was located."

When discussing what he meant by "being questioned", it became clear that these questions mainly came from members of the EuroCorp enterprise level union and the international union movement. At this time, few, if any, other stakeholders discussed these issues with EuroCorp. The EuroCorp manager then responsible for these issues confirmed this picture claiming that there was, at this time, no pressure from customers, investors, media or stakeholders other than the unions for adopting a code of conduct and/or international framework agreement.

As noted above, the international framework agreement idea was first officially discussed at a EuroCorp union World Works Council. After internal union discussion, representatives from the EuroCorp union approach the relevant corporate manager. As this manager recalled:

> "In conjunction with a EuroCorp labour union World Works Council meeting, the question about an agreement arose. It was probably the global union federation that pushed for this issue and then the question came to me. The EuroCorp enterprise-union representatives posed the question: Shouldn't EuroCorp have such an agreement that more formally regulates how we, the union, and you, EuroCorp management, work together? I responded: It is possible. Leave the issue with me and I will consider it."

Internal Debate: Stopped Processes

Shortly after this approach by the EuroCorp enterprise union, the relevant EuroCorp managers discussed the idea of an IFA. Although the managers saw few direct problems of having such an agreement, there was a general scepticism towards codifying workers' rights issues. As one manager explained:

> "We discussed it internally, and my opinion was that there was nothing really stopping us from formalising what we were doing anyway. There is always, however, a risk when you start formalising, that things will become too rigid. I mean, it was not that the [EuroCorp enterprise level] union was trying to fix something that was not working, and it was not that we wanted to fix something that was not working. Rather, I guess both parties felt that things were working very well. At that time, we had rules and agreements at the European level that regulated European corporate–union relations. If you really followed all these rules to the letter, it would become extremely bureaucratic and we felt that we had a more natural and productive way of working. So there was some fear or scepticism regarding what such an agreement would yield. But for some reason I felt that maybe we should have an agreement,

> because they [i.e., the EuroCorp enterprise level union] would not let this idea go. However, it should include more than simply our corporate-union relation."

At this time, numerous international firms had already adopted unilateral codes of conduct. The EuroCorp managers started collecting different codes of conduct and talked to relevant individuals outside the firm. Once they had gotten a fairly good idea of what a code of conduct would mean, they presented the idea to top management. However, some key top managers had the same objections that codifying practices and responsibilities would make it very rigid. As one of the involved EuroCorp manager recalled:

> "We talked to top management, who were sceptical about the code of conduct idea. They basically reasoned as we did, but as top management they could decide that we should not have such an agreement. It would become too rigid."

This led the process to somewhat of a halt. At the same time, the EuroCorp manager mainly responsible for union relations perceived that the EuroCorp union would simply not accept a negative answer to the development of an IFA. This perception seemed to be correct with union representatives continuing to on a regular basis inquire into if it would be possible to develop an agreement.

Moving Forward with a Working Group

In the end of the 1990s, the process regained momentum with a working group being created with the purpose of developing a code of conduct. Hence, the focus had at this time been shifted from a corporate-union agreement to a unilateral code of conduct. The enterprise level union representatives were though still convinced that the workers' right part of the code of conduct eventually would turn into an agreement. The working group consisted of two EuroCorp representatives, one external consultant and a national union representative. Hence, the union movement was represented in the process, but not in the form of either the enterprise level union or the global union federation. This might be somewhat surprising given that it was these two actors that had instigated and driven the IFA question at EuroCorp up to that point. One of the EuroCorp managers explained why they had chosen a national rather than enterprise union representative:

> "Our idea was probably not to get into negotiations. If it had been the enterprise level union representative, it would have turned into negotiations. He would have taken the EuroCorp union position, so in retrospect it feels like it was the right choice. The chosen national-level union representative was also the person responsible for EuroCorp in the national union."

The enterprise level union representatives saw no problems with having this particular national union representative participate in the code of conduct process as a representative for the union movement's agenda. As one enterprise level union representative explained:

> " He [i.e., the national level union representative] was our union expert. He had an impeccable reputation, was extremely knowledgeable, and had an outstanding network. From my perspective, he might as well have been at EuroCorp. We were supportive of having him in

> the working group. It was our relationship with him that made all the difference, so from our perspective there was no big difference if it was he or I who was involved in the process … We talked weekly about all sorts of issues, met at least monthly, and travelled around the world together three–four times a year."

Once the code of conduct process was initiated there were four main issues remaining that were related to the workers' right section of the code and the signing of a corporate-union agreement. First, it was the issue of what actor within the union movement that should sign the agreement. Second, it was the issue of specificity of the content of the code. Third, it was the issue of inclusion of suppliers' operations in the agreement and, forth, it was the issue of how to monitor the agreement.

Issue I: What Union Representative Signs the IFA?

One key issue in developing the EuroCorp IFA was to decide what union representative that should sign the IFA. The global union representatives perceived that the agreement should be signed between the GUF and EuroCorp potentially with the enterprise level union co-signing the agreement. As one GUF representative explained:

> "The question was who should sign the agreement – if it should be we [i.e., the GUF], the European union federation or the enterprise level union. But it was totally clear, to have a world wide legitimate agreement, the only option was that we [i.e., the GUF] signed such an agreement. This was the appropriate solution according to us. However, we also believed that the union organization at the company headquarter location that in practice had negotiated the agreement should be allowed to co-sign the agreement in order to give them recognition for their role."

The enterprise level union recognised, and seemed to accept, this position by the GUF, understanding the symbolic importance of IFAs for GUFs. As one enterprise level union representative explained:

> "If the GUF is to play a role in society and show its union strength, this [IFAs] was a good opportunity. If the GUF could establish a number of these agreements where the GUF was the signatory, then the GUF establishes itself as the instigator and driver of union issues on an international level. So signing IFAs would increase the GUF's influence in many many other issues. It has to find legitimacy for its role. IFAs became a way for them to move beyond abstract discussions into bargaining at the enterprise level. GUFs have tried to influence national unions that in turn influence enterprise level unions, but even though GUFs have instigated initiatives they have not received credit for it because agreements are so local. Signing IFAs was a way to put the GUF on the map – a way to show that they are doing something."

Another union representative highlighted the symbolic importance of who signs the IFA, when explaining why this question was so important.

"The most important aspect [of IFAs] is that the global union level becomes recognised [by the companies] as a negotiation partner. We have a problem internationally that companies, even if thy recognise unions at the national and enterprise level, not necessarily recognise the global level unions. This is one of the weaker parts in the entire international [industrial relations] system. Therefore, we believe that if we can reach these agreements then we have received recognition of the role of the global union federations as negotiation partners."

At the same time, the enterprise level union representatives perceived that the signing of an IFA was more important than it necessarily being signed by the global union federation. While recognising the downside of an agreement that was not signed by the GUF, they perceived that the value of signing an agreement was greater than the loss of it not having a GUF signing it.

"The GUF claimed to have the right to sign the agreement, because without their signature the document would not be worth anything. We had to try to explain to them that if we did not find a solution there would no agreement at all, and this was not our aim and could not be the GUF's aim either. The alternative was to have no agreement at all. It was that bad. We would then have had to move forward ourselves without the GUF."

Similarly, some GUF representatives valued the symbolic importance of a EuroCorp agreement so greatly that they were prepared to deviate somewhat from their initial position as signatories of international framework agreements.

"I fought really hard to convince people in the union movement that despite this not being a good agreement it was still a start and that we needed to break the ice in EuroCorp's headquarter country. I thought that the agreement would provide us with a small, small opening to further expand our work in this country."

The issue of who should sign the IFA was made even more complicated with EuroCorp management being unwilling to sign an agreement with the GUF. One manager explained:

"We [i.e., EuroCorp management] did not want to sign an agreement with a global union. It was not that type of agreement. I mean regardless, it was never a possibility. But I know that they raised this matter. It was what they wanted. To this I responded, 'Never'. Our agreements are for our employees, and this [the IFA] specifies a way to act towards our employees. This was not a cunning strategy to avoid any legal responsibility, but rather an emotional decision. Why should we make an agreement with a GUF? Implicitly: the GUF does not really have anything to do with what we do. If they [i.e., the GUF] feel that they have this, they can use their available channels. However, we are not going to encourage the GUF to step in to our operations with opinions regarding how we work. They can of course use their legal channels the way they want, but we are not going to sign anything with them ... Our questions are our questions. And our [i.e., enterprise level] union is a part of EuroCorp."

The enterprise level union was well aware of this corporate position. As one union representative put it:

"We faced a dilemma as enterprise level union representatives. We really wanted this agreement and EuroCorp refused to enter into an agreement signed by the GUF."

This corporate position regarding signing agreements with GUFs is not unique for EuroCorp. For example, several union representatives claimed that companies are sceptic of signing agreements with GUFs. As one representative explained:

> "I think that the reason they [i.e., the corporations] do not want to sign agreements is that they by signing agreements recognise global union federations as an international negotiation partner and legitimize a union organization at the global level. There have even been instances when industry organizations have almost forbidden their company members to sign these agreements."

This apparent deadlock was innovatively solved when the enterprise and global level unions identified the possibility for the enterprise level union to sign the agreement as representatives of the EuroCorp workers and as representative of the GUF. Since the EuroCorp enterprise level union is, at least indirectly, a part of the GUF, it could be seen as representing both the enterprise and global level. From the enterprise level union and EuroCorp perspectives this was an acceptable solution, since it meant that the agreement would be between EuroCorp and its enterprise level union. From the global union federation perspective this was not an optimal, but acceptable, solution.

> "We were very sceptic and unsure of whether to support the agreement or not, but we understand that the agreement is important. We would really have liked to see a different kind of agreement ... That we allowed the enterprise level union to sign as a representative of the GUF was due to the fact that we had reached a point where we did not want to ruin our relations with EuroCorp that has an exemplary history regarding workers' rights."

Issues II - IV: Content, Suppliers and Control Structures

While negotiating who should sign the agreement was a key issue where the tension within the union movement was illustrated, this tension was also present in other issues. For example, the EuroCorp enterprise level union and the global union federation also had diverging opinions on the level of detail in the agreement. As one enterprise level union representative explained:

> " Representatives of the GUF argued that all the details should be regulated in the agreement. Everything that is not regulated is a restriction, while we saw it the other way. The agreement should include as little detail as possible, to give us as much freedom as possible. Their ideas were based on the notion that you [i.e., the company and the union] cannot trust each other so everything should be regulated. Our ideas were based on the notion that you should trust each other. If there are some problems, you have to sit down in a working group and solve them. I said that I would not approach the company representatives with such a detailed agreement that they proposed."

A similar recognition of the differences in perspective regarding the level of detail in the agreement between the enterprise and global level is provided by global union representatives:

> "We do not think that the EuroCorpo agreement is a good agreement. It is good in principle, but to be a real agreement it should be more extensive and detailed regarding certain areas such as suppliers and have explicit references to all ILO conventions. This is why we were somewhat unsure of whether to sign this agreement or not. We would never have signed a similar agreement with any other company, but we know that EuroCorp has a history of not signing detailed agreements and I trust them."

Hence, there was a tension within the union movement – not necessarily regarding the content of the agreement – but regarding the level of detail of the actual written agreement. In similarity to the outcome regarding who signed the agreement, the outcome in this issue was much in favour of the enterprise level union's preferences with the EuroCorp agreement being fairly short and not extensively detailed.

The third tension was regarding how strict the agreement should be in terms of suppliers' operations. The GUF representatives opted for strict inclusion of the suppliers in the agreement. However, EuroCorp representatives were reluctant to including strict regulations regarding the applicability of the agreement at suppliers' operations. The EuroCorp enterprise level union occupied a middle position as one enterprise level representative explained:

> "I fully understand their [i.e., EuroCorp's] position. To exert control over the largest suppliers is reasonable, because they buy so much and should then make demands. And they [i.e., EuroCorp] were not against that. But this was not the demand of the GUF: [they wanted] every supplier and sub-supplier should be included, and it should be possible for the GUF to monitor the working conditions at these suppliers. Of course, EuroCorp claimed: we are doing a good thing here, trying to sign and abide by these rules, and then someone would be able to enter through the back door, throwing more dirt at us than at any other company because we are in the front line. We will be one of the first companies with such an agreement. So there was fear from the corporate counterpart. We [i.e., the enterprise level union] were telling the GUF to tone down these supplier demands, because it is not going to happen. It was one of the biggest issues in the negotiations."

The outcome of this negotiation was (in similarity to who sign and level of detail issues) an agreement close to the position of the enterprise level union and EuroCorp. As one GUF representative phrases it:

> "The problem is all the suppliers that EuroCorp is dependent on. We have not been able to include them in our work and therefore we have not been able to pressure them ... If you look at other agreements, they are really tough regarding suppliers. The issue with suppliers really has to be much stronger regulated than in EuroCorp's agreement."

Finally, there was also a tension in how the implementation of the agreement was to be controlled. EuroCorp representatives strongly felt that they and the enterprise level union were to be responsible for the implementation of the agreement.

> "The GUF representatives involved in the discussions were of the opinion that there should be a working group with union representatives [i.e., including GUF representatives] that should monitor compliance globally. We [i.e., EuroCorp] basically said that this was never going to happen. Anyone from the enterprise level union knows that they are allowed to go anywhere they want: EuroCorp has opened and will open all possible doors for them. They can look at

whatever they want, whenever, but we are not going to create some sort of task force that attempts to expose non-compliances. This is not the way we want to run EuroCorp. The GUF representatives still felt that it had to be an external working group – this was the only way to provide trustworthy monitoring. And then we simply had to explain that if this was their absolute demand, we would not reach an agreement. Then we would not even have to discuss IFAs any more, since it is we who decide how to run EuroCorp. We have nothing to hide, but we are not going to change our corporate culture into a culture of ambushing."

This strong sense of implementation ownership residing within EuroCorp was to a great extent (although in a more moderate version) shared by the enterprise level union.

"We [i.e., the enterprise level union] felt that it was appropriate to use the already established structures within the EuroCorp group and expand these committees with issues related to the agreement. Both the company and we do continuous monitoring of the agreement mainly separately but we can also do it together. Our big advantage is that we already have established structures and an established global forum in our World Works Council."

Eventually, the chosen control structured was mainly based on existing EuroCorp structures, i.e. in line with the corporate and enterprise level union preferred option. In these existing structures, the GUF is partly included (mainly in the World Works Council) so the GUF is still a part of the advisory group for the monitoring of the agreement but the GUF plays a more limited role than it had opted for in the negotiations.

In sum, there were numerous issues in which the enterprise level union and the GUF did not have the same opinion regarding the content, form, monitoring and so on of the EuroCorp IFA. In all of the main issues, the outcome was an IFA closely linked to the enterprise level union's preferences. Hence, the enterprise level union had substantial influence over the IFA signing process in this particular case.

The Formation of Roles within the Union Movement

The Role of National Unions

The conducted study shows that the construction of IFAs can be a multi-level union process with enterprise level, national level and global level unions participating. In itself, this illustrates the unclarity of what actor within the union movement that should drive the development of transnational industrial relations on the enterprise level. Interestingly, the involvement of the national union in the process was due to the fact that the EuroCorp wanted to avoid negotiations at the initial stages of the process. Hence, since neither the company nor the enterprise and global level unions considered the national union as a bargaining partner in the formation of transnational industrial relations systems, the national union was able to participate in the process and influence the code of conduct and IFA content. In this respect, this study adds to the more general argument that the national level of union organizing is loosing bargaining influence by showing how increased union focus on developing transnational industrial relations systems at least implicitly implies a move of bargaining influence from the national union level to either the enterprise or global level (e.g. Katz, 1993; Bean, 1994; Jeong, 2001; Gregory and Nilsson, 2004).

However, while developing IFAs symbolize a move of formal bargaining from a national level to a transnational level, the conducted study also shows that this does not necessarily mean that national level unions are becoming obsolete. Rather, it simultaneously opens up for a new national union role in the form of being a consulting partner as compared to a more traditional negotiation partner. In terms of influencing the actual content of IFAs, such a consulting role could be as central as the actual bargaining role. Hence, even though the traditional *national* tripartite system that so far has dominated industrial relations in Western countries is being complemented with a *transnational* system (e.g., Dunlop, 1958; Emery and Thorsrud, 1969; Hedlund and Otterbeck, 1977; Bamber and Lansbury, 1998), the influential actors within the national systems seem to still retain influence in the emergent transnational system.

The Role of Global Union Federations

Since national unions are not considered to be a legitimate bargaining partner in the signing of IFAs, the question still remains: what actor in the union movement is allowed to assume the bargaining role in IFAs? As shown in the case description, this was an important and complicated question in the negotiations of EuroCorp's IFAs. Much of this is likely due to the relatively newness and legal unclarity of IFAs. Sobczak (2007: 479) concludes that given "the lack of a legal framework in the field of transnational collective bargaining, no power has been explicitly conferred by labour law to any actor to negotiate such agreements. Consequently, those who want to adopt IFAs act in an unclear context and have to invent new solutions." Hence, there is no given answer to the question of who should assume the bargaining role.

When Sobczak (2007) reviewed how actors have responded to this uncertainty, he found that there are three different actors that have signed IFAs: i) global union federations, ii) national unions (mainly from country where the company has its headquarter), and iii) European Works Councils. Of these actors, Sobczak (2007: 480-481) noted that all "existing IFAs have been signed by a global union federation, but some have been co-signed with other workers' representatives, either by the European Works Council, by national unions or by both." Hence, Sobczak (2007) clearly argues that GUFs are the key bargaining actor, although other actors could be involved as well. This argument is supported by other authors that claim that it is a minimum requirement for a document to be considered an IFA that a GUF has signed it (Hammer, 2005; Riisgaard, 2005). For example, Hammer (2005:524) notes that "a key innovation of IFAs lies in the recognition of GUFs as negotiation and bargaining partners by MNCs."

This attempt by GUFs to assume the role as bargaining partner is also clearly evident in the EuroCorp case. During the process, the GUF representatives attempted to influence the EuroCorp IFA content to include a role for the GUF as a signatory of the IFA and as well as a role in the monitoring of the implementation of the agreement. However, the EuroCorp corporate representatives were reluctant to provide the GUF with such an extensive role. Especially the demand for the GUF to sign the IFA was rejected by the corporate representatives based on the argument that GUFs are not recognized as a bargaining partner in

EuroCorp's home market, i.e. only enterprise and national level unions are recognized as bargaining partners in this country. This deadlock between the GUF, the enterprise level union and the company risked jeopardizing the signing of a EuroCorp IFA or at least risked making the enterprise level union signing an agreement without GUF involvement.

One way to understand why GUFs consider it so important to be the recognized bargaining partner in IFAs is that IFAs provide GUFs with an opportunity to revitalize its role in the union movement. Several authors argue that GUFs historically have been under-funded, with limited resources and capacity (e.g., Garver et al., 2007; Lerner, 2007). The stated reason for this is both that national unions retain extensive political power in GUFs and/or that national unions do not channel sufficient resources and support to GUFs to support global activities and carry out a global union strategy (e.g., Garver et al., 2007; Lerner, 2007). As Fairbrother and Hammer (2005:405) put it, GUFs have historically been "small and relatively remote international union secretariats with limited capacity to mobilize and speak on behalf of local members. However, with the changing architecture of international capital and nation states, these union bodies have started to renew themselves." In their attempt to renew themselves and increase their influence, one of GUFs key activities is the signing of IFAs (e.g., Fairbrother and Hammer, 2005; Royle, 2005; Andersen, 2006; Turnbull, 2006; Waddington, 2006; Bergene, 2007; Doellgast and Greer, 2007). Hence, the recognition as the legitimate bargaining partner embedded in the possibility to be the signatory of an IFA is of central symbolic importance to GUFs. It shows that GUFs are key actors in the emerging transnational industrial relations systems.

One argument supporting GUFs strive to be the bargaining partner of IFAs is that GUFs as responsible at a sector level for representing workers in all companies in the world while an enterprise level union only can legitimately represent workers in that enterprise (Sobczak, 2007). With most IFAs (including EuroCorp's) encompassing paragraphs either encouraging or demanding that the company's suppliers adhere to the IFA principles, a GUF could argue to represent these supplier workers as well. However, having GUFs as bargaining partners also creates problems, since "the signature of an IFA by a global union federation creates a problem of asymmetry between the two actors involved in the process. Whereas the workers' representatives are organized at the sector level, their partner is an individual company and not the employers' association at the sector level" (Sobczak, 2007: 482). Hence, IFAs locate bargaining at the enterprise level and serves as a vehicle for GUFs to enter into bargaining at this level (cf. Fairborther and Hammer, 2005). In this way, GUFs emerge as an alternative bargaining partner at the enterprise level along side enterprise level unions. This would allow a more active GUF involvement in negotiations and disputes with corporate managers than what GUFs previously have had (cf. Wills, 2002).

In sum, there are arguments and empirical data indicating that GUFs attempt to become the union bargaining partner in IFA processes, that GUFs often have succeeded in this attempt and that their ability to represent workers throughout the supply chain is advantageous for legitimizing such a bargaining role. However, there are also arguments against GUFs assuming the role of the bargaining partner mainly in the form of GUFs not being recognized in certain countries as a bargaining partner and that it creates an asymmetric relationship with sector level GUFs signing IFAs with individual companies. The conducted study also shows that GUFs are not always signatories of the IFAs (at least not in any other than symbolic way) and that companies in some cases are reluctant to including GUFs in the signing and monitoring processes.

The Role of Enterprise Level Unions

The alternative to locating IFA bargaining at the global union level is to locate it at the enterprise union level. This was also the main outcome in the studied EuroCorp case. Such a decentralization of industrial relations to the enterprise level in *transnational* industrial relations systems follows the current decentralization trend in *national* industrial relations systems. Numerous authors have showed that there has been a decentralization of industrial relations and bargaining on the national level from national to regional, industrial and enterprise levels (e.g. Katz, 1993; Bean, 1994; Jeong, 2001; Gregory and Nilsson, 2004). For example, recent studies show that most of EU's member states were characterised by a decentralisation of their bargaining systems (Beori et al, 2001; Ferner and Hyman, 1998). Similarly, Bamber and Lansbury (1998) reviewed industrial relations trends in ten industrial countries and showed that the enterprise level has become a more important locus of dialogue and bargaining. Evidence of the decentralization development has also been found in a US setting (e.g., Deutsch, 1994; Appelbaum and Batt, 1994), in Sweden (Nilsson, 1999; Hammarström et al, 2004), Ireland (von Prondzynski, 1998), and Italy and Spain (Elvander, 2002). Although this is a general trend, Traxler (1995) argues that this trend does not develop the same way all over the globe with some countries not undergoing change, some undergoing "disorganized decentralization", some undergoing partial decentralization and some becoming more centralized. Traxler's (1995) categorization of countries decentralization process has since then been challenged by numerous other authors' findings and arguments (e.g. Walsh, 1995; Iversen, 1996). For the purpose of this chapter, we need not dwell into the details of current trends in *national* industrial relations systems. Here, it is enough to simply note that bargaining and influence is becoming more and more decentralized in most national systems.

Hence, placing bargaining power at the enterprise level in an IFA *transnational* system would further the ongoing decentralization at the national level. It would also address the asymmetry problem associated with having sector level GUFs sign contracts with individual TNCs. The conducted study provides another important argument in favor of why enterprise level unions actually in practice are equipped with bargaining mandates: the trustful relationship between the corporate counterpart signing the agreement and the enterprise level union. At least in the EuroCorp case, this trustful relationship was key to an agreement being signed.

Hence, to understand why the outcome of the EuroCorp IFA process was that the bargaining mandate ended up at the enterprise level rather than the global level (as exemplified in who signed the agreement, the level of detail in the agreement, the strictness of supplier inclusion and the structure of the monitoring system), an understanding is needed of the EuroCorp corporate-union relation. This relationship has developed over a long period of time. As one corporate manager explained:

> "Since the 1980s – well really long before then – there has been very productive collaboration between the management of EuroCorp and the enterprise union. I think that many can testify that this is the case."

Indeed, most, if not all, interviewed EuroCorp managers highlighted the good corporate-union relation. This does not mean that there have not been conflicts between management and union representatives, only that these conflicts have been handled in such a way that a trustful relationship has developed between corporate managers and union leaders. Interviews with union representatives confirm this picture with, for example, one representative claiming that:

> "I think that it is relatively unique, even internationally, to have the type of relationship that we have [with corporate management]. This relationship has been nurtured over the years – it is not something that emerges from one year to another. Historically, we have had an understanding of one another's differences and have respected one another. The goal has always been the same, but we have been very aware of one another's roles."

Given the legal uncertainty of IFAs, the corporate-union relationship was – at least in the EuroCorp case – of utmost importance for the realization of an IFA. Even though the EuroCorp management recognized the importance ascribed to an IFA by its enterprise level union, some managers were still skeptical to actually signing an IFA in addition to having a unilateral code of conduct. Key to overcoming this internal skepticism was a recognition that the EuroCorp union would use the IFA in a responsible way, and as one manager said when reflecting on the legal nature of the signed agreement:

> " I don't know if it is legally binding. Well, I don't think so. Maybe I am naïve if I ask 'Does it matter?' If EuroCorp formally codifies something, it should be followed. And I cannot imagine a situation in which we would say that we did not wish to follow such and such a document simply because it was not legally binding. I know that some managers were scared of exactly such questions, thinking that they [i.e., the enterprise level union] would use them against us. However, if you have lived with EuroCorp you understand that the EuroCorp union is not sitting and waiting for an opportunity to drive a dagger into your back because you agreed to something. It is not that kind of relationship that we have, and we need to be careful that we do not create such a relationship either. You have to put aside your suspicions regarding what they [i.e., the union] mean and why they are doing this."

When asked to reflect upon the time after the signing of the IFA, the same manager noted that:

> "We eventually signed it, and it has of course not been any problems with the agreement."

In addition to the corporate conviction that the enterprise level union would use the IFA in a responsible way, another reason why the trustful corporate-union relation was so important was that the main driver for EuroCorp to sign an IFA was to foster its relations to the enterprise level union. While there is, and have been, extensive external pressure from investors, NGOs, media and other stakeholders for TNCs to adopt unilateral codes of conduct regulating responsibilities in terms of workers' rights (e.g., Frenkel, 2001; van Tulder and Kolk, 2001; Braun and Gearhart, 2004; Ählström and Egels-Zandén, 2008), there is, and have been, little external pressure except from that of the union movement for adopting IFAs. Hence, while corporate adoption of codes of conduct could be described as an isomorphic process in which TNCs relatively passively due to institutional pressures embrace the general rationalized solution of codes of conduct (Meyer and Rowan, 1977; DiMaggio and Powell, 1983; Long and Driscoll, 2007), the adoption of IFAs is a more active strategic corporate choice with the effect of creating differences to other firms (since so few firms have signed IFAs) rather than similarity (as is the case of adoption of codes of conduct).

The question is then why companies – such as EuroCorp – take this additional step and adopt IFAs and not only codes of conduct? Previous research into IFAs has stressed the importance of obtaining improved legitimacy in the eyes of customers, NGOs and other external stakeholders as the key driver for TNCs to adopt IFAs (Riisgaard, 2005). Although certainly relevant in other IFA signing processes, a strive for improved legitimacy in the eyes of external stakeholders was not the key reason for EuroCorp to adopt its IFA. Instead, the main reason was to retain the perceived fruitful relationship with EuroCorp's enterprise level union. Throughout the development of the code of conduct and the IFA, EuroCorp's enterprise level union had consistently stressed the importance of an IFA. The EuroCorp managers also recognized that an IFA was an important issue for its enterprise union and that to retain the trustful and fruitful corporate-union relationship an IFA was one important element. Since the reason for signing the IFA was to foster the relation with the enterprise level union, EuroCorp was interested in supporting its enterprise level union throughout the process rather than the global level union. Hence, the corporate driver for adopting IFAs seemed to affect where the locus of influence is shifted to within the union movement.

The above discussion has shown that integral to understanding why EuroCorp was prepared to take the extra step and adopt an IFA even though the legal status of an IFA was unclear and there were little external pressures (except from the union movement) to sign an IFA was the trustful relationship between the managers of EuroCorp and the EuroCorp union representatives. The flipside of trust being such an important element for the signing of the IFA is that this trust was from the corporate side mainly in its relation to its enterprise level union – not the global level union. As the case description illustrates, EuroCorp managers were uncertain and worried regarding how GUF representatives would act were they given an extensive role in the IFA process while they were confident that the enterprise level union (and the national level union) representatives would act in what the managers would describe as a responsible way.

Hence, a key reason why enterprise level unions – at least in the EuroCorp case – could gain more influence in IFA processes than global level unions is that they can draw on long term trustful relations with corporate management. More generally, the results from the conducted study indicate that in companies with trustful corporate-enterprise level union relations and/or when corporate managers have distrustful relation to GUF representatives we could expect the locus of influence to be decentralised to the enterprise level. Logically, in companies with distrustful corporate-enterprise level union relations and/or with trustful corporate-GUF relations we could expect the opposite, i.e. that the locus of influence is centralised to the global union level. The results also indicate that if the corporate motive for signing an IFA is mainly to foster its relation with the enterprise level union, the local of influence could be expected to be decentralised to the enterprise level. Conversely, when the corporate motive for signing an IFA is mainly to improve external legitimacy (as the case presented in Riisgaard (2005) illustrates), we could expect the influence to be centralised to the global level.

Conclusion

In the ongoing globalization of business, *transnational* industrial relations systems are emerging as complements to the traditional *national* systems. These transnational systems are mainly based on two tools: codes of conduct and international framework agreements (IFAs). This chapter has focused on the latter of these arguing that previous research into IFA has disregarded a central issue in IFAs: the tension between global, national and enterprise level unions. With industrial relations issues moving from a national to a transnational setting, the locus of influence in the union movement could either be *centralised* to global union federations or *decentralised* to enterprise level unions.

This chapter has shown that the answer to the centralization-decentralization question is far from straightforward. While most previous research has argued that IFAs mainly lead to centralization, the conducted study of EuroCorp shows that there are also cases of IFAs leading to decentralization. Central to understanding why the locus of influence was decentralised in this particular case was the already existing trustful relationship between EuroCorp and its enterprise level union (combined with a somewhat distrustful relationship between EuroCorp and the global level union). More generally, the findings from this study indicate that the locus of influence will be decentralised to the enterprise level union when: i) there is a trustful corporate-enterprise level union relation, ii) there is a distrustful corporate-global level union relation, and iii) the corporate driver for adopting an IFA is to foster its relations with its enterprise level union. On the other hand, the locus of influence will be centralized to the global level when: i) there is a distrustful corporate-enterprise level union relation, ii) there is a trustful corporate-global level union relation, and iii) the corporate driver for adopting an IFA is to improve its external legitimacy.

References

Ählström, J., & Egels-Zandén, N. (2008). The Processes of Defining Corporate Responsibility: A Study of Swedish Garment Retailers' Responsibility. *Business Strategy and the Environment* (in press).

Andersen, S. K. (2006). Nordic Metal Trade Unions on the Move: Responses to Globalization and Europeanization. *European Journal of Industrial Relations, 12*(1), 29-47.

Anner, M., Greer, I., Hauptmeier, M., Lillie, N., & Winchester, N. (2006). The Industrial Determinants of Transnational Solidarity: Global Interunion Politics in Three Sectors. *European Journal of Industrial Relations, 12*(1), 7-27.

Appelbaum, E., & Batt, R. (1994). *The New American Workplace*. Ithaca, NY: ILR Press.

Asia Monitor Resource Centre (2007) *Report on Industrial Relations and Working Conditions in IMF-related TNCs in China*. Geneva: International Metalworkers' Federation.

Bamber, G. J., & Lansbury, R. D. (Eds.) (1998). *International and Comparative Employment Relations*. St Leonards, Austrialia: Allen & Unwin.

Bartley, T. (2005). Corporate Accountability and the Privatization of Labor Standards: Struggles over Codes of Conduct in the Apparel Industry. *Research in Political Sociology, 14*, 211-244.

Bartley, T. (2007). Institutional Emergence in an Era of Globalization: The Rise of Transnational Private Regulation of Labor and Environmental Conditions. *American Journal of Sociology, 113*(2), 297-351.

Bean, R. (1994). *Comparative Industrial Relations: An Introduction to Cross-national Perspectives*. London: Routledge.

Beck, U. (1992). *Risk Society: Towards a New Modernity*. London: Sage.

Beori, T., Brugiavini, A., & Calmfors, L. (Eds.) (2001). *The Role of the Unions in the Twentieth Century*. Oxford: Oxford University Press.

Bergene, A. C. (2007). Trade Unions Walking the Tightrope in Defending Workers' Interests: Wielding a Weapon Too Strong? *Labour Studies Journal, 32*(2), 142-166.

Bhagwati, J. (2005). *In Defence of Globalization*. New York, NY: Oxford University Press.

Braun, R., & Gearhart, J. (2004). Who Should Code Your Conduct? Trade Union and NGO Differences in the Fight for Workers' Rights. *Development in Practice, 14*(1–2), 183–196.

Chan, A. (1998). Labor Standards and Human Rights: The Case of Chinese Workers Under Market Socialism. *Human Rights Quarterly, 20*(4), 886–904.

Chang, D., & Wong, M. (2005). After the Consumer Movement: Toward a New International Labour Activism in the Global Garment Industry. *Labour, Capital and Society, 38*(1-2), 127-155.

Chen, F. (2003). Between the State and the Labour: The Conflict of Chinese Trade Unions' Double Identity in Market Reform. *The China Quarterly, 176*, 1006-1028.

Christerson, B., & Appelbaum, R. P. (1995). Global and Local Subcontracting: Space, Ethnicity, and the Organization of Apparel Production. *World Development, 23*(8), 1363–1374.

Christmann, P., & Taylor, G. (2002). Globalization and the Environment: Strategies for International Voluntary Environmental Initiatives. *Academy of Management Executive, 16*(3), 121-135.

Cohen, D. (2006). *Globalization and Its Enemies*. Cambridge, MA: MIT Press.

Compa, L. (2004). Trade Unions, NGOs, and Corporate Codes of Conduct. *Development in Practice, 14*(1–2), 210–215.

Cooke, F. L. (2004). Foreign Firms in China: Modelling HRM in a Chinese Toy Manufacturing Corporation. *Human Resource Management Journal, 14*(3), 31-52.

Cooney, S., Lindsey, R., Mitchell, R., & Zhu, Y. (Eds.) (2002). *Law and Labour Market Regulation in Eastern Asia*. London: Routledge.

Cowton, C. J., & Thompson. P. (2000). Do Codes Make a Difference? The Case of Bank Lending and the Environment. *Journal of Business Ethics, 24*(2), 165-178.

Deutsch, S (1994). New Union Initiatives on Technological Change and Work Organization. In S. Deutsch, & R. Broomhill (Eds.), *Recent Developments in U.S. Trade Union Strategies*. Adelaide, Australia: University of Adelaide.

DiMaggio, P. J., & Powell, W.W. (1983). The Iron Cage Revisited: Institutional Isomorphism and Collective Rationality in Organizational Fields. *American Sociological Review, 48*(2), 147-160.

Ding, D. Z., & Warner, M. (1999). Re-inventing' China's Industrial Relations at Enterprise-Level: An Empirical Field Study in Four Major Cities. *Industrial Relations Journal, 30*(3): 243-260.

Doellgast, V. & Greer, I. (2007). Vertical Disintegration and the Disorganization of German Industrial Relations. *British Journal of Industrial Relations, 45*(1), 55-76.

Dunlop, J. T. (1958). *Industrial Relations Systems*. New York, NY: Henry Holt.

Egels-Zandén, N. (2007). Suppliers' Compliance with MNCs' Codes of Conduct: Behind the Scenes at Chinese Toy Suppliers. *Journal of Business Ethics, 75*(1), 45-62.

Egels-Zandén, N., & Hyllman, P. (2006). Exploring the Effects of Union-NGO Relationships on Corporate Responsibility: The Case of the Swedish Clean Clothes Campaign. *Journal of Business Ethics, 64*(3), 303-316.

Egels-Zandén, N., & Hyllman, P. (2007). Evaluating Strategies for Negotiating Workers' Rights in Transnational Corporations: The Effect of Codes of Conduct and Global Agreements on Workplace Democracy. *Journal of Business Ethics, 76*(2), 207-223.

Elvander, N. (2002). The Labour Market Regimes in the Nordic Countries: A Comparative Analysis. *Scandinavian Political Studies, 25*(2), 117-137.

Emery, F. E., & Thorsrud, E. (1969). *Form and Content in Industrial Democracy* London: Tavistock.

Emmelhainz, M. A., & Adams, R. J. (1999). The Apparel Industry Response to 'Sweetshop' Concerns: A Review and Analysis of Codes of Conduct. *Journal of Supply Chain Management, 35*(3), 51–57.

Esbenshade, J. (2004). *Monitoring Sweatshops: Workers, Consumers, and the Global Apparel Industry*. Philadelphia: Temple University Press.

Fairbrother, P., & Hammer, N. (2005). Global Unions: Past Efforts and Future Prospects. *Relations Industrielles/Industrial Relations, 60*(3), 405-431.

Ferner, A., & Hyman, R. (Eds.) (1998). *Changing Industrial Relations in Europe*. Oxford: Blackwell Publishers.

Frenkel, S. (2001). Globalization, Athletic Footwear Commodity Chains and Employment Relations in China. *Organization Studies, 22*(4), 531–562.

Frenkel, S., & Kim, S. (2004). Corporate Codes of Labour Practice and Employment Relations in Sports Shoe Contractor Factories in South Korea. *Asia Pacific Journal of Human Resources, 42*(1), 6–31.

Frenkel, S., & Scott, D. (2002). Compliance, Collaboration, and Codes of Labor Practice: The *adidas* Connection. *California Management Review, 45*(1), 29-49.

Gallin, D. (2000). *Trade Unions and NGOs: A Necessary Partnership for Social Development*. Geneva: United Nations Research Institute for Social Development.

Garver, P., Buketov, K., Chong, H., & Martinez, B. S. (2007). Global Labor Organizing in Theory and Practice. *Labor Studies Journal, 32*(3), 237-256.

Gregory, D. & Nilsson, T. (2004). Seconds Away: Naming and Framing the Book. In T. Huzzard, D. Gregory, & R. Scott (Eds.), *Strategic unionism and partnership: Boxing or Dancing?* Basingstoke: Palgrave Macmillan.

Guillén, M., Melé, D., & Murphy, P. (2002). European vs. American Approaches to Institutionalization of Business Ethics: The Spanish Case. *Business Ethics: A European Review, 11*(2), 167-178.

Hammarström, O., Huzzard, T., & Nilsson, T. (2004). Employment Relations in Sweden. In G. J. Bamber, & R. D. Lansbury (Eds.), *International and Comparative Employment Relations: A Study of Industrialised Market Economies*. Sydney: Allen & Unwin.

Hammer, N. (2005). International Framework Agreements: Global Industrial Relations between Rights and Bargaining. *Transfer, 11*(4), 511-530.

Hathcote, J., & Nam, I. -J. (1999). Advantages of Sourcing Apparel from China, Taiwan, South Korea and Mexico. *International Trade Journal, 13*(2), 157–185.

Hedlund, G., & Otterbeck, L. (1977). *The Multinational Corporation, The Nation State and the Trade Unions: An European Perspective*. The Comparative Administration Research Institute: Kent University Press.

Huzzard, T., Gregory, D., & Scott, R. (Eds.). (2004) *Strategic unionism and partnership: Boxing or Dancing?* Basingstoke: Palgrave Macmillan.

IDE (Industrial Democracy in Europe). (1981). *Industrial Democracy in Europe*. Oxford: Clarendon P.

Iversen, T. (1996). Power, Flexibility, and the Breakdown of Centralized Wage Bargaining: Denmark and Sweden in Comparative Perspective. *Comparative Politics, 28*(4), 399-436.

Jeong, J. (2001). Pursuing Centralised Bargaining in an Era of Decentralisation? A Progressive Union Goal in Korea from a Comparative Perspective. *Industrial Relations Journal, 32*(1), 55-70.

Jones, M. T. (2005). The Transnational Corporation, Corporate Social Responsibility and the 'Outsourcing' Debate'. *Journal of American Academy of Business, 6*(2), 91–97.

Justice, D. W. (2003). Corporate Social Responsibility: Challenges and Opportunities for Trade Unionists. *Labour Education, 130*, 1–13.

Kaptein, M. (2004). Business Codes of Multinational Firms: What Do They Say?. *Journal of Business Ethics, 50*(1), 13-31.

Katz, H. C. (1993). The Decentralisation of Collective Bargaining: A Literature Review and Comparative Analysis. *Industrial and Labor Relations Review, 47*(1), 3-22.

Klein, N. (2000). *No Logo: No Space, No Choice, No Jobs*. London: Flamingo.

Kolk, A., & van Tulder, R. (2002). The Effectiveness of Self-Regulation: Corporate Codes of Conduct and Child Labour. *European Management Journal, 20*(3), 260–271.

Lau, R. W. K. (2001). Social-Political Control in Urban China: Changes and Crises. *British Journal of Sociology, 52*(4), 605-620.

Leahy, J. T. (2001). Making Room for Labor in Business Ethics. *Journal of Business Ethics, 29*(1–2), 33–43.

Lee, T. W. (1999). *Understanding Qualitative Methods in Organizational Research*. Thousand Oaks, CA: Sage.

Lerner, S. (2007). Global Unions: A Solution to Labor's Worldwide Decline. *New Labor Forum, 16*(1), 23-37.

Liew, L. H. (2001). What is to be Done? WTO, Globalisation and State-Labour Relations in China. *Australian Journal of Politics and History, 47*(1), 39-60.

Lipschutz, R. D. (2004). Sweating It Out: NGO Campaigns and Trade Union Empowerment. *Development in Practice, 14*(1–2), 197–209.

Long, B. S., & Driscoll, C. (2007). Codes of Ethics and the Pursuit of Organizational Legitimacy: Theoretical and Empirical Contributions. *Journal of Business Ethics* (in press).

Maguire, S., Hardy, C., & Lawrence, T. B. (2004). Institutional Entrepreneurship in Emerging Fields: Hiv/Aids Treatment Advocacy in Canada. *Academy of Management Journal, 47*(5), 657–679.

Marshall, C., & Rossman, G. B. (1995). *Designing Qualitative Research*. Thousand Oaks, CA: Sage.

Meyer, J., & Rowan, B. (1977). Institutionalized Organizations: Formal Structure as Myth and Ceremony. *The American Journal of Sociology, 83*(2), 340-363.

Michalos, A. C. (1997). Issues for Business Ethics in the Nineties and Beyond. *Journal of Business Ethics, 16*(3), 219–230.

Miller, D. (2004). Preparing for the Long Haul: Negotiating International Framework Agreements in the Global Textile, Garment and Footwear Sector. *Global Social Policy, 4*(2), 215-239.

Morsing, M., Midttun, A., & Palmås, K. (2007). Corporate Social Responsibilty in Scandinavia: A Turn to the Business Case?. In S. K. May, G. Cheney, & J. Roper (Eds.), *The Debate over Corporate Social Responsibility* (pp. 86-104). Oxford: Oxford University Press.

Muller-Camen, M., Almond, P., Gunnigle, P., Quintanilla, J., & Tempel, A. (2001). Between Home and Host Country: Multinationals and Employment Relations in Europe. *Industrial Relations Journal, 32*(5), 435-448.

Nijhof, A., Cludts, S., Fisscher, O., & Laan, A. (2003). Measuring the Implementation of Codes of Conduct: An Assessment Method Based on a Process Approach of the Responsible Organisation. *Journal of Business Ethics, 45*(1), 65-78.

Nilsson, T. (1999). The Future Role of the Swedish Unions – Increased Local Cooperation for Production Development. *Economic and Industrial Democracy, 20*, 461-482.

O'Rourke, D. (2003). Outsourcing Regulation: Analyzing Nongovernmental Systems of Labor Standards and Monitoring. *The Policy Study Journal, 31*(1), 1-29.

Piazza, J. (2002). *Going Global: Unions and Globalization in the US, Sweden and Germany.* Lanham, MD: Lexington Books.

Prieto, M., & Quinteros, C. (2004). Never the twain shall meet? Women's organisations and trade unions in the maquila industry in Central America. *Development in Practice, 14*(1-2), 149-157.

Provis, C. (2006). Industrial Relations, Ethics and Conscience. *Business Ethics: A European Review, 15*(1), 64-75.

Riisgaard, L. (2005). Industrial Framework Agreements: A New Model of Securing Workers Rights?. *Industrial Relations, 44*(4), 707-737.

Roman, J. (2004). The Trade Union Solution or the NGO Problem? The Fight for Global Labour Rights. *Development in Practice, 14*(1–2), 100–109.

Rosenau, J. N., & Czempiel, E.-O. (Eds.). (1992). *Governance Without Government: Order and Change in World Politics*. Cambridge, UK: Cambridge University Press.

Radin, T. J. (2004). The Effectiveness of Global Codes of Conduct: Role Models That Make Sense. *Business and Society Review, 109*(4), 415–447.

Royle, T. (2005). The Union Recognition Dispute at McDonald's Moscow Food-Processing Factory. *Industrial Relations Journal, 36*(4), 318-332.

Schlegelmilch, B., & Houston, J. (1989). Corporate Codes of Ethics in Large UK Companies: An Empirical Investigation of Use, Content and Attitudes. *European Journal of Marketing, 23*(6), 7-24.

Schrage, E. (2004). *Promoting International Workers Rights Through Private Voluntary Initiatives: Public Relations or Public Policy?* Iowa City: The University of Iowa Human Rights Center.

Sethi, S. P. (1999). Codes of Conduct for Multinational Corporations: An Idea Whose Time has Come. *Business & Society Review, 104*(3), 225-241.

Sethi, S. P. (2002). Standards for Corporate Conduct in the International Arena: Challenges and Opportunities for Multinational Corporations. *Business and Society Review, 107*(1), 20–40.

Shanahan, S., & Khagram, S. (2006). Dynamics of Corporate Responsibility. In G. S. Drori, J. W. Meyer, & H. Hwang (Eds.), *Globalization and Organization: World Society and Organizational Change* (pp. 196-224). Oxford: Oxford University Press.

Sobczak, A. (2007). Legal Dimensions of International Framework Agreements in the Field of Corporate Social Responsibility. *Relations Industrielles/Industrial Relations, 62*(3), 466-491.

Spooner, D. (2004). Trade Unions and NGOs: The Need for Cooperation. *Development in Practice, 14*(1-2), 19-33.

Stiglitz, J. P. (2003). *Globalization and Its Discontents*. New York, NY: Norton & Company Ltd.

Strange, S. (1996). *The Retreat of the State: The Diffusion of Power in the World Economy*. Cambridge, UK: Cambridge University Press.

Sullivan, R. (2003). NGO Expectations of Companies and Human Rights. *Non-State Actors and International Law, 3*, 303-322.

Taylor, T. (2005). In Defence of Outsourcing. *CATO Journal, 25*(2), 367–377.

Thörnqvist, C. (1999). The Decentralization of Industrial Relations: The Swedish Case in Comparative Perspective. *European Journal of Industrial Relations, 5*(1), 71-87.

Traxler, F. (1995). Farewell to Labour Market Associations? Organized versus Disorganized Decentralization as a Map for Industrial Relations. In C. Crouch, & F. Traxler (Eds.), *Organized Industrial Relations in Europe: What Future?* Aldershot: Avebury.

Turnbull, P. (2006). The War on Europe's Waterfront: Repertoires of Power in the Port Transport Industry. *British Journal of Industrial Relations, 44*(2), 305-326.

Walsh, J. (1995). Convergence of Divergence? Corporatism and the Dynamics of European Wage Bargaining. *International Review of Applied Economics, 9*(2), 169-191.

van Tulder, R., & Kolk, A. (2001). Multinationality and Corporate Ethics: Codes of Conduct in the Sporting Goods Industry. *Journal of International Business Studies, 32*(2), 267–283.

Waddington, J. (2006). Contesting the Development of European Works Councils in the Chemical Sector. *European Journal of Industrial Relations, 12*(3), 329-352.

Warner, M. (1996). Economic Reforms, Industrial Relations and Human Resources in the People's Republic of China: An Overview. *Industrial Relations Journal, 27*(3), 195-210.

von Prondzynski, F. (1998). Ireland: Corporatism Revived. In A. Ferner, & R. Hyman (Eds.), *Changing Industrial Relations in Europe* (pp. 55-73). Oxford: Blackwell Publishers.

Wills, J. (2001). Uneven Geographies of Capital and Labour: The Lessons of European Works Councils. *Antipode, 33*(3), 484-509.

Wills, J. (2002). Bargaining for the Space to Organize in the Global Economy: A Review of the Accor-IUF Trade Union Rights Agreement. *Review of International Political Economy, 9*(4), 675-700.

Zhu, Y., & Fahey, S. (1999). The Impact of Economic Reform on Industrial Labour Relations in China and Vietnam. *Post-Communist Economies, 11*(2), 173-192.

In: Corporate Social Responsibility
Editor: Adam R. Timpere, pp. 111-134
ISBN: 978-1-60456-284-2

Chapter 5

Mining, Corporate Social Responsibility and Pluralism in Papua New Guinea

Benedict Y. Imbun*

School of Management, University of Western Sydney, Locked Bag 1797 Penrith South, DC NSW 1797, Australia

Abstract

This chapter discusses the emergence of an embryonic form of pluralism in the negotiation of development projects between local communities and multinational mining companies (MNMCs) as part of (the latter's) corporate social responsibility (CSR) commitments in Papua New Guinea (PNG). The author draws on data gathered through long periods of fieldwork and observation of MNMCs, state and local communities interactions in the development and day to day operations of mines in PNG. The chapter identifies factors which have led to the emergence of eager and sometimes restless local communities which host large mining projects and their unrelenting pressures on developers for tangible development projects. This has led to the establishment of appropriate institutional arrangement and therefore legitimizing the entry of local communities into the pluralistic negotiation process. The background to mining, complexity characterizing PNG mining and CSR and discussion of three mines' CSR commitments are just some of the topics pursued in this chapter.

One theme is the pluralistic institutional framework facilitating local community participation and influencing in development agenda setting for MNMCs to honor whilst at the same time mining for ore. This unique arrangement giving unprecedented voice to formerly neglected spheres of state and MNMC concern has become exceptional for PNG local communities. This chapter contends that this mode of community participation at the peak decision making and influencing CSR function of MNMCs is both pluralistic and exceptional which is not common in most developing countries with mining economies. Therefore, Papua New Guineans have become active partners in mining

* Tel +61 2 9685 9624 Fax + 61 2 96885 9593; Email b.imbun@uws.edu.au www.uws.edu.au

development and had legitimized the process for a pluralistic approach to management and operation of mining projects in the country.

Introduction

The advent of large scale mining operation in many developing countries has largely become a collective affair in mist of generally receptive and sometimes restless local host communities. This has become particularly the case in PNG where MNMCs have embraced a pluralistic approach to management of operations under the watchful eyes of local communities, government, trade unions, and community at large. It seems to have occurred because of the way the political and economic structure of the country is shaped, together with a cynical perception of MNMCs. The mining operations are influenced by a complex web of issues and concerns emanating from the local 'stakeholders' which requires delicate attention by management. They have responded accordingly by embracing the function of CSR in a big way and find at times that the neglect of being appropriately responsive is detrimental to the continued safe and sound operation of their projects. Therefore, this chapter argues that Papua New Guineans have become active partners in mining development and had legitimized the process for a pluralistic approach to management and operation of projects in the country.

This chapter will explore the post-Bougainville dispute period in the relationship between local community and mine operators to understand the current status quo where community relations is treated as one of the core responsibilities of management of mines. The inherent forces of local community pressure and an emergence of the current receptive thinking of MNMCs tend to be the case in PNG. Second, the chapter examines the emergence of local community as a development pressure group in mine development negotiation process. Their role, in the broader context of development agenda setting and involvement of provincial and national government representation is explored to understand how mine operators are convinced to implement projects as part of their CSR role. This chapter contends that an embracement of pluralistic mine development negotiation framework has laid the foundation for legitimised mining aided development in mainly rural areas of PNG.

Research Methodology

This chapter is based on the author's long scholarly association with the PNG mining industry. He has investigated workers, management, state and local communities engagement with MNMCs in the course of operations of many mines (i.e. Imbun, 1998, 1999a, b, 2000, 2000). For the works he has utilised multifaceted methodology and techniques suited to exploring history, politics, culture, mining economic imperatives and social and economic change associated with general mining and the stakeholders. The nature of research involving particularly local tribal communities adjacent to mining operations and beyond allowed him to require an ethnographic approach to documenting their perceptions and attitudes to MNMCs and development. A combination of fieldwork, ethnographic techniques, in-dept interview methods and qualitative survey had allowed him to address the approach and methodological requirement of his previous works.

However, this chapter is the product of ethnographic information with integration of primary documentary evidence from local communities, MNMCs, and other sources. The existing primary and secondary literature take the form of current literature on PNG mining, select mine literature pertaining to individual projects as well as general mining policy and socio-economic policies. Not only that as the review of secondary literature existing literature also acknowledge other works done pertaining to MNMCs and local communities in other developing countries. The tying in of both primary and secondary data to the ethnographic information allow the author to explain the intricacies and peculiarities of underpinning the issue of MNMCs led development in rural PNG.

THE PNG MINING CONTEXT

PNG is a country heavily dependent on mineral revenue and records more than 70 per cent of export income annually from a small number of world class mines. Since gaining political independence from Australia in 1975, it had relied on a mineral policy of maximizing government revenue from resource developers and utilizing them on facilitating infrastructure development in rural areas. The policy had appeared best on paper, yet worst in practice, as little funding if any, had been spent in rural areas, let alone in mining regions (Imbun and McGavin, 2001; Filer and Imbun, 2004; Imbun, 2003, 2006a,b). Consequently, a three-generation of disgruntled and disenchanted rural communities of mining areas have emerged forming a formidable power base to influence the PNG Government on mineral policy. Yet, in PNG generally the element of discontent is not only confined to local mining communities as it is also pervasive where ever large exploitation of primary resources and development of urban areas is situated. Often the discontentment is between customary landowners and 'outsiders' (migrants) (Koczberski and Curry, 2004). In such cases, it is the landowners who sometimes use violence against migrants and they do it in fear of being marginalized by an unprecedented influx of migrants converging into the 'progressive' areas. While concerning mining in acknowledging this predicament, the Government has included provincial government and landowners as legitimated stakeholders, and therefore has made policy making more expensive, time-consuming and often frustrating. In practice, the impact of inclusion of other stakeholders in the negotiations has embraced a wide scope for project-by-project negotiation and exercise of government discretion rather than the earlier basic policy regime with general applicability.

As for the MNMCs, only recently have they come to maintain a challenging role in the presence of the host government and local indigenous community, particularly landowners in PNG. Although in the Pacific region, the reflection of tensions and social complexities had become apparent in Australia (an exception to many advanced countries with indigenous communities) following the passing of the Native Titles Act in the early 1990s (Trigger, 2000; Keen 1993; McEachern, 1995; O'Faircheallaigh, 2002; Crawley and Sinclair, 2003). In PNG some of the tensions and challenges have led to the collapse of the CRA operated giant Bougainville copper mine in the late 1980s due to civil uprising, and the BHP Billiton's Ok Tedi mine environmental debacle in the late 1990s (Connel and Howitt, 1991; Banks and

Ballard, 1997; Filer; 1990). Consequent of these episodes, MNMCs in PNG seem to have cultivated a favourable relationship with the indigenous local communities. In other words, they tend to have embraced the CSR role into their main pursuit of operations. This is done deliberately in order pacify the local communities' expectations and have a sense of social security in their operations.

Therefore in PNG, MNMCs are under constant pressure to live up to the commitments have with government, while being responsible for the diverse impacts them generate in the host communities (Filer, 1999; Banks and Ballard, 1997). More importantly, the local indigenous community in the host region insist that MNMCs address their demands for more tangible benefits from the mining operations, as a means of 'compensation', in order to guarantee them peace and safety for the life of the mine (Howard, 1988, 1991). This chapter will shed light on the emergence of this development role of MNMCs and the role of local communities as they are instrumental in imposing themselves as a partner to be reckoned of and thus influencing a pluralistic process of shaping and operation of CSR practice and mining policies in general. This seems to be the current norm and obviously the local communities are acknowledged as an inseparable partner to the MNMCs and PNG Government in facilitation and operation of successful mines in the country.

Complexity of Mining and CSR in PNG

Mining in PNG for many MNMCs is challengingly complex assignment unlike any experience they could have encountered elsewhere, least in their own countries. The multitude of roles and responsibilities emanating from various sections of the local communities and host government (s) in many ways exert immense pressure on the resource developers to be receptive and accommodating to their extra curricular needs and demands. The review of literature on PNG mining identify however several themes which contribute to the complexity of mining and CSR and are worth stating.

First, in PNG mining the roles local community wield and play is integral to that of MNMCs and government in formulation of policies directed towards rural development in mining project negotiation and implementation. The issue of local community initiated development, therefore, is an understanding of government policy failure and an emergence of a willing (but sometimes reluctant) resource developers giving into the demands of its host development 'deprived' communities. In fact, a significant number of development projects have been implemented which reflect the pluralistic policy formulation process. These projects, although sanctioned by the PNG Government, much typified its own failure. In an earlier paper, Imbun (1994) argued that the infrastructure and economic projects of Ok Tedi and Porgera mines implemented in local communities resulted of their sheer resource strength and efficiency. Similarly in a very recent paper (Imbun, 2007) he also contended that the PNG Government lacked the necessary resources and therefore it was shifting its civic role to the resource developers to undertake socio-economic development responsibilities. While this chapter acknowledges the assertion and contends that current concerns, issues and dilemmas between local communities, the government and MNMCs in juggling development policy issues and mining is becoming too predictably inevitable. This mode of pressured development will continue as long as the snail pace of general economic and social development in the country is still in order. However, a multi-dimensional analysis of the issue is required to understand the contextual variables and forces that drive the current local community led mineral policy making in PNG.

Similarly, several observations (Chand and Levantis, 2000; Lea, 2004 and others) suggest that a rapid drop has occurred in government social and economic services in not only rural areas of mining operations but in the entire rural areas of the country. Although in some mining adjacent areas, government services had been non-existent until the arrival of mining projects, which often later see a trickling of postal, school and health services. The subsequent part of this chapter will shed light on three mines led subsidized national development occurring on a scale, in some cases unparalleled by government services. The implications of this mode of development on overall government policy framework seem to obviously place an addictive 'begging' culture on the local communities

Third, current literature portrays a context where local communities (and host Government) seem to develop a 'love-hate' relationship with the MNMCs (Imbun, 1999, 2006b). For example, many of the studies (Springgs and May, 1990; Oliver, 1991; Wesley-Smith, 1993) documenting the Bougainville mine saga and others (Jackson, 1991; Filer, 1999; Filer, Henton and Jackson, 2000) on existing and new mine developments theorized of an emergence and eventual entrenchment of a legitimized role of landowners as 'the other stake holder' in PNG mining. Some (Filer, 1990, 1992; Havini, 1992; Springgs and Denoon, 1992) concluded that the arrogance and ignorance by MNMCs and therefore neglect of landowners and local community development aspirations would be a serious blunder, as the continued safe operation of a project in the long term would not be a guarantee. Others (Wesley-Smith and Organ, 1992; Imbun, 1994, Imbun and Morris, 2001) have observed that resource project developers are initially welcomed as the messiahs to isolated communities' development woes and therefore held in high regard than their government (s). Notwithstanding, one of their notable presences have been in enhancing the skill formation of previously unskilled local people through a systematic recruitment and training pattern favouring them to work at the mines at the expense of other Papua New Guineans (Imbun, 1997, 1998, 1999a, 2000, 2006b, 2006c; McGavin, Jones and Imbun, 2001; Hess and Imbun, 2003). However, this positive treatment of local people in employment is also overlapped into the mainstream of management of the mine workforces. Imbun (2007) argued that the different mine managements have effectively embraced the aspirations of local workers from within the vicinity of the project areas to influence positive employment relations amongst the entire workforces therefore inevitably creating a 'them' and 'us' situation with the rest of the workforce. This type of ploy effectively demonstrates the strategic moves MNMCs undertake in addressing both general local communities and workers issues to guarantee their longevity.

Fourth, review of literature on PNG mining indicate that the salient features such as location, local community, politics, development status and other contextual variables of each mining project which may impinge on a mine's CSR function. The current cooperation regime in setting local development agenda shed light on the broader context of development agenda setting and involvement of provincial and national government representation, and particularly local community pressure to understand how mine operators are convinced to implement CSR projects. While the current literature portray a scenario where local communities (and host government) seem to develop a 'love-hate' relationship with the MNMCs (Imbun, 1999a). For example, many of the studies (Springgs and May, 1990; Oliver, 1991; Wesley-Smith, 1993a, b) documenting the Bougainville mine saga and others (Jackson,

1991; Filer, 1999; Filer, Henton and Jackson, 2000) on existing and new mine developments theorized of an emergence and eventual entrenchment of a legitimized role of landowners as 'the other stake holder' to the dismay of many MNMCs. Some (Filer, 1990, 1992; Havini, 1992; Springgs and Denoon, 1992) concluded that the arrogance and ignorance by MNMCs and therefore neglect of landowners and local community development aspirations would be a serious blunder, as the continued safe operation of a project in the long term would not be a guarantee. Others (Wesley-Smith, 1993a, b; Wesley-Smith and Organ, 1992; Imbun, 1994, Imbun and Morris, 2001) have observed that resource project developers are initially welcomed as the messiahs to isolated communities' development woes and therefore held in high regard than their government (s). Notwithstanding, one of their notable presences have been in enhancing the skill formation of previously unskilled local people through a systematic recruitment and training pattern favouring them to work at the mines at the expense of other Papua New Guineans (Imbun, 1997, 1998, 1999a, b, 2000, McGavin, Jones and Imbun, 2001; Hess and Imbun, 2003).

Moreover, the general PNG mining literature (i.e. Imbun and Morris, 2001), agree that community demand for social and economic projects from MNMCs is identified as a significant determinant of effectiveness in the delivery of projects. Demands by various local communities of mining project sites varies and therefore reflecting the size and life span of the project, management attitude, physical geography, culture, politics and host of other factors. On the same token, the satisfaction levels of each community of MNMC's projects also vary. Therefore, no one mine is same as the other, however what is evident is the magnitude of CSR projects arising from pluralistic project negotiation process is similar, including outcomes.

Finally, the impact of infrastructural developments and other social projects has been great for the people of mining project areas. The MNMC's opportunity to deliver projects in rural areas has unreservedly acknowledged by government, observers and the recipients (Imbun, 1994). Most importantly, they seem to create a certain perpetuating social atmosphere where local recipients and others view the governments (national, provincial and lower-level governments) with contempt, because they have failed to provide basic services, and economic development. Conversely, the local communities tend to view the mining projects as the medium that has brought development and they would favour MNMCs to provide more services. This chapter discuss three projects' approach to implementing and sustaining development projects and assess their significance in the general context of social and economic progress of PNG.

Emergence of Pluralistic Practice of CSR in PNG Mining

This chapter contends that CSR is becoming an indispensable part of managing large mines by MNMCs in PNG. And most importantly it is increasingly influenced by an advent of pluralistic form of development negotiation between particularly local communities, MNMCs and host government (s). As the existing literature and evidence of CSR projects of MNMCs demonstrate overwhelmingly that an emergence and stranglehold of local communities in development negotiations with mineral resource developers is gaining huge currency in PNG. So what has transpired is the emergence of pluralistic practice of CSR.

However, the unique character of PNG's mining aided development system with history, issues and limited economic parameter is not explained in the general CSR theories. There are important areas of community, workers, government and management (developer) interest where participatory involvement by the parties occurs because of the way the political and economic structure of the country is shaped together with a cynical perception of MNCMs. The inter-play of the elite parties of managers, unionists, bureaucrats and tribal headmen may demonstrate participation at the highest level. But they are not at all indicative of the day to day pressures on MNMCs by exercised by the newly exposed backward villager in the less spectacular, mundane areas of adjacent local communities in PNG. Nevertheless, it is obvious the current developments in local communities engagement in project negotiations in articulation of interests is occurring within a global framework of CSR cohesion represents a basic form of 'pluralism'.

Notwithstanding the difficulties of applying theoretical concepts from the advanced countries, this chapter supports the claims of pluralist theorists (Fox, 1966; Clegg, 1976) who argue that conflict is a product of diverse interest groups and sources of loyalty. Contrary to the widely reported governments of developing countries trend towards a unitarist perspective in acknowledging and supporting multinational company natural resource exploitation, this chapter will demonstrate that pluralism in CSR development agenda setting and implementation is relatively strong and gaining rapid momentum in PNG. Despite the imperfections in the PNG bureaucratic and generally political system, various social disputes resulting of mining developments demonstrate that functioning representative machinery is capable of pressurising MNMCs to engage in CSR activities within the existing framework of the law. In particular, pressure on MNMCs for development projects indicate the genuine ambition of the various independent groups like traditional landowners of mine projects to take up community grievances and to fight them through to a pluralist compromise.

While on the international literature, the major debate in CSR over the past decade has been over whether or not accountability and fairness as prerequisites are part of the process of management of CSR by MNCs in countries of operation (Holliday et al, 2002; Kapelus, 2002). Most of the analysis supporting these debates (of either viewing CSR as benevolent role of MNCs for a better society or rhetoric and environmental initiatives as 'greenwash') has taken place in parallel, within different countries. While this has an important step in the process of robust discussion in redefining concepts and models, analyses of CSR activities in developing countries by critics from mainly developed countries think otherwise. They argue "CSR as primarily about projecting a suitable image in order to placate critics and ensure 'business as usual' (Friends of the Earth International, et al., 2002). With respect to mining, critics (Hamann and Kapelus, 2004; Rivas-Ducca 2002:4; Hamann and Acutt, 203:255; Levy, 1997 and others) complain of the environmental devastations mining corporations cause to local indigenous communities and disappear without adequately compensating them. However, what the critics and general international literature on CSR seldom acknowledge is that each developing country embodies certain historical patterns of developmental, institutional and civic or community features which varyingly influence MNMCs and their voluntary activities. An international perspective, is therefore, needed in order to compare the impact of these and other variables.

Yet international research on issues concerning CSR requiring deep knowledge of local culture, history, institutions and developmental needs is extremely difficult to do well. In deed, this chapter will be one attempt to accommodate this challenge and point out that there is local variation and distinctive local features influencing the character and implementation of CSR of MNMCs. Theoretically, the empirical discussions from CSR of MNMCs in PNG mining will have novel implications. Unlike the usual case in developing countries, PNG government system exhibit strong signs of 'pluralism' as traditionally understood by the advocates of pluralist scholars. In addition, PNG offers a relatively eager role for local communities in development matters, and is again, for this reason, something of an exception when measured against the general pattern for developing countries. Moreover, in contrast to the empirical cases, which inform Kerr et al. (1962)'s model, PNG's mineral policy is structured in MNMCs recognition of local pressure group action and its claims. Hence, in short, this chapter wants to emphasize that PNG local communities are, to a considerable degree, 'exceptional' actors putting pressure on MNMCs and consequently influencing their CSR in mining developing countries. This is evidenced by the level of pressure imposed on MNMCs by local communities for development assistance.

Emergence of Institutional Arrangements Supporting Pluralistic Participation

Unlike many developing countries with mining economies, PNG is an exception with an institutional arrangement which legitimizes local community participation in mine development negotiation process and regular review meetings which have direct implications for the CSR agenda. This arrangement has paved the way for compulsory local community participation as acknowledging them as one of the significant actors (others being government (s) and developer). Thus, interaction of the three main players has established a pluralistic forum to bandy mainly equity and development agendas between them. Bigg and Ward (2003) argue that the absence of such arrangements (in many countries) have held back progress in some important areas as a result hindering the potential for CSR to deliver its goals. However, in the case of PNG the emergence of a dynamic relationship between the MNMCs and local communities has stemmed from the existence of the Mine Development Forum (MDF) where anticipated distribution of benefits from mine is discussed prior to its development and operation. The MDF is an extraordinary meeting of mine stakeholders and outcomes are reflected in contracts between each of the parties. This binds them to fulfil and adhere to the conditions of agreement mainly during the operation of the projects. The parties include the PNG Government, mine developers, respective provincial government and local communities hosting the particular projects. The outcomes take the form of an agreement between the developer and local community, provincial government and National PNG Government where specific infrastructural development agendas and other benefits are identified for the mine to deliver during the course of its operation. In fact, the agreement in many ways ensures that the parties share the risks and rewards of mining. What mining does to the national economy is evident in the form of fiscal revenues employment however costs associated with the activity are not equally distributed. Obviously, the investor bears the financial risks but local communities are often understated (Hancock, 2002). That is where their participation is legitimised in MDF as they would be the bearers of environmental, social and cultural impacts and increased population pressures due to in-migration to once stable and tranquil as a result of mining activity.

However, MNMCs and other resource developers often carry out projects in local communities over and beyond their requirements stipulated in the Mining Act and MDF agreements. In a landmark publication on landowner compensation in PNG mining and petroleum sectors, Filer, Henton and Jackson (2000) defined compensation as 'community benefit at company cost'. The study of 106 individuals representing 26 organisations found that as it was hard to quantify the adversely affected communities as a result of resource exploitation (mining) companies were pressured to do more to cover large areas adjacent to projects and beyond (view Table 1). They observed that resource exploration companies and operators were compensating local communities for various reasons at their own expenses however they formed part and partial of the overall compensation regime. The responses recorded in Table 1 overwhelmingly acknowledge compensation payment has become integral to the management and operation of large MNMC run projects in PNG.

Table 1.

In addition to statutory compensation as required by law, some organisations (resource developers) provide other benefits to landowners at their own cost. These may include community benefits such sas education and health programmes, business development support, sponsorships etc.		
	Yes	No
Does your organisation provide community benefits at its own cost?	92%	8%
In your opinion, are these benefits a form of compensation?	46%	54%
Do you think that these kinds of benefits should become part of the formal compensation system?	34%	66%

Note: Q 1 responses were tabulated to show the percentage of participating organisations providing community benefits. Questions 2 and 3 aggregate the response of the individual respondents.

Source: Filer, Henton and Jackson, 2000:2

Further, MNMCs fulfil their contractual obligations in delivery of infrastructural and other projects as well as additional social and economic activities in order to gain project security. Acknowledged as non-income components of the fiscal regime for mining, in PNG the local communities utilise the MDF to bargain for goods and services which results from the distributional mechanisms for sharing portions of centrally collected mineral revenues. All local mining communities harbouring projects have been able to share portions of royalty revenues, Special Support Grants (SSG) from central government to local provincial governments, Tax Credit Schemes (TCS) and miscellaneous other support programmes. It is also through negotiations during the MDF that local communities ensure that the MNMCs acknowledged them as "preferred area status" in having access to education, employment and development assistance. This is often above and beyond compensation and relocation payments, mine equity participation and prescribed infrastructure which are part and parcel of every agreement involving local communities. All in all, the MDF has legitimised local community participation in PNG mining that at the same time imposed a development role on MNMCs as part of their CSR in return for mine security.

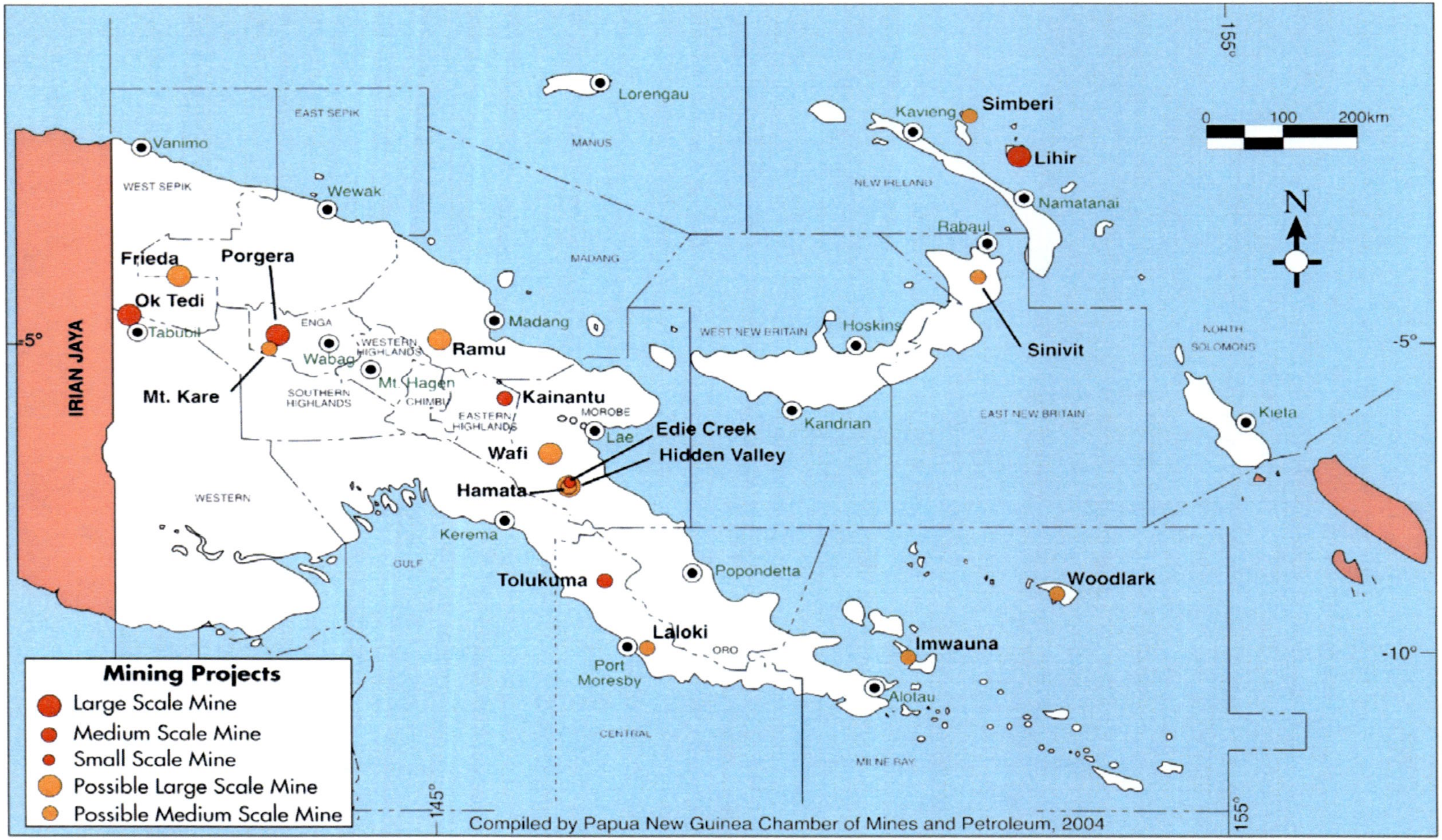

Figure 1. The PNG Mining Industry.

PLURALISM IN ACTION: EVIDENCE FROM THREE PNG MINES

The evidences of pluralistic involvement allowing for local community participation in influencing development agenda and also CSR activities is best highlighted by accounts of three PNG mines: Porgera, Ok Tedi and Lihir (See Figure 1 for location of these and other mines). They also provide a microcosm of developer and local community relationship in identification and implementation of development projects. Further, the case discussions also document the perceptions and experiences of MNMCs and local communities and explain how the three projects cope and maintain the social relationship on a day-to-day basis with their host communities. It also points out the various modes of approaches and strategies of each project developers in assessing development needs of the communities and responding accordingly. Based on the three mines' experiences, this chapter will be in a position to highlight at least some general practices and trends in mining aided economic and social development in rural PNG. The three mines are discussed accordingly.

ACCOUNT ONE: PORGERA MINE

Porgera is in the top ten of Australasian large gold mines with a current average annual production of 304,858 tonnes. Upon production in 1989 it was managed by Canadian miner, Placer Dome until 2005 when it was absorbed by Barrick, one of the current top three world goldminers. Operated under a joint venture arrangement, with equity representation held by South African, Australian, PNG Government and local Porgeran community, the mine has been mostly profitable. The mine commenced production after three years of construction and compulsory negotiations with local and PNG Government stakeholders. It has a current workforce of little under 2000 with large part of it being local Porgerans. However, if the mine had any obviously immediate impact, it has been the local Porgeran community more than others.

Like most people of PNG's interior Highlands, the Porgeran people who host the huge mine have a relatively short history of European contact. But during this period they have had almost continuous contact with the white alluvial gold miners who frequented this outback since the mid-1930s (Imbun, 1999a). Numbering over twenty thousand, they occupy the second largest district in area, which is more spacious than other five populated districts which make up the province of Enga. They are scattered in small defensive hamlets in contrast to the larger, denser populations adjacent to large populated areas. They value social bonds (like marriages and kinship linkages) as crucial to the incorporation of individuals into clan groups. Meggit (1958:46) mentioned that a clever manipulation of the social network has provided a defensive system with the result that the neighbouring tribal warfaring clans found it hard to conquer the Porgerans.

Unlike other earlier PNG mines, in 1989 Porgera became the first mine to go through a pluralist style of mine development negotiation process to devise policies on the anticipated distribution of the benefits from the mine. The negotiating parties were made up of representatives from the Porgera Landowners Association, the Enga Provincial Government (EPG), developer representatives and the PNG Government. The policies of the Porgera Forum, as it was called, were also to be applicable to all major mining projects to be developed in PNG. For the two existing major mining projects (Ok Tedi and Misima) it was too late. Nonetheless there were community expectations that benefits would in some way be provided (West, 1992). Out of the several policies on the distribution of benefits ranging from royalty distribution to infrastructure and social improvements funding, the forum also called for preference in employment, training and business to be given to local people. They argued they were most affected by the adverse impacts such as disruptions to lives, culture and environment by the mining activity. Above all, they were the traditional owners of the mining lease land and they argued that, as such, they were to have first preference in receiving the material benefits from the mine (Porgera Agreement, 1989:45). In Porgera's case, subject to normal commercial and operating requirements, priority was to be given, in order, to landowners, people from the mining areas, from the (Enga) province and finally to nationals (other Papua New Guineans).

In the context CSR Porgera Joint Venture (PJV), the mine operator has done more for Porgeran community in the last eighteen years of mining operation than the EPG and PNG Government combined in their social and economic service delivery. Much of the mine's CSR work is often credited with the first PJV Managing Director who had the foresight and ability to convince the National Government that a lot of tangible development could occur in Porgera and Enga Province in general if the mine attended to development needs of the communities in return for tax credit. The freshness of the closure of the Bougainville mine by disgruntled landowners and the distressingly backwardness of Porgera had arguably spurred on PJV to give increasingly positive attention to the wishes and aspirations of local communities as well as to the Enga province, in general.

Under the TCS PJV spends up to two per cent of the project income on up-grading existing infrastructure and build new schools and medical centres in its areas of operation and beyond. This amounts to millions of dollars and the company is entitled to a tax rebate for this type of expenditure. However, the amount of commitment and effort into achieving tangible development outcomes demonstrates it is one of the best policy outcomes that have emerged in the PNG mining industry (Imbun, 2006). The scheme is working extremely well and projects have been undertaken in upgrading health, education and physical infrastructure and currently it is emphasing cash cropping and other economic ventures for local Porgeran and Engan communities. In the period of some eighteen years of operation of the mine more than three hundred million dollars have been spent on such projects. It demonstrates how PJV has ventured beyond a narrow operating role and is providing services which are normally provided by the public sector.

The identification of projects and approval for implementation are the result of collaboration between the local communities, local and provincial government and appropriate National Government institutions. Usually, the projects reflect EPG's Five Year Plan for the province however local communities have a significant say in the actual determination of the projects. On going maintenance of the projects remain the responsibilities of governments however there are still concerns expressed by some sections of the local communities on the quantity of projects. Talepakali (1999) acknowledged the differing opinions where PJV was excelling on a public relations exercise by some critics whilst the company claims of playing a legitimate role and in the process has become *the* government. All in all, as he concluded "TCS expenditure has had at least come visible impact in various communities", however the mine income going back to the EPG has not made its marks since the mine's operations in 1990.

ACCOUNT TWO: OK TEDI MINE

Unlike Porgera mine, Ok Tedi mine has had an environmentally troublesome short history since its production in 1984. The mine took almost eight years to construct in one of the least developed provinces in PNG. The construction posed a huge engineering feat contributed largely by the remote location of the site and the unstable terrain. After some US$1, 400 million construction expenses, the Australian giant miner, BHP took the helms with significant equity and other partners being Canadian, German and PNG Government. Considered one of the World's largest low-cost open cut copper mines with an average of 220, 000 tonnes mined daily, it also became for many years *the* biggest export earner as typified by 25.7 per cent of PNG's export earnings in 2004 (http://www.oktedi.com/aboutus/). Under current mining operations, the mine is expected to go on until 2013 when it is expected to cease operations as a result of depletion of accessible ore. Unfortunately the mine had been in the international media spot light and therefore emerged as one of the hot topics of local and international environmental critique since establishment as a result of handling or mishandling of its tailings. The relentless adverse publicity both internally and externally ultimately took its toll on BHP. Finally, the mining company admitted that the mine's impact on the Ok Tedi and Fly River systems where some 50, 000 villagers draw their livelihood was irreparably impacted upon by the mine. This conclusion was contrary to what had been held and the company claimed there was no possible solutions it investigated were able to alleviate the situation. In 2002 BHP surrender its majority shareholding of 52 per cent and transferred it to a new company, the PNG Sustainable Development Limited (PNG SDL). Despite its chequered performance, the mine which directly employs more than 2000 workers arguably stands out in the department of sustainable development and CSR pursuits.

However, the introduction of MDF by Porgera mine legimitised the tacitly pluralistic negotiation arrangements Ok Tedi mine had with development issues with its landowners and other local communities. Unlike Porgera and other PNG mines, Ok Tedi had the mammoth task to appease particularly local community dissent as a result of its adverse environmental degradation. After the collapse of the construction of its tailings dam by massive landslides in 1984, the mine had been disposing its tailings along the Fly River system which had reached unbelievable sediment levels that have killed off vast tracks of vegetation. In 1994 the local people and their community leaders successfully sued Ok Tedi Mining Limited (OTML), the mine Management Company and BHP in the Australian Supreme Court for environmental damages. The case was settled out of court with a $75 million compensation payment to the Ok Tedi/Fly River landowners. Despite the legal battle over environmental compensation, OTML had a healthy and robust relationship with its local communities in bringing tangible development benefits to once isolated and time forgotten communities. Prior to the operation of the mine, the Ok Tedi and Fly River people of the Western Province of PNG, numbering some 200, 000 people were mostly hunters, gathers and subsistence farmers with virtually no contact with the outside world. The advent of Ok Tedi mine has brought huge socio-economic benefits through mainly employment opportunities, business spin offs and above all, mine initiated development projects. These projects have resulted of extensive negotiations between the OTML and local communities.

In 1990 OTML put a stoppage to its previously ad hoc management of development projects and formed the Lower Ok Tedi/Fly River Development Trust (FRDT) as a result of extensive negotiations with people who were adversely affected by the tailings of the mine. As part of its CSR package, OTML provided source of funding for community and economic development assistance to 107 villages along 1, 000 kilometres of the Ok Tedi and Fly Rivers. Initially the trust fund was meant for village infrastructure projects, education, health infrastructure, later it was extended to agribusiness-related programs designed to benefit collective communities. Some 50 million dollars had been spent so far until it was superseded by the PNG PNGSDL. The FRDT supplemented the TCS and SSG projects also managed by OTML in consultation with local level governments in the Western Province which were overseen by PNG Government. In addition to the projects, the mine also manage several trust funds also geared towards attending to specific development projects along mine impact areas and in the entire Western Province (Simpson and Goie, 1999).

Yet, OTML sensing the nearing of the ceasation of its operations has embarked on embracing the concept of sustainable development as part of its CSR and enforcing it in its numerous community projects in a big way. It was first debated in two key company sponsored workshops for all stakeholders, including local community participants in 1999 and 2001. The two workshops set the blue print for the OTML assisted development of mine affected people and rest of the population in Western Province. A host of mainly agricultural and other economically projects sprouted as part of the OTML supported sustainable development initiate and its biggest allay came with the establishment of the PNG SDL in 2002. The PNGSDL through its ownership of 52 per cent previous BHP equity in the mine allowed it to use proceedings sustainable development projects in the Western Province and PNG generally. Two thirds of the company's earnings are going into a long-term fund for post-closure and one-third for annual project expenditure. This arrangement allows the local communities and provincial and local governments to identify possible projects while OTML is principally responsible for design and construction of the actual projects. PNGSDL is providing a significant and long-term source of development project for the Western Province which is complemented by other OTML's community development projects. At the end of 2005 PNGSDL had $175.5 million in its long term fund for post mine closure activities and 81.8 million in its Development Fund for pre-mine closure. The latter was divided between funding projects in the Western Province (27.6 million) and PNG generally (54.2 million) (PNG SDP Information Booklet, 2005). Although depending on the price of copper the pool of development funds is going to vary however one thing is obvious. That is the PNGSDP is a unique organisation and in fact is one of the first kind of mining influenced pro-development and pro-community orientated organisation in the world (Perkins, 2007).

Account Three: Lihir Mine

The third case of mining assisted development in local communities involves Lihir mine. It commenced open-cut gold production since 1997 and located on the Lihir Island north-east of mainland PNG. The British mining giant, Rio Tinto through a public registered company (Lihir Management Company) operates the project where significant equity is dominated by Australian institutions and general public including local Lihirian participation under the terms of the Lihirian Equity Trust. The mine has sufficient ore deposit that its life span has been estimated to go beyond 2020 (Imbun, 2007). With a workforce of a little over 2000, most of them local lihirians work mainly in manual and lower white-collar jobs. The mine has become in recent years one of the most profitable operations in PNG. Like Porgera mine, it is operated on fly-in-fly-out mode of operations for other Papua New Guineans and sizable number of expatriates while a key skeleton workforce lives on the island.

Before mining, like almost all local communities in PNG harbouring mining and other major resource extraction sites, Lihir Island was a backward area deprived of basic services. The population of over 4000 people had little external contact and lived an overwhelming subsistence life characterised by farming and fishing. Only their embracement of the Catholic faith on the island provided some limited exposure to mainly educational opportunities. However, the long isolation has assisted in the widespread of a cargo cult movement where the people believed that their small island would be submerged with modern goods and services trigged by a vague benevolent figure (Filer and Jackson, 1989; Macintyre and Foale, 2003; Macintyre, 2003).

The advent of mining in the 1990s on the island became prophetic to the cargo cult obsessed community who had yearned so long for modern goods and services. Most of those materialistic yearnings have been realised through the Integrated Benefits Package (IBP), a comprehensive agreement between the mine and the people of Lihir Island, New Ireland Provincial Government and the PNG National Government. Mainly a compensation agreement for the mine to provide infrastructural and other development projects, it also paved the way for unlimited CSR related input into the local communities as the mine saw fit. However, IBP was a creation of four years of extensive negotiations between the Lihir (Mine) Management Company (LMC) and Lihir local community representatives which were often fraught with deadlocks that required the occasional intervention of national government as mediators. The testimony of the first Managing Director of the mine echoed the formidable challenges he was facing in the numerous negotiations with the local communities and three levels of PNG Governments.

"I often say that having spent ten years in Africa and another ten in the Middle-East, I thought I was an expert in dealing with under-developed communities. But I threw the book away soon after I arrived here. You have to take PNG on its own merits. You cannot rely on pass experience and expect it to fit in with what you have here. Certainly Lihir was totally different from anything I had experienced beforehand.

You have to get up a fairly steep learning curve, and you have to get your team up a steep learning curve, that you understand the community and that they understand where you are coming from, and that strike that happy medium fairly quickly" (Prime, 1998:22).

The IBP was renegotiated after an interval of five years and recently in 2005 the agreement was reviewed to assess the benefits that have been going to the Lihir people from the gold mine. Apart from compensation and royalty payments, infrastructural and economic projects mandated by the agreement, the LMC had gone beyond the duty of call to ensure tangible development priorities are met and provided on the island. Such extra-curricular commitments include employing external managers and workers to oversee local businesses, leasing mine staff to setting up and running local organisations and a host of other assistances. The mine has provided in access of several millions of dollars on community projects on an annual basis on top of those commitments laid out in the IBP. As long as the Lihirian communities are aggressive and articulate of their developmental demands it seems the LMC is prepared to accommodate them as part of fulfilling its statutory commitments and also as part of being a benevolent corporate citizen in a previously predominant subsistence economy.

DISCUSSION

As this chapter contended, PNG's mining and CSR regime have developed (embryonic) pluralistic independent local community groups, capable of operating and negotiating with MNMCs in advocating for tangible social and economic projects. In this PNG is an 'exception' when contrasted with a number of developing countries with mining as part of revenue generating activities. In these countries it is usually the prerogative of the resource developers to entertain extra circular projects, let alone acknowledge them. In other words, they do not view it as part of their primary objectives and therefore they exercise unbridled authority over what they do and who they interact with within the vicinity of their special mining leases. For example, in African mining there is very little participation by local communities of mining project sites in expressing their development needs in mining development negotiations which are strongly guarded by state and developer interests (i.e. Kapalus, 2002). Often solutions are offered favoring MNMCs whenever there is a dispute with local communities which reflects the pro-capital style of government. In arguing for a structuralist explanation of the general weakness of African local communities' bargain for tangible development presence Eweje (2006) points out the prevalence of formidable MNMCs' obsession with ore production leaves little room for community consultation at the expense of compromising and weak governments.

While Filer, Banks and Burton (forthcoming) acknowledge that there is "a strange contradiction" in Melanesia where there is robust interaction between MNMCs, State and local communities in PNG than in West Papuan side of Indonesia. In the latter, they argue that such as the role of Freeport mine, world's largest open cut mine located in West Papua has not been decisive in engaging in CSR activities particularly in local communities, partly because of the lack of an articulate and well-organised local communities and local governments. In contrast to these countries and others in Africa and South America, a pluralistic legal and political framework exists in PNG.

The three PNG evidences of mines in partnership with local communities demonstrate that large scale mining can not begin and operate on a daily basis without contributing tangibly to development pursuits and fulfilling their CSR roles. This allows for a liberal environment that encourages the exercise of freedom of association and collective bargaining for tangible development projects by local communities. The right to negotiate with MNMCs is not seen as a barrier to foreign direct investment by the PNG Government. In fact, the three evidences provide a microcosm of the current trend of MNMC advocated CSR projects in particularly rural areas of PNG. It results from the existence of institutional arrangements allowing for healthy pluralistic negotiations between stakeholders which provide a win-win situation for everyone. It is evidently more so for the previously neglected and backward local communities whose only introduction to the cash economy have been through the advent of mining operations in their backyards. They seem to relentlessly and aggressively negotiate for tangible development programs particularly during MDFs because of not only the backwardness of their communities but also for a host of other reasons (see Figure 2 below).

However, many developing countries with mineral and other natural resource base form an authoritarian view of mineral development policy thus regard local communities as 'undesirables' and therefore their demands would inhibit the development and operation of mining projects. To them accelerated mineral extraction and development can only be achieved by suppressing and belittling the role of local communities so that the state and developers can discuss what *is* best for them and the country (Eweje, 2006). This is contrary to the PNG situation where institutional arrangements and political process supporting community involvements exists independently in the mining industry and the role of the state resembles more that of a mediator for competing interests. In this sense, PNG, and its 'pluralism' is an exception.

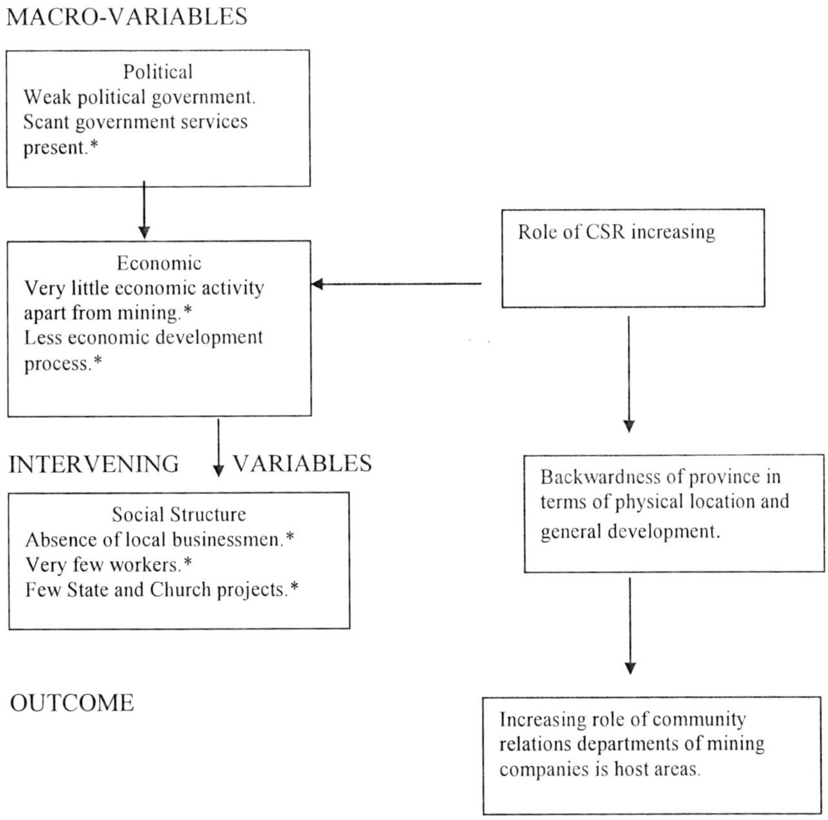

Note: *CSR role increasing.
Source: Imbun, 2007:189.

Figure 2. The CSR function of MNMCs in PNG.

Although there could be arrangements between local communities and MNMCs facilitating development projects in some developing countries, what is unfolding in PNG, is in a different way, 'exceptional'. PNG has a liberal pluralistic mining policy framework that is quite different from those found in most of the developing countries including its nearest neighour Indonesia. 'Exceptionalism' is demonstrated in PNG's 'pluralism' with the existence of independent local communities, local and provincial governments and MNMCs all of which pursue their interests in a relatively liberal and democratic environment. In contrast, in much of Asia, Africa and Latin America, local communities are generally seen as 'distracters' and hinderers of foreign investment in resource extraction, and therefore they are dealt harshly by the administrative arms of the state, in a typically unitarist approach, favouring capital (i.e. Filer, Banks and Burton, forthcoming; Szablowski, 2002; Eweje, 2006). This is often done to the exclusion of any effective interest in their demands for compensation and development projects. Surprisingly for a newly developing country, PNG is something of an exception with a legal and political framework which allows a pluralistic environment that encourages local communities to exercise the freedom of association and right to negotiate for tangible development outcomes with MNMCs.

Conclusion

This chapter contended that MNMCs that are operating in PNG continuously maintain a challenging role in the presence of both the Government and the people. They exist in the dual situation of being foremost an economic agent for the shareholders, which almost all MNMCs practise elsewhere. However, equally significant and occurs increasingly in PNG, they are also seen as a social agent for bringing development to the host local communities and the country. In the latter role, they find themselves willingly (and sometimes reluctantly) as agents for making tangible contributions to these often backwards communities. This facet of mining aided social and economic development in PNG has rapidly gained momentum arguably after the premature closure of Australian mining company CRA operated giant Bougainville copper mine in the late 1980s and the recent unceremonious departure of BHP, another Australian mining company from Ok Tedi copper mine, in the late 1990s. The sudden and unprecedented input (in some cases millions of dollars) for infrastructure, economic and social services has heralded a new dimension of mining-aided development, especially in rural PNG. It seems the MNMCs consciously do it as a prerequisite to operating socially and politically sound mines. Their increasingly positive role in creating and maintaining 'socially healthy environments' in host local communities and the country has also added a new dimension to the theory and practice of CSR in PNG.

However, the voluntary development activities resulting from perceived and sometimes overt pressures from particularly local host communities have been never critically understood nor recorded for academic and public consumption. This chapter explained how and why local communities have (suddenly) become a 'significant other' in exerting pressures on MNMCs to seriously attend to their developmental demands as a priority to mining for ores. The embracement of a developmental role to their usual mining operational pursuits is redefining the parameters of CSR in a huge way unprecedented in PNG. Although other actors like social and environmentally conscious citizens of mostly developed countries and non-governmental organisations (NGOs) are well documented of their pressures on multinational companies (MNCs) to increase their CSR role. Yet, this chapter in way of contribution to the field of CSR - by examining the unheralded role local indigenous communities (of PNG mining projects) – highlight the significant role they are playing in influencing MNMCs, which increasingly influence their CSR activities. This 'new' actor coupled with weak government presence in rural areas seem to result of a pluralistic mine development negotiation process where all stakeholders in mining as accorded with some kind of equal status and respect.

In course of explaining of this mining driven rural development, this chapter investigated what seems to be the indispensability of CSR activity in provision of developmental projects to local indigenous communities by MNMCs. As it seems this is purposely done as a requirement to the continued and safe operations of the mines. This has effected of the unrelenting pressure exerted increasingly by local communities. In the process, they have become a "significant other" or one of the major stakeholders in the operations of the mines in PNG. The author having extensive periods of ethnographic research in PNG mining discussed the issues and explored history, politics, culture, economic imperatives and social and economic change in rural communities brought about by the advent of large scale mining.

Above all, theoretically a concept of relevance to PNG mining assisted development is pluralism. Unlike many developing countries which do not enjoy this privilege of directly influencing mining policy, the pluralistic approach to mine development in PNG recognises the settlement of conflict by collective negotiation as central to the relationship between MNMCs, PNG Government (s) and local communities. As the evidence of mining aided development illustrates, the emergence of pluralistic institutional framework allows for a participative approach towards improving MNMC in conduct of its CSR, changing attitudes and possibly significantly reordering the power relations between local communities and MNMCs. In fact, MNMCs' increasingly positive role in creating and maintaining 'socially healthy environments' in host local communities and the country has also added a new dimension to the theory and practice of CSR in PNG.

ACKNOWLEDGMENT

This work is a product of various funding over the years from several organisations. They include AusAid, University of PNG, Oceania Development Network, and the University of Western Sydney. The author is grateful for their support, however any errors or misrepresentations remains his responsibility.

REFERENCES

Arnold, D. 2003. Libertarian Theories of the Corporation and Global Capitalism. *Journal of Business Ethics* 48(2):155-170.

Ballard, C. & Banks, G. 2003. Resource Wars: The Anthropology of Mining. *Annual Review Anthropol* 20(15): 287-313.

Banks, G. & Ballard, C. (Eds.). 1997. *The Ok Tedi Settlement: Issues, Outcomes and Implications*. Canberra: Australian National University.

Bigg, T. & Ward, H. 2003. Linking Corporate Social Responsibility, Good Governance and Corporate Accountability Through Dialogue, Discussion Paper, International Institute for Environment and Development, London.

Chand, S. & Levantis, T. 2000. Dutch Disease and the Crime Epidemic: an investigation of the mineral boom in PNG'. *Australian Journal of Agricultural and Resource Economics* 44:129-146.

Clegg, H.A. 1975. Pluralism in the Industrial Relations. *British Journal of Industrial Relations* 13(3):309-16.

Connel, J. & Howitt, R. (Eds.). 1991 *Mining and Indigenous Peoples in Australasia. Sydney*: Sydney University Press.

Crawley, A. & Sinclair, A. 2003. Indigenous human resource practices in Australian Mining Companies. *Journal of Business Ethics* 45(4):361-370.

Eweje, G. 2006. The Role of MNEs in *Community* Development Initiatives in Developing Countries, *Business & Society* 45 (2): 93-129.

Filer, C. 1990. The Bougainville rebellion, the mining industry and the process of social disintegration in Papua New Guinea. *Canberra Anthropology* 13:1-39.

Filer, C. 1992. The Escalation of Disintegration and the Reinvention of Authority. In: Springgs and Denoon (Eds). *The Bougainville Crisis: 1991 Update.* Canberra: Political and Social Change Monograph 16.

Filer, C. (Ed.). 1999. *Dilemmas of Development: the social and economic impact of the Porgera gold mine 1989-1999*. Canberra and Waigani: Asia Pacific Press and INA. Port Moresby.

Filer, C. Banks, G. & Burton, J. (forthcoming). The Fragmentation of Responsibilities in the Melanesian Mining Sector. In O'Faircheallaigh, C & Ali, S (Eds.) *Indigenous Peoples, Corporate Social Responsibility and Resource Development.* Greenleaf Publishing: London. (forthcoming).

Filer, C. Henton, D.& Jackson, R. 2000. *Landowner Compensation in Papua New Guinea's Mining and Petroleum Sectors*. Port Moresby: PNGCMP.

Filer, C. & Imbun, B.Y. 2004. A Short History of Mineral Development Policy in Papua New Guinea, Resource Management in Asia-Pacific Studies, *Working Paper No. 55,* Research School of Asia and Pacific Studies, The Australian National University, Canberra.

Fox, A. 1966. Industrial Sociology and Industrial Relations, *Research Paper No. 3.* Royal Commission on Employer Associations and Trade Unions, London, HMSO.

Friends of the Earth International. 2002. *GroundWork and CorpWatch Greenwash Awards.* Pietermaritzburg:Groundwork.

.Hamann, R. & Acutt, N. 2003. How Should Civil Society (and the Government) Respond to Corporate Social Responsibility? A Critique of Business Motivations and the Potential for Partnerships. *Development Southern Africa* 20(2):255-270.

Hamann & Kapelus, P. 2004. Corporate Social Responsibility in Mining in Southern Africa: Fair accountability or just greenwash. *Development* 47(3):85-92.

Hancock, M. 2002. Sharing the Risks and Rewards of Mining, WMMF Workshop on Mining and People, 13-15 March.

Havini, M. 1992. A Bougainvillean Perspective on the Crisis. In: Springgs and Denoon (Eds). The Bougainville Crisis: 1991 Update. Canberra: Political and Social Change Monograph 16.

Hess, M. & Imbun, B.Y. 2003. Papua New Guinea. In: Zanko, M. (Ed*). Handbook of Human Resource Management Policies and Practices in Asia-Pacific Economics* Vol. 2. London: Edward Elgar.

Holliday, C.O., Schmidheiny, S. & Wattas, P. 2002. *Walking the Talk, the Business Case for Sustainable Development*, Sheffield, UK: Greenleaf Publishing.

Howard, M.C.1988.*The Impact of the International Mining Industry on Native Peoples*: Sydney: University of Sydney.

Howard, M.C. 1991. *Mining, Politics, and Development in the South Pacific*, Colorado: Westview Press.

http://www.oktedi.com/aboutus/. Ok Tedi Mine Website.

Imbun, B.Y. 1994. 'Who said mining companies take and do not give?': The mining companies' role of Social Responsibility in Papua New Guinea, *TaimLain*: *A Journal of Contemporary Melanesian Studies* 2(1):27-42.1997.

Imbun, B.Y. 1997. The Emergence of An Industrial Workforce: Recruitment and Training in the Papua New Guinea Mining Industry. *International Journal of Employment Relations* 5(2):35-54.

Imbun, B.Y. 1998. Human Resource Management Issues in Papua New Guinea Mining: The Case of Porgera. *International Employment Relations Review*. 4 (2):1-18.

Imbun, B.Y. 1999a. *Industrial and Employment Relations in the Papua New Guinea Mining Industry*. Waigain: University of Papua New Guinea Press.

Imbun, B.Y. 1999b. The Dynamics of Industrial Relations in the Papua New Guinea Mining Industry: Implications for Trade Union Policies. Waigani: National Research Institude.

Imbun, B.Y. 2000. Mining workers or 'opportunist' tribesmen?: A tribal workforce in a Papua New Guinea mine. *Oceania* 4(2):16-32.

Imbun, B.Y. 2003. The dynamics of policy making in Papua New Guinea's mining and petroleum sectors. *PNG Resources: Reporting on PNG's Petroleum, Mineral & Forestry Industries*. Issue Four. 30-43.

Imbun, B.Y. 2006a. Multinational mining and petroleum companies' perceptions of the policy framework in Papua New Guinea. *Pacific Economic Bulletin*. 21(1): 225-245.

Imbun, B.Y. 2006b. Local laborers in Papua New Guinea Mining: Attracted or Compelled to Work?. *The Contemporary Pacific: A journal of island affairs*. 18 (2): 315-334.

Imbun, B.Y. 2006c. Multinational mining companies and indigenous workers in Papua New Guinea: Tensions and challenges in employment relations *Labour, Capital & Society*. 39 (1): 114-147.

Imbun, B.Y. 2007. "Can not manage without the "significant other": Mining, corporate social responsibility and local communities in Papua New Guinea, *Journal of Business Ethics* 73:177-192.

Imbun, B.Y. & McGavin, P.A. (Eds.). 2001. *Issues in Papua New Guinea Mining: Analsysis and Policy Implications*, Waigani: University of Papua New Guinea Press.

Imbun B.Y. & Morris, R. 2001. Labour and Mining in Remote Areas: Towards an Assessment of Benefits. In: Imbun and McGavin (eds.). *Mining in Papua New Guinea: analysis and policy implications*, Port Moresby: University of Papua New Guinea Press. Pp. 81-96.

Jackson, R. 1991. Not without influence: villages, mining companies, and government in Papua New Guinea. In: in Connell, J. and Howitt, R. (eds.). *Mining and Indigenous Peoples in Australia*. Sydney. Sydney University Press. Pp. 63-76.

Kapelus, P. 2002. Mining, corporate social responsibility and the "community": The case of Rio... *Journal of Business Ethics* 39(3):275-296.

Keen, I. 1993. Aboriginal beliefs vs. mining at Coronation Hill: the containing force of traditionalism. *Human Organisations* 52:344-355.

Kerr, C., Dunlop, J., Harbison, F.H. & Myers, C.A. 1962. Industrialism and Industrial Man: The Problems of Labour and Management in Economic Growth, London: Heinemann.

Koczberski, G. & Curry, G.N. 2004. Divided communities and contested landscapes: mobility, development and shifting identities in migrant destination sites in Papua New Guinea. *Asia Pacific ViewPoint* 45(3) 357-371.

Lea, D. 2004. Can democratic reform enhance PNG's economic performance. *Pacific Economic Bulletin* 19 (1) 23-29.

Levy, D.E. 1997. Environmental Management as political Sustainability. *Organization & Environment* 10 (2):126-147.

Macintyre, M. 2003. Petztorme Women: Responding to Change in Lihir, Papua New Guinea. *Oceania* 7(1/2):120-133.

Macintyre & S. Foale. 2002, *Politicised ecology: local responses to mining in Papua New Guinea, Resource Management in Asia and Pacific Program.* Australian National University, Paper No. 3.

McEachern, D.1995. Mining meaning from the rhetoric of nature: Australian mining companies and their attitudes at home and abroad. *Policy Organisation and Society* 10: 48-69.

McGavin, P.A., Jones, M. & Imbun, B.Y. 2001. Long-distance commuting and national human resource development: evidence from Papua New Guinea. *Asia Pacific Journal of Human Resource Management* 39 (2):98-114.

Meggit, M.J. 1958. The Ipili of the Porgera Valley, Western Highlands District, *Oceania* 28 (1):31-55.

O'Faircheallaigh, C. 2002. *A New Approach to Policy Evaluation: Indigenous People and Mining*. Aldershot: Ashgate.

Oliver, D. 1991. *Black Islanders: A Personal Perspective of Bougainville 1937-1991.* Honolulu: University of Hawaii Press.

PNG Sustainable Development Program Information Booklet. 2005. Ok Tedi, Tabubil.

Perkins, D.H. 2007. Review of PNGSDP: *Papua New Guinea Sustainable Development Program,* Harvard University.

Porgera Mine Agreement. 1989. Port Moresby: PNG Government Printing Service.

Prime, 1998. News on PNG Mining and Petroleum. April-June.

Rivas-Ducca, G. 2002. *Less Mining for a Better World.* LINK, 101. London: Friends of the Earth International.

Simpson, G. And Goie, A. 1999. Ok Tedi: Planning for Sustainable Development: Summary of Issues and Options, Ok Tedi Mining Limited, Tabubil.

Springgs, M. & May, R. 1990. The Bougainville Crisis. Bathurst: Crawford House Press.and Denoon, D. (Eds). 1992. The Bougainville Crisis: 1991 Update. Canberra: *Political and Social Change Monograph 16.*

Szablowski, D. 2002. Mining, Development and the World Bank: A Case Analysis of Compania Minera Antamina's Operations in Peru, *Journal of Business Ethics*. 39 (3): 247-273.

Talepakali, S. 2001. Replacing the mountain: Resource revenue accessing and utilisation in Enga Province. *Development Bulletin* 50:22-24.

Trigger, D. 2000. Aboriginal responses to mining in Australia: economic aspirations, cultural revival and the politics of indigenous protest. In: P. Schweitzer and Biesele, M. & Hitchcock (Eds.). *Hunders and Gathers in the Modern World: Conflict Resistance and Self-Determination*. New York: Berghahn. Pp.192-205.

Wesley-Smith, T. 1993a. The politics of access: mining companies, the state, and landowners in Papua New Guinea, *Political Science* 42:1-199.

Wesley-Smith, T. (Ed). 1993b. A Legacy of Development: Three Years of Crisis in Bougainville. Special Issue. *The Contemporary Pacific* 4(2):121-134.

Wesley-Smith, T. & Organ, E. 1992. Copper, Class, and Crisis: Changing Relations of Production in Bougainville. *The Contemporary Pacific* 4(2):245-246.

West, R. 1992. Development Forum and Benefits Package: A Papua New Guinea Initiative, Institute of National Affairs, Working Paper, No. 6.

In: Corporate Social Responsibility
Editor: Adam R. Timpere
ISBN: 978-1-60456-284-2

Chapter 6

NATIONS, CULTURES, AND CORPORATE SOCIAL RESPONSIBILITY: THE PUBLIC RELATIONS OF BROADCASTING ADVOCATES IN A DIVERSE, DEVOLVING U.K.

Rachel (Randy) Kovacs*
York College, CUNY, One Bernard Baruch Way, New York, NY 10010, USA

ABSTRACT

This paper discusses how public relations is used to elicit greater corporate social responsibility (CSR) in support of U.K. regional and national cultures, culture-specific representations in electronic communication and, in particular, "endangered genres" in that country. It explores some of the prescient issues in this field and the technological and industry changes that have catalyzed U.K. activists. Its primary focus is on the strategies and impact of NGO viewer and listener broadcasting advocacy groups, community media associations, coalitions, and informal groups that seek to advance indigenous culture and get government and media corporations to both respond to these stakeholders and commit to policy and regulatory changes. The chapter also references pressure group activities with respect to the current crisis in children's television throughout the U.K.'s nations. Particular emphasis will be placed on CSR structures and vehicles for cultural expression in the nations of Scotland and Wales, the North of England, and other underrepresented regions. It will also examine if, and how, political devolution is intertwined with cultural agendas. Finally, it will also touch on the larger crisis in children's television, which will have further impact across the U.K., and which is a growing arena of CSR for NGOs throughout the U.K.

* 646-312-3700; rkovacs@york.cuny.edu

Problem

When we discuss public relations and corporate social responsibility (CSR), it begs a chicken-and-egg question: Does the global push for CSR stem from attention drawn to poor public relations practices or have effective public relations practices spawned an interest in CSR? Perhaps some practitioners would prefer to think the latter but, historically, CSR has largely emerged from less-than-stellar practices generating negative public reaction and consequently, organizational change. This author (2006) described CSR as a "push from within," a higher commitment to public interest than accountability, which frequently is externally-driven. There also has been an historical, perceived inability, or even unwillingness, by broadcasters, government, regulators, and other institutions to address and represent the needs and interests of diverse viewing and listening constituencies. In the U.K, especially in underrepresented and less-empowered communities, this failure has provoked skepticism and anger at Westminster, the seat of U.K. government, where decision-making powers concerning broadcasting have been "reserved" for Parliament. Given the limited, devolved power of the Scotland Parliament and Welsh Assembly, activists there and in the English North have developed alternative vehicles for public discourse, consensus building, and action about cultural issues. Consequently, a fine line exists between public relations and advocacy around public interest CSR issues.

This lack of empowerment is a common thread has among well-established as well as newer and disparate cultural entities with different agendas. Those aggrieved may organize as formal or informal non-governmental organizations (NGOs). As NGOs, broadcasting and cultural activists have followed environmental and other activists by taking into their hands what they feel others, including the nation state and business interests, cannot or will not do (Castells, 2000). A range of strategies and alliances gives these NGOs a competitive "edge" in setting their agendas, raising public awareness of compelling issues, and in their impact on policy processes.

The study will explore how U.K. NGO broadcasting/cultural advocates, community media groups, and ad hoc coalitions in Scotland , Wales and secondarily, in the English North, practice public relations to preserve regional and national cultural identity. U.K. activists have also acted on a perceived failure by government and business to protect their distinct identities. Their role in increasing CSR in the public interest is not to be underestimated. Even though their achievements are sometimes intangible, they build relationships with targets that are themselves positive outcomes. Their events generate discourse, pique interest in public policy issues and provide forums for debate. Their cumulative strategies are likely to achieve long-term goals.

This study stems from over research beginning in the early 1990s into U.K. broadcasting activism at home, in Europe, and in global forums. Of the six U.K.-wide groups (Voice of the Listener and Viewer [VLV], Consumers Association, National Consumer Council, Mediawatch UK [formerly National Viewers and Listeners Association], Campaign for Quality Television, and the Deaf Broadcasting Council) in the original study (Kovacs, 1998), some have forged ad hoc alliances with each other. Mediawatch UK, CQT, and DBC, quite visible and all successful at one time, appear far less active than before. Only VLV maintains a high, consistent profile on cultural issues and active chapters with directorships in Scotland

and Wales. Other ad hoc alliances and smaller, less-renowned groups (particularly in Scotland) will also be tracked.

British NGOs and CSR in a Larger Context

The concerns of the NGOs studied here are considered CSR issues. Although they are not violations of human rights, fair labor standards, environmental regulations, or similar norms, British broadcasters have a public service mandate. Cultural representation clearly falls within their remit and activists expect them to fulfill it. Devolution has underscored this obligation.

Recently, the author researched the emergence, nature, goals, activities, and impact of NGOs. The focus was on their origins and how they became increasingly legitimized in a world where multinationals' powers may surpass those of governments (Kovacs, 2004, 2005). NGO, like CSR, literature, cuts across business, management, political science, and other fields. To put U.K. NGO efforts to increase CSR into perspective, the author (Kovacs, 2006) studied interdisciplinary frameworks for CSR and the role of the Global Compact, Global Alliance, and Business for Social Responsibility in raising the CSR bar. With this grounding in normative CSR frameworks and principles in mind, the author traveled to the U.K. in spring 2006 and 2007. Prominent stakeholders in communication and cultural policies in England, Scotland, and Wales identified competing U.K. cultural interests in the Nations and the North.

METHODS

The initial 1996-97 study involved over 43 interviews of broadcasters, activists, politicians, regulators, civil servants, academics and other interested parties (Kovacs, 1998). Many interviewees had served in more than one of the above capacities and many were also consulted on subsequent trips to the U.K. and/or on their visits to the U.S. This provided a longitudinal perspective. In addition, archival research at the now-defunct Independent Television Commission (ITC) Library, the British Film Institute (BFI, now home to the ITC collection), the Yale Libraries, and the U.N.'s DPI/NGO Resource Center provided formal, informal, and unobtrusive documentation. The author, for over a decade, attended public meetings of activist groups, conferences, Media Society forums for debate, hearings in Parliamentary committees, the Houses of Lord and Commons, and the European Commission, and was a participant observer at the U.K. headquarters of VLV, the most widely recognized of the groups. The author also traveled to Welsh and Scottish broadcasting and regulatory offices (e.g., OFCOM, Scottish Consumer Council in Scotland). In addition, activist, national consumer advocacy, government, and related Web sites provided updated information on issues, legislation, consultative documents and activist responses to them, White (policy) Papers, initiatives and hearings, and newsletters/brochures. The broadsheets' media pages publicized policy debates and dilemmas and the journalists themselves often "led the charge" or became a conduit through which credible groups, such as the VL V, generated key debates.

Issues at Stake: Cultural Integrity in Devolving Scotland

Mitchell (2006), a veteran consumer advocate, founder of the Telecommunications Ombudsman service, and an appointee to the U.K. regulatory Office of Communications (Ofcom), identified unresolved concerns that Scottish telecommunications and content needs were not being addressed. Recalling the 2006 hearings on the future of the BBC, held in 2006, in the Scottish Parliament (with testimony on behalf of VLV) as "not without difficulty," he felt that these policy matters should be co-determined by the U.K. and Scottish Parliaments. Nevertheless, Mitchell indicated, it would be impossible and not necessarily desirable for all Scottish content to be generated at home. Certain key areas, such as local news he said, should be local in origin and express a distinctly Scottish view. Pointing to Spain and Germany as models of choice for devolved yet balanced broadcasting power, he noted the oscillation of broadcasting decision making among the Basque and Catalan provinces and the Madrid seat of Spanish government, and German federal government and lander, respectively. (Such power sharing, among the latter avoids total media control, as under the Nazis regime). Thus, there exist viable alternative models that vest power in local and regional bodies and are testable for the future.

A Crash Course in Demographic Divisions

Beveridge (2006), VLV Director for Scotland, outlined several socio-cultural issues at the heart of current cultural debates—and their linguistic and religious origins. Among the Gaelic speakers, largely in the remote Highlands, coast, and Scottish islands, there are many Catholics, and they are far poorer than the Protestants in developed Scotland. Historical hostilities and religious/economic divisions are palpable among broadcasting policy issues. Gaelic speakers, who number around 20,000+, are facing off against the Anglo-Protestant lowlanders who have dominated Scotland for over 250 years. These differences, Beveridge maintained, today play out in decisions over Gaelic hours and programming, obscured by stereotypes of "Loch Ness" Scots.

This monolithic perception of Scots is compounded by the fact that English domination contributed to a Scottish "inferiority complex," with all things English perceived as superior. Scots who want to achieve, Beveridge (2006) said, have always gone to London. This notion has been reinforced by historical accounts, such as LaMont's (2002), which illustrate Scots' influence as administrators in the British Empire and expatriate inventors and industrialists.

Issues of Scottish culture are intertwined with those of independence. Despite the strong possibility of a U.K. breakup in the next 50 years, Beveridge (2006) reported that factionalism impedes prospects for an independent state. The dominant Scottish Labour Party, which opposed devolution, does not want to be seen helping the Scottish nationalists. Thus, he noted, Scottish factionalism, or rather English use of it, has weakened Scotland and Scottish interests. There are likely to be more concentrated and urgent efforts to provide forums for Scottish representation and cultural expression, given the resurgence of Nationalists' power in Scotland's Parliament (Vass, 2007; Smith, 2007) and the likelihood of a sympathetic ear by the EU (Gallagher, 2007; Global National, 2007). It is also unclear how much of a role the restructured BBC will play.

The BBC and Scottish Broadcasting

Much of what was Scottish drama and news in British broadcasting has been made available courtesy of the BBC, and secondarily, ITV's Grampian Television, which was absorbed into other ITV franchises during the merger craze of recent years. Granada, the remaining, reconstituted ITV channel, has essentially divested itself of its public service obligations. That leaves the BBC as the bulwark of public service and thus, CSR.

This is not without complications. The BBC, which will take the lead in building a digital Britain, was recently restructured to include a BBC Trust. The Broadcasting Council for Scotland is an advisory body to the BBC Governors. The new Trust will have national representatives for Scotland but it is unclear how accountable it will be to the Scottish Parliament. In addition, there is concern, said Beveridge (2006), that the Scottish Consumer Council, whose mandate includes, but is not restricted to, broadcasting, will be configured into a different and less independent body. If these changes should transpire, there are still avenues for a Scottish consumer/viewer and listener voice, but many of them are small local radio and other media outlets that have just begun to network in the past few years (Gray, 2006, Rushton, 2007). It appears that where the fallout from industry changes and political winds is unclear, activist groups are more likely to turn to each other for support and to jointly advocate for their goals.

According to Hay (2006), VLV, the most vocal of the larger, more established groups, planned "....a country-wide campaign and a range of special events to raise awareness of the crucially influential role that broadcasting plays in British culture and democracy...." Hay suggests that this influence and the resources needed to promote it will be generated through social and fundraising events (such as a VLV evening of Gershwin played by the BBC orchestra), grants, the VLV Trust, and individual, smaller donations. The group's national chapters, such as the one in Edinburgh, meet with local broadcasters and regulators around issues of cultural autonomy (Beveridge, 2006; Mitchell, 2006). They have also opened forums for dialogue among the above targets, Scottish parliamentarians, and activists (Beveridge, 2007).

The New Scotland: CSR in the Face of Cultural and Communication Differentials

In Scotland, historical divisions have survived with varying levels of intensity—Labor vs. Nationalists, Catholic vs. Protestant, Highlander vs. Lowlander, Islander vs. Mainlander, Gaelic vs. English speaking, to name some. The predominant cultural mix included Scottish, English, Irish, with some French nobility of Norman descent. Now, Scotland and Wales (which was almost exclusively-white) are experiencing the immigration of Asians, Muslims, and Africans, which occurred on a larger scale and earlier in the rest of the U.K, including the North. A recent influx of Poles (mostly in Wales) and other East/Central Europeans has further changed that mix.

Broadcasters have a responsibility to promote social integration through programming that credibly represents the lives of a highly diverse immigrant population and the cultural needs of indigenous U.K. nationals. The North, although historically underrepresented in terms of news and drama production, has at least had, for some decades, a Granada TV series that functioned as a glimpse of mainstream Northern English life. The Scots, more so even than with the Welsh,. have lacked a voice in and about their media Thanks to the Internet and local radio, these needs are being addressed in ways heretofore unknown (See Rushton, 2007, on the Digital Dividend)

Catalyzing Responsibility: Activist Responses to New Developments and Challenges

Broadcasting has been recognized as a potent vehicle for the public sphere (Garnham, 1994) and similarly, a catalyst for social integration in a pluralistic society. As such, it is subject to scrutiny and performance norms (McQuail, 1992). Although few could have anticipated the technical and regulatory complexities brought about by the advent of digital television, concerns about a "digital divide" that favors the economically and geographically privileged have resurfaced. There is an historic BBC precedent establishing public service broadcasting as a public good in the public interest. Broadcasters' social responsibility (Crawford Commission, 1927) to viewing and listening publics should, in principle, be met, regardless of the technology, or the difficulty of maintaining consistent standards in peripheral areas of the U.K.

The digitalization of the broadcasting spectrum has presented nearly unlimited options for distribution (some would say democratization) of the broadcasting spectrum. At the same time, the costs of producing and distributing digital services is beyond many communities' budgets, and poorer constituents may only be able to access free-to-air and not subscription services. The Digital Dividend is one alternative that may alleviate both the spectrum shortage and the poor's inability to pay for additional services. Groups across the UK have voiced their views as to if and how the analogue spectrum available after digital switchover may be put to pro-social uses..

CSR and the Airwaves: Democratization through the Digital Dividend

As digital rollover (set to begin in Wales in 2008) gets underway, activists would like to see the analogue spectrum used for "citizen-centric, in addition to this consumer-centric broadcasting," This is according to Public Voice (2007), a coalition of activist and voluntary encouraged civic participation in submitting consultative materials to Ofcom, the national regulator, for decision as to future spectrum allocation. In addition to an independent reviewer, Ofcom had additional input--a three-month consultation process in which broadcasting activists and voluntary group voiced their concerns and proposed alternatives for the freed-up spectrum.

Rushton (2007) heads the Edinburgh-based Institute of Local Television and lobbies for community television access. He published a series of documents and held meetings to discuss how the new spectra would connect local communities and their cultures. He has networked with local radio stations nationwide, academics, consumer advocates, government-funded bodies, civil servants and others to this end. The London-based Public Voice (2007), a coalition of voluntary groups, hosted a conference on the Dividend in February 2007. On its site, it created both links to related public interest and community broadcasting organizations sites and a brochure that outlined the voluntary sector's interest in and possible uses for the spectrum.

Rushton (2007) articulated the function and reach of analogue spectrum:

> ...to explore new ways to regulate Spectrum as a flexible, inalienable social asset which becomes immediately of interest to whose who can receive a range of signals which might be many different channels to be sourced from the local transmitter (p.3).

Furthermore, without a CSR label, Rushton makes it clear that the reduction of regional and local television programs by national television networks is a CSR issue and is culturally problematic:

> Bigger structures which ignore and eradicate differences are not the rational way ahead for a country that has lost touch with itself and with its communities—smaller, more flexible public service operations have greater capacity to survive, to reflect on local aspirations and to transform and innovate (p. 6).

By quoting J. Clay Shirky, he also sets this issue in public service and CSR contexts:

> A public good, in economic terms, is something that is best provisioned by everyone (an economic characteristic called non-excludability) and which anyone can use without depleting the resource (a characteristic called non-rival use)—individual users aren't rivals for the resource (p.3).

In other words, activists' rhetorical approach posits that it is a win-win situation for communities to gain access to analogue spectrum, since no one person loses and everyone gains when information and local interest programming are made accessible to all.

Pushing the borders: Lobbying at the European level. The largest constituencies/voices in the "Digital Dividend" debate are U.K-wide ("national") organizations, and they have set their sights on a piece of the broadcasting spectrum. At the same time, numerous small, spontaneous community-linked groups both in urban centers and at the geographic outposts of Scotland and Wales have emerged and tapped into yearnings for cultural expression. At one extreme, Europe has provided an outlet for smaller Scottish groups, such as the Saltire Society, which promotes indigenous expression across literary and cultural genres. The Internet has provided an open-ended forum for such expression. Despite this, lobbying at the European: level has been a prime strategy of choice (Beveridge, 2005). Many advocates of Scottish cultural representation believe that as a result of their historical kinship with the Flemish, they will elicit more support in the EU than they would achieve in the U.K. (see Kovacs, 2005). This influence has enriched Scotland's cultural tapestry and has legitimized, in part, its case for greater cultural and media representation and its call for CSR by broadcasters and regulators alike.

The Welsh take great pride in their language and have struggled for its public support and preservation through cultural programming. The relatively small, Gaelic-speaking, Scottish population also fought to increase funding for indigenous language programming, though its tactics were less dramatic than in Wales, where a 1980s hunger strike catalyzed support for Welsh language channel S4C. In both nations, strategic public relations has been used to inform, mobilize, and advocate for increased CSR in terms of representation and allocation of resources. Each country's approach differs according to geography, demography, culture, and economics.

Wales, Scotland, and the Industrial North as per Language, Politics, and Representation

To some extent, both Wales and Scotland have been "stepchildren," so to speak, of England, especially when it comes to cultural dominance and available indigenous production resources. Recently, though, there has been some national leap-frogging. Wales has expressed a strong desire to capitalize on Web-based learning and cultural opportunities through the Internet. Note:

> A paradoxical outcome of Internet internationalism is the increased opportunity that now exists for the local and the specialist—for example, local cultures and languages, and specialist disciplines and hobbies—to claim their rightful place in cyberspace. Wales is no exception. We have a new stage on which to appear and project our individualities. (Green, 2005, p. 6)

The Institute for Welsh Affairs is one "rubric" organization that supports efforts towards maximizing Welsh use of the Web and immersion in cyberspace. Wales shares with Scotland the desire for greater online engagement and the difficulties in implementing and maximizing Web learning and digital TV. Wales and Scotland are both mountainous and in large expanses of both countries, there is difficulty in getting quality television reception. The mountainous areas and those with poor reception are also those with the poorer constituencies, so in effect, it is a "double whammy" for groups that are on the low end of the socioeconomic scale. Perhaps that is why the first trial digital rollout of broadcasting services will take place in a mountainous region of Wales. If digital works there, it is a "plus" but will still not address other areas of deficit in which those parts of Wales lag. Scotland also faces similar difficulties.

Despite this, Wales has made substantial gains in terms of a Welsh language revival and support for Welsh broadcasting. The initial success that resulted in S4C Welsh language channel came about through hard-line activist tactics (a hunger strike in the 1980s). The nationalist call for political independence is far stronger in Scotland than in Wales. Thus, Welsh demands on its governing Assembly and on Westminster for cultural expression and resources are relatively de-politicized, non-partisan, and unlikely to result in any confrontation. This may, in part, be due to the relative homogeneity of the Welsh, as compared to the Scots, as per culture, religion, and level of comfort with Westminster. In reality, it may be the fact that the Welsh have already achieved a formidable victory in terms of their language/cultural preservation that accounts for their activists' relatively de-politicized efforts in the communication realm. Welsh efforts appear to lack the sense of urgency shared by diverse Scottish local media associations petitioning for a slice of the Digital Dividend. This discrepancy in NGO CSR activity and also in the demographic makeup of those who call for greater representation in communication, may also explain why the Scots have forged more alliances, at home and in Europe, than the Welsh (Beveridge,

2006;Gray, 2006).. Despite the geographic dispersion of Scotland's minority Gaelic speakers and their relative lack of economic empowerment, Scottish demands and support for representation in the soon-to-be launched Gaelic-language channel are stronger, though not nearly as extensive or well-funded, as in Wales. In both countries, though, public relations and efforts to increase CSR are about strategic relationship building with key elites, opinion leaders, and like-minded citizens, creating awareness through framing policy issues in the press, public forums, and legislatures, and coalition building through networking and coordinating initiatives with other culturally-focused and community-based organizations.

Power and Coalitions

Schlesinger, Miller, and Dinan (2001) explored the relationship between the newly-devolving power of the Scottish Parliament and allied political entities after 1999 and communication around emergent political processes and among key players. Although eight years later, the devolved and "reserved" powers remain basically the same, some of those players and groups seeking broadcasting and cultural change have navigated around and identified politicians, civil servants, and other key individuals in the Parliamentary committee system, advisory boards, and other entities. They have also had the opportunity to develop alliances. Some organizations have folded—for example, The Scottish Advisory Committee on Telecommunications (SACOT), a consumer-centered advisory body, defunct since Ofcom took over as a single regulator (Mitchell, 2004). There have been, though, increased opportunities for joint public relations and lobbying projects with groups whose precise agenda may differ but support either greater Gaelic language programming or some other form of cultural expression, such as the literary-centered Saltire Society, mentioned above. Many of these groups are too small, under-resourced, or otherwise unrepresentative to be able to bring about change on their own. In addition to Public Voice, the U.K.-wide coalition of which VLV and CQT were a part, other ad hoc group alliances exerted influence. Gray (2006) described how radio stations in the Hebrides and other remote locations, and poetry and fine/performing arts groups, networked to influence policy ad legislative change.

CSR and the Role of the Public Broadcaster

Much that concerns broadcast news and cultural representation in the nations and regions has historically fallen to the public broadcasters. This refers mainly to the BBC, which has obligations to "inform, educate, and entertain" (BBC, 1992). Channel 4 has a clear mandate for cultural representation and diversity but is itself essentially a publisher, not a program producer.

Green (2005) documents the BBC's efforts to expand Welsh-language program offerings on the Web: The BBC, he said, has "built a formidable array of online services" and "In Cardiff, BBC Cymru/Wales has more than played its part." He points to three BBC-launched Welsh initiatives: Cymru r'Byd, a rolling Welsh-language newspaper, Digital Storytelling, Real Media movies recorded by lay citizens in studios around Wales, and Where I Live, which provides directories, information, and feedback on specific regions of Wales. Nevertheless, new online resources largely supplement the vast BBC radio and television archives. The BBC's joint project with a Welsh company seeks to digitalize this radio and broadcasting material (Green, 2005).

At the same time, the real challenge is to provide permanent access for the public to these archives. Despite digitalization, much programming is what Green (2005) refers to "ephemeral," (p.12). In other words, the broadcast may be a one-off experience because there will be no way of recalling the data. Thus, there is a heavy debt owed to the BBC for its programs in both Wales and Scotland, but what is really needed is a "democratization" of BBC cultural and educational resources to make them accessible across populations and class and economic barriers.

Pan-U.K. Activism: CSR around Digitalization and the Distribution of Media Resources

When one looks at capital investment into and output from Wales, Scotland, and the industrial North, it pales by comparison with the London-centric South, In addition, Green (2005) points to the "shortage of expertise in Wales on assessing and exploiting the commercial viability" of publicly-owned content (p. 14). Such an investment would give more autonomy to the North. Despite a substantive BBC relocation to Manchester, investment in regionally-representative productions and employment of area residents, in comparison to that in London, are low. Justifying this is a major public relations dilemma for the BBC, on whom the lion's share of CSR falls. This is because ITV, the commercial broadcaster, has essentially relinquished its PSB obligations and Channel 4, which has a remit to reflect diversity, is essentially a broadcaster/publisher for programs made by independent producers (Paterson, 2007).

Nevertheless, if the commitment to diversity and regional production infrastructure and output is to be seen as more than lip service, broadcasters will need to come to grips and engage more proactively with these CSR issues. Perhaps NGOs might collectively call for a unified summit on the issue, or, at least, a thorough assessment of the relative broadcasting/digital stakes and needs of each nation and the regions. Many groups, such as VLV, have already written consultative documents and presented oral evidence. Perhaps such an ad hoc effort might swing the CSR pendulum further in the direction of the nations and regions.

Activist concerns about regional and national (Scottish and Welsh) representation and indigenous production have always been particularly pronounced when it comes to drama, language (historically, Welsh language activism resulted in the creation the Welsh Fourth Channel [S4C]) and news. In particular, the costs of drama productions are so high that in budget crunches, they are the first to be cut. Similarly, one ongoing issue for NGO activists has been the dumbing down, London-centric nature of the news and its pre-emption by prime-time programming that generates higher ratings.

The investment in infrastructure needed for local news, while not as costly as for drama, is substantive. The consolidation of the ITV franchises in recent years, in which one of the original 15 producer/broadcasters (Carlton/Granada) basically remains, has also contributed to U.K. news' more generic nature. In addition, in Scotland, Wales, and the North, there has arisen a particular manifestation of a pan-U.K. dilemma--the near-demise of quality children's programs, with potentially dire consequences for this and future generations.

In the Best Interests of Children

Livingstone (2007), Tongue (2007), and Childs (2007) all described the cutbacks, policy recommendations, and campaigns centered on production and maintenance of quality children's television. They have participated, together with various children's advocacy organizations, in identifying the major issues comprising and possible solutions for the current children's television crisis. This has involved considerable time and effort, testimony in front of Houses of Parliament, and written submissions to Ofcom's (2007) newly-published (October 3) consultation on the future of children's television. According to Voice of the Listener & Viewer (VLV) (2007), one NGO submitting evidence to Ofcom, the BBC announced it would cut 5% of its children's programming budget for six years.

This represents, to activists, insult after injury and a gross breach of its CSR as a public broadcaster, given that ITV decided earlier this year to preempt children's programming for more commercially viable adult shows. Activists fear that British children will not experience homegrown, pluralistic, quality, indigenous programming. The obvious alternative, imported, largely American-made programming, has been considered culturally threatening by most European countries. General concerns about cultural integrity catalyzed the protectionism of the *Television Without Frontiers Directive* (1989; revised 1997; current revisions underway), which established quotas for the maximum amount of programming any EU member could import from outside the EU. The U.K., as a member state of the EU, must abide by its directives. In recent years, children's issues have come to the fore and organizations like the European Alliance of Listeners and Viewers Associations (EURALVA) and VLV, its principal founding member, have tackled such concerns as junk food advertising. This has clearly had an impact on advertisements of junk foods on U.K. Television. Nevertheless, the it is the content of children's television that currently weighs the most heavily on activists and parents. They worry about what will follow next when British television-viewing children who were surveyed thought the U.K. emergency number was 911, rather than 999, the actual number (Tongue, 2007). Now fears run more deeply. Program cuts mean that few, if any, new U.K. children's programs can be made.

Even after having submitted its views in the most recent consultation (Ofcom, 2007), VLV framed its agenda as follows: "It is vitally important therefore that we not only alert all those with an interest in the welfare of children to the dangers that these cuts pose but also encourage them to engage in debate at this time" (VLV, 2007). One cannot possibly do justice in this space to the children's issues at stake, but many NGOs, among them Public Voice and Save Kids' TV, have "colluded" to maintain quality children's television. If the recent children's television policy and programming crisis is a U.K.-wide, issue, then it certainly has relevance in Scotland, Wales, and the North already culturally vulnerable and/or under-resourced on a local level. Its importance to cultural continuity and distinctiveness is undisputed, as seen below.

Discussion and Suggestions for Further Research

This issues and concerns raised in this article are, in part, a function of a broadcasting and electronic landscape that is changing at a dizzying speed and also of the political, social, and industry economic backdrop against which it is set. There is ongoing restructuring and redefinition of the BBC's significant role in shaping program production and broadcasting in the North and the Nations. As its own financial base and structure may be modified yet again, the Beeb's role as perpetual torchbearer for cultural CSR may be questionable. In addition, with a burgeoning of Asian, Eastern European, and other minorities and a call by Scottish nationalists for independence, a re-prioritization of CSR and resources for cultural representation in electronic communication may be warranted. Such demographic and political shifts may not decrease support for Gaelic and other homegrown productions but will increase calls for greater representation of diversity as well. Public relations will need to deal, to an even greater extent, with requisite variety and demands for more custom tailoring of programs to the needs of niche, multicultural publics. In this newer tableau, the multicultural current may run in a different direction from that envisioned by nationalists or romanticized in Braveheart. It may require as much or more training in conflict resolution as in environmental scanning and research.

Given the uncertainty of the evolving, complex electronic communication environment, it is also unclear whether the Nations and the North will be able to rely as heavily as before on the BBC for both financial and technical help in developing and disseminating a plurality of cultural perspectives and representations. NGOs may have to continue their lobbying at the Westminster, Welsh National Assembly, and Scottish Parliamentary levels. In addition, NGO efforts at the European (European Commission, Brussels, or perhaps through Media Programme or other agencies funding EU member creative endeavors) and global levels may be necessary.

NGO activists will continue to play a critical role in monitoring CSR in the electronic environment and in dealing with publics in Scotland and the North. Their assessment will help to ascertain the adequacy of production and distribution resources for showcasing multicultural content. Their efforts may also catalyze greater interest by politicians in these issues, including the future of children's television. The government-business-NGO triangle, which has been recognized (Doh, 2003) as evidence of the emergent power of NGOs in global policy and decision making. This new configuration warrants careful attention, as does the question of whether newly-empowered NGOs will, in the long run, be absorbed into or co-opted by their targets.

In the case of the national and regional issues mentioned above, NGOs have a CSR stake in the future of the U.K and its viewing and listening audiences. It is their public relations--implemented through events, public forums for debate, research and consultation papers, strategic relationship building, lobbying and testimony and Web-based outreach and networking with members and targets publics-- that is the cornerstone of effective policy change and a potent voice for the representation of national and regional diversity. Regardless of devolution's ultimate outcomes, NGOs' voice should reflect and insist on the cultural public interest.

References

A complete list of interviews is available from the author upon request.

BBC. (1992). *Guide to the BBC.* London: BBC.

BBC. (2006). *Defining a Nation: Wales and the BBC.* Llandysul, Wales: Gomer Press.

Beveridge, R. (2006, June). Interview-links between broadcasting/Scots cultural groups.

Beveridge, R. (2006, June). Interview regarding Scottish broadcasting activism.

Castells, M. (2000). The power of identity (Vol. II). *The information age: Economy, society, culture*. Oxford, UK: Blackwell.

Commission of the European Communities. (1989; revised 1997; further revisions underway). *Television.Without Frontiers* (COM [84] 300). Brussels: The Commission

Doh, J. (2003). Nongovernmental organizations, corporate strategy, and public policy: NGOs as agents of change. In J. P. Doh & H. Teegen (Eds.) *Globalization and NGOs: Transforming business, government, and society* (pp. 1-18). Westport, CT: Prager.

Garnham, N. (1994). The media and the public sphere. In C. Calhoun (Ed.), *Habermas and the public sphere* (pp. 359-376). London: MIT Press.

Gallagher, E. (2007, Jan. 12). *It's inconceivable the EU wouldn't welcome an independent Scotland with open arms.* Retrieved on 1/12/07 from Sundayherald.com/news/heraldnews/display.var.1201131.0.its_inconceivable_t...

Global National. (2007). *Scottish nationalists poised to sweep elections.* Retrieved on 5/3/07 from www.canada.com/globaltv/national/ html

Gray, J. (2006, June). *Interview regarding Scottish cultural history and activists.*

Green, A. (2005). *The Gregynog Papers* (Vol. 4, No. 1). Cardiff: Institute of Welsh Affairs.

Hay, J. (2006). Letter to VLV members.

Herbert, S. (2006, May 24). *SPICe briefing: Media and broadcasting industries.* Edinburgh: Scottish Parliament.

Institute for Welsh Affairs. (2006). *Wales on the Web.* Cardiff: Institute for Welsh Affairs.

Kovacs, R. (2004). Public relations and politics: NGOs and national/global Broadcasting Policy. *Proceedings of the Seventh Annual PRSA Educators' Academy International, Interdisciplinary Conference, Miami, FL*

Kovacs, R. (2005). Driving the 'greater good': NGOs, broadcasting, and the case for CSR. *Proceedings of the Eighth Annual International Public Relations Research Conference,* Miami, FL.

Kovacs, R. (Winter 2006). An Interdisciplinary Bar for the Public Interest: What CSR and NGO Frameworks Contribute to the Public Relations of British and European Activists. *Public Relations Review.*

LaMont, S. (2002). *When Scotland ruled the world: The story of the golden age of genius, creativity, and exploration.* New York: Harper Collins.

McQuail, D. (1992). *Media Performance: Mass Communication and the Public Interest.* London: Sage.

Mitchell, J. (2006, June). *Interview concerning Scottish consumer, cultural, and programming interests.*

Public Voice (2007). *The digital dividend review. London: Public Voice.* Retrieved on 5/4./07 from www.public-voice .org/uk.

Rushton, D. (2007). *Who owns red: ACTO digital dividend review edition.* Edinburgh: Institute of Local Television.

Small, M. (2007). It will be the web wot won it. *The Guardian.* Retrieved on 5/3/07 from http.commentisfree.guardian.co.uk/mike_small/2007/05

Vass, S. (2007, Jan. 12). *Nationalists reveal their vision for Scottish Broadcasting Corporation.* Retrieved on 1/12/07 from www.sundayherald.com/dislay.var.1185254.0.0.php?utag=30411.

Voice of the Listener and Viewer. (2007, Jan. 18). *Letter to members regarding Public Voice consultation* (Email to members)

Welsh Assembly Government. (2007). *Broadcasting.* Retrieved on 1/22/07 from http://new.wales.gov.uk/topics/cultureandsport/mediapublishing/broadcastradio/?lang=en

In: Corporate Social Responsibility
Editor: Adam R. Timpere

ISBN: 978-1-60456-284-2

Chapter 7

Incorporating Stakeholder Perspective into Entrepreneurship Research

Francesco Perrini *

Bocconi University, Department of Management, Viale Filippetti, 9, Milan 20122, Italy

Clodia Vurro †

Bocconi University, Department of Management, Viale Filippetti, 9, Milan 20122, Italy

Abstract

Starting from the assumption that entrepreneurship does not occur in a vacuum but the external environment has relevant impacts on the entrepreneurial activity and is in turn affected by it, the paper aims at exploiting the relational side of entrepreneurship proposing the stakeholder theory of the firm as a bridge between entrepreneurship and *business in society* research. It adopts a dual perspective considering the external environment as either an antecedent or as a *receptor* for entrepreneurial outcomes. The contribution of stakeholder theory to entrepreneurship is presented both in general terms using the concept of value as the common basis shared by the two fields and detailing the analysis along the three broad perspectives on stakeholder approach: normative, descriptive and instrumental lenses.

Introduction

Undoubtedly, entrepreneurs are vital to the life of society. As they fulfill their economic tasks, entrepreneurial organizations increase employment, stimulate innovation progress, and enhance material well-being, in the constant cycles of creative destruction which fuels economic growth (Schumpeter, 1942).

---

* Tel +39-02-58363622; Fax +39-02-58363691; francesco.perrini@unibocconi.it
† Tel +39-02-58363641; Fax +39-02-58363691; clodia.vurro@unibocconi.it

Despite differences in the way they tackle the contribution of entrepreneurial efforts to society and development, studies that aim at capturing the complex relationship between entrepreneurship and the external environment share an attempt to exploit the 'relational' side of entrepreneurship, starting from the following underlying assumption: entrepreneurship does not occur in a vacuum but the external environment has relevant impacts on the entrepreneurial activity and is in turn affected by it. This dual perspective, that is, the external environment as either an antecedent or as a *receptor* for entrepreneurial outcomes, can be increasingly found in the literature, still missing a systematic and comprehensive definition of what the context of reference exactly is and how new ventures interact with it.

This means that notwithstanding its important insights, the mainstream view of entrepreneurship, with its focus on the dynamics of discovery, evaluation and exploitation of opportunities (Shane and Venkataraman, 20000), has rarely attempted to go beyond the environmental factors that affect new business activities or the creation of new firms, still mainly investigated according to either a resource dependence or a population ecology perspective. As argued by Gnyvali and Fogel (1994), in a comprehensive review of the studies on the relationship between entrepreneurship and the external environment, an integrated and theoretically driven framework is still missing for studying the complexity and the relevance of this issue.

Starting from these premises, our paper aims at filling this void in current literature on the relational dimension of entrepreneurship, proposing the stakeholder theory of the firm as a bridge between entrepreneurship and *business in society* research. In so doing, this study clarifies how new ventures affect and are affected by their context of reference, defined not in general terms but with regards to its constituencies, namely, the different categories of stakeholders.

If we adopt a definition of entrepreneurship as the process by which "opportunities to bring into existence 'future' goods and services are discovered, created and exploited" (Venkataraman, 1997, p.120), entrepreneurship inevitably involves joint production where several different stakeholders have to be brought together to create new combinations (Shane and Venkataraman, 2000). As a result, the ability to offer an attractive value proposition to actual (especially in the case of corporate entrepreneurship, or serial entrepreneurs) and potential stakeholders is part of the creative task of the entrepreneur, as well as part of the entrepreneurial process in broad sense. At the same time, the entrepreneurial process may lead to numerous outcomes. Here is where the external environment, namely, the societal level, comes again as a crucial part of the discourse. To date, although entrepreneurship is widely recognized as a major propeller for economic advancement, studies suffer from what has been defined an oversimplification (Baumol, 1990) due to the fact that mainstream research seems to rely on an often unstated assumption: although a risky game, entrepreneurship always benefits those who succeed in playing the game. This means that micro-level outcomes are too readily, directly translated to the aggregate level without a more broad assessment of the social and environmental impacts of such a rule-breaking exercise.

This theme has recently been identified as a research priority by leading scholars in the field of entrepreneurship (see for example Dess et al., 2003). In fact, as firms become increasingly complex nexus of contracts with multiple constituencies within their social context of reference (Freeman & McVea, 2001), or, alternatively, sets of relationships among groups which have a stake in the activities that make up the business (Freeman and Velamuri, 2006), it becomes crucial to start a new business keeping clear in mind the necessity to deal with criteria that sooner or later in the process will be weighted differently by the different stakeholders. In this sense, stakeholder theory (Freeman, 1984, Donaldson & Preston, 1995) and stakeholder management approach (Post, Preston & Sachs, 2002; Cummings & Doh, 2000, Mitchell et al., 1997) can provide further insights on the multiple dimensions and challenges that come along the entrepreneurial act.

The remainder of the paper is structured as follows. First, the literature on the relationship between entrepreneurship and the external environment is reviewed and systematized, in order to highlight the missing points that justify the integration of the stakeholder theory. In this regard, the external environment is considered either as an antecedent of the entrepreneurial process or as the receptor for the entrepreneurial outcome. Second, the stakeholder theory of the firm is presented, with an emphasis on the specific research question, assumptions and levels of analysis that determine the distinctiveness of the field. Third, the contribution of stakeholder theory to entrepreneurship is presented both in general terms using the concept of value as the common basis shared by the two fields and detailing the analysis along the three broad perspectives on stakeholder approach: normative, descriptive and instrumental lenses.

Entrepreneurship and the External Environment

Entrepreneurship is how the opportunity to create value is discovered and acted upon by some individuals. It occurs at the nexus of enterprising individuals and valuable opportunities (Eckhardt and Shane, 2003), even though boundaries of entrepreneurship research have changed over time so that it is still difficult to find a clear, shared definition of what entrepreneurship is all about as a field of study and how it is possible to distinguish entrepreneurial acts in practical terms when looking at them.

Although researchers in this area still continue to ask themselves questions about levels of analysis and the focus of the field, a tendency to consider more closely and systematically the environment in which entrepreneurial acts take place clearly emerges looking throughout the pages of the special issues periodically published by academic journals and devoted to these themes.

The idea that entrepreneurship does not occur in a vacuum, but is characterized by what we call a relational dimension (i.e., the relationship between entrepreneurship and the external environment) is certainly not new (Stinchcombe, 1961), whatever entrepreneurial act is considered as resulting into the formation of new firms (Gartner, 1988) or as occurring within an established organization (Lumpkin and Dess, 1996; Zahra, 1991). As argued by Gartner (1985), in his attempt to systematize entrepreneurship research, the environment is one of the four dimensions relevant to study and describe the field, together with the entrepreneur, the process and the organization.

In more details, looking at the literature on this issue a double perspective characterizes the relationship between entrepreneurship and the external environment: the latter is seen either as a way to predict entrepreneurial performance, defined alternatively as survival, economic success, innovation and so on, (i.e., as antecedent of entrepreneurial process) or as the receptor for the outcomes of entrepreneurship (i.e., as the setting where the consequences of the entrepreneurial process apply). Additionally and according to the multidimensionality that characterizes entrepreneurship as a field of study and application, research on the relational dimension has focused on different levels of analysis: the individual, the firm and more aggregate levels, such that the industry, the network or the societal level in general terms.

The External Environment as a Predictor of Entrepreneurship

Considering first the environment as an antecedent to the entrepreneurial process, research at the firm level of analysis is characterized by two different perspectives. One side includes a more deterministic approach focused on a notion of environment as a set of external conditions, namely environmental variables, to which new organizations must adapt (Hannan and Freeman, 1982), or, more generally, that affect the creation process. Examples are venture capital availability, government influences, proximity to university, and so on. Basically, resource dependence and population ecology theory has driven research in this area, providing explanations as to how the environment can affect firm formation rate (Ucbasaran, Westhead and Wright, 2001).

The other side includes those studies that consider the environment not as given but as resulting from the interaction between organizations and the prevailing social framework of norms, values, and taken-from-granted assumptions. Institutional theory clearly belongs to this group, relying on the assumption that conformity to social expectations contributes to organizational success and survival (Oliver, 1991; DiMaggio and Powell, 1983).

At a glance, although the study on the interaction between entrepreneurship and the external environment is well established, literature belonging to the two perspectives presented above either does not clearly provide an explanation of what the environment actually is or it introduces a partial view of the context of reference stressing one out of many possible contingent characteristics. In different words, the multiple constituencies that compose the context are introduced only indirectly into the discourse. Examples are available financial capital, public regulation, presence of attractive markets, and so on. What is missing in this regard is a more comprehensive normative and descriptive framework for the environment and its components.

Increasingly, however, research on the relational dimension of entrepreneurship tends to move beyond the firm-level of analysis, giving particular emphasis at more aggregate levels: the industries (especially emergent industries) and the role of networks, based on the concept of social embeddedness (Granovetter, 1985; Shane and Cable, 2002). The main idea is that contrary to the mainstream asocial economic perspective, entrepreneurial acts benefit from what comes along social obligations between connected parties and information spill-over through social relationships (Shane and Cable, 2002). Recent studies (Sine, Haveman and Tolbert, 2005) have also explored the role of different types of institutions (i.e., normative, regulative and cognitive) in altering the mix of organizations entering a new industry, explicitly linking their impact on perceived risk due to *liability of newness* that characterizes entrepreneurship in general.

In this regard, what is worth emphasizing is how concepts like legitimation, trust and reputation become relevant even though attention remains focused on inter-firm relationships without taking into consideration, in a systematic fashion, the multiple constituencies that characterize the new ventures' social context of reference.

Finally, external environmental conditions can be predictors of the entrepreneurial process with a focus on the individual level. Such perspective remains centered on the importance to take into account socially-driven dimensions of economic activity. The network-based concept of social embeddedness is then translated at the individual level in the form of social capital of the entrepreneur. As defined by Putnam (2000, p.19), social capital is concerned with the connections among individuals (i.e., social networks), and the broadly defined resources that can arise from them due to norms of reciprocity and trustworthiness. Recently, the theory of social capital has been expanded to the field of entrepreneurship, with an emphasis on the impact of the personal network of the entrepreneur on firm survival and success. Yet, research on this issue is still in its infancy, with social capital treated as a one-dimensional construct (Liao and Welsch, 2005), regardless of the specific context of reference and of the differences in the relationships that entrepreneurs possess. In other words, so far the potential of investigating how relationships with each category of the entrepreneurs' stakeholder network have an impact on the level of social capital has not been fully exploited.

The External Environment as a Receptor for Entrepreneurial Outcomes

The external environment is not only the locus of opportunities, constraints and resources from which entrepreneurial processes can result. Considering the existence of a relational dimension of the entrepreneurial activity necessarily implies that the interaction between entrepreneurship and the external environment is double-sided. In other words, the external environment, intended as the societal context of reference, is a receptor for the entrepreneurial activity and its outcomes. As explained in the introduction, current research seems to share the belief that, value creating processes like the entrepreneurial ones can lead to positive economic growth and development in absolute terms.

In more detail, entrepreneurship continues to be considered a major driver of economic development as a whole (Baumol, 1990; Corriveau, 1994; Powell, 1990), a viable opportunity to foster economic advancement in developing regions of the world (El-Namaki, 1988; Harper, 1991; Jarrillo, 1989), and recently as the most powerful and innovative way to deal with complex social problems and explicitly initiate social change (Austen, Stevenson and Wei-Skillern, 2006, Mair and Martì, 2005; Perrini, 2006) starting from perceived social entrepreneurial opportunities.

However, what emerges looking at the ongoing academic debate on this issue, while entrepreneurship is, for sure, one of the most important factors in global economic development, bringing together labor, capital and business know-how, not surprisingly, there is wide disagreement among economists and business scholars about its precise relationship to such development.

This situation can be read as the result of two biases in the literature: one side includes the tendency to consider only value creating entrepreneurial acts or, alternatively, to read entrepreneurial acts as value creating by assumption. Even though entrepreneurship is acknowledged as a disequilibrium force (Eckhardt and Shane, 2003; Shane and Venkataraman, 2000), namely, an activity that introduces, or initiates new patterns in business and society, conflicts that may arise due to the fact that the new patterns can unexpectedly or dramatically change business environments and relationships (Hannafey, 2003) are not explicitly considered. The other side includes the tendency to oversimplify outcome evaluation, translating micro-level outcomes directly to more aggregate levels (i.e., the societal level in this case, Davidsson and Wicklund, 2001).

Assuming the importance of entrepreneurship economic function in terms of its impact on societal development, recent research at the nexus of entrepreneurship and ethics is attempting an answer to the following question: Do entrepreneurs and entrepreneurial organizations have moral obligations to or responsibility within society? In more details, research agenda has been addressed to the ethical problems faced by entrepreneurs (Hannafey, 2003; Fisher et al., 2005; Freeman and Venkataraman, 2002; Mahoney, 1997). Studies on ethics and entrepreneurship have been mainly focused on raising awareness on this topic, thorough the identification of broad critical moral issues specific to entrepreneurial decision making. For example, unlike managers, entrepreneurs face entirely new ethical dilemmas when introducing new products or entering new markets. Moreover the lack of track records makes it difficult, for entrepreneurs, to rely on established guiding norms in addressing their behavior.

Yet, the ongoing debate on the social side of entrepreneurship is still in its infancy, focusing exclusively on the individual level of analysis (i.e., in term of the moral orientation of the entrepreneurs) and missing all the potential of incorporating leading perspectives in the field of business in society. Moreover, even though such research aims at exploiting the view on the social side of entrepreneurship, in terms of both positive contributions to society and harms, the external environment is defined as a one-dimensional construct in aggregate terms and considered only as the locus of necessary resources for the entrepreneurial process. In fact, using the Gartner's four-dimensional framework (1985) and as highlighted by Hannafey (2003) in her literature review of the entrepreneurship and ethics research, at the individual level attention remains centered on the ethical dilemmas of the entrepreneur in raising resources for the new venture. At the organizational level, the characteristics of new ventures (e.g., small dimension, constantly changing organizational settings, limited cash flows) and the high level of uncertainty become the sources of possible ethical problems and reduce moral tone in order to win stressful environments. The studies at the environment level share this same perspective, looking at the characteristics of the business environment (e.g., external time pressure, scarce resources and competition) that can force unethical behavior. Finally at the process level, research takes a resource dependence perspective in order to understand how to reduce risk perceived by key resource controllers. How much to disclose and which kind of information are the major themes addressed in this regards, related to the newness, small size, risks of innovation and limited availability of resources in startup firms.

Summarizing, a more broad assessment of entrepreneurial outcomes and a clearer, more comprehensive definition of what a societal level exactly is are still missing in current research.

The Stakeholder Theory of the Firm

To date many aspects of the business-society relationship (Altman, 1998) have been studied, shifting from an initial, vague awareness of the relationship between companies and their social relevance to the identification of more defined taxonomies and identifiable streams of research.

Starting in the eighties with Freeman's seminal contribution (1984), stakeholder theory of the firm represents now the theoretical mainstay of *corporate social responsibility research*, having its fulcrum in the location and classification of 'those groups who can affect or are affected by the achievement of an organization's purpose' (Freeman, 1984, p. 49).

The bridge between corporate social responsibility and the stakeholder view of the firm clearly emerges form the definition of socially responsible behavior provided by the European Commission in the well-known *Green Paper: "Promoting a European Framework for Corporate Social Responsibility"*: "A concept whereby companies integrate social and environmental concerns in their business operations and in their interactions with their stakeholders on a voluntary basis" (CEC, 2001, p.6).

Recognizing the presence of different and complementary perspectives on stakeholder approach, the statement that best summarizes stakeholder theory is: 'Business can be understood as a set of relationships among groups which have a stake in the activities that make up the business' (Freeman, Wicks et al., 2004, p. 9). In other words, it is no longer a matter of value distribution among stakeholders, but rather a radical change in the basic way of thinking about modern corporations. In support of this view, the capacity of a firm to generate sustainable value over time is claimed to be determined by the relationships with critical stakeholders (Post, Preston and Sachs, 2002).

Stakeholder theory has still its main field of application in large corporations. This clearly reflects its origins, resulting from the unprecedented increase in size and bargaining power of multinational firms during the last fifty years, as well as from higher-level, interrelated phenomena, from globalization to the gradual affirmation of the concept of sustainable development. Just think about how acting globally allows firms to manage an enormous pool of resources. But their responsibilities simultaneously become global and local mistakes can wield an unprecedented ripple effect. It follows that conventional concepts of the corporation based on input-output perspective become descriptively inaccurate and ethically unacceptable (Post et al. 2002), claiming for the related necessity to enlarge the scope of managerial responsibility and the adoption of socially responsible business practices.

However, all the debate on the firms' social and environmental responsibility is clearly a consequence of finding out an answer to the following question: "*for whose benefit and at whose expense should the firm be managed?*" This represents the starting point of the stakeholder theory of the firm, namely, the central research question setting its boundaries as a distinct and legitimate research area. The stakeholder theory of the firm is about creating value for stakeholders through the integration of business, ethics and societal considerations. It remains a managerial theory about how business works, in terms of value creation and trade. In order to catch these multiple dimensions, Freeman and Velamuri recently (2005) proposed the expression "company stakeholder responsibility", in an attempt to extend the stakeholder approach to value creation to all businesses, beyond corporations, and take into consideration the inseparability of business from ethics.

To be more specific and in an attempt to summarize the different approaches that have been adopted over time, the distinctiveness of the stakeholder theory domain can be traced back to the following assumptions. First of all, corporations are open systems that interact with a wider system – the external environment of reference – on a continuative basis. The external environment or, alternatively, context of reference is not treated as an aggregate construct, but in its constituents groups – stakeholders – that affect and are affected by firms' decisions and operations (Freeman, 1984). Stakeholders have been classified in different ways (for a review see Mitchell, Agle and Wood, 1997) as having a legal, moral or presumed claim on the firm, as well as the ability to affect its processes, decisions and so on. Moreover, they have been treated either as resource providers or as risk bearers and residual claimants for the value created by the firm (Jones, 1995). Management and strategy research has long emphasized the internal stakeholders such as employees, customers and stockholders, that is, those that have a direct stake in the firm's activity and operations. However, increasingly secondary stakeholders (e.g., community activists, public institutions, media, and other non-governmental organizations), namely, those that do not have a formal contractual bond with the firm or direct legal authority over the firm, are raising research attention in the name of their ability to pressure the firm (Eesley and Lenox, 2006), imposing either operational costs (e.g., public relation expenses) or losses in terms of intangible resources (e.g., trust and reputation).

The second crucial assumption is that the interests of all legitimate stakeholders have intrinsic value, no set of interests is assumed to dominate the others (Clarkson, 1995; Donaldson and Preston, 1995; Phillips, Freeman and Wicks, 2003). This means that stakeholder theory is different from other theories because it is driven by taking morals and values (i.e., ethics) explicitly into consideration, as a central feature of the organization. Such assumption defines stakeholder theory's normative foundation, namely, each stakeholder is considered "for its own sake and not merely because of its ability to further the interests of some other groups, such as the shareowners" (Donaldson and Preston, 1995, p. 67). According to this perspective, relationships with stakeholders are not means to an end but the end themselves.

However the assumption above does not imply that stakeholders are the same for each firm, as well as relationships treated in the same way by all firms. Here comes the third main feature of the stakeholder theory: its concern is with the nature of these relationships in terms of both processes and outcomes for the firm and its stakeholders. The instrumental and descriptive traditions (Donaldson and Preston, 1995) of the stakeholder theory are focused on these issues, the former on the link between responsiveness to stakeholder and success or performance (Jones, 1995; Wood, 1991), the latter on investigating the way firms and stakeholders interacts in actual terms. The power, legitimacy and urgency framework, developed by Mitchell, Agle and Wood (1997) in order to explain stakeholder identification and prioritization is a leading example of the descriptive side of entrepreneurship research. What is worth emphasizing at this point is what emerges from the many studies on processes and outcomes: even though the interests of all stakeholders are normatively legitimated, firms have to be able to develop a balancing ability between often conflicting, costly interests, in light of the respective contributions, costs and risks of each stakeholder group.

INCORPORATING STAKEHOLDER THEORY INTO ENTREPRENEURSHIP RESEARCH

The Stakeholder View of the Entrepreneurial Process

At a glance entrepreneurship and the stakeholder theory of the firm seem to speak different languages and to be focused on different, unrelated issues. However, although they have developed largely independently of each other, stakeholder theory can contribute to shape entrepreneurship domain, enriching our understanding of the entrepreneurial process in its relational dimension and outcomes.

If we look more in depth at what is behind the general research questions the two research fields attempt to address, while entrepreneurship is broadly about how the opportunity to create value is identified and exploited, the stakeholder theory of the firm is about the basis starting from which the value can be created, as well as how the value created is distributed among the different categories of stakeholders that compose the firm's external environment of reference. The value that results from the entrepreneurial process is what makes entrepreneurship and stakeholder theory complementary: together they represent "two sides of the same coin: the coin of value creation and sharing" (Venkataraman, 1997, p.6).

However, arguing that value is what links stakeholder theory to entrepreneurship still does not explain where the contribution of the former to the latter is. It is widely held that the creation of a new venture is the result of, and results in disequilibria and conflicts (Eckhardt and Shane, 2003; Baumol, 1990). Moreover, along the entire entrepreneurial process the entrepreneur does not own or control all the necessary resources, thus dealing with multiple, potentially conflicting interests in order to gather them. Finally, what remains as a result of the entrepreneurial process – the value or surplus – is a complex set of related dimensions: from new occupation to innovation, from new markets to new modes of organizing, and so on. On the other hand, in its attempt to understand for whom benefit and at whom expenses the firm should be managed, stakeholder theory looks at the firm as an equilibrating mechanism. If we extend the boundaries of stakeholder theory outside the corporation and, precisely, to entrepreneurial ventures (Phillips, Freeman and Wicks, 2003), it can provide further insights into the mechanisms of fair and efficient equilibrating rules, that is, how to manage disequilibrium processes, thus reconciling conflicting claims.

To this end, the stakeholder theory offers a single managerial framework that allows entrepreneurs to deal with the external environment, starting from a fine grained understanding of the particular stakeholders of each new venture (Freeman and McVea, 2001). Moreover, going beyond the one-by-one stakeholder identification, managing stakeholder from the very beginning of the entrepreneurial process enables the entrepreneurs to develop an attitude to offer solutions that balance the interests of multiple stakeholders over time. The basic tenet of the stakeholder approach to business is in fact the following: since interests will sooner or later conflict, a diverse collection of stakeholders will cooperate over the long term only if they share a common set of values. This result can be reached only if entrepreneurs develop the ability to scan the environment, map stakeholders, prioritize requests, interests and needs, develop cooperative solutions that balance those interests and monitor effectiveness of responsiveness actions. Finally, stakeholder theory integrates economic, social, political and ethical considerations, enabling a broader evaluation of the entrepreneurial impacts, beyond the mainstream, one-way value creating proposition.

In a more systematic fashion, the contribution of integrating the stakeholder theory into entrepreneurship field can be seen at different levels: normative, descriptive and instrumental lenses along the entire entrepreneurial process, from the existence of the opportunity to the exploitation stage.

The Normative Contribution

At the most basic level and from a normative point of view, the integration of the stakeholder theory into entrepreneurship research enables shaping the ethical context of entrepreneurship, providing a renewed interpretation of the function of the entrepreneurial process, as well as of the new ventures that emerge from it (Donaldson and Preston, 1995), on the basis of moral and philosophical principles. In so doing, it is the very reason for the existence of the firm to be broadened, shifting attention from the firm as meeting conventional economic and financial criteria to the firm as creating value for multiple stakeholder interests (Venkataraman, 1999). This means that the coexistence between personal profit motive and societal wealth, more or less implicitly acknowledged since Schumpeter and Adam Smith, becomes explicit providing both a normative foundation for the entrepreneurial activity and the need for performance measures that take simultaneously into consideration economic and social outcomes, per stakeholder group. In this regard, frameworks, tools, and managerial instruments developed within the stakeholder theory field (e.g., social, environmental and sustainability reporting, social return on investment, ethical indexes, social and environmental management systems, and so on) can provide guidance both at the level of opportunity assessment, thus supporting the decision to exploit an opportunity, and at the level of overall evaluation of the impact of entrepreneurial activity on stakeholders. Compared to the traditional entrepreneurial setting, the decision to exploit entrepreneurial opportunities will be based, not only on the nature of the opportunity and individual differences, but also on the characteristics of the external environment, in term of a fine-grained, stakeholder-based characterization.

In an even more extreme case, taking stakeholders into normative consideration can broaden the definition of entrepreneurial opportunities itself. Keeping in mind moral, ethical principles, the tenet that opportunities are those situations in which new goods, services, raw materials, and organizing methods can be introduced and sold at greater than their cost of production (Casson, 1982) not necessarily hold in absolute terms. There can be situations, in which stakeholder relationships can push towards opportunities that even though not consistent with the definition above, are socially desirable. In these cases, failing in managing stakeholders' expectation, balancing their requests with traditional entrepreneurial motives can be detrimental for the survival or success of the new venture.

The reasoning above makes it clear how normative foundation provides the starting base for further descriptive and instrumental integration of the stakeholder theory into the entrepreneurship field.

The Descriptive Contribution

The descriptive side of the stakeholder theory emerges from those studies that try to explain firm's characteristics and behaviors: from the nature of the firm to the way managers interpret the interaction with the environment or the conditions under which firms are more likely to take a certain stakeholder group into consideration (i.e., urgency, legitimacy and power framework, Mitchell et al. 1997).

In this regard, extending the descriptive application of stakeholder theory to entrepreneurship field can enable an understanding of the conditions under which the discovery and exploitation of entrepreneurial opportunities are fostered. In particular, stakeholder theory can provide a better mapping of information corridors based on which entrepreneurs discover opportunities, as well as how entrepreneurs learn within their stakeholder network.

In line with this argument, stakeholder theory's descriptive frameworks can be used to distinguish between situations in which entrepreneurs are pressured by the environment and those in which active manipulation is more likely to occur. These contexts can be defined as based on the specific characteristics of the stakeholders (e.g., power measured in term of resource dependence of the new venture), the characteristics of the stakeholder requests or needs (e.g., legitimacy and urgency, Eesley and Lenox, 2006), or the position of the entrepreneurs within their stakeholder network.

The fine-grained description of the way entrepreneurs interact with their stakeholders can also help clarify what are the necessary or contingent relations, as well as those that are compatible with the entrepreneurial process and those that have to be managed because of being potentially conflicting (Friedman and Miles, 2002).

Summarizing, the contribution of integrating descriptive studies relies on the possibility to better clarify both the composition of the external environment, as well as how and under what conditions the entrepreneurs actually interact with their context.

The Instrumental Contribution

The last broad area of contribution is the one based on the instrumental perspective, namely, the connection between stakeholder management and entrepreneurial performance.

First of all stakeholder theory can help explaining differences in new ventures' survival rates. In fact, given the liability of newness that characterizes entrepreneurial activities (Stinchcombe, 1961), it could be worth understanding what characteristics of the new ventures are assessed by stakeholders in deciding whether or not develop or maintain a certain relationship, as well as whether or not bear a certain risk or provide a certain resource. The reference here is, for example, to the reliability of the entrepreneur, to the accountability in the way resources are used, to the legitimacy of the entrepreneur's value proposition and the commitment s/he is able to mobilize.

However the ability to manage stakeholder relationships can predict other measures of entrepreneurial performance. In this sense, the focus is on the relationship between stakeholder management and the decision to exploit entrepreneurial opportunities. The presence of stakeholder relationship can support entrepreneurs in managing risks. In fact, in dynamic and risky setting, like the entrepreneurial one, do not taking into consideration a certain stakeholder claim from the beginning can lead to higher risk of future claims (McGuire, Sundgren and Schneeweis, 1988). The ability of the entrepreneurs to manage multiple stakeholder relationships decreases risk, providing signal of successful attempts at satisfying stakeholders groups and being a reliable partner.

Summarizing, webs of cooperative interdependencies with stakeholders and among stakeholders can enable entrepreneurs in coping with complex and uncertain environments, not only in term of an increased ability to collect the necessary resources but also as raised control in the face of uncertainty.

Conclusion

Entrepreneurship is an important and relevant force of economic and societal development. It is exactly for this reason that the relational dimensions of entrepreneurship have to be taken into consideration, since legitimacy, survival, success and performance of any new venture depend on them. So far, the idea that entrepreneurial processes do not occur in a vacuum has been developed in entrepreneurship research. However, either the environment has been taken for granted or considered as a one-dimensional construct. Moreover, even acknowledging the complexity of the entrepreneurial outcomes, the value creation proposition has been taken for granted, directly translated into benefits for the whole society. Starting from highlighting the missing points in entrepreneurship research, the purpose of this study was to focus research attention explicitly on the relational dimension of entrepreneurship, providing a fine-grained view of the environment in which the entrepreneurial process takes place based on the stakeholder theory of the firm.

We recognize that we may have offered some uncertain assumptions or potentially flawed logical arguments. Nevertheless, this study provides a starting point from which further investigation might proceed. Throughout the paper, entrepreneurship was defined as new venture creation (i.e., new business activity). However, normative, descriptive and instrumental settings can be applied to develop specific propositions and empirical research questions distinguishing between organizations and business creation, as well as across different levels of innovativeness and uncertainty. Given the lack of previous theoretical basis on the integration between the two fields, a deeper understanding of the conditions under which integration is feasible, necessary, beneficial would enable a better understanding of this new research area.

References

Altman, B.W. 1998. Corporate community relations in the 1990s: A study in transformation, *Business and Society*, 37(2): 221-228.

Austin, J., Stevenson, H., Wei-Skillern, J. 2006. Social and commercial entrepreneurship: some, different or both? *Entrepreneurship Theory and Practice*, 30(1): 1-22.

Baumol, W.J. 1990. Entrepreneurship: Productive, Unproductive, and Destructive. *Journal of Political Economy*, 98(5): 893-921.

Clarkson, M.B.E. 1995. A stakeholder framework for analyzing and evaluating corporate social performance. *Academy of Management Review*, 20: 92-117

Commission of the European Communities (CEC). 2001. *Green Paper 'Promoting a European Framework for Corporate Social Responsibility'*, Brussels: COM(2001) 366 final.

Corriveau, L. 1994. Entrepreneurs, Growth, and Cycles. *Economica*, 61 (February): 1-15.

Cummings, J.L. and Doh, J.P. 2000. Identifying who matters: Mapping key players in multiple environments. *California Management Review*, 42(2): 83-104.

Davidsson, P. and Wiklund, J. 2001. Levels of analysis in entrepreneurship research: Current research practice and suggestions for the future. *Entrepreneurship Theory and Practice*, (summer): 81-89.

Dess, G.G., Ireland, R.D., Zahra, S.A., Floyd, S.W., Janney, J.J. and Lane, P.J. 2003, Emerging issues in corporate entrepreneurship. *Journal of Management*, 29(3): 351-378.

DiMaggio, P.J. and Powell W.W. 1983. The iron cage revisited: Institutional isomorphism and collective rationality in organizational fields. *American Sociological Review*, 48: 147-160.

Donaldson, T. and Preston, L.E. 1995. The stakeholder theory of the corporation: Concepts, evidence and implications. *Academy of Management Review*, 20(1): 65-91.

Eckhardt, J.T. and Shane, S.A. 2003. Opportunities and entrepreneurship. *Journal of Management*, 29(3): 333-349.

Eesley C. and Lenox, M.J. 2006. Firm responses to secondary stakeholder action. *Strategic Management Journal*, 27: 765-781.

El-Namaki, M.S. 1988. Encouraging entrepreneurs in developing countries. *Long Range Planning*, 21(4): 98-106.

Fisscher, O., Frenkel, D., Lurie, Y. and Nijhof, A. 2005. Stretching the frontiers: Exploring the relationships between entrepreneurship and ethics (special issue), *Journal of Business Ethics*, 60: 207-209.

Freeman, R.E. and Velamuri, S.R. 2006. A new approach to CSR: Company stakeholder responsibility, in Kakabadse A. and Morsing M. (eds.) *Corporate Social Responsibility: Reconciling aspiration with application*, Palgrave Macmillan

Freeman, R.E. 1984. *Strategic management: a stakeholder approach*. (Pitman, Boston).

Freeman, R.E. and McVea, J. 2001. A stakeholder approach to strategic management, In M.A. Hitt , R.E. Freeman and J.S. Harrison (eds.) *Handbook of strategic management*: 189-207, (Blackwell, Oxford, UK)

Freeman, R.E. and Venkataraman, S. 2002, Ethics and entrepreneurship, *The Ruffin Series No.3, Business Ethics Quarterly*: 1-246.

Freeman, R.E., A. Wicks, B. Parmar, and McVea, J. 2004. Stakeholder Theory: the State of the Art and Future Perspectives. *Politeia*, 74: 9-22.

Friedman A.L. and Miles S. 2002. Developing stakeholder theory. *Journal of Management Studies*, 39(1): 1-21.

Gartner, W.B. 1985. A conceptual framework for describing the phenomenon of new venture creation. *Academy of Management Review*, 10(4): 696-706.

Gartner, W.B. 1988. "Who is an entrepreneur" is the wrong question. *American Small Business Journal*, (Spring): 11-31.

Granovetter, M. 1985. Economic action and social structure: The problem of embeddedness. *American Journal of Sociology*, 91(3): 481-510.

Hannafey, F.T. 2003. Entrepreneurship and Ethics: A literature review. *Journal of Business Ethics*, 46: 99-110.

Hannan, M.T. and Freeman, J. 1982. The population ecology of the organizations. *American Journal of Sociology*, 82(5): 929-964.

Harper, M. 1991. Enterprise development in poorer nations. *Entrepreneurship Theory and Practice*, 15: 7-11.

Jarrillo, J.C. 1989. Entrepreneurship and growth: The strategic use of external resources. *Journal of Business Venturing*, 4: 133-147.

Jones, T.M. 1995. Instrumental stakeholder theory: A synthesis of ethics and economics. *Academy of Management Review*, 20: 404-437.

Liao, J. and Welsch, H. 2005. Roles of Social Capital in Venture Creation: Key Dimensions and Research Implications. *Journal of Small Business Management*, 43(4): 345-362.

Lumpkin, G.T. and Dess, G.G. 1996. Clarifying the entrepreneurial orientation construct and linking it to performance. *Academy of Management Review*, 21(1): 135-172.

Mahoney, J. 1997, Spheres and limits of ethical responsibilities in and of the corporation, in G. Enderle (ed.) *People in Corporation* (Kluwer Academic Publishers, Dordrecht)

Mair, J., Marti, I., 2006. Social entrepreneurship research: a source of explanation, prediction, and delight. *Journal of World Business* 41: 36-44.

Mitchell, R.K., Agle, B.R. and Wood, D.J. 1997. Toward a theory of stakeholder identification and salience: Defining the principle of who and what really counts. *Academy of Management Review*, 22(4): 853-886.

Oliver, C. 1991. Strategic responses to institutional processes. *Academy of Management Review*, 16: 145-179.

Perrini, F., 2006. *The new social entrepreneurship: What awaits social entrepreneurial ventures?* London: Edward Elgar Publishing.

Phillips, R., Freeman, R.E. and Wicks, A.C. 2003. What stakeholder theory is not. *Business ethics quarterly*, 13:479-502.

Powell, S.S. 1990. *The entrepreneur as the mainspring of economic growth*. Stanford, CA: The Hoover Institution, Stanford University.

Putnam, R.: 2000, *Bowling Alone: The Collapse and Revival of American Community* (Simon and Schuster, New York, NY).

Rowley TJ. 1997. Moving beyond dyadic ties: a network theory of stakeholder influences. *Academy of Management Review*, 22: 887–910.

Schumpeter, J.A. 1942. *Capitalism, Socialism, and Democracy*. New York and London: Harper

Shane, S. and Cable, D. 2002. Network ties, reputation, and the financing of new ventures. *Management Science*, 48(3): 364.381.

Shane, S., Venkataraman, S. 2000. The promise of entrepreneurship as a field of research. *Academy of Management Review* 25(1): 217-226.

Sine, W.D., Haveman, H.A. and Tolbert, P.S. 2005. Risky business? Entrepreneurship in the new independent power sector. *Administrative Science Quarterly*, 50: 200-232.

Stinchcombe, A.L. 1961. Social structure and organizations. In J.G. March (ed) *Handbook of organizations*: 142-193, Chicago, IL: Rand McNally.

Ucbasaran, D., Westhead, P. and Wright, M. 2001. The focus of entrepreneurial research: contextual and process issues. *Entrepreneurship Theory and Practice*, Summer: 57-80.

Vandekerckhove, W. and Denchev, N.A. 2005, A network perspective on stakeholder management: Facilitating entrepreneurs in the discovery of opportunity, *Journal of Business Ethics*, 60: 221-232.

Venkataraman, S. (1999), *Stakeholder value equilibration and the entrepreneurial process*, Ruffin Lecture Series of the Olsson Center for Applied Ethics, Darden School of the University of Virginia.

Wood, D.J. 1991. Corporate social performance revisited. *Academy of Management Review*, 16: 691-719.

Zahra, S. 1991. Predictors and financial outcomes of corporate entrepreneurship: An explorative study. *Journal of Business Venturing*, 6/4, 259-275.

In: Corporate Social Responsibility
Editor: Adam R. Timpere

ISBN: 978-1-60456-284-2

Chapter 8

CORPORATE SOCIAL RESPONSIBILITY AND HYDROPOWER DEVELOPMENT

Risako Morimoto*
CERMAS, Toulouse Business School, France

ABSTRACT

This chapter develops a cost benefit analysis model, which considers corporate social responsibility aspects of hydropower development projects. This cost benefit analysis model is empirically applied to controversial hydropower projects in Malaysia, Nepal and Turkey. The model emphasizes the importance of assessing not only economic impacts, but also environmental and social impacts in order to achieve sustainable hydro power development. The study covers diverse cases in terms of characteristics of the dams including size, their geographical locations, and the development stage in each country. According to the model results, the mean cumulative net present value at the 100th year of the analysis with the 5% discount rate for the Sharada-Babai dam in Nepal shows a positive figure, whereas the mean cumulative net present value after 100 years for both the Bakun dam in Malaysia and the Ilisu dam in Turkey are negative. The sensitivity analysis indicates that the significant positive impact of the generation capacity parameter on net present value for Bakun dam; and the parameter expressing initial expected increase in economic output for the Sharada-Babai dam and the Ilisu dam.

1. INTRODUCTION

Incorporating corporate responsibility (CR) into daily business operations is perceived to be significantly important (Morimoto *et al.* 2005). CR initiatives should be an essential part of business practice and decision making processes need to include environmental and social considerations. Large hydropower development projects often draw criticisms over their

* Tel: + 33561294712; Fax: +33561294994; Email: r.morimoto@esc-toulouse.fr

serious environmental and social impacts. Importance of studying environmental and social consequences of dam projects is emphasized in many literatures (e.g., WCD 2000; Scholtz 2002; Nakayama 1998). However, there are not many academic studies explicitly address CR and dams. For example, Bhattacharyya (2007) has reported the CR practices that Indian dam project had initiated including local education and community supports.

This chapter illustrates how we can effectively and efficiently manage to balance economic, social as well as environmental impacts of hydropower projects by introducing a project assessment model that include not only economic, but also social and environmental evaluations. It is a responsibility of industries to take care of overall impacts of their operations affecting local communities and the environment. By quantifying the environmental and social impacts of dam projects, policy makers can make a fairer judgment in project evaluations since at present only economic impacts are mainly quantitatively evaluated and other impacts are just mentioned qualitatively at a planning stage. Although such initiative is useful, difficulties of evaluating environmental and social impacts still remain, as these evaluations are more subjective values compared to more easily quantifiable economic or financial impacts. However, we believe this challenging initiative is a step forward for a better CR practice in hydropower development.

Currently, there seems to be a lack of adequate environmental and social considerations during a planning process of dam projects (e.g., Morimoto and Hope 2004). Although environmental impact assessments are compulsory in many countries, more attentions and emphasis seem to be given to economic benefits associated to hydropower project developments. This chapter critically addresses the importance of incorporating quantified environmental and social impacts of dam projects into a decision making process at a planning stage. The study develops an extended cost benefit analysis (CBA) that assesses not only economic impacts of a dam project, but also associated key environmental and social impacts. In order to illustrate the functionality and the validity of the model, this study empirically applies such probabilistic CBA (cost benefit analysis) to much debated hydroelectric projects in Nepal, Malaysia and Turkey as case studies. Various cases in terms of main characteristics of dams, geographical locations of each dam, and the development stage of each country are selected. The study brings together all the major issues attached to each hydropower project and estimates the quantitative impacts of these controversial dams. The CBA model in this study is extended from the previous version in Morimoto and Hope (2004a, 2004b), in order to take into account the correlation between the generation capacity, the total construction cost and the construction period.

This chapter consists of the following four sections. The next section describes the background of the three hydropower projects used as case studies. The third section explains the environmental, social and economic impact assessment model developed in this study and lists the variables used in the model. The fourth section presents the findings from the study including Net Present Value (NPV), sensitivity analysis and the variation of cumulative NPV against the pure rate of time preference. The last section provides summaries of this chapter and concludes the study.

2. Case Studies

2.1. Malaysia: Bakun Hydro Project

The main Malaysian energy provider - Tenaga National Berhad (TNB)[1] - reports that the electricity demand in Malaysia in 2005 was met mainly by three major sources; gas (47%), hydro (10%), and coal (43%). The government intends to balance this ratio and tries to increase hydropower generation, which has led to the controversial Bakun Hydroelectric Project construction plan. The Bakun dam on Balui River in Sarawak state on Borneo Island will be the largest dam in South East Asia with a generation capacity of 2.4GW, and is supposed to cater for the rising industrial demand for electricity in Malaysia. Electricity consumption in Malaysia grew at 5.6 % between 2000 and 2005 together with rapid economic growth, according to *APEC Energy demand and Supply Outlook 2006*. Although this development of a remote part of Malaysia might improve the regional economy through increased employment and infrastructure development, such as access roads and airports, there are also massive costs associated with it. The dam is estimated to flood 70,000 hectares of rainforests and abundant timber sources, equivalent to the size of Singapore, and fertile agricultural lands. The construction costs for this gigantic project will be huge, despite the possibility of insufficient demand to absorb its enormous electricity generation. Another serious concern of the project is the displacement of 10,000 indigenous people. The entire ecosystem of the area might also change; such as large negative effects on downstream fishery are anticipated. The area is already suffering from siltation problem due to timber extraction, which is forecasted to restrict electricity generation capacity in the near future. The project has been delayed due to serious environmental, social and financial problems. The project was originally scheduled to complete in 2003, however was revised to 2007.

2.2. Nepal: Sharada-Babai Hydro Project

Nepal has a great hydropower potential and its theoretical generation capacity is 83 GW, according to the Nepal Electricity Authority (NEA). There are currently numerous planned hydropower projects in Nepal in order to utilize such abundant resources. Lack of electricity may restrict economic growth, especially in the industrial and service sectors that are the fastest growing economic sectors in Nepal (Pokharel 2001). The electrification rate in Nepal is still very low – only about one third of the population has access to electricity, and the rate is much lower for rural population (ADB 2004). The country's major sources of energy for rural population are fuelwood and kerosene (Mahapatra 2001). The government in Nepal plans to provide electricity to 55% of the population by 2007, which requires rapid expansion of electrification in the country (ADB 2004). The electricity demand in Nepal is estimated to grow at 7.5% annually until 2020 (ADB 2004).

The Sharada-Babai hydropower project in the Mid Western Region of Nepal has an installed capacity of 93MW, and requires a 5-year construction period. The project is located between the tropical and sub-tropical climatic regions of the country. The dam site is very

[1] http://www2.tnb.com.my/tnb/pdf/GenStats.pdf

fertile land, whose main crops are paddy and wheat. More than 300 families will be relocated from the core project area. The major impact of the project is the submergence of rich forest and agricultural land. The impoundment and reduced flow of the downstream would change the hydrology of the basin, which is likely to affect the aquatic environment of the river. The holy pond and the Kali Vhagwati (a temple of religious and cultural importance) will be inundated due to the reservoir formation. Infrastructure relocation such as a school, a post office, and suspension bridges are also required.

2.3. Turkey: Ilisu Hydro Project

The electricity demand in Turkey is met by oil (38%), coal (27%), gas (23%), and hydro and renewable (12%), according to Turkish Ministry of Foreign Affairs (2006). The electricity consumption in Turkey has been growing by the rate of 6 % per annually as a result of rapid urbanization and industrialization, according to the report *Turkey's Energy Strategy* by Ministry of Foreign Affairs (2006).

The Ilisu hydro project is a part of the Southeastern Anatolia Project which aims to improve the living standards and develop the agricultural potential of the nine southeastern Anatolia provinces and to bring their socio-economic level up to the national average. The Ilisu dam is presently the largest hydro project in Turkey with a generation capacity of 1,200 MW. The dam site is located on the Tigris River in South-East Anatolia, 65 km upstream of the Syrian and Iraqi border. The project plan was stopped in 2002 as it is extremely controversial for a variety of political, social, environmental, economic, and archeological reasons. However, the project resurfaced in 2005 and began construction on 5 August 2006 with the completion being expected in 2013 (*BBC news 5 August 2006*).

The project will submerge approximately 52 villages and 15 small towns and could affect between 25,000 and 78,000 people mainly ethnic Kurds[2]. The people living in the project area are mainly farmers who grow cereals, vegetables, fruits, cotton, tobacco as well as herbs and a small number of shepherds. Although there is no real commercial fishing in the River Tigris, farmers fish for local consumption. Local residents moving to cities will face sharp changes in their daily activities and traditional ways of life which often cause significant problems of adaptation to the urban environment, family tensions, psychological stress and social disruption.

Hasankeyf, the main town to be inundated is the only town in Anatolia which has survived since the middle ages without destruction, and is also known as an important pilgrimage center. The town's history dates back at least 2,700 years, and it hosts a formidable array of monuments, including cave churches, ornate mosques, and Islamic tombs. An astounding complexity of architectural and religious heritage spanning several civilizations has been created. Being a rich treasure of Assyrian, Christian, Abassidian-Islamic and Osmanian history in Turkey, Hasankeyf was awarded complete archeological protection by the Turkish department of culture in 1978, and 22 monuments have been entered on the Turkish Cultural Inventory List in 1981. The lack of funds and time would result in difficulties in relocating the treasures that will be inundated. Moreover, even after successful relocation, they may not create the same aesthetic impact in a new site. Hasankeyf

[2] http://www.rivernet.org/turquie/ilisu.htm

is also a tourist destination and a holiday resort, so inundation of this town is likely to affect on tourism in the area.

The area to be flooded by the reservoir includes 7,353 hectares of rich agricultural land, 4,820 hectares of medium-low quality land, and 15,675 hectares of land not suitable for growing crops[3]. Since, the amount of trees and shrubs in the area to be flooded is relatively small, the carbon dioxide release from the reservoir is assumed to be small compared to the other reservoirs of the same size in dense forest (IEG 2001). Solid waste and wastewater of major cities are being dumped into the Tigris River without any treatment. The Ilisu reservoir is expected to reduce vastly the auto-purification capacity of the Tigris. This is therefore highly likely to cause water quality degradation and possibly to affect the downstream fishery negatively.

3. Model

The CBA model developed in this study is extended from the previous versions in Morimoto and Hope (2004a, 2004b) in order to take into account the correlation between the generation capacity, the total construction cost and the construction period. Table 1 lists the variables used in the CBA model. The core variables included in all the case studies are PG (power generation), CP (clean power), EG (economic growth), CC (construction cost), OM (operation & maintenance cost), RE (resettlement cost), IN (losses due to inundation of land), AC (accident cost). The project specific variables are FI (impacts on downstream fishery) for Bakun; IF (infrastructure cost) for Sharada-Babai; and LT (tourism loss) and AS (archaeological loss) for Ilisu. How archaeology is perceived is different from place to place and generation to generation (Carver 1996). Although there are many studies on how to place values on archaeological sites, there is no simple conclusion for this argument (see Carman et al (1999); Carver (1996); Darvil et al. (1987); Lipe (1984); Schaafsma (1989)). A brief summary of the equations used in the model, and all the parameters in the model and their values are listed in Appendix A-I and A-II respectively. Dixon *et al.* (1994) argue that the appropriate time horizon should be long enough to encompass the useful life of the proposed project, therefore the project life of 100 years is selected in this study.

Some inputs in the CBA model seem to be clearly correlated to each other. If the generation capacity were to be reduced, the total construction cost and the construction period would also be reduced accordingly. Hence, we assume that a minimum value for one of these variables implies a minimum value for the others. The same assumption is made for most likely and maximum values. The correlation coefficients for each project are shown in Table 2[4]. There is a wide range in the data input for GC (generation capacity) in the Bakun case, as the project size might be drastically reduced due to the protests. The minimum, most likely and max values are 0.5, 0.7 and 2.4 GW respectively. Therefore the consideration of this input dependency would be particularly important for Bakun.

[3] http://www.rivernet.org/turquie/ilisu.htm

[4] The calculation is based on the following formula, Correlation coefficient [x,y] = {covariance [x,y]}/{(standard error [x]*(standard error [y])}

Table 1. Variables used in the CBA model

Variable (core variables in bold)	Description
EG (economic growth)	The forgone economic costs for electricity not served, which will occur during the time when an alternative power generation technology is not available.
PG (power generation)	Calculated by multiplying the quantity of electricity generated by the price of electricity. A possible reduction in the quantity of electricity generated due to sedimentation, and changes in electricity prices, are also included in the equation.
CP (clean power)	The environmental benefit of avoiding damage from air pollution when generating an equivalent amount of power by thermal power. This benefit will occur during the time when an alternative power generation technology is available.
IN (losses due to land inundation)	Financial values of forests and agricultural lands to be inundated
AS (archaeological loss)	Approximated by the values of cultural antiquities being sold on the market.
CC (construction cost)	Construction costs of the power station and transmission facilities.
FI (impacts on downstream fishery)	Decline in revenues from fishery due to dam construction.
LT (tourism loss)	Losses in tourism revenue as a result of the dam construction
OM (operation & maintenance cost)	O&M costs for running the hydropower station.
RE (resettlement cost)	Compensation to individuals and development costs for new houses and infrastructure. Theoretically, estimations of what resettled people are willing to accept are preferred as better estimates. However, those data are difficult to obtain and their results are not very reliable, especially in developing countries.
IF (infrastructure relocation cost)	Costs required to relocate infrastructures to be inundated
AC (accident cost)	During construction, O&M & special circumstances (technical failure, terrorism attack or earthquake). Calculated by multiplying the estimated number of deaths and injuries due to the project by the economic value of deaths and injuries. Assumes that accident risks are not internalized in wages[5].

Table 2. Correlation coefficients

	GC-TCC	GC-Tc	TCC-Tc
Bakun	0.996	0.996	0.983
Sharada-Babai	0.98	0.9	0.79
Ilisu	0.99	0.82	0.9

Note: GC=generation capacity parameter; TCC=total construction cost; Tc=construction period.

Each data are given as ranges, collected mainly from the existing project reports including Environmental Impact Assessment (EIA) reports and energy reports. Supplementary data are based on an extensive collation of information from past studies on

[5] This method does not take into account accident costs for alternative sources of supply for simplicity, as different risks are included for the alternative cases.

similar topics, newspapers, internet and other relevant sources. The most appropriate data for each parameter are selected using our best knowledge on the energy policy of each country, their current situation and future direction of power generation. Best efforts are made to find as accurate and representative data as possible. Visiting the project site and interviewing relevant key individuals being involved in the dam projects, government officials, energy experts, policymakers, researchers, academics, environmentalists and locals during our fieldtrip in Malaysia, Nepal and Turkey have greatly facilitated such decision making process.

Many of the values in Table A-1, A-2, and A-3 are tentative. However, this is inevitable, as many variables are not readily quantifiable and some data have a limited availability because of the project complexity or simply they do not exist. Repeated runs of the model provide a probability distribution of expected outcomes, which is a more reliable procedure than just using single values for inputs that are in reality not well known.

Table 3. Mean cumulative present values for the variables at t=100 years

	(Units are all in US$ billion)	**Bakun**	**Sharada-Babai**	**Ilisu**
PVEG	**Economic growth**	**+13**	**+0.18**	**+13.8**
PVPG	**Power generation**	**+3.6**	**+0.21**	**+3.3**
PVCP	Clean power	+0.9	+0.03	+0.5
PVIN	**Inundation loss**	**-10.5**	**-0.09**	-0.2
PVAS	**Archaeological loss**	-	-	-9.5
PVCC	**Construction cost**	**-4.5**	**-0.14**	**-4.9**
PVFI	Fishery loss	-4.4	-	-0.9
PVLT	Tourism loss	-	-	-3.5
PVOM	O & M cost	-0.4	-0.03	-0.5
PVRE	Resettlement	-0.1	-0.003	-1.0
PVIF	Infrastructure relocation	-	-0.02	-
PVAC	Accident cost	-0.03	-0.0004	-0.04

Note: Significant variables are expressed in bold letters.
Source: CBA model runs.

4. Findings

4.1. Net Present Values

The impacts of each variable on the NPV for each project are depicted in Table 3 and Figure 1. The notable variables to be mentioned are: EG (economic growth), PG (power generation), and CC (construction cost) that are significant in all the projects; IN (inundation loss) for Bakun and Sharada-Babai; and AS (archaeological loss) for Ilisu. The impact of CC (construction cost) is huge as much as EG (economic growth), but not as prolonged. The sharp decay of the positive impacts of EG (economic growth) and PG (power generation) can be explained as a result of serious sedimentation problems. In comparison, AS (archaeological loss) and LT (tourism loss) are long lasting negative impacts, and are not recoverable once the dam is constructed.

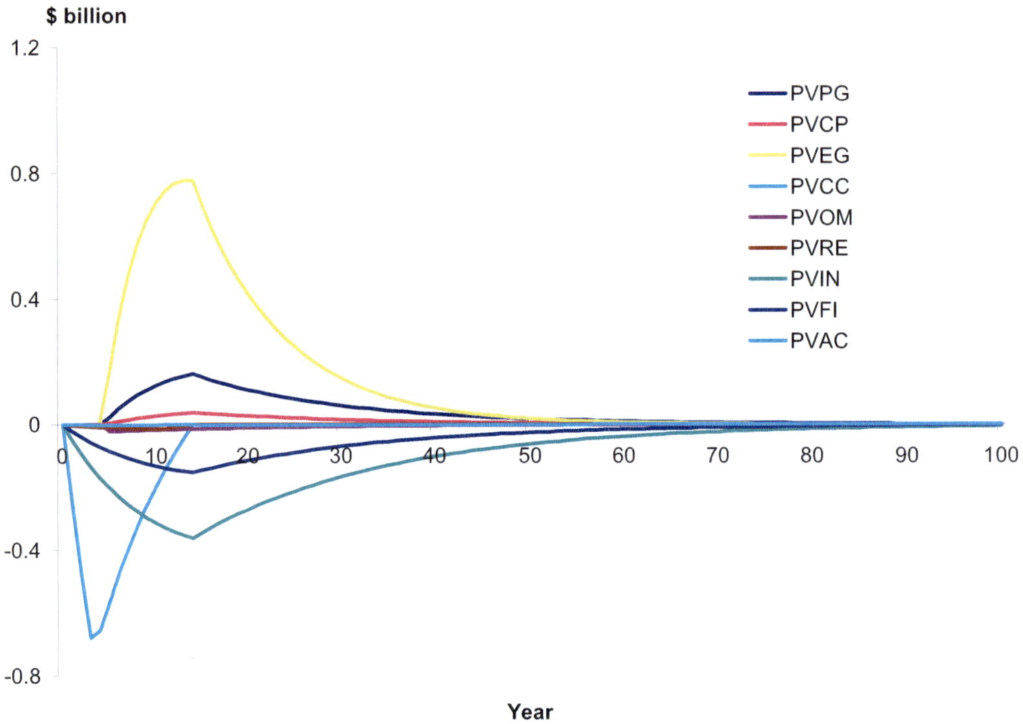

Bakun

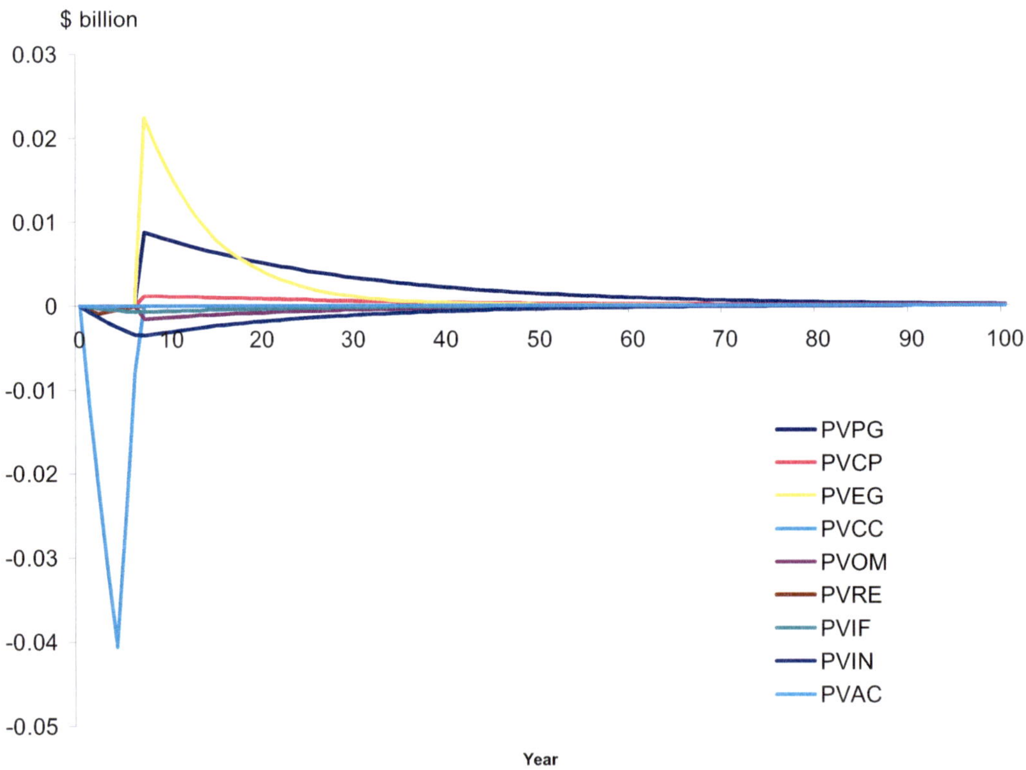

Sharada-Babai

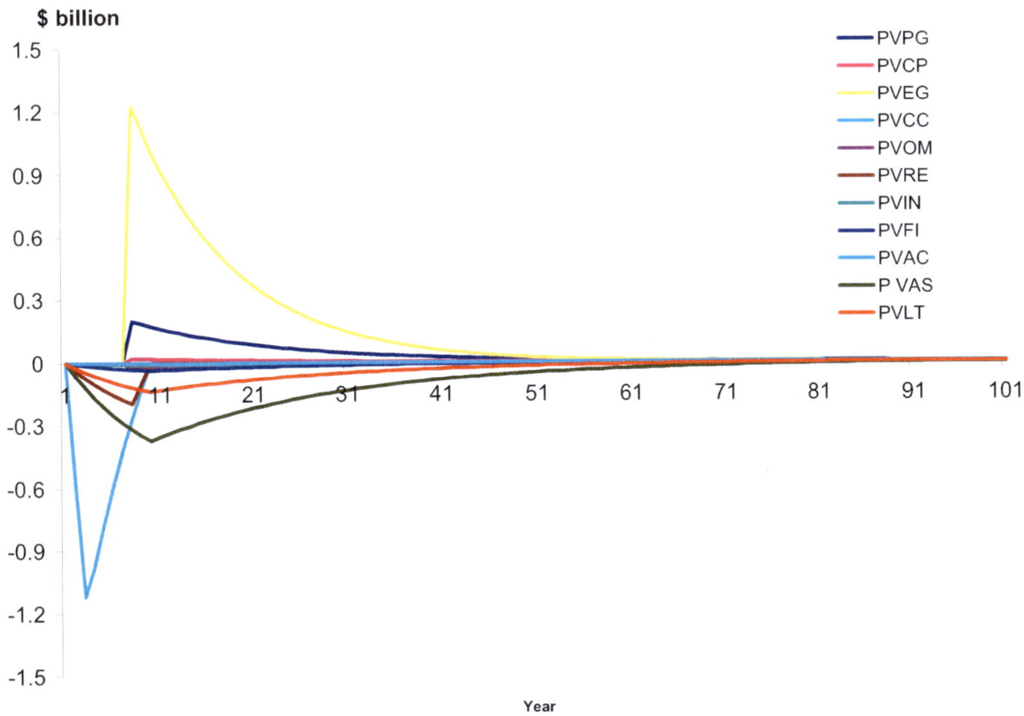

Ilisu

Source: CBA model runs.

Figure 1. Present value of the variables by year.

For Bakun, the 5th percentile, mean and the 95th percentile of cumulative NPV with a premature decommissioning option at a 5 % discount rate at t=100 years are $ -9.6, -2.8, and 7.0 billion respectively (without decommissioning they are $ –9.9, -2.9, and 7.0 billion respectively; showing that the option of premature decommissioning gives a slight improvement)[6]. The mean, the 5th and the 95th percentiles of the cumulative NPV are all initially significantly negative due to the large construction cost as shown in Figure 2. The 95th percentile recovers quickly after the construction is complete since the benefits of increased economic growth soon outweigh all the costs. Its peak is at t = 40 years, as after this date the revenue is insufficient to cover the total annual costs. The 5th percentile and the mean values both remain negative throughout the life of the project. The mean shows a slight recovery from year 10 until year 30 followed by a permanent downward movement. The 5th percentile shows a similar pattern to the mean, though it already starts declining at t = 20 years due to the large anticipated costs such as inundation and fishery losses.

For Sharada-Babai, the 5th percentile, mean and the 95th percentile of the NPV at the 5% discount rate at t=100 years with premature decommissioning option are $ -0.009, 0.14, and 0.34 billion respectively. The results without the premature decommissioning option are exactly the same since the recoverable costs such as AC (accident costs during operation & maintenance period) and OM (operation & maintenance cost) are small for this specific

[6] The premature decommissioning option allows the dam to be closed early if the annual revenue drops below the annual avoidable costs

project. The range of cumulative NPV over time in Figure 2 shows that the huge initial capital costs are gradually outweighed by the anticipated large benefits from power generation and increased economic growth.

For Ilisu, The 95th percentile is positive whereas the mean and the 5th percentile are negative as shown in Figure 2. The mean, the 5th percentile and the 95th percentile of the cumulative NPV at the 5% discount rate with the premature decommissioning option at t = 100 years are $ –9.9, -3.5, and 4 billion respectively. As Figure 2 illustrates, the benefits never outweigh the costs throughout the period for the 5th percentile and the mean, while the 95th percentile turns to be positive soon after the completion of construction. The 95th percentile starts declining gradually after its peak at t = 40 years. The NPV are all negative at the beginning because of large construction and resettlement costs. The NPV increases rapidly once electricity starts to be generated, however the mean and the 5th percentile remain negative as a result of huge archaeological losses from the destruction of this important area in Turkey which has numerous unique archaeological sites as well as tourist and pilgrim attractions. The result also shows that the consideration of premature decommissioning would not improve the result, since those recoverable costs after premature decommissioning such as operation & maintenance cost, accidents costs during operation, and land inundation loss for this project are relatively small.

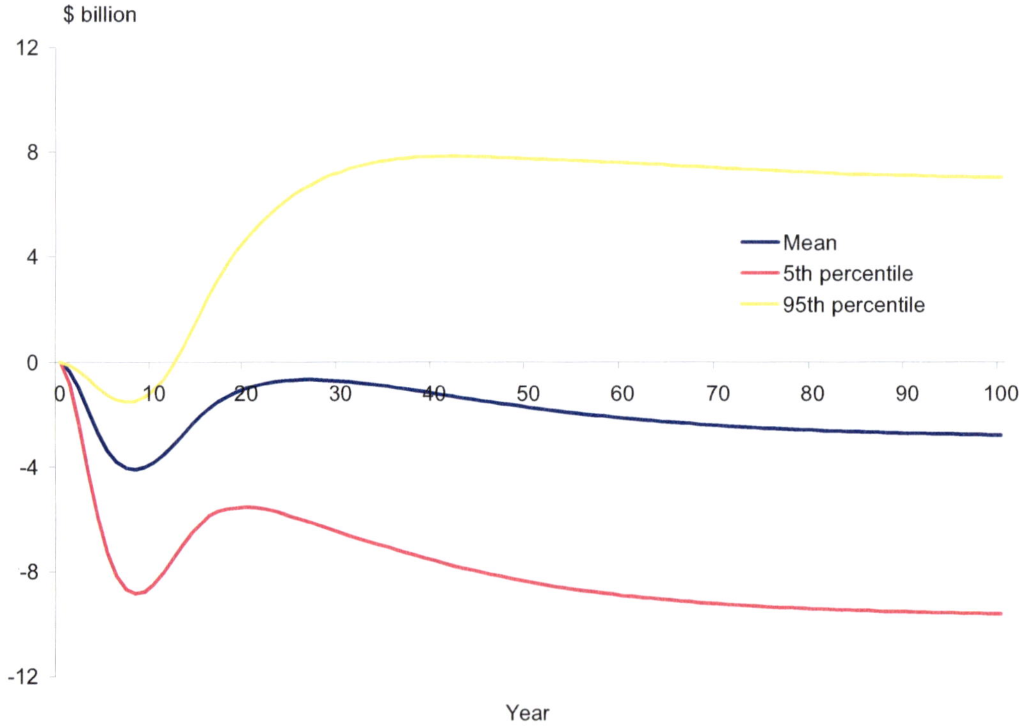

Bakun

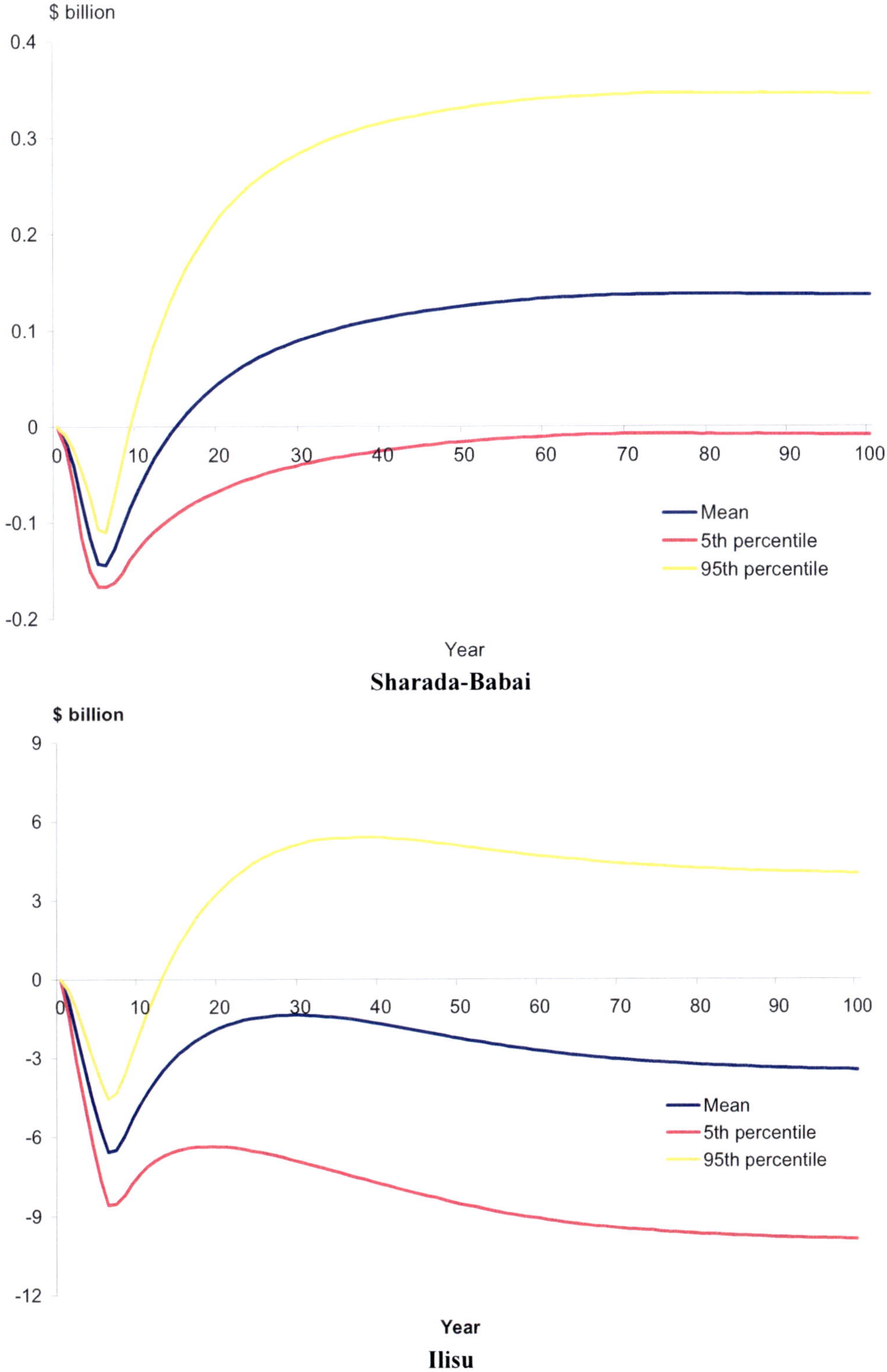

Source: CBA model runs.

Figure 2. Ranges of cumulative NPV at the 5% discount rate by year.

Table 4. Sensitivity analysis (student b coefficients)

Bakun		Sharada-Babai		Ilisu	
GC	**+0.96**	**EO**	**+0.78**	**EO**	**+0.83**
EO	+0.63	P0	+0.34	NT	-0.33
TCC	-0.61	GC	+0.30	TCC	-0.28

Note: The input parameter values are regressed against the output (NPV). The student b coefficient is a coefficient calculated for each input parameter in the regression equation. The most significant variables are expressed in bold.

Source: Sensitivity analysis runs.

4.2. Sensitivity Analysis

The sensitivity analysis illustrates the dominant positive impact of the parameters GC (generation capacity) on NPV for Bakun, and EO (initial expected increase in economic output) on NPV for both Sharada-Babai and Ilisu as presented in Table 4. The parameters TCC (total construction cost), P0 (Initial proportion of time during which an alternative power generation technology is not available), and NT (number of tourists visiting the dam site in absence of the dam) also have significant impacts on NPV for at least one of the sites.

4.3. Cumulative NPV against Pure Rate of Time Preference

Figure 3 depicts the cumulative NPV against the pure rate of time preference, which illustrates the sensitivity of the NPV to the changes in discount rates. These discount rates are calculated in the same manner as the ones in Morimoto and Hope (2004a & 2004b).

$$r(t) = g(t) + p,$$

where r(t) = variable discount rate at time t, g(t) = annual growth rate at time t, and p = pure rate of time preference.

The mean value of the cumulative NPV for all projects converges to zero as the pure rate of time preference becomes larger. The 95th percentile of the cumulative NPV for Bakun becomes negative when the pure rate of time preference is larger than 11%. The mean value of the cumulative NPV for Sharada-Babai is positive when the pure rate of time preference is low, and becomes negative when the pure rate of time preference is larger than 6%. The 95th percentile of the cumulative NPV for Ilisu becomes negative when the pure rate of time preference is larger than 8%.

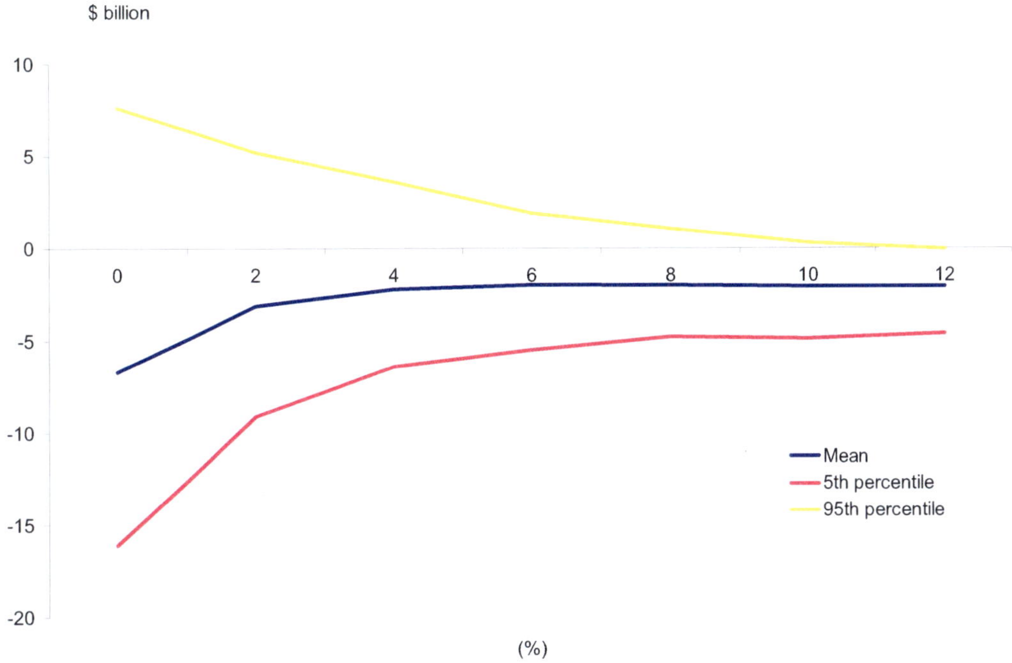

Bakun

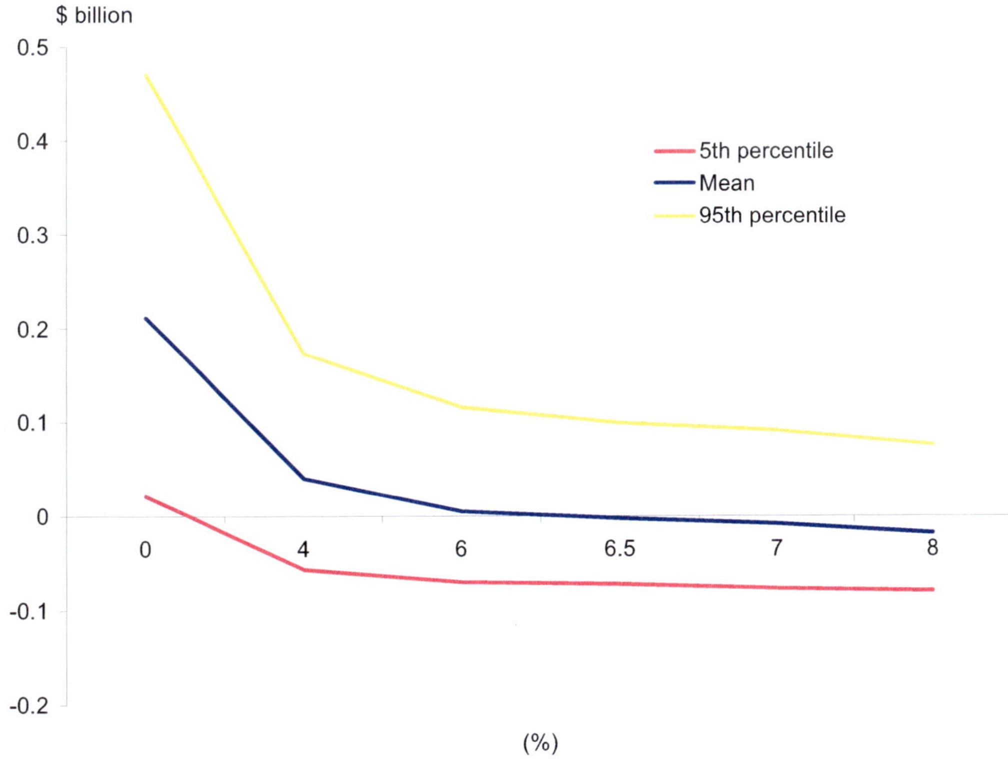

Sharada-Babai

Figure 3. (Continues)

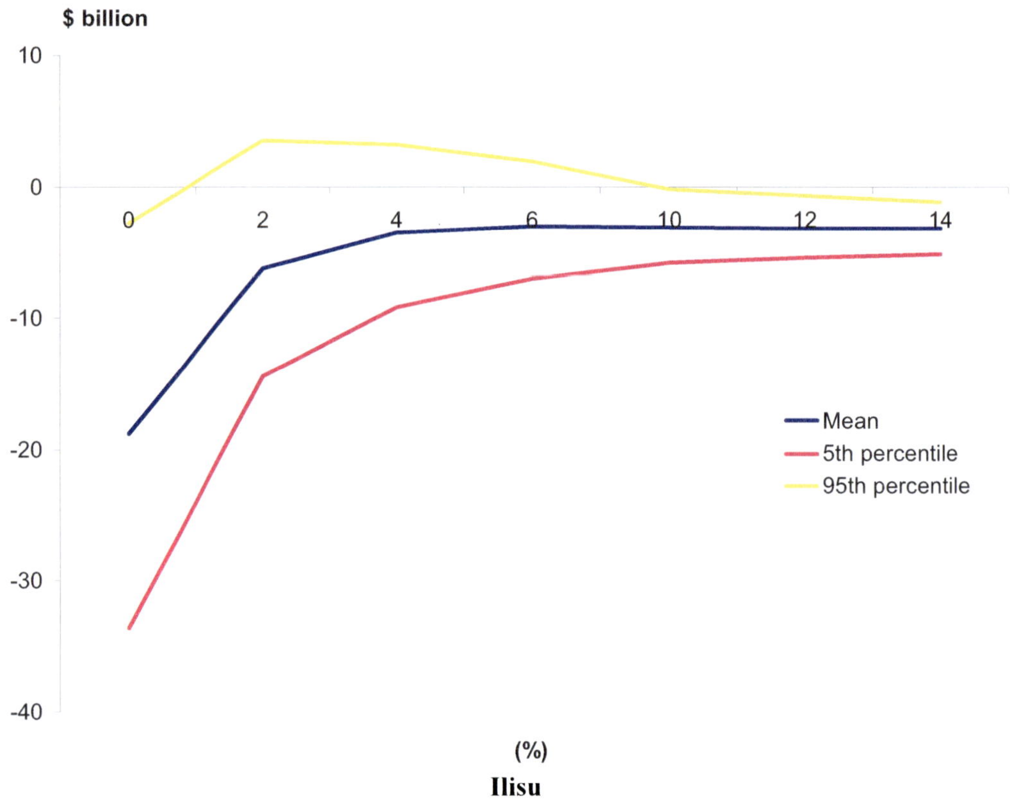

Source: CBA model runs.

Figure 3. Cumulative NPV against pure rate of time preference.

5. Conclusion

This chapter has addressed the significance of practicing corporate responsibility in hydropower industry. The study suggests incorporating environmental and social impacts into project assessments that are generally economic impact focused. This is a challenging task, as environmental and social impacts are usually difficult to quantify. However, the model provides a first step forward to initiate corporate responsibility at a planning stage when building dams. The probabilistic CBA model, developed in Morimoto and Hope (2004a & 2004b) with further modifications, has been applied to the case studies. The updated CBA model takes into account the correlation between the generation capacity, the total construction cost and the construction period. The model developed in this chapter has a potential to support policy makers in their decision-making process, as an overall picture of a project can be captured at a glance, and the annual movements of each impact is visually very clear to see. The possible environmental, social and economic impacts of three highly controversial dam projects in Malaysia, Nepal and Turkey have been quantified in this chapter. Characteristics of each dam differ in terms of size, geographical locations, and the level of economics development. The validity of this type of project assessment models seems to be well proved by previous applications (Morimoto and Hope 2004a; 2004b).

The result for the Bakun dam in Malaysia shows expected huge losses mainly due to the inundation of the dense rainforest and the fertile agricultural lands, and the significant negative impacts on downstream fishery. The benefit of 2.4GW electricity supply and facilitated economic growth might outweigh these massive losses. However, this is unlikely to occur during any feasible period, as can be seen from the 5th percentile and the mean of the cumulative NPV being negative even after 100 years.

The result for the Sharada-Babai dam in Nepal presents more positive outcome. There are large benefits from the increased economic growth due to an increased power supply as the country presently suffers from a seriously shortage of electricity, large revenues from electricity sales, and the benefits of clean hydropower, in exchange for a large construction cost and the unrecoverable loss of submerging fertile agricultural land as well as forest. This study seems to support the improvement of hydropower development in Nepal, given the careful consideration of the consequences to the community and the environment.

The main finding for the Turkish Ilisu dam is the significant impact of the loss of unique archaeological sites, some of which date back at least 2,700 years. The losses are not only the value of these cultural heritages and artifacts to be submerged, but also the significant number of tourists and pilgrims visiting the sites. Both the 5th percentile and the mean of the cumulative NPV show that the proposed project benefits will not outweigh the large costs of the project. This result is coherent with the project being postponed in 2002, due to significant social and environmental concerns.

The overall results indicate that large scale dams generally tend to create large social and environmental impacts. The Nepalese dam case illustrates that smaller scale dams seem to be more sustainable than gigantic scale dams. Furthermore, huge costs are involved in each project discussed above, therefore an increase in electricity prices might not be avoidable. However, this may not be the case for the Sharada-Babai Project in Nepal, as the benefit is likely to outweigh the cost soon after the construction. The advantage of the model developed here is its flexibility. Developers could choose from an array of variables that most closely fit the constraints and conditions of their individual case. Some of the listed variables are either included or excluded in order to serve the differences in each project. These case studies with diverse individual concerns has demonstrated that the generalized model can be a highly practical tool, with the great advantage of its simplicity and a capability to cater for almost any kind of hydropower project assessment under uncertainty. Moreover, the application of this type of probabilistic CBA model is not limited to assess only hydropower projects, but it is also possible to extend its ability to assess other engineering or infrastructure projects, such as new aircraft, water pipes or tunnels (for example, Morimoto and Hope (2005)).

The limitations of the model are such that some impacts could be much larger than the impacts included in the above model, though may not be accurately quantifiable. For example, the scale of the resettlement for the Bakun dam is enormous and the resettlement impact is therefore expected to be huge, though this impact seems to be not fully reflected in our results. This suggests that current estimates of the resettlement cost might be too low, and that alternative approaches such as 'willingness to pay' or 'willingness to accept' could better estimate the true resettlement cost. Furthermore, some evaluations in the model might be over-simplified. There would be other possible impacts for each project not being considered; some of these could be significant. Such examples are increased malaria infection, health problem caused by reduced water quality, negative impacts on biodiversity in the area. Displaced people are further impoverished economically, and suffer from cultural decline, high rates of sickness, malnutrition, deaths, and great psychological stress in nearly every case[7]. Some of the dam sites, such as Bakun dam, are a home of many unique species of fauna and flora, which may disappear due to the project's impact. The Bakun dam site is located in dense forest; therefore the CO_2 release from the reservoir might also not be negligible. These impacts are omitted from the current analysis due to lack of data and the difficulty in quantifying them. Including every single impact is not possible, therefore the variables entered into the model are prioritized in each project assessment in this research. They could, however, be included in the future analysis, if relevant, with sufficient background information.

APPENDIX

A-I Model

The brief summary of the equations used in the model is as follows[8];

EG =	(proportion of time during which an alternative generation technology is unavailable)*(quantity of electricity)*(increased economic output due to increased electricity supply)
PG =	(quantity of electricity)*(price of electricity)
CP =	(proportion of time during which an alternative generation technology is available)*(benefit of avoiding air pollution due to reduced thermal power use)
IN =	economic value of lost land
AS =	valuation proxies for lost cultural resources
CC =	annual construction cost
FI =	annual lost profit from fishery due to the dam
LT =	annual lost tourism revenue with absence of the dam
OM =	annual operation & maintenance cost
RE =	annual resettlement cost
IF =	annual infrastructure relocation cost
AC =	(number of deaths/injuries during construction, O&M, and under special circumstances)*(economic valuation of death/injury) + (annual economic damage cost of dam collapsing)
NPVt =	$(1 + \text{discount rate})^{-t}$*(EGt+PGt+CPt-INt-ASt-CCt-FIt-LTt-OMt-REt-IFt-ACt)

[7] http://www.caa.org.au/campaigns/adb/fact_sheets/dams.html

[8] The complete set of equations are presented in details in Morimoto (2004a, 2004b).

A-II Data

Table A-1. Parameters and descriptions for Bakun [BHP] ($1= 3.8 Ringgit Central Bank of Malaysia 2002)

(min, most likely, max)	Description of each value
GC (0.5, 0.7, 2.4)	Original plan is 2.4GW, but might be scaled down to 0.5-0.7GW (www.earthisland.org).
EO (380, 760, 1500)	In China, each kWh of power shortage results in a loss of economic output of $0.38-1.5 (MOF 1990)
TCC (0.7, 0.8, 32)	The planned figure is $4 billion (www.idsnet.org). If we consider the possibility of GC being scaled down as above, the min and most likely should be reduced to $0.083 and 0.1 billion. Since the BHP is financially highly uncertain project, set the worst case like the latest India's Narmada dam cost estimate being more than 8 times of the original figure for all the min, most likely and max (McCully 1996).
φ (0.01, 0.04, 0.05)	The planned installed capacity in Malaysia will grow at 11% per annum on average up to 2007, while power demand is expected to grow by 8-10%, or in reality the demand has registered an even slower growth of 6-7% (Shabat Alam Malaysia Press Release; www.surforever.com/sam/pressrelease/lipis.htm).
P0 (0.33, 0.5, 0.66)	Malaysia consumes 1/3 of electricity consumption in Singapore (www.mint.gov.my/policy/nuc_energy/metp95_asli.htm). Thus, they may need to increase their electricity supply by 2/3 to bring their economic development to the Singapore level. The min value is assumed to be ½ of this value, taking into account the possibility of electricity over-supply they have experienced before. The most likely is valued at ½, assuming equal possibility of over-supply and demand growth.
FP (0.005, 0.3, 0.6)	US Fish and Wildlife Service studies show Savage Rapids Dam in Oregon has destroyed at least $5 million/year in fisheries benefits (The Pacific Coast Federation of Fisherman's Associations 'From Fisherman's News May 1998). 'The National Marine Fisheries Service estimated the losses of Salmon fishery due to dams in the Colombia basin to be $6.5 billion in 1960-80 alone' (McCulley 1997). The max value is assuming twice as much as the most likely value. These are also used for SBHP.
Tc (12.5, 13.5, 17.5)	The min is the original plan (www.idsnet.org). The WCD Survey (2000) shows about 40% of the delayed projects shows 1-year delay, and 5% shows 5 years delay.
Peo (30, 50, 80)	These are min, average and max TNB tariff rates in 1999 (www.tnb.com.my/newtnb/custom/tr/et1.html).
α (0.1, 0.2, 0.5)	Generally, the distribution of CC skewed to the left due to large costs at an initial stage. These are also used for IHP.
β (0.6, 0.8, 0.9)	The distribution is likely to be skewed to the right, as the resettlement process often delays. These are used for IHP
a (0.001, 0.02, 0.03)	The average annual loss rate of active storage due to sedimentation in WCD Survey is 0.1% (WCD 2000). Some experts say the dam will not last for more than 50 years, i.e., 2% (www.earthisland.org). The max rate in WCD Survey is 3%. A relatively high rate is set in order to challenge project optimism

Table A-1. Continued

(min, most likely, max)	Description of each value
EL (0.6, 0.7, 0.9)	70000ha of affected rainforests including rich agricultural lands are valued based on the following studies. Projected economic value of the Peruvian Amazon if intact forest is sustainably harvested for fruits, latex, and timber is \$6820/ha/year with the 5% discount rate based on the annual yield in the region (Peters 1989). Constanza (1997) placed a value of \$1660/ha/year on the 'ecological services' provided by rainforests excluding any rewards from harvesting forests for food or raw materials[9]. The most likely and max are 20% and 50% higher, as there should be other benefits from the forest which are not valued.
f20 (-0.001, 0.001, 0.02)	The attempt by TNB to raise tariff was not successful in 2001, so assume very tiny deviations for the min and most likely. These are also used for the following periods (max will be reduced by 20% every period). The tariff rate was increased by 8% in 1997, i.e., 8%/4=2% (TNB Annual Report 2001).
σ (0.1, 0.5, 0.8)	For the min, assuming the peak of the distribution is at the beginning while completing fundamental work; for the most likely, in the middle period during complicated and large-scale work; for the max, at the end of the period. These are used for SBHP & IHP
TRE (0.08, 0.16, 0.32)	The planned figure is 0.08 (www.earthisland.org). Assume the cost overrun of 2-4 times (McCully 1996).
C1 (660, 730, 880)	The most likely is calculated with the same procedure in Morimoto and Hope (2004b). The min and max are 10% lower and 20% higher than the most likely.
C2 (13, 14, 17)	Ibid.
CM1 (14.5,15.7, 19.3)	The same values in Morimoto and Hope (2004b). These are also used for IHP.
CM2 (414, 60, 552)	Ibid.
OMC (20, 28, 39)	The min is the calculated value by Battelle (1998 Table 5.11). Cost overrun of 40% is assumed (WCD 2000).
VD (0.4, 0.8, 6.7)	The same values in Morimoto and Hope (2004b). These are also used in SBHP and IHP.
VM (0.0001, 0.0004, 0.04)	Ibid.
DCR (0.3, 0.8, 1.9)	Ibid.
MCR (170, 310, 340)	Ibid.
DCR' (0.32, 0.57, 0.63)	Ibid.
MCR' (7, 12, 13)	Ibid.
DCR'' (6750, 12150, 13500)	Same in Morimoto and Hope (2004b). These are also used in IHP, but excluded for SBHP, as the scale is small.
MCR'' (34750, 62550, 69500)	Ibid.
ECL (2, 3.6, 5.1)	See Morimoto and Hope (2004a). Cost overrun of 40% is assumed for max (WCD 2000). These are used also for IHP.
π (0.06, 0.2, 0.6)	The min and the most likely are 1/10 & 1/3 of the max. The removal of the Marmot and Little Sandy dams which generate 22 MW is estimated to be \$22 million. Based on this, the Bakun needs 2.4 GW / (mean TCC = 4) = 0.6.

[9] The 'ecosystem' refers to climate/disturbance/water regulations, water suplí, erosion control, soil formation, nutrient cycling, waster treatment, genetic resources, recreation and cultural services. His estimation is based on past studies and a few original calculations (mostly, willingnesss to pay of individuals for ecosystem services).

(min, most likely, max)	Description of each value
TDC (50, 75, 100)	The expected life of a dam is 50 years. About 5000 large dams in the world are now more than 50 years old (McCully 1997; Wade 1999). Assume 50% more than the min for the most likely. The max is the final year of the analysis.
$P = 10^{-4}$; $P' = 10^{-5}$; $P'' = 10^{-5}$	The same values in Morimoto and Hope (2004b). These are also used for IHP.

Note: PERT distribution (a special form of Beta distribution) is used for all the parameters apart from EO, f20, DCR, MCR, DCR', MCR', DCR'', MCR'' for which Triangular distribution is used instead. The same distributions are used for SBHP and IHP.

Table A-2. Parameters and descriptions for Sharada-Babai [SBHP] ($1=NRS76 Central Bank of Nepal 2002)

(min, most likely, max)	Description
EO (110, 280, 1300)	The min and the most likely are estimated losses to the Sri Lankan economy for energy not served in 1990 prices & 1998 prices respectively (CEB 1994). The max is a loss of economic output per kWh of power shortages in China (MOF 1990).
P0 (0.1, 0.75, 0.9)	The min and max are same as the ones in Morimoto and Hope (2004a). About ¾ of the yearly precipitation in the subcontinent of South Asia falls within just 3 months (Lincoln 1989).
GC (0.06, 0.08, 0.093)	The energy output of Victoria Dam in Sri Lanka is about 31% lower than the planned figure (WCD 2000). The WCD Survey shows that the most likely case is 10% below the target (WCD 2000). The max is the current planned installed capacity (WRC and SILT 2001).
Tc (5, 6, 10)	The original plan is 5 years (WRC and SILT 2001). According to the WCD Survey, about 40% of delayed projects show a 1-year delay; 5% shows 5-year delay (WCD 2000).
f20 (-0.013, 0.01 0.026)	The electricity price is increased by 1% in 1999-2001 (NEA 2000)[10] The same values in Morimoto and Hope (2004a) for the min and max[11].
φ (0.077, 0.08, 0.09)	The number of electricity consumers increased by 0.09% (1998), 0.08% (1999), and 0.077% (2000) annually (WRC and SILT 2001).
PEo (69, 77, 92)	Average electricity price in 2000 is 5850 NRs (NEA 2000). Assume 10% lower than the most likely value for the min and 20% higher than the most likely for the max.
TCC (0.13, 0.17, 0.18)	The min is the planned figure (WRS). 70 hydropower projects commissioned in 1915-1986 financed by the World Bank show average cost overruns of 30% (Bacon and Besant-Jones 1998). Average cost overruns excluding extreme cases are 40% (WCD 2000).
α (0.2, 0.7, 0.8)	The peak is likely to be at the end of the construction period. See Morimoto & Hope (2004a).
β (0.2, 0.3, 0.5)	The peak is more likely to come near the beginning of the construction period. See Morimoto and Hope (2004a).
BD (0.01, 0.018, 0.019)	The min is the damage caused by particulates CO_2 (CEB 1994). The most likely is the total damage caused by air pollution (SO_2, NOx, particulates, & CO_2) emitted by diesel (CEB 1994). The max is 10% higher than most likely.

[10] See also www.nea.org.np/tariffrate.htm.

[11] The same minimum and maximum values are used for every period. The most likely value is assumed to decrease by 20% every period.

Table A-2. Continued

(min, most likely, max)	Description
IN (0.004, 0.005, 0.006)	The min is the estimated losses (WRC and SILT 2001)[12]. The same cost overrun rates as for TCC, 30% & 40%.
IF (0.0008, 0.0011, 0.0012)	The min value is the estimated cost (WRC and SILT 2001)[13]. The same cost overrun rates as for TCC, 30% & 40%.
TRE (0.0026, 0.0036, 0.0039)	The min is the planned figure (WRC and SILT 2001). The actual number of resettled people is 35% higher than the estimated figure according to the WCD Survey (WCD 2000). The actual number is 47% higher than the estimated figure among the projects financed by the World Bank (World Bank 1996).
OMC (0.0018, 0.0023, 0.0026)	The min is the planned figure (WRC). The same cost overrun rate as for TCC are used, 30% & 40%.
a (0.0005, 0.001, 0.002)	The most likely is same as the min for BHP. This issue involves huge uncertainty. Assume the min and max are ½ and twice of the most likely.
π (0.07, 0.23, 0.7)	The max is calculated in the same manner as in Morimoto and Hope (2004a). The min and the most likely values value are 1/10 and 1/3 of the max value respectively. The removal of the Marmot and Little Sandy dams which generate 22 MW is estimated to be $22 million. Based on this figure, the SBHP needs 0.093GW / (TCC = 0.13)
TDC (50, 75, 100)	Same as in Morimoto and Hope (2004a)

Table A-3. Parameters in the CBA model and descriptions for Ilisu [IHP] ($1= 1360000 TL Central Bank of Turkey 2002)

(min, most likely, max)	Description of each value
EO (380, 760, 1500)	Same as BHP above.
NT '0000 (13, 28, 103)	About 30,000 pilgrims visit Hasankeyf annually (www.khrp.org/publish/p1999/ilisuReport.htm). 1 million tourists are predicted to visit GAP region in 2005 (www.international.icomos.org/risk/turkey_2000.htm), and assume of which 10% and 25% for min and max.
TCC (1.52, 6.08, 9.12)	The original plan (http://www.rivernet.org/turquie/ilisu.htm); assumption of cost overrun of 4 & 6 times (2-4 times China TGP; 6 times Brazil Itaipu; McCully 1996).
GC (0.8, 1.1, 1.2)	The energy output of Victoria Dam in Sri Lanka is about 31% lower than the planned figure (WCD 2000 Report). The WCD Survey shows that the most likely case is 10% below the target. The max is the current planned installed capacity
φ (0.012, 0.026, 0.029)	The annual rates of decrease in the proportion of hydro and renewable planned installed capacity out of total capacity in Turkey are 0.012 (1997-2010), 0.026 (2010-2020), and 0.029 (2010-2020) (http://www.dolph.com.tr/energy.htm). The max is triple of the min.

[12] Land acquisition [Agricultural land (268ha) and Forest land (33ha)] = 0.311 GNRs

[13] 2 suspension bridges = 5,000,000Rs; 2 temples = 40,000 Rs; 1 school = 1,400,000 Rs; 5 roads = 50,000,000 Rs; 5 foot trails = 500,000 Rs; 6 irrigation schemes = 6,000,000 Rs; 1 health post = 100,000 Rs; 1 post office = 80,000 Rs; 1 police office = 1,300,000 Rs; 3 water mills = 150,000 Rs; 1 telephone office = 50,000 Rs.

(min, most likely, max)	Description of each value
P0 (0.52, 0.7, 0.75)	The domestic energy production can only meet 48% of the requirements (www.parliament.the-stationery-office.co.uk/pa/cm200001/cmselect/cmtrdind/360/36008.htm). The potential of hydropower in Turkey is presently < 30% developed (IEG 2001). The IHP is a peak power plant, so assume 75%.
FP (0.0025, 0.005, 0.3)	The most likely is same as the min for BHP above. The min is ½ of the most likely as fishery in this area is mainly for locals. The National Marine Fisheries Service estimated the losses of Salmon fishery due to dams in the Colombia basin to be $6.5 billion during 1960-80 alone' (McCulley 1997).
a (0.001, 0.02, 0.033)	The min is same as the min for IHP above. Experts foresee 30-50 years of functional life for the dam due to the high possibility of the dam being filled with rubble.
AL (0.5, 0.55, 0.75)	A four-foot bronze candelabrum dating to the Han Dynasty was sold for $2.5 million at the International Asian Art Fair in New York (www.archaeology.org/online/news/china.html). At least 200 or even some hundreds more sites would be inundated by Ilisu Dam (CHR et al 2001). The exact number of antiquities in the sites is unknown. Assume 10% (most likely) and 50% (max) as many antiquities exist in the area.
EL (0.008, 0.013, 0.016)	CEB (1994) estimated the value of land at 26-764 $/ha/year. Thus, assume the followings. The dam will submerge 7353ha of good agricultural land ($764/ha/yr), 4820ha of medium-low quality land ($500/ha/yr), 15675ha of land not suitable for growing crops ($26/ha/yr). The most likely and max are assumed to be 50% and 100% higher than the min.
ε (0.8, 0.9, 1)	Since Hasankeyf is the main attraction of both tourists and pilgrims, assume very high reduction rate of visitors.
RS (560, 620, 680)	The 1999 tourism recipient in Turkey is 620 (http://www.gso.org.tr/turkey.htm). 10% lower and higher for min and max.
Tc (7.5, 8.5, 12.5)	The min is the original plan (IEG 2001). The WCD Survey (2000) shows about 40% of the delayed projects shows 1-year delay; 5% shows 5 years delay.
PEo (72, 80, 88)	The most likely figure is the tariff rate effective from March 2002 (www.tedas.gov.tr). The min and max are 10% higher and lower than the tariff.
f20 (0, 0.001, 0.02)	An average rate of change in electricity tariff in Turkey is 0.02 from Oct to Nov 2001(Turkish electricity Distribution Corporation). The min and most likely assume small negative and no deviations in tariff rates.
TRE (0.57, 1.14, 2.28)	The planned figure is 0.57 (http://www.dsi.gov.tr/ilisu1.htm). Assume 2 & 4 times cost overrun (McCully 1996).
C1 (700, 780, 940)	The most likely is calculated in the same manner as in Morimoto and Hope (2004b). The min and max are 10% lower and 20% higher than the most likely.
C2 (18, 20, 24)	Ibid.
OMC (20, 28, 39)	The min is the calculated value by Battelle (1998 Table 5.11). 40% cost overrun is assumed (WCD 2000).
π (0.079, 0.26, 0.79)	The removal of the Marmot and Little Sandy dams which generate 22 MW is estimated to be $22 million. Based on this figure, the IHP needs 1.2 GW / (TCC = 1.52). The min & the most likely are 1/10 & 1/3 of the max value respectively.
TDC (30, 50, 100)	The expected life of a dam is 30-50 years. The max value is the final year of the analysis.

Acknowledgement

Useful comments and feedback from Dr Chris Hope (University of Cambridge) are greatly acknowledged. We would like to thank Dr Yusof Ahmad, Mr Ir Nordin Bin Ismali, and Mr Mohd Zekri Yaakob from Malaysia TNB Hydro for their support towards our data collection and the field visits in Malaysia in December 2001. Many thanks also go to Mr Arjun Aryal (University of Hawaii, US) and Mr Bhupendra Aryal from WRC (Water Resource Consultant, Nepal) who provided us with useful data, information, and the project report on the Sharada-Babai project, and for their great help during the field visit in Oct 2001. Finally, financial supports from the World Bank and the University of Cambridge which enabled us to pursue this project are well noted.

References

ADB: Asian Development Bank (2004) *Technical Assistant Report for Nepal*, Manila.

Battelle (1998) *China's Electric Power options: An analysis of economic and environmental costs*, Battelle Memorial Institute.

Bhattacharyya, S, S, (2007), 'CHEP-1 Khairi: Looking beyond the horizon of hydro electricity & profits, giving new meanings to life, The Journal of Business Perspective, 11(1), Jan-March.

Carman. J, Garnegie. GD, and Wolnizer. PW (1999) 'Is archeological valuation an accounting matter?' *Antiquity* 73 143-8.

Carver. M (1996) 'On archaeological value' *Antiquity* 70 45-56CTGPC (1995) *Environmental Impact Statement for the Yangtze Three Gorges Project* (A Brief Edition) Science Press.

CEB (1994), Environmental Impact Assessment for the Upper Kotmale Hydro Project Lincoln.K 'Subcontinent: The Wasted Waters; Himalayan Plunder; Resources and Rights; Buyer's.

Constanza.R et al (1997), 'The value of the World's ecosystem services and natural capital', *Nature*, 387, 253-260.

Corner House Research (CHR), et al (2001) *Cultural Heritage: review of the EIA Report for the Ilisu Dam and HEPP*, September.

Dervil. T, Saunders, A, and Startin, B (1987) 'A question of national importance: approaches to the evaluation of ancient monuments for the monuments protection programme in England' *Antiquity* 61 393-408.

Dixon, J.A. Scura, LF. Carpenter, RA. and Sherman, PB. (1994), 2nd ed, *Economic Analysis of Environmental Impacts*, The Asian Development Bank and the World Bank, London.

IEG: Ilisu Engineering Group (2001) *Ilisu Dam and HEPP Environmental Impact Assessment Report* April.

Lincoln.K (1989) 'Subcontinent: The Wasted Waters; Himalayan Plunder; Resources and Rights; Buyer's Market', *Far Eastern Economic Review*, Feb 2.

Lipe,WD (1984) 'Value and meaning in cultural resources' in Cleere. HF (1984) (ed.) Approaches to the Archaeological Heritages, Cambridge University Press 1-11.

Mahapatra.R (2001), 'Power the people', *Appropriate Technology*, Jan-Mar.

McCully, P (1996), *Silenced Rivers: The ecology and politics of large dams*, Zed Books: London & New Jersey.
McCulley, P (1997) 'Taking Down Bad Dams' *World Rivers Review* 12 (4) August.
MOF (1990), *Energy in China*, Ministry of Energy Press, Beijing.
Morimoto R and Hope C (2004a) 'The CBA model for the Three Gorges Project in China', *Impact Assessment and Project Appraisal Journal*, 22(3), 205-220.
Morimoto R and Hope C (2004b) 'An extended CBA model of hydro projects in Sri Lanka', *International journal of global energy issues: special issue on energy and renewable energy with economic development in developing countries*, 21 (1/2), 47-64.
Morimoto R and Hope C (2005) 'Making the case for developing a silent aircraft' *Transport Policy* 12 (2) 165-174.
Morimoto R, Hope Ash, J and Hope C (2005) 'Corporate Social Responsibility: from theory to practice' *Journal of Business Ethics* 62 (4) December 315-325.
Nakayama, M (1998) 'Post-project review EIA for Saguling Dam for voluntary Resettlement' *Water Resources Development*, 14 (2), 217-229.
NEA (2000) *NEA Financial Year 1999/2000: A year in Review*, August.
Pokharel.S (2001) 'Hydropower for Energy in Nepal', *Mountain research and Development*, 21 (1).
Peters.C.M, Gentry.A.H, and Mendelsohn.R.O (1989), 'Valueation of an Amazonian Rainforest', *Nature*, 339, 655-656.
Schaafsma. CF (1989) 'Significant unit proven otherwise: problems versus representative samples' in Cleere (1984).
Scholtz, B (2002) 'Role of dams in irrigation, drainage and flood control' *Water Resources Development*, 18(1), 147-162.
TNB (2001), *Kenyir Hydroelectric Power Plant Project II – preliminary works, Progress Report 10*, February.
Wade, B (1999) 'Brining down the dams' *The Ameican City & County*, Pittsfield, June.
WCD (2000), *Dams and Development: A new framework for decision-making*, Earthscan, London and Sterling.
World Bank (1996) 'Resettlement and Development: The Bankwide Review of projects involving involuntary resettlement 1986-1993' *Environment Department paper* 32 The World Bank, Washington DC.
WRC and SILT (2001) *Environmental Impact Assessment Study Final Report.*

In: Corporate Social Responsibility
Editor: Adam R. Timpere
ISBN: 978-1-60456-284-2

Chapter 9

THE DIVULGATION OF INFORMATION ON CORPORATE SOCIAL RESPONSIBILITY VIEWED THROUGH THE THEORY OF POLITICAL COSTS

García Sánchez*[†]*, Isabel María, Gallego Álvarez*[*]*,
***Isabel and Prado Lorenzo and José Manuel*[‡]**
Universidad de Salamanca, School of Economics and Business, Campus Miguel de Unamuno, Edificio FES, 37007 Salamanca

ABSTRACT

The Theory of Political Costs affirms that the information which a company provides is used to draft the regulations affecting them; as a consequence the executives of that company will attempt to choose the disclosure policies which most contribute to eliminating political interference and to producing a decrease in costs such as taxes, fees and regulated charges, as well as others. This paper is an attempt to determine whether the reduction in costs is one of the goals pursued by companies when divulging information on Corporate Social Responsibility.

This information, established as a dependent variable, has been subjected to multivariate analysis, using a dependence model based on the estimation of a linear regression by ordinary least squares.

The independent variable was the measure of industrial concentration because the greater the monopolistic power of a firm, the greater the public scrutiny it is subjected to. Thus, in order to avoid or reduce political costs, companies would reveal more information with a view to showing their behavior to the State and to society at large.

Confirming the cases defended by the Theory of Political Costs, the results found indicate that companies with clearer monopolistic positions reveal a greater volume of unregulated information on Corporate Social Responsibility.

[†] lajefa@usal.es
[*] igallego@usal.es; Phone: 923-294400
[‡] jmprado@usal.es

1. Introduction

The increase in the public's sensitivity towards certain social and environmental problems is forcing companies to behave properly and include their activities in these fields within their annual reports, which have traditionally revealed only economic and financial information.

As part of this *social legitimation* process, the drafting and divulgation of a social responsibility report is a vital component in terms of the community's perceptions of its executives' level of responsibility (i.e. Patten, 1992; Gray et al. 1995; Deegan and Rankin, 1996). Nevertheless, as Lindblom (1994) points out, the process may pursue socially disparate and ethically reproachable objectives such as manipulating the perceptions of certain stakeholders.

At the same time, if, in accordance with the Theory of Political Costs, the information which the company provides is used to draft the regulations affecting them, executives will attempt to choose the revelation policies which most contribute to eliminating political interference and to producing a decrease in costs such as taxes, fees and regulated charges, as well as others (Leventis and Weetman, 2000). Empirically, severally studies, i.e., Deegan and Carroll (1993) and Rodríguez (2004), have made it clear that there is a positive relationship between a monopolistic position and the existence of information divulgation practices oriented towards reducing political costs.

This study is an attempt to determine, considering social demands and political costs, whether the reduction of the latter is one of the goals pursued by companies when divulging information on Corporate Social Responsibility.

In order to perform the analysis, criteria were followed which are similar to those used in prior studies (i.e. Guthrie and Parker, 1990; Hackston and Milne, 1996), with the selection of the largest 117 non-financial Spanish companies that are traded on the stock market, entities which commonly include information on Corporate Social Responsibility.

The reports were obtained through the companies' websites, and we have assessed their contents in accordance with three criteria: (i) their match with the Global Reporting Initiative model; (ii) auditing of the information by an independent professional; and (iii) access to the reports from the last three years. Likewise, the information divulged was analyzed in terms of the degree to which the social and environmental standards allowing the company to possess the ISO14001, ISO9001, OHSAS and AENOR (accreditation of product safety) certifications are adhered to.

The information has been subjected to multivariate analysis, using a dependence model based on the estimation of a linear regression by ordinary least squares, establishing as a dependent variable the rate of divulgation of information on corporate social responsibility – produced by assigning values on the basis of whether the aforementioned items are adhered to– and as an independent variable the measure of industrial concentration, which is defined as the Herfindahl Index for the industry in which each of the companies studied does business. Moreover, four business characteristics were included as control variables: size, profitability, sector of activity and trading on other stock markets.

Confirming the cases defended by the Theory of Political Costs, the results found indicate that companies with clearer monopolistic positions reveal a greater volume of unregulated information on Corporate Social Responsibility. The goal of these practices of divulgation is to reduce potential political costs entailed by any increase in regulation (such as laws aimed at equal hiring by gender, reconciling work and family life, etc.), as well as any increase in taxes or fees resulting from socially unacceptable behavior.

2. Corporate Social Responsibility

In recent years, the protection of the environment and other social issues has been a continuing object of concern for all kinds of individuals, companies, organizations and governments.

Both the social and the environmental aspects directly affect the concept of sustainable development, defined by the World Commission on Environment and Development (the Brundtland Commission) in 1987 as the kind of development that meets "the needs of the present without compromising the ability of future generations to meet their own needs".

In the business field, the growing concern with encouraging behavior oriented to sustainable development comes under the rubric of Corporate Social Responsibility. The importance of such behavior is due to the fact that "the private sector is the dominant engine of growth – the principle creator of value and managerial resources – and [] it has an obligation to contribute to economic growth and opportunity – equitable and sustainable -. CSR is therefore founded on a stronger recognition of the role of business as an active partner in a world of scarcity and dwindling resources" (Jamali and Mirshak, 2007, p. 244).

According to Moon (2007, p. 298), the definitions of Corporate Social Responsibility vary, not simply by virtue of its essentially contested status but also as a reflection of the different practical orientations of corporations towards their responsibilities: (i) it has been associated with different *underlying strategic purposes* (e.g. legitimacy, responsibility for externality, competitive advantage); (ii) it varies according to its *substantive content* (e.g. economic, legal, ethical, discretionary – Carroll, 1991); and it can vary according to the *approach* deployed to identify responsibilities and evaluate practices, specifically to which stakeholders the policies are oriented (Clarkson, 1995) or around which ethical principles or values they have been developed.

In general, the concept of Corporate Social Responsibility refers to the set of legal and ethical obligations and commitments, both national and international, deriving from the impact that the activity of organizations has on the social, labor, environmental, and human rights areas.

Its consideration entails an extension of the goals pursued by companies, completing the traditional objective of maximizing profits with the consideration of the interests of any individual or group that affects or is affected by the actions of the organization (Fleege and Adrian, 2004).

The origins of Corporate Social Responsibility are usually linked to one country, the United States, and one era, the end of the 1950s and beginning of the 60s. Within the framework of this time and place there was a rapid rise in public awareness relating to whether certain political regimes were maintained or certain ethically censurable economic practices were condoned either through the work of specific companies or through the purchase of certain products.

As a consequence, society began to call for changes in the behavior of companies and a greater involvement of business in solving social and environmental problems.

In Spain, Corporate Social Rresponsibility came into being at the end of the 1990s. At that time, the Association of Institutions of Collective Investments and Pension Funds (Asociación de Instituciones de Inversión Colectiva y Fondos de Pensiones - INVERCO) introduced the concept of Responsible Social Investment in order to foster responsible savings among investors.

Currently, there are more and more Spanish companies which believe that they should contribute to sustainable development by planning their operations with a view to favoring their economic growth and increasing their productivity and competitiveness at the same time that they guarantee the protection of the environment and foster social responsibility, thus complying with general interests.

Nevertheless, it must be pointed out that the internationalization of Spanish firms had a great impact on this process, both because of the demands imposed on them by the countries they were operating in and because of the concern of Spanish society with respect to the behavior of Spanish firms outside Spain's borders. In short, it can be said that interest groups have applied suitable pressure, favoring the gradual transformation of the values and objectives of the Spanish business sector.

Moreover, efforts have also been made on the part of different organizations and institutions, which have carried out a variety of initiatives that promote and foster the socially responsible behavior of companies.

Generally, these initiatives or projects contain a series of norms or recommendations to be observed on a voluntary basis and which incorporate a commitment on the part of the States adhering to them to foster their application by businesses in their respective countries.

These projects, in short, attempt to set out uniform principles, actions and indicators of Corporate Social Responsibility that will allow us to rate the corporate contribution both in the geographical area closest to the company and internationally.

In the sphere of Corporate Social Responsibility the most outstanding international initiatives are the following:

- The World Pact of the UN aimed at promoting the reconciliation of business interests with social values and demand.
- The Organization for Economic Cooperation and Development (OECD) guidelines for multinational firms included in the "Declaration on International Investment and Multinational Enterprises" aimed at promoting responsible action on the part of these firms in the communities in which they operate.
- Guides for the drawing up of Sustainability Reports issued by the Global Reporting Initiative. This organization was created in 1997 by the non-governmental organization CERES (Coalition for Environmentally Responsible Economies) in conjunction with the United Nations Environment Programme (UNEP), with the support of many private institutions, businesses, trade unions, NGOs and other organizations in order to foster quality, precision and usefulness in reports on Corporate Social Responsibility.

At the regional level, we must point out the publication of the Green Book by the European Union, which establishes a common framework for member States with respect to CSR. It fosters the development of social responsibility in European firms by means of an increase in the transparency and quality of corporate information and their contribution to sustainable development.

3. Corporate Social Responsibility Report

Within this new corporate behavior there is a stage or process of legitimization of the company based on the communication of their activity to the outside by drawing up and divulging a corporate social report, by which they hope to strengthen the perceptions and expectations of the community with respect to the responsibility of the firm and its executives (e.g.. Patten, 1992; Gray et al. 1995; Deegan and Rankin, 1996). In short, we are talking about a strategy aimed at showing society how suitable the behavior of an organization is.

According to the Global Reporting Initiative (GRI), the report on corporate social responsibility or triple bottom line entails a description of the economic, environmental and social performance of organizations.

Longitudinal studies on the divulgation of corporate social information point to an increase over time of both the number of companies doing so and the information contents they report on (Deegan and Gordon, 1996).

Initially, this report provided almost anecdotal information (Hogner, 1982; Guthrie and Parker, 1989), closely linked to the political structure of society, as well as to occasional environmental or social crises that occurred (Hopwood, 1987; Loft, 1988). Subsequently and especially over the last two decades, informative practices regarding environmental and social information have increased in volume and complexity (Gray et al., 2001), and have gone from being mere national initiatives, extensions of annual accounting reports, to become an authentic model of international corporate social information.

Generally, the contents and quality of these reports is linked to the different business characteristics. Specifically, these characteristics differ according to activity sector (i.e., Cowen et al, 1987; Patten, 1991; Roberts, 1992; Hackston and Milne, 1996; Deegan and Gordon, 1996), and improve as the size of the firm grows (i.e., Trotman and Bradley, 1981; Cowen et al, 1987; Patten, 1991; Hackston and Milne, 1996; Adams et al., 1998). On the other hand, a clear relationship has not been detected between the contents of the report and profitability, since although Bowman (1978) and Roberts (1992) show evidence of a strong positive relation, Cowen et al. (1987) and Patten (1991) found that this relationship was not significant.

Likewise, it has been observed that certain general contextual factors, mainly the country of origin (i.e. Lynn, 1992; Niskala and Pretes, 1995; Adams and Kuasirikun, 2000) and the cultural, social, political and economic context (i.e., Guthrie and Parker, 1989; Hogner, 1982; Burchell et al, 1985; Adams and Harte, 1998), are the source of differences between the different informative practices analyzed.

According to Lindblom (1994), this could be because this process of legitimization may be pursuing socially disparate goals such as: reporting on changes in business operations and performance; modifying the perceptions of the main stakeholders and even manipulating the perceptions of those stakeholders, distracting their attention from critical points to other more positive aspects of the firm; and changing the external expectations about its behavior and performance.

In this sense the Theory of Political Costs affirms that the companies most sensitive to regulation, nationalization, expropriation, etc., will be more inclined to reveal information in order to reduce those costs. Thus, according to this paradigm, firms would disclose more environmental and social information in order to reduce or avoid regulations or norms that would impose restrictions on their behavior.

4. The Theory of Political Costs: Research Hypothesis

Along with numerous other rationales (e.g., decision usefulness, legitimacy theory, stakeholder theory, critical or political economy theory—see Gray et al., 1995 for a review), positive accounting theory or the political cost hypothesis has been suggested to explain why firms make voluntary social disclosures. Based on the original work of Watts and Zimmerman (1978, 1986), several empirical studies (e.g., Belkaoui and Karpik, 1989; Ness and Mirza, 1991; Panchapakesan and McKinnon, 1992; Lemon and Cahan, 1997) have directly sought to establish evidence for the political cost hypothesis as an explanation for firms' social disclosures. Several related empirical studies have also sought to use the political cost hypothesis to explain other types of voluntary disclosure, including value added statements (Deegan and Hallam, 1991), disclosures by statutory authorities (Lim and McKinnon, 1993), and disclosures in pursuit of reporting excellence awards (Deegan and Carroll, 1993).

The Theory of Political Costs starts from the supposition that politicians need funds to perform their actions, actions which in turn allow them to increase their power of influence at the same time favoring their re-election. These funds are obtained through regulations that mainly affect business enterprises, since regulation operates as a medium for transferring wealth from companies to society.

In this political process, the information or data issued by companies are used to justify and draft regulations that affect these same companies (Giner, 1997) and can turn into political costs –taxes, price intervention, quality norms, monopoly regulation, etc.-, and political advantages – grants, subsidies, etc.

To eliminate the potential interference of institutions, company executives will select information disclosure policies that will lead to a reduction in political costs (Leventis and Weetman, 2000) or foster advantages such as receiving government grants; they may even exert pressure on the government to act in their favor (Giner, 1997).

Based on the theoretical reasoning of the Theory of Political Costs that the voluntary disclosure of information would be aimed at reducing those costs by minimizing transfers of wealth from the firm to governments (Leventis and Weetman, 2000), we established the followed alternative hypothesis:

H_1: The voluntary disclosure of corporate social information is aimed at minimizing the political costs borne by the firm.

5. Methodology

5.1. Population and Sample

The population that formed the object of study was comprised of 117 non-financial Spanish firms quoted on the Spanish stock exchange in 2005. It was selected taking into account the criteria of size and quotation on the stock market used in previous studies (e.g. Guthrie and Parker, 1990; Hackston and Milne, 1996).

Subsequently, we obtained the companies' reports on corporate social responsibility through their web pages, as well as information relating to how well they have complied with certain social and environmental requirements that have led to their having certifications such as ISO14001, ISO9001, OHSAS and AENOR.

The analysis of how businesses disclose information through their web pages is a consequence both of the importance that the Internet has acquired internationally as a channel of information and the legal obligations that demand the online publication of certain information for investors and shareholders. In the case of Spain this is specified in Circular 1/2004 of the Comisión Nacional del Mercado de Valores (Spain´s equivalent to the SEC).

5.2. Variables

Dependent Variable: Practices in Corporate Social Responsibility (PCSR)

In practically all of the previous studies on the topic the dependent variable is usually built using the content analysis of corporate social responsibility reports. This method consists of defining various items related with general lines defined in the preceding bibliography.

The disclosure of information on each item is usually expressed numerically, measured by means of different units of analysis, such as the number of pages, the number of sentences (Hackston and Milne, 1996), or the number of words (Neu et al., 1998). Recently, indices have been created that assign a score of 1 if the firm reports on said item, and zero otherwise. On occasion this measurement can be improved by using a score of 1 to 3 to refer to the characteristics of the information, i.e. whether it is qualitative, quantitative or monetary.

The process of synthesizing the efforts of firm disclosure is characterized by highly objective metrics; nevertheless, the rating of the items entails the subjectivity of the person who has drawn up the information. That is, if those in charge of the firm decided not to disclose bad news regarding business behavior, or to use more favorable expressions[1] even though they are not the most accurate ones, it would not be penalized.

In order to overcome these limitations, in the present study we decided to classify CSR reports according to whether the information they provide is in line with the format and contents of the most widespread international model, the Global Reporting Initiative (GRI).

---

[1] Adams (2002) points out how some business executives have doubts about whether or not it is a good idea to publish in their reports negative data that could damage the firm's reputation.

Table 1. Items on *Corporate Social Resonsibility*

1	Report on Corporate Social Responsibility	2 points if complete (economic, social and environmental information) 1 point if the information is only environmental or social
2	Report on the three previous fiscal years	1 point
3	Follows GRI format	1 point
4	RSC information has been audited	1 point
5	Accreditation of environmental behavior (ISO 14001)	1 point
6	Accreditation of behavior regarding human resources (OHSAS)	1 point
7	Quality accreditation (ISO 9001)	1 point
8	Product safety accreditation (AENOR)	1 point

This model was selected because it obliges firms to report on all aspects of the firm – economic, social and environmental- even if this entails the inclusion of negative data or non-optimal situations of the firm. Furthermore, certain information must be expressed in numerical and monetary terms in order to facilitate comparisons. Finally, it is a harmonized report, understandable for all firms regardless of their country of origin. For this reason business is highly interested in having CSR reports standardized in accordance with the GRI format (Adams, 2002).

Furthermore, the GRI also takes into account whether the information has been audited by an independent professional and whether historical data on CSR are available on the web pages.

As pointed out earlier, we also considered it important to analyze another typology of information disclosed, this time relating to the degree to which the social and environmental behavior of the company has fulfilled the requirements of the ISO14001, ISO9001, OHSAS and AENOR certifications.

Thus, the dependent variable PCSR will be a numerical variable that takes values between 0 and 8, depending on the sum of the scores assigned to the disclosure of information collected in the items commented on above and which appear in Table 1.

Independent Variable

Subsequent to Watts and Zimmerman (1978), empirical studies have tended to use or suggest a wider range of measures to proxy for political costs. These include: profits, rates of return, risk, capital intensity, industry concentration, industry membership, effective tax rates, number of employees, number of shareholders, labor intensity, press coverage, and even social responsibility disclosures themselves. In some cases, the metrics involve alternative measures of *firm size* (e.g. number of employees). In other cases, however, they represent attempts to find alternative measures of *political visibility or political cost* (e.g., capital intensity).

But it can be said that *industry concentration* is the variable most employed empirically to demonstrate whether a firm's interest in reducing political costs determines the practices of voluntary disclosure of information.

Its use can be justified in that the greater the monopolistic power of a firm, the greater the public scrutiny it will be subject to. In order to reduce or avoid political costs related to taxation and controls such as the issuing of regulations that would penalize them, companies will reveal more information in order to show society and the State their position in the market and their conduct.

Deegan and Hallam (1991), Deegan and Carroll (1993) and Rodríguez (2004), when analyzing market concentration and the presentation of different voluntary information –state of added value, excellence prizes, information on intangibles- confirm the hypothesis that there is a positive relationship between seeking a reduction in political costs and information disclosure practices.

Thus, the effect that market concentration has on online corporate social information disclosure practice is tested using a variable representing the degree of industry concentration which a firm faces. This is measured as the Herfindahl Index. The Herfindahl Index for firm i was established as:

$$H_i = \Sigma (R_{ij} / R_j)^2 \text{ con } i = 1 \ldots n_j$$

where R_{ij} is the income obtained by firm i in industry j (following the industry classification of the CNMV, Spain's equivalent to the SEC), n_j is the number of firms in industry j and R_j is the sum of the incomes of all the firms in industry j.

Control Variables: Business Characteristics

As indicated in the preceding sections, different studies have shown the relationship between the volume of corporate social information disclosed and the business characteristics. We chose to introduce these characteristics as control variables, selecting three that clearly identify firms and have shown their importance in previous studies: SIZE, PROFITABILITY and SECTOR. They are described in Table 2.

Size was selected because previous studies (Trotman and Bradley, 1981; Belkaoui and Karpik, 1989; Patten, 1991; Deegan and Gordon, 1996; Hackston and Milne, 1996; Gray et al., 2001; Archel and Lizarraga, 2001; Archel, 2003 and Ochoa and Aranguren, 2005) have detected a direct positive relationship with firm size.

Business profitability has been repeatedly considered in analyses, even though the results obtained have been unequal (i.e. Cowen et al., 1987; Belkaoui and Karpik, 1989; Hackston and Milne, 1996).

Finally, the last of the variables, that of a firm's pertaining to certain activity sectors, has been identified as an explanatory factor in works such as those of Cowen et al. (1987), Freedman and Jaggi (1988), Roberts (1992), Adams et al. (1995 and 1998), Hackston and Milne (1996) and Deegan and Gordon (1996).

We additionally considered the variable OTHER STOCK MARKETS, which represents the international quotation of the firm and reflects the fact that companies may have to adhere to rules and regulations pertaining to this kind of information or adopt good practice and respond to the pressures of various interest groups (Haniffa and Cooke, 2005).

Table 2. Control Variables

Size	Numerical variable represented by means of the firm's market capitalization
Profitability	Numerical variable representing the return on assets
Services sector	Dummy, takes a value of 1 if the firm's activity pertains to the services sector and 0 otherwise
Transpsector	Dummy, takes a value of 1 if the firm's activity pertains to the transport and communications sector and 0 otherwise
Indussector	Dummy, takes a value of 1 if the firm's activity pertains to the industrial sectors and 0 otherwise
Enersector	Dummy, takes a value of 1 if the firm's activity pertains to the energy sector and 0 otherwise
Constsector	Dummy takes a value of 1 if the firm's activity pertains to the construction sector and 0 otherwise
Other stock markets	Dummy, takes a value of 1 if the firm is quoted on international stock markets and 0 otherwise

5.3. Proposed Explanatory Model

After obtaining a corporate social information disclosure index through the Internet, the working hypothesis was tested by analyzing the influence that industry concentration could have on the amount of information disclosed.

To do this we proposed the following model [1], in which the amount of information disclosed on web pages is a function of firm size, industrial sector, profitability and industrial concentration.

$$PCSR = f\,(Size, Sector, Profitability, OtherStockMarkets, Concentration) \qquad [1]$$

Model [1] can be estimated empirically based on model [2]:

$$PCSR_i = \beta_0 + \beta_1 SIZE_i + \Sigma\beta_{2k} SECTOR_K + \beta_3 PROFITABILITY_i + \beta_4 OTHERSTOCKMARKETS + \beta_5\, CONCENTRATION_i + \varepsilon \qquad [2]$$

where:

$PCSR_i$ is the disclosure index obtained after analyzing the web page of company i; it takes values between 0 and 9

Size is the market capitalization of firm i, as the variable relating to size;

$\Sigma\beta_{2k} Sector_{ik}$ are dummy variables. $SECTOR_K$ which takes a value of 1 if the firm pertains to sector k and a value of 0 otherwise; following the sector classification established by the CNMV, the sectors considered are: Services, Transport, Industrial, Energy and Construction;

Profitability is the economic profitability of firm i, defined as the quotient between operating profit and total volume of assets;

Other stock markets$_i$ dummy variable that reflects the international presence of firm i in stock markets;

Concentration$_i$ is the measure of industrial concentration, defined as the Herfindahl Index for the industry in which firm i operates.

Model [2] was tested empirically using a linear regression estimated by ordinary least squares. As stated earlier, the dependent variable was obtained from the study of the sections on corporate social disclosure practices on the corresponding web pages. The independent variables were obtained from the AMADEUS database.

6. Empirical Results

6.1. Description of the Statistics

According to the data presented in Table 3, practically 42% of the firms analyzed make a complete disclosure of corporate social responsibility on their web pages, whereas 13% present a partial report.

This document generally follows a specific format for each firm, and 32.66% of the firms that published a complete document, 13.70% of the total, used the GRI guidelines. Furthermore, 36.73% of these firms, 15.40% of the total, have their corporate social responsibility report audited.

Regarding the degree to which certain social and environmental conduct was observed on the part of the firm, 30.80% have an ISO14001 or EMAS certification of environmental behavior and almost 18% have the ISO9001 quality certification.

On the other hand, accreditation of product safety (AENOR) and, to a lesser extent, conduct with respect to human resources (OHSAS) is practically irrelevant.

6.2. Univariate Analysis

Table 4 summarizes the bivariate correlations between the dependent variable and the independent and control variables proposed.

Table 3. Item Frequency of Corporate Social Responsibility

	Corporate Social Responsiblity	Frequency	Percentage
1	Corporate Social Responsibility Report	49	41.90
	Environmental or social report	15	12.80
2	Report on the three previous fiscal years	7	6.00
3	Follows GRI format	16	13.70
4	RSC information has been audited	18	15.40
5	Accreditation of environmental behavior (ISO 14001)	36	30.80
6	Accreditation of behavior regarding human resources (OHSAS)	7	6.00
7	Quality accreditation (ISO 9001)	21	17.90
8	Product safety accreditation (AENOR)	2	1.70

Table 4. Bivariate correlation between variables: Pearson's coefficient

	PCSR
Concentration	**0.385*****
Size	**0.462*****
Profitability	0.014
Services sector	-0.070
Transport sector	0.146
Industrial sector	-0.066
Energy sector	0.224
Construction sector	0.063
Otherstock markets	**0.384****

** p- value <0.05
*** p-value < 0.01

As can be seen, the variables CONCENTRATION, SIZE AND OTHERSTOCK-MARKETS have a significant positive relationship with the dependent variable representing the disclosure practices analyzed.

Prior to estimation of the explanatory model proposed, we analyzed the effect of each one of the independent variables, considered individually, on online corporate social disclosure practices.

In Table 5 we show the results of the Kruskal-Wallis test for several independent samples. The variables that cause differences according to the different practices of CSR information disclosure observed are marked in bold.

Concretely, it was detected that the control variables SIZE and OTHERSTOCK-MARKETS, at a confidence level of 99% (p-value < 0.01), and the independent variable CONCENTRATION, at a confidence level of 95% (0.01 < p-value < 0.05), are factors that allow us to distinguish between firms catalogued according to the volume of data and the quality of CSR information they disclose on their web pages. These data confirm the significant correlations detected by means of Pearson's coefficient.

The rest of the control variables were not significant (p-value > 0.05), and therefore in principle it can be affirmed that they do not have a differentiating capacity that would allow us to group firms according to their level of social transparency.

6.3. Multivariate Analysis

The results derived from the estimation of the model proposed are shown in Table 6. the explanatory power of these models (R^2) is 34.50 %, for a confidence level of 99% (p-value < 0.01).

Regarding the variables, three of the nine analyzed turned out to be statistically significant. CONCENTRATION shows a positive and statistically significant effect at a confidence level of 99% (p-value < 0.01). This result makes it possible to accept the hypothesis proposed. Moreover, the SIZE and ENERGYSECTOR variables have a positive and statistically significant effect at the confidence level of 95% (0.01< p-value < 0.05).

Table 5. Individualized effects on online CSR disclosure practices: Kruskal-Wallis Test

Concentration	
Chi-squared	16.803
p-value	0.032
Size	
Chi-squared	35.951
p-value	0.000
Profitability	
Chi- squared	8.446
p-value	0.391
Services sector	
Chi- squared	5.466
p-value	0.707
Transport sector	
Chi- squared	11.793
p-value	0.161
Industrial sector	
Chi- squared	9.951
p-value	0.268
Energy sector	
Chi- squared	10.652
p-value	0.222
Construction sector	
Chi- squared	12.664
p-value	0.124
Other stock markets	
Chi- squared	37.474
p-value	0.000

The rest of the dummy variables representing the activity sectors and whether or not the firm is quoted internationally have a positive effect on the online disclosure of corporate social information, but are not statistically significant. Likewise, the PROFITABILITY variable is not statistically significant, although its effect on the estimated model was negative.

These results are quite similar to the ones obtained in the univariate analysis in the previous section. Specifically, the individual differentiating effect of the CONCENTRATION and SIZE variables was observed.

Furthermore, the explanatory capacity of the ENERGYSECTOR variable should be mentioned, as it is a variable that individually does not have an effect on the different online CSR disclosure practices. On the other hand, the effect of the variable representing quotation on international stock markets has disappeared. These two effects may be due to the explanatory power derived from the interrelation between the CONCENTRATION and SIZE variables.

Table 6. Effect of concentration on online CSR disclosure practices: Linear regression

Variables	Coefficient	t
Constant	0.000	-0.379
Concentration	**0.264**	**2.645*****
Size	**0.327**	**2.344****
Profitability	-0.064	-0.685
Services sector	0.331	1.309
Transport sector	0.025	0.236
Industrial sector	0.369	1.420
Energy sector	**0.428**	**2.319****
Construction sector	0.252	1.379
Other stockmarkets	0.075	0.550

$R^2 = 0.345$

F = 4.734***

Significant values in bold.

** p-value < 0.05

*** p-value < 0.01

The dependent variable is the disclosure index obtained after analysis of the web page of company i and takes values between 0 and 9.

Size: the market capitalization of firm i;

Profitability: the economic profitability of company i defined as the quotient between operating profits and total volume of assets;

Other Stock markets dummy variable that takes a value of 1 if the firm is quoted on international stock markets and 0 otherwise;

Concentration: the Herfindahl Index for the industry in which firm i operates, as a measure of sector concentration.

The influence of 5 sectors has also been considered (Services, Transport, Industrial, Energy and Construction), following the sector classification of the CNMV.

As regards the interpretation of the results obtained, we would point out that, in accordance with the suppositions of the Theory of Political Costs, it was confirmed that firms with greater monopolistic positions and thus the most visible firms voluntarily disclosed a greater amount of information on Corporate Social Responsibility. These disclosure practices could be aimed at reducing possible political costs such as an increase in regulation of these matters (e.g. legislation addressed to sexual parity, harmonizing family and work aspects, emissions reductions, etc.), as well as an increase in taxes deriving from unacceptable environmental and social conduct.

In relation to the SIZE variable, just as in previous studies (e.g., Patten, 1991; Niskala and Pretens, 1995), it was found that the larger firms are the ones that disclose a greater volume of corporate social information. These results also coincide with those of studies on the voluntary general disclosure of information on the Internet (e.g. Craven and Marston, 1999; Oyelere et al., 2003; Marston and Polei, 2004; Giner et al., 2003; Bonsón and Escobar, 2004)

As regards sector, it was found that the drawing up of economic, social and environmental information is determined by the firm's activity sector. Thus, firms in the energy sector are those that issue the most corporate social information.

CONCLUSIONS

The disclosure of corporate social information is a key element used by firms to recover, maintain or improve their reputation or social image, although it can also be used to modify external expectations regarding behavior and performance.

In this sense, the Theory of Political Costs affirms that the firms most exposed to political scrutiny, generally those holding monopolistic positions, will disclose more environmental and social information in order to reduce or avoid regulations or norms that would restrict their behavior.

The present study has shown the primacy of the hypothesis defended by the Theory of Political Costs in that the most monopolistic firms, which in turn are more visible, voluntarily disclose a greater volume of information on Corporate Social Responsibility on their web sites.

These disclosure practices could have as their objective, on the one hand, to reduce possible political costs such as an increase in regulation in these matters and a rise in taxes derived from unacceptable social and environmental practices, and on the other, to obtain certain advantages associated with subsidies or favorable treatment from the government.

BIBLIOGRAPHY

Adams, C.A. (2002). Internal organisational factors influencing corporate social and ethical reporting. *Accounting, Auditing and Accountability, 15(2)*, p. 223-250.

Adams, C.A., & Harte, G. (1998). The changing portrayal of the employment of women in British banks' and retail companies' corporate annual reports. *Accounting, Organizations and Society, 23(80)*, p. 781-812.

Adams, C.A., & Kuasirikun, N. (2000). A comparative analysis of corporate reporting on ethical issues by UK and German chemical and pharmaceutical companies. *European Accounting Review, 9(1)*, p. 53-80.

Adams, C.A., Hill, W.Y., & Roberts, C.B. (1995). *Environmental employee and ethical reporting in Europe*. ACCA Research Report 41, Chartered Association of Certified Accountants, London.

Adams, C.A., Hill, W.Y., & Roberts, C.B. (1998). Corporate social reporting practices in Western Europe: Legitimating corporate behaviour?. *British Accounting Review, 30 (1)*, p. 1-21.

Archel, P. (2003). La divulgación de la información social y medioambiental en la gran empresa española en el período 1994-1998: Situación actual y perspectivas. *Revista Española de Financiación y Contabilidad, 32 (117)*, p. 571-601.

Archel, P., & Lizarraga, F. (2001). Algunos determinantes de la información medioambiental divulgada por las empresas españolas cotizadas. *Revista de Contabilidad, 44 (7)*, p. 129-153.

Belkaoui, A., & Karpik, P. (1989). Determinants of the corporate decision to disclose social information. *Accounting, Auditing and Accountability Journal, 2 (1)*, p. 36-51.

Bonsón, E., & Escobar, T. (2004). La difusión voluntaria de información financiera en Internet. Un análisis comparativo entre Estados Unidos, Europa del Este y la Unión Europea. *Revista Española de Financiación y Contabilidad, 33*, p.1063-1101.

Bowman, E.H. (1978). Strategy, annual reports and alchemy. *California Management Review, Spring*, p. 64-71.

Burchell, S., Clubb, C., & Hopwood, A.G. (1985). Accounting in its social context: towards a history of value added in the United Kingdom. *Accounting, Organizations and Society, 10(4)*, p. 381-413.

Carroll A. (1991). The pyramid of corporate social responsibility: toward the moral management of organizational stakeholders, *Business Horizons, 34(4),* p. 39–48.

Circular 1/2004, (2004) Comisión Nacional del Mercado de Valores, 17 de Marzo.

Clarkson M. (1995). A stakeholder framework for analyzing and evaluating corporate social performance. *Academy of Management* Review, *20(1), p. 92–117.*

Commission of the European Communities. (2001). Green Paper: Promoting a European Framework for Corporate Social Responsibility 366. Brussels. http://europa.eu.int [November 2003].

Cowen, S., Ferreri, L., & Parker, L.D. (1987). The impact of corporate characteristics on social responsibility disclosure: A typology and frequency-based analysis. *Accounting, Organizations and Society, 12 (2)*, p. 111-122.

Craven, B.M., & Martson, C.L. (1999). Financial reporting on the Internet by leading UK companies. *European Accounting Review, 8*, p. 321-333.

Deegan, C., & Carroll, G. (1993). An analysis of incentives for Australian firms to apply for reporting excellence award. *Accounting and Business Research, 23,* p. 219-227.

Deegan, C., & Gordon, B. (1996). A study of the environmental disclosure practices of Australian corporations. *Accounting and Business Research, 26 (3)*, p. 187-199.

Deegan, C., & Hallam, A. (1991). The voluntary presentation of value added statements in Australia: a political cost perspective. *Accounting and Finance, 3 (1)*, p. 1-21.

Deegan, C., & Rankin, M. (1996). Do Australian companies report environmental news objectively? An analysis of environmental disclosures by firms prosecuted successfully by the Environmental Protection Authority. *Accounting, Auditing and Accountability Journal, 9 (2)*, p. 50-67.

Fleege, E., & Adrian, E. (2004). The implementation of corporate ethics: a comparative study between Motorola and Ericsson. *UW-L Journal of Undergraduate Research, 7,* p. 1-9.

Freedman, M., & Jaggi B. (1988). An analysis of the association between pollution disclosure and economic performance. *Accounting, Auditing and Accountability Journal, 1 (2)*, p. 43-58.

Giner, B. (1997). The Influence of company characteristics and accounting regulation on information disclosed by Spanish firms. *European Accounting Review, 6*, p. 45-68.

Giner, B., Arce, M., Cervera, N., & Ruiz. A. (2003). Incentivos para la divulgación voluntaria de información: evidencia empírica sobre la información segmentada. *Revista Europea de Dirección y Economía de la Empresa, 12*, p. 69-86.

Gray, R. H., Kouhy, R., & Lavers, S. (1995). Methodological themes: constructing a research database of social and environmental reporting by UK companies. *Accounting, Auditing and Accountability Journal, 8 (2)*, p. 78-101.

Gray, R. H., Javad, M., Power, D., & Sinclair, C.D. (2001). Social and environmental disclosures and corporate characteristics: A research note and extension. *Journal of Business Finance & Accounting, 28 (3 and 4)*, p. 327-356.

Guthrie, J., & Parker, L.D. (1989) Corporate social reporting; a rebuttal of legitimacy theory. *Accounting and Business Research, 19(76)*, p. 343-352.

Guthrie, J., & Parker, L.D. (1990). Corporate social disclosure practice: a comparative international analysis. *Advances in Public Interest Accounting, 3*, p. 159-175.

Hackston, D., & Milne, M.J. (1996). Some determinants of social and environmental disclosures in New Zealand companies. *Accounting, Auditing and Accountability Journal, 9 (1)*, p. 77-108.

Haniffa, R.M., & Cooke, T.E. (2005). The impact of culture and governance on corporate social reporting. *Journal of Accounting and Public Policy, 24*, p. 391-430.

Hogner, R.H. (1982). Corporate social reporting: eight decades of development at US Steel. *Research in Corporate Social Performance and Policy, 4*, p.45-55.

Hopwood, A. (1987). The archaeology of accounting systems. *Accounting, Organizations and Society, 12(3)*, p. 207-234.

Jamali, D., & Mirshak, R. (2007). Corporate Social Responsibility (CSR): Theory and Practice in a Developing Country Context. *Journal of Business Research, 72,* p. 243-262.

Lemon, A.J., & Cahan, S.F., (1997). Environmental Legislation and Environmental Disclosures: Some Evidence from New Zealand. *Asian Review of Accounting, 5 (1),* p. 78-105.

Leventis, S., & Weetman, P. (2000). Exploring and explaining variations in voluntary disclosure in a European emerging capital market: evidence from the Athens Stock Exchange, *Working paper*. BAA 2000 Regional Conference.

Lim, S., & McKinnon. J.(1993). Voluntary Disclosure by NSW Statutory Authorities: The Influence of Political Visibility. *Journal of Accounting and Public Policy, 12*, p. 189-216.

Lindblom, C.K. (1994). The implications of organizational legitimacy for corporate social performance and disclosure, paper presented at the Critical Perspectives on Accounting Conference, New York.

Loft, A. (1988). *Understanding accounting in its social and historical context: The case of cost accounting in Britain, 1914-1925,* New York: Garland Publishing.

Lynn, M. (1992). A note on corporate social disclosure in Hong Kong. *British Accounting Review, June*, p. 105-110.

Marston, C., & Polei, A. (2004). Corporate Reporting on the Internet by German Companies. *International Journal of Accounting Information Systems, 5,* p. 285-311.

Moon, J. (2007). The contribution of Corporate Social Responsibility to Sustainable Development. *Sustainable Development, 15,* p. 296-306.

Ness, K.E., & Mirza, A.M. (1991). Corporate Social Disclosure: A Note on a Test of Agency Theory. *British Accounting Review, 23 (3),* p. 211-217.

Neu D., Warsame, H., & Pedwell, K. (1998). Managing public impressions: Environmental disclosures in annual reports, *Accounting, Organizations and Society, 23(3)*, p. 265-282.

Niskala, M., & Pretes, M. (1995). Environmental reporting in Finland: A note on the use of annual reports. *Accounting, Organizations and Society, 20 (6)*, p. 457-466.

Ochoa, E., & Aranguren, N. (2005). Divulgación de información social y medioambiental. Un estudio empírico de las empresas del IBEX 35, Comunicación presentada al XIII Congreso AECA, Oviedo.

Oyelere, P., Laswad, F., & Fisher, R. (2003). Determinants of internet financial reporting by New Zealand companies. *Journal of International Financial Management and Accounting, 14*, p. 26-63.

Panchapakesan, S., & McKinnon, J., (1992). Proxies for Political Visibility: A Preliminary Examination of the Relation Among Some Potential Proxies, *Accounting Research Journal, Spring*, p. 71-80.

Patten, D. (1991). Exposure, legitimacy and social disclosure. *Journal of Accounting and Public Policy, 10 (4)*, p. 297-308.

Patten, D. (1992). Intra-industry environmental disclosures in response to the Alaskan oil spill: a note on legitimacy theory. *Accounting, Organizations and Society, 17 (5)*, p. 471-475.

Roberts, R.W. (1992). Determinants of corporate social responsibility disclosure: an application of stakeholder theory. *Accounting, Organizations and Society*, 17 (6), p. 595-612.

Rodríguez, G. (2004). Factores explicativos de la revelación voluntaria de información sobre fuentes de ventaja competitiva empresarial. *Revista Española de Financiación y Contabilidad, 122*, p. 705-739.

Trotman, K.T., & Bradley, G.W. (1981). Associations between social responsibility disclosure and characteristics of companies. *Accounting, Organizations and Society, 6 (4)*, p. 355-362.

Watts. R.L., & Zimmerman. J.L. (1978). Towards a Positive Theory of the Determination of Accounting Standards. *The Accounting Review, 53 (1)*, p. 112-134.

Watts. R.L., & Zimmerman. J.L. (1986). *Positive Accounting Theory*, London: Prentice-Hall.

In: Corporate Social Responsibility
Editor: Adam R. Timpere

ISBN: 978-1-60456-284-2

Chapter 10

Transferring Corporate Social Responsibility to the School Context: Teachers' Perceived Responsibility for Students' Failure*

Maria Cristina Matteucci†
Department of Education, Faculty of Psychology, University of Bologna, Italy

Abstract

The concept of Corporate Social Responsibility (CSR) has a variety of definitions and, within the academic literature, there is some confusion about how CSR should be operationalized and measured (Godfrey & Hatch, 2006). CSR generally refers to the obligations that organizations have toward society (Fisher, 2004). This chapter focuses on school as a particular but real formal corporation, and it explores the social responsibility related to the school "mission", i.e., the accomplishment of school curriculum. School (i.e., its legal representatives, such as teachers and headmasters) fulfills its social obligations when students achieve school goals. But what happens when students are not successful at school? Teachers are most directly responsible for learning, and the social contract assigns responsibility for education to schools (Del Schalock, H. 1998). This chapter identifies the relationship between causal and responsible ascription in the case of failure, and stresses the role of effort as "cutting edge" in the discussion of accountability for student/pupil learning. Perceived social responsibility for failure in teachers and students is taken into account, and results of previous studies concerning teachers' perceived responsibility in case of school failure are presented and discussed (Matteucci, 2007; Matteucci & Gosling, 2004). According to Weiner (1995) it is argued that effort attribution and responsibility ascription are mutually related, although teachers are

* This research was financially supported by the Italian Ministry of University and Research (ex 40% 2004; ex 60% 2005).

†* Address for correspondence: Dipartimento di Scienze dell'Educazione, Università di Bologna, via Filippo Re, 6, I 40126 Bologna, Italy. mariacristina.matteucci@unibo.it.

reluctant to accept their responsibility for students' failure, thus assigning responsibility to the failing students. The issue of responsibility and accountability for student learning will be discussed, and implications of the results for teachers' work will be considered.

INTRODUCTION

The concept of Corporate Social Responsibility (CSR) has not an accepted definition and, within academic literature, there is some confusion about how CSR should be operationalized and measured (Godfrey & Hatch, 2006). Carroll (1999) mapped the evolution of the modern concept of CSR, and showed that its definitions have expanded and proliferated since the 1960s.

If CSR is generally referred to as the obligations that organizations have toward society (Fisher, 2004), a Green Paper of the European Commission, published in 2001, provides a wide-ranging definition of CSR, underlying that "*Being socially responsible means not only fulfilling legal expectations, but also going beyond compliance and investing "more" into human capital, the environment and the relations with stakeholders*". The concept of CSR is usually applied to large private corporations or companies even though socially responsible practices exist in public institutions as well.

Is it reasonable to consider school as a particular form of corporation, and teachers as professionals of education? Vanderstraetem (2007) has recently provided an analysis, where teaching is conceived of as a profession, whereas Perrenoud (1994) already developed a study in which school is compared to a formal organization. He considers school as a particular, but real formal corporation, whose mission is the pursuit of pupils' school achievement. School is, in fact, a formal organization which is in no way inferior to or different from a "genuine" company. In school, as well as in an enterprise, life is structured, personnel are submitted to a conduct code, and a reference model is usually present and shared by human resources. Furthermore, working time, systems and methods, as well as evaluation standard, quality control and disciplinary sanctions (for teachers and pupils as well) are imposed and foreseen both at school and in private corporations.

Within the private sector, socially responsible practices primarily engage employees and shareholders (the so-called "internal dimension" of the CSR), but also the local community ("external dimension"), involving a wide range of stakeholders (European Commission, 2001). Now, following the parallel between school and corporation, we can ask ourselves two essential questions: who are the school's stakeholders? What are the main issues involved in social responsibility practices related to educational institutions?

This chapter explores the social responsibility of school as related to its main mission, i.e., the accomplishment of a formal curriculum. In particular, results of two studies concerning teachers perceived responsibility in case of school failure are presented and discussed.

SOCIAL RESPONSIBILITY IN SCHOOL CONTEXT

By transferring to the school context the idea of CSR as a social responsibility applied to the school mission, we argue that if school is a particular corporation, we can study the theme of social responsibility in its main actors: pupils/students and teachers. Obviously, other subjects might be involved in this matter: families, headmasters, school board members, school administrators, the local community, and the society at large. But the "receivers" (pupils, students) and the "providers" of education (the school by means of teachers) are the main subjects involved in this analysis.

If, on the one hand, we consider that a company is answerable especially to its stakeholders, i.e., those who have an interest in the company and/or who are affected by the organization's business (i.e., WBCSD, 1999; Vallverdu Calafell et al. 2006), we come to the view that pupils, students, and their families may represent the principal stakeholders of the school-company. Actually, they are the subjects and "users" that are most involved in the services offered by the educational corporation.

On the other, we can wonder what kind of "mission" education providers can be considered responsible for? What is the social obligation of school? As a matter of fact, teachers are responsible for their pedagogical and educational task, for the dissemination of knowledge, and, ultimately, for the application of the formal curriculum. Thus, social expectations concerning school are related to the "mission" of this particular company devoted to the education of its stakeholders: its formal curriculum. According to Unesco (2007), the formal or official curriculum is "the planned program of objectives, content, learning experiences, resources and assessment offered by a school". In fact, curriculum documents define what students should be taught in schools by detailing the knowledge and skills that students are expected to acquire in each subject at each grade level.

The law concerning responsibility and liability in education has been explored in several European countries (e.g., Legrand, 2002; Poulis, 2002; Glendenning, 2002; Gounalakis, 2002) with a particular focus on the liability of education "providers" (teaching staff; school headmasters) and with regard to quality care as well (e.g. not following the curriculum). Besides legal liability (e.g. for wrongful acts), the teaching staff is considered to be responsible for its pedagogical and educational task, for the dissemination of knowledge and for the strict application of the school program set by the State.

Thus, the school (and its representatives, i.e., teachers) fulfils its social obligations as far as students' school achievement is concerned. In fact, "teachers and schools do have an impact on learners and are bound by a broader social contract to ensure this happens" (Del Schalock, M. 1998, p. 281).

A survey on the social responsibility of teachers, which was conducted with a sample of more than 3,000 American respondents (MIDUS; see Rossi, 2001), gives us an idea of the social acknowledgment of the strict connection between teaching profession, and young people who are granted to them for learning, and educational purposes. The MIDUS survey tapped different domains and dimensions of social responsibility (Rossi, 2001), and the "generativity" was one of those. Authors (Colby, Sippola, & Phelps, 2001) make use of Erikson's definition of generativity (1963), who considers that "it involves commitment to the well-being of the next generation and activities that aim to contribute a positive legacy that will outlive the self". In this research we have adopted the Loyola Generativity Scale which includes several items referring to the teaching directly (e.g., "Other would say that you have made unique contributions to society", " You feel that other people need you", "you like to teach things to people"). The results of this study showed a relation between social responsibility and generativity. In particular, it was found that teachers were similarly likely to cite concerns for others or the common good in talking about the meaning their work has for them. Authors claim that teaching is a profession that seems to naturally call forth a concern for contributing to others' welfare and that teaching is a "quintessentially generative profession". Thus, teachers and educational providers are invested not only with a "curricular" responsibility towards pupils/students, but also with a more general responsibility (see also Fischman et al., 2006).

So, teaching is a generative profession, which is deeply concerned with the well-being of adolescents and children in development. This feature may be a source of job and personal satisfaction, but the teaching profession is a highly stressful occupation as well. As a matter of fact, several studies indicate that teachers often find themselves beleaguered by disruptive and non-achieving students (Chan, 1998). This perception of being under pressure is quite due to the characteristics of this job, holding teachers accountable for their students' attainments and well-being, and depending on others (e.g., parents, colleagues and the principal) to accomplish tasks. Teachers' responsibility can therefore be a source of distress and psychological troubles, since the exposure to chronic occupational stressors, with low sense of efficacy to manage job demands increases vulnerability and usually lead to burnout. According to Friedman (2003), teacher efficacy is defined as the extent to which a teacher believes that she/he can influence student behavior and academic achievements, especially students with difficulties or those with particularly low learning motivation.

Summing up, teachers are the most directly responsible for learning, and the social contract assigns responsibility for education to schools. Quoting Del Schalock H. (1998, p.238)

"...the purpose of schooling is learning and the purpose of teaching is to foster the progress of students in their learning. Teachers are hired to fulfil this primary mission of schooling and there are few parents, school-board members, school administrators, or teachers who would view their job otherwise."

According to this author, school and teachers' responsibility for education goes hand-in-hand with educator accountability for student progress in learning. The school's mission is so important for its individual and social relevance that a debate about accountability is inevitable. The main dimensions of responsibility that may be recognized are three: agency, accountability and obligation. Agency refers to individuals being answerable for their actions to other members of the community; accountability refers to the individual being subject to sanction when acting incongruently with formal guidelines, rules or laws; obligation refers to the duty of carrying out a moral requirement (see Witt, 2001).

All of these aspects of social responsibility fit the teaching profession, even if accountability especially fits with the professional responsibilities of teachers. A debate about standard of performance, and quality evaluation of educational systems, is the most important caveat for institutions of schooling of all Western nations in this century, which is defined as "accountability era". Thus, teachers have to answer for their actions to the headmaster, to their colleagues, and to pupils/students as well. In the last years, a great number of contributions have discussed accountability policies and their effects, in terms of "culture of fear" (McGhee M.W & Nelson S.W., 2005), spur vs. discourage to good teaching (e.g. Karen Seashore, et al., 2005), and of increasing of individual work rather than collaborative work (Valli et al. 2007).

Causality and Responsibility for School Failure

Teachers and school are recognized by the society in general, and by the contract of employment as well (i.e., National Union of Teachers, 2003), as responsible and accountable for pupils/students learning. We can now take into consideration what happens when students do not achieve knowledge and skills that they are expected to acquire. In other words, what happens when pupils are not successful at school? To whom is the cause of this failure ascribable and, consequently, who is responsible for it?

Assuming or accepting personal responsibility for a failure is actually not so obvious. If, from the viewpoint of the accountability for quality, teachers are considered as responsible and accountable for pupils/students' failure, a potential sanction towards those who failed in their mission of being an effective facilitator of learning is necessarily implied. Given that the learning goals have not been achieved, the standard of performance has not been achieved either.

From the origin of social psychology, the process that leads to the ascription of responsibility has been a subject matter of several theories (i.e., Heider, 1958; Fincham & Jaspars, 1980; Fisher & Ravizza, 1998; Hamilton, 1978, 1980; Shaver, 1985; Shaver & Drown, 1986; Schlenker et al. 1994). In order to understand the responsibility ascription process, theoretical and empirical literature in social psychology clearly distinguishes "causality" from "responsibility" and both of those concepts are distinguished from blame (e.g., Shaver, 1985; Shaver & Drown, 1986). In this tradition, causality refers to the production of an effect and applies to all factors that might have contributed to the occurrence. The cause of an event is the antecedent sufficient for the occurrence of the effect. On the contrary, responsibility and blameworthiness come into play only after the occurrence of events with negative consequences. Responsibility is a moral judgment about an event made by an individual and blame is the moral opprobrium attached to a person who has intentionally committed a negative event without adequate excuse or justification.

Weiner's attributional theory of social conduct (1995), applies in educational and school contexts, and investigates the social-psychological mechanism which influences responsibility attribution. According to Weiner, in case of students' failure teachers ascribe a cause to this negative event. The cause ascribed to the failure is directly linked and influences the responsibility attribution. In particular, if the cause ascribed to the effort is "internal" to the actor of the negative event (i.e. the failing student) and directly controllable by him/her, the person is considered also responsible for the outcome. In other words, if you have caused the event and you could have done otherwise, you are responsible of the consequence obtained.

A particular cause which is usually ascribed to school failure is the lack of effort by the pupil/student. In achievement situation, the student who does not put effort to achieve (an internal and controllable cause), is deemed responsible of the subsequent failure. Thus, effort attribution and responsibility assignment are mutually related. In particular, putting effort into study might be considered a fundamental aspect of the "moral curriculum" (or implicit curriculum) (Matteucci, 2007).

The moral curriculum consists of those subjects which pupils learn through the experience of attending school rather than through the stated educational objectives of such institutions. The so-called "unofficial curriculum" is the ensemble of accidental lessons that students learn at school, and includes lessons about behavior, personal relationships, sources of motivation and so on (Unesco, 2007). At the same time, effort would be a defensive attribution: it relieves the teacher from responsibility by ascribing it to the diligence of the student's work (Matteucci & Gosling, 2004).

Thus, the causes attributed to failure and particularly the pupil's effort play the role of "cutting edge" of discussion about accountability for student/pupil learning. According to Weiner (2003), the principle influencing the teacher's decision about discipline and classroom interventions is the "ethic of effort": students have to work hard and try to do as well as possible in school work. The violation of this moral norm by a student results in the teacher's behavioral reaction, which Weiner and colleagues have described as a process involving both emotional feedback and responsibility assessment.

Two experimental studies focusing on the responsibility ascription in case of school failure will be presented below. Results show that most teachers do not assume responsibility for their student's failure and, moreover, they assign responsibility to the failing student. The role of pupils' effort- as a cause ascribed for failure - emerges as "cutting edge" of discussion about accountability for student/pupil learning and the responsibility for school failure shifts from teachers to students.

Study 1. Causal and Responsibility Attribution for Failure. May Teacher Intervene on Failure Causes?

Within the framework of causal attribution theory and of social conduct theory, a study conducted on 213 high school teachers (66.8% women; average age: 45.8, *SD* = 7.5) of Italian high schools, has investigated the teachers' causal and responsibility attribution for their pupil's failure.

The research was presented to the teachers as a study on academic failure. The instrument utilized was an anonymous questionnaire aimed at recalling a real situation of failure: one of his/her failed students.

After reading the instructions, teachers were asked general questions about the targeted student (sex, class, etc.). Then the questionnaire presented several items, which were meant at assessing:

- A list of the most frequent causes of failure. Participants rated the extent to which each cause fit the pupil's situation of failure, ranging from 0 to 6
- The cause ascribed by the teacher to the failure. Participants rated on a 7-point scale (semantic differential) ranging from "completely ascribed to the pupil" to "completely ascribed to other causes/conditions (not under pupil's personal volition)"

- The influence that the teacher considers to have, ranging from 0 (not at all – "All depends on pupil") to 6 (a lot – "I can exert a significant influence")
- The student's responsibility for the failure. Participants rated the extent to which the student was deemed responsible on a 7-point scale ranging from 0 ("not at all") to 6 ("very much").
- The teacher's personal responsibility. Participants rated the extent to which they held themselves responsible on a 7-point scale ranging from 0 ("not at all") to 6 ("very much").

As far as the responsibility for school failure is concerned, results indicated that teachers ascribe the most significant responsibility to the failing student (M=4.1, SD = 1,2) rather than to themselves (M = 1.9. DS=1.3), t(205) = 19.9; $p < .001$.

The pupil's responsibility is negatively correlated to the item concerning the internal versus external cause of the failure, P(206)= -.498, p< .001. thus confirming the link between ascription of responsibility and causal attribution of failure. In particular, when the cause of failure is perceived as resulting from the pupil's volition or action, the pupil's responsibility increases in the teachers' opinion. No significant results emerged as for the teacher responsibility in this case.

As for the link between cause and responsibility, results suggest a strong association between causes referring to the pupil's effort (i.e., lack of interest, will, effort, or hard work) and the responsibility ascribed by the teacher to the pupil him/herself. On the contrary, teachers' responsibility is weakly correlated only with two causes (see Table 1 and Figure 1).

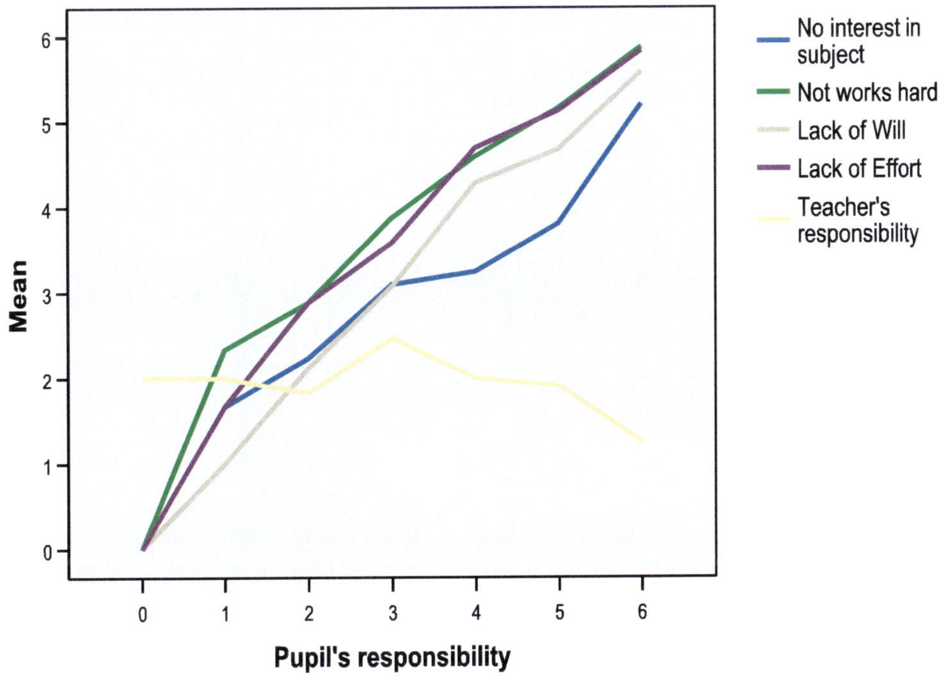

[minimum score: 0 ; maximum score: 6]

Figure 1. Causes attributed to failure and teachers' self-ascribed responsibility according to responsibility level ascribed to the failing pupil.

Table 1. Spearman's Correlations matrix (among causes attributed and responsibility ascription) (N=197)

	1	2	3	4	5	6
Pupil's responsibility	1	-.189(**)	.525(**)	.547(**)	.550(**)	.415(**)
Teacher's responsibility		1	-.183(**)	n.s	-.162(*)	n.s.
Lack of Effort			1	.788(**)	.816(**)	.509(**)
Lack of Will				1	.774(**)	.488(**)
Pupil does not work hard					1	.522(**)
No interest in subject						1

** Significant at the 0.01 level (2-tailed).
* Significant at the 0.05 level (2-tailed).

After having ascribed the cause of the failure, teachers were asked to express themselves on whether they consider themselves to be able of influencing causal antecedents of failure. Findings reveal a correlation between the responsibility ascription and the perception to be able to modify the antecedents of failure. In particular, results confirm that teachers that ascribe themselves more responsibility deem themselves to be more able to influence the causes or antecedents of failure as well. In these cases no linkage with the pupil's responsibility was found (see Figure 2).

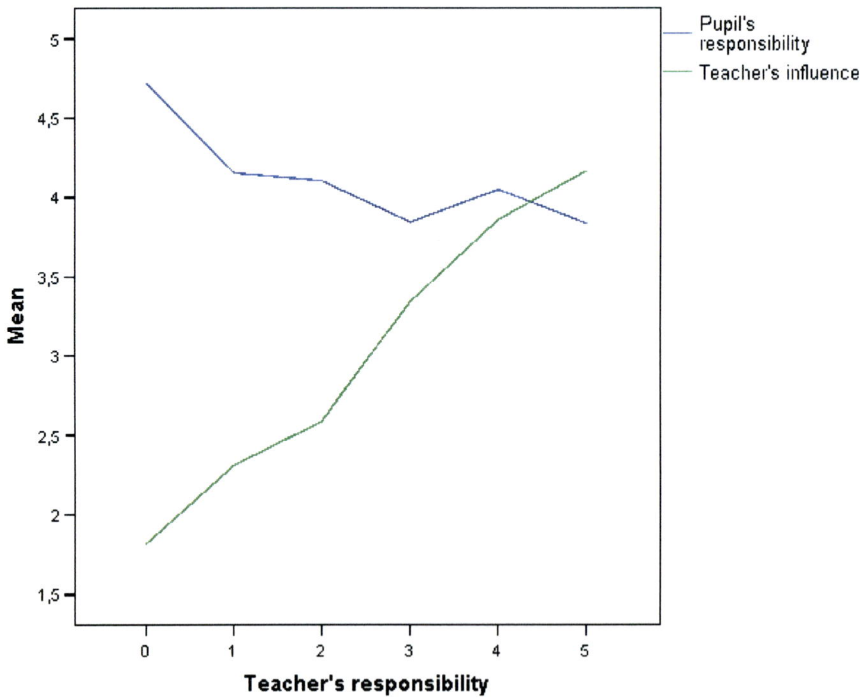

[minimum score: 0 ; maximum score: 6]

Figure 2. Teachers' perception to be able to influence the causes of failure according to responsibility level ascribed to the failing pupil and to themselves.

Summing up, the causal attribution of failure is directly linked to the responsibility ascription, whereas the perception of being able to remove or to influence the causes of failure is positively correlated to the responsibility. A closer look at the results allows us to notice that pupil's responsibility ascription is driven by causal attribution for failure, while personal responsibility is refused by teachers. Despite these findings, if teachers assume their role on the failure (in terms of responsibility) they believe, as a result, to be able to influence causal antecedents and consequently, as we suppose, student behavior and academic achievements as well.

We can affirm, therefore, that the causal ascription is central in the of accountability process in case of failure and confirm that when teachers are asked to express their opinion about how their pupils fail, the predominance of causes evoking pupils' effort, will, personal volition of success is considerable.

The results of the following study may be helpful to appreciate the role of a *contra-posit* cause to the effort of pupils evoked in case of achievement failure, i.e., pupil's lack of ability. Moreover, other variables will be studied as co-influencing the responsibility ascription: the type of school and the differences due to the nationality of participants in a cross-cultural comparison.

Study 2: Are Pupils or Teachers Responsible for Failure?

In order to study teachers' perceived responsibility for students' failure in two particular conditions of causal ascription, a study on 115 teachers (88% women, 12% men; average age: 47.3, s.d. 6.5) of junior high schools (42.6%) and high schools (57.34%) situated in a central region of Italy was conducted by Matteucci & Gosling (2004).

The research was presented to the teachers as a study on academic failure. The instrument employed was an anonymous questionnaire, which was aimed at recalling a real situation of failure. After a presentation of the research, teachers were asked to fill in the questionnaire regarding one of his/her failed students.

Two versions of the questionnaire were created and submitted to the subjects: the first version asked the teacher to answer the questionnaire by referring to a student with achievement failure caused by lack of effort (but with sufficient ability); in the second version the teacher was asked to answer the questionnaire by considering a student with achievement failure caused by lack of ability (but who put effort into study). 59 subjects (51.3%) received the first version of the questionnaire (concerning the "lack of effort" student); 56 subjects (48.7%) received the second version (concerning the "lack of ability" student).

After the instructions, teachers were asked general questions about the student (sex, class, etc.) and then the questionnaire presented one item assessing the student's responsibility for the failure (participants rated the extent to which the student was responsible on a 7-point scale ranging from 0 to 6), one item assessing teacher's personal responsibility (participants rated the extent to which they held themselves responsible on a 7-point scale ranging from 0 to 6).

The results concerning the responsibility ascription showed that teachers ascribe themselves a portion of responsibility for students'/pupils' failure (M=1.97, SD=1.3), which is significantly inferior to the responsibility they ascribe to students/pupils themselves (M= 3.54, SD=1.3), t(113) = 8.65, p < .001.

The cause ascribed to the failure influences in a significant way the responsibility ascription as well. As a matter of fact, our results show that in case of failure ascribed to lack of effort, pupils/students are judged as more responsible for failure (M=1.97, SD=1.3), than in case of lack of ability (M= 3.54, SD=1.3), t(113) = 8.65, p < .001. (see figure 3)

Next, the types of school were examined as independent variables. The answers about responsibility attribution were compared between high school teachers and junior high school teachers. The latter ascribed to themselves a responsibility for the failure of their pupils (M= 2.37, SD=1.3), which was significantly higher than the responsibility indicated by their colleagues of high schools (M= 1.68, SD=1.3), t(112) = 2.78, p < .01. No significant results emerged about responsibility assigned to failing pupils.

If we examine the responsibility that teachers perceive and assert to have about the students/pupils who do not achieve the objectives of formal curriculum, and, at the same time, we consider the school level and the antecedents of results in terms of causal ascription, we observe that both factors modulate responsibility ascription (see figure 4).

A comparison between Italian and French subjects was conducted as well, with the aim of studying teachers' social responsibility with a cross-cultural approach (cfr. Matteucci & Gosling, 2004). A sub-sample of 65 Italian high school teachers (55.1%) was confronted to 53 French high school teachers (44.9%). According to the results, French teachers held themselves more responsible for the failure of their students (M = 2.3, SD = 1.6) than Italian teachers did (M = 1.7, SD = 1.3). However, as in the case of the first research, the mean value of the teacher's personal responsibility (M= 1.9, SD = 1.4) was significantly much lower than the mean value of the student's responsibility (M = 3.7, SD = 1.4), t(116) = 9.4; p < .001.

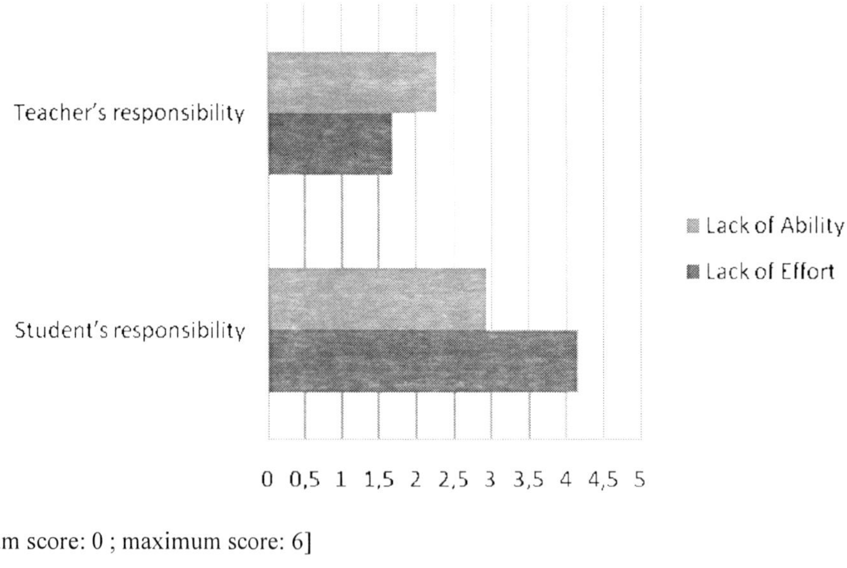

[minimum score: 0 ; maximum score: 6]

Figure 3. Responsibility ascribed by teachers to themselves and to the failing pupil according to the causal attribution for failure.

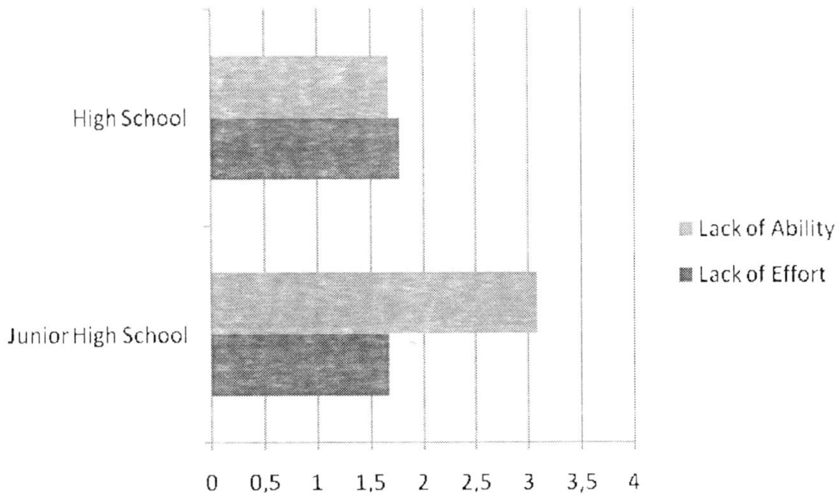

[minimum score: 0 ; maximum score: 6]

Figure 4. Teacher's responsibility as a function of causal attribution and type of school.

The results of this study illustrate the role of causal attribution and of effort as steering cause of responsibility ascription. Furthermore, other variables appear as part of the process: teachers' perception about responsibility depends on the level of the school in which they work and also on the country they belong to. It is noteworthy that teachers' vs. pupils' responsibility have an opposite trend: teachers' responsibility decreases when the pupils' age increases; on the contrary, pupils' responsibility increases with the school level attended. This result seems to suggest a sort of making-responsible process, where the only factor which is influencing is the age of the pupil. As for the cross-cultural comparison, we need more investigations on this topic, in order to understand the socio-psychological determinants of this process in which, as we argue, social representation and social valorization of the teaching profession are concerned, as well as other micro-factors like school climate might be involved (e.g. Freiberg, 1999).

CONCLUSION

With the purpose of transferring the concept of CSR to the school setting, we attempted to provide a parallel between school and enterprise, considering students as stakeholders and teachers as "legal delegates" of the school- company. In this effort we argue that the social responsibility of educational institutions, and particularly of teachers, is rooted on the achievement of their main mission: the formal curriculum or, in other words, pupils' school success.

Within this framework we have presented some observations focusing on social responsibility of teachers concerning the formal and informal curricula, and we have explored the fundamental role of causal attribution for school failure.

Following this line of reasoning, we have described the results of two studies conducted with teachers with the aim of illustrating responsibility ascription and the link between responsibility and causes of failure.

Findings confirm that teachers who were asked to explain pupils' low achievement indicate causes suggesting the pupil's main role in failure, in terms of lack effort, lack of hard-work or/and lack of will to success in school, thus assigning prevalently responsibility to the failing pupil/student.

These results confirm and extend some of the findings of previous works, which have shown that teachers are willing to accept credit for students' success, but they are reluctant to accept blame for students' failure to achieve (e.g. Martin et al., 2001). Moreover, they contribute to clarify the antecedents of responsibility ascription in school failure by suggesting and describing some relevant implications for teachers' work. As a matter of fact, findings show that teachers who bear their responsibility or accept their role in students' failure are convinced to be able to influence the antecedents of failure as well, and thus prove to have high sense of efficacy to manage job demands, also with low-achieving students.

In light of the fact that teaching is considered as a highly stressful profession (Friedman, 2003), it may be suggested that the avoidance of responsibility can be a strategy to keep away from distress, burnout, and to protect professional identity. Other factors that may be relevant to this process may be identified, e.g., in teachers' social representation of pupils' intelligence (Mugny & Carugati, 1989), as well as in social valorization of the teaching profession and school culture. Further studies are needed to comprehend all the determinants involved in the responsibility ascription process.

Implications related to the broader theme of accountability for student learning might be discussed as well. As a matter of fact, teachers of the contemporary "accountability era", have to pursue the main goal of closing the "achievement gap," while answering for their actions. The debate about teacher accountability in case of school failure will certainly continue to dominate the sphere of education in the years ahead. Teachers will have to play their part by starting taking responsibility, thus opening the debate about practices and strategies to achieve their mission as far as school improvement is concerned.

When schools and teachers will have achieved their principal purpose, that is "letting no one more child behind", they will be able to dedicate themselves to more typical subjects of CSR (e.g. stimulate ecological behavior in pupils, improve the school environment), which are concerned with the school moral curriculum.

References

Carroll, A. (1999) Corporate Social Responsibility. Evolution of a Definitional Construct . *Business & Society, 38(*3), 268-295.

Chan, D.W. (1998). Stress, coping strategies, and psychological distress among secondary school teachers in Hong Kong. *American Educational Research Journal, 35,* 145–163.

Colby, A., Sippola, L., & Phelps, E. (2001). Social responsibility and paid work on contemporary American life. In A. Rossi (Ed.), *Caring and doing for others. Social responsibility in the domains of family, Work, and Community* (pp. 463-501). Chicago/London: The University of Chicago Press.

Cooper, S. (2004). *Corporate Social performance: A Stakeholder approach.* Burlington/ Aldershot: Aschgate.

Del Schalock, H. (1998). Student progress in learning: Teacher responsibility, accountability, and reality. *Journal of Personnel Evaluation in Education, 12(3*), 237-246.

Del Schalock, M. (1998). Accountability, student learning, and the preparation and licensure of teachers: Oregon's teachers work sample methodology. *Journal of Personnel Evaluation in Education, 12(3*), 269-285.

Fincham, F.D., Jaspars, J.M. (1980). Attribution of Responsibility: From Man as the Scientist to Man as Lawyer. In: L. Berkowitz (Ed), *Advances in Experimental Social Psychology, vol. 13,* New York, Academic Press.

Fischer, J.M., Ravizza, M. (1998). *Responsibility and control: a theory of moral responsibility.* Cambridge, Cambridge University Press.

Fischman, W., DiBara, J., & Gardner, H. (2006). Creating good education against the Odds. *Cambridge Journal of Education, 36*(3), 383-398.

Fisher, J. (2004). Social responsibility and ethics: Clarifying the concepts. *Journal of Business Ethics, 52,* 391-400.

Freiberg, H.J. (1999) (Ed.), *School climate: Measuring, improving and sustaining healthy learning environments.* Philadelphia: Falmer Press.

Friedman, I.A. (2003). Self-efficacy and burnout in teaching: the importance of interpersonal-relations efficacy. *Social Psychology of Education, 6,* 191-215.

Glendenning, D., (2002). Responsibility and liability in education: Ireland. *European Journal for Education Law and Policy, 6,* 99-101.

Godfrey, P.G. & Hatch, N.W. (2006). Researching corporate social responsibility: An agenda for the 21th Century. *Journal of Business Ethics, 70,* 87-98.

Gounalakis, G. (2002). Responsibility and liability in education: Germany *European Journal for Education Law and Policy, 6,* 83-92.

Hamilton, V.L. (1978). Who is Responsible? Toward a Social Psychology of Responsibility Attribution. *Social Psychology, 41,* 316-328.

Hamilton, V.L. (1980). Intuitive Psychologist or Intuitive Lawyer? Alternative Models of the Attribution Process. *Journal of Personality and Social Psychology, 39,* 767-772.

Heider, F. (1958). *The psychology of interpersonal relations.* New York:Wiley.

Karen Seashore, L., Febey, K., & Schroeder. R. (2005). State-Mandated Accountability in High Schools: Teachers' Interpretations of a New Era. *Educational Evaluation and Policy Analysis, 27 (2), 177-204.*

Legrand, A. (2002). Responsibility and liability in education: France. *European Journal for Education Law and Policy, 6,* 75-81.

Martin, B.N., Crossland, B., &Johnson, J.A. (2001). Is there a connection: Teachers empowerment, teachers' sense of responsibility, and student success? *Paper presented at the Annual meeting of the Mid-South Educational Research Association* (30th, Little Rock, AR, November 14-16, 2001).

Matteucci, M.C. (2007). Teachers facing school failure: social representations of intelligence and behavioural feedback. Social *Psychology of Education, 10*(1), pp.29-53.

Matteucci, M.C., & Gosling, P. (2004). Italian and French teachers faced with pupil's academic failure: the norm of effort. *European Journal of Psychology of Education, 19*(2), 147-166.

Mugny, G. & Carugati, F. (1989) *Social representations of intelligence.* Cambridge: Cambridge University Press.

National Union of Teachers (2003). Education, the law and you. Retrived October 15, 2007, from www.teachers.org.uk

Poulis, P., & Fortsakis, T. (2002). Responsibility and liability in education: Greece. *European Journal for Education Law and Policy, 6,* 93-97.

Rossi, A. (2001). (Ed.), *Caring and doing for others. Social responsibility in the domains of family, Work, and Community.* Chicago/London: The University of Chicago Press.

Schlenker, B.R., Britt T., Pennington, J., Murphy, R. (1994). The triangle model of responsibility. *Psychological Review, 101,* 632-652.

Shaver, K.G. (1985), *The attribution of blame: causality, responsibility, and blameworthness.* New York, Springer-Verlag.

Shaver, K.G., & Drown, D. (1986), On causality, responsibility, and self-blame: a theoretical note. *Journal of Personality and Social Psychology, 50,* 697-702.

Unesco (2007). *The curriculum.* Retrived October 03, 2007, from http://www. unesco.org/education/tlsf/TLSF/theme_a//mod05/uncom05t01s01.htm

Valli, L., Croninger R.G., & Walters, K. (2007). Who (else) is the teacher? Cautionary notes on teacher accountability systems. *Americal Journal of Education, 113(4), 635-662.*

Vallverdu Calafell, J., Moya Gutierrez, S., & Somoza Lopez, A. (2006). Social responsibility and accountability : A possible binomial. *International Advances in Economic Research, 12,* 125-130

Vanderstraetem, R. (2007). Professions in organizations, professional work in education. *British Journal of Sociology of Education, 28*(5), 621-635.

Weiner, B. (1995). *Judgment of responsibility. A foundation for a theory of social conduct.* New York, London: Guilford Press.

Weiner, B. (2003). The classroom as a courtroom. *Social Psychology of Education, 6,* pp. 3-15.

Witt, L.A. (2001). Responsibility in work organizations. In A. E. Auhagen & H. W. Bierhoff (Eds.), *Responsibility: the many faces of a social phenomenon* (pp. 139-147). London: Routledge

Word Business Council for Sustainable Development (1999). *Corporate Social Responsibility: Meeting changing expectations.* Cambridge: The MIT Press. Available from: http://www.wbcsd.org

In: Corporate Social Responsibility
Editor: Adam R. Timpere

ISBN: 978-1-60456-284-2

Chapter 11

HELPING SMEs TO TAKE CSR: RESPONSIBLE BUSINESS SCRUB BRUSH CAMPS IN SRI LANKA

Tarja Ketola [*]
University of Vaasa, Finland

ABSTRACT

Devastating experiences can turn companies as well as individuals responsible. A consultant of a Finnish company, Novetos Consulting Ltd, survived the Asian Tsunami in 2004. Her experience changed the course of Novetos Consulting, which started to organize responsible business high-altitude camps in Sri Lanka. These camps are called Scrub Brushes because Finnish business managers go there as hands-on groups to build something useful for local orphans. Many managers of small and medium-sized enterprises (SMEs) have embraced this initiative and learned a great deal about themselves, co-operation and mutual solidarity. They have then brought their individual sense of responsibility into their SME businesses. Unfortunately, managers of large companies seem avoid individual involvement in social responsibility issues. Large companies only observe laws and donate relatively small amounts of money. It is suggested in this paper that top managers' individual sense of responsibility could change the course of not only SMEs but also large companies.

INTRODUCTION

Devastating experiences change individuals. As a result of their deepened understanding, they often try to change others, too, even at their workplaces. Seldom do they succeed because the colleagues have not experienced a similar awakening. But if a major catastrophe

[*] tarja.ketola@uwasa.fi

hits and affects thousands, even hundreds of thousands, of people, something may move even inside those not directly affected.

However, it seems that only incidents with either geographic or ethnic or personal proximity have a potential to move most people. Most Europeans remain cold to the sufferings of Asian victims to floods and mud slides resulting from deforestation and climate change, and few Asians warm up to the distress of European workers for the mass lay-offs resulting from companies removing their production operations to developing countries. Furthermore, any induced feeling of empathy usually fades away fast. The more your initial emphatic feeling is influenced by a justified sense of responsibility, the faster it seems to disappear. It is mentally easier to ignore hardships faced by others, if you or your group of people has affected their occurrence, and particularly if you benefit from their outcome. Denial, devaluing and projection of these incidents are commonplace defences against the feelings of guilt. The vicious circle of the market mechanism is based on these primitive reactions: triumphant winners suppress their guilt and humiliated losers quietly swear retaliation.

It seems that only acts of nature fully independent on acts of humans can derive open, global empathy. According to current scientific knowledge, earthquakes occurring at the bottom of seas and tsunamis caused by them are acts of nature that are independent on preceding human acts. The human consequences of tsunami waves caused by earthquakes at the bottom of the Indian Ocean on 26 December 2004 resulted in unprecedented global wave of sympathy. Some of the countries affected were overwhelmed by charity work, donations of materials by companies, donations of money through charities, and offers for assistance by governments. Relative to human and material loss and damage, Thailand received by far the greatest amount of emotional and practical sympathy from Europe because of the high number of European tourists affected by the tsunami on their Christmas holiday there. Also Sri Lanka gained much sympathy for this reason, but because of its politically instability and undeveloped infrastructure, much less aid reached the victims. The worst affected country, Indonesia, was virtually forgotten by European citizens, if not by charities.

Jaffe and Pasternak (2006) studied moral intensity as a predictor of social responsibility. They talked about the following factors: probability, proximity, magnitude, harm, consensus and temporal immediacy. While their study dealt with the research subjects predicting their reactions to the possible closing down of a glass-making factory, this study draws conclusions on social responsibility after the tsunami incident had taken place. Despite the time difference – possibly in the near future vs. definitely in the recent past – the factors influencing social responsibility are the same with some modifications.

Many Northern Europeans know someone who either died, lost a relative, or was physically or mentally damaged by the Boxing Day tsunami in 2004. People felt that it could have just as well happened to them or their family. Such a probability factor of personal involvement in an incident works also in hindsight. This *retrospective probability* was coupled with *ethnic proximity*. Although the tsunami took place in a geographically distant area for North Europeans (geographic non-proximity), it affected people of their ethnic origin staying there as tourists or expatriates (ethnic proximity). The live coverage by the reporters and the video clips filmed by the tourists displayed on all television channels showing explicitly the powers of the tsunami and the resulting devastation and human suffering added a third and fourth factor: magnitude and harm. The *magnitude* of the tsunami waves and their destruction powers surprised most people – except for some experts and victims of earlier tsunamis (e.g., in Japan). The massive human, environmental and material *harm* done by the tsunami waves was quite unexpected because there had never before in the memorable history of humankind arisen such a large-scale tsunami: it affected nearly all the coasts of the Indian Ocean. At first there was very high *consensus* of the fact that action should be taken to avoid similar disasters in the future. Many different kinds of precautions were planned, including advance warning systems, alarm systems, new building standards and protection of coastal areas with mangrove forests. After a few months, however, enthusiasm faded, people went back to their earlier ways, building standards were not modified and natural coastal protection was forgotten. Only the use of scientific warning systems was adopted more extensively in the area. Thus temporal immediacy affected people's sense of responsibility but only for a short time. *Retrospective temporal immediacy* shows how short our memory is.

The combined effect of the retrospective probability, ethnic proximity, magnitude, harm, consensus and retrospective temporal immediacy of the tsunami evoke a storm of emotions in Europe. This was evident immediately after the tsunami. Millions of Europeans were upset, wanting anxiously to do something. Most of them ended up donating money to charities working in the area, so that they could feel that they had contributed to the "solving of the problem"; some took more active part in these "solutions". *Sympathy* was overwhelming. The upsurge of feelings lasted for a few weeks, after which most people became hardened to the relentless bombarding by the media. Sympathy never lasts long – it is an intense feeling, the stocks of which are soon exhausted, if not externally by constant reminders, then internally by burnout (which many amateur helpers eventually found out). If we sympathize with other human beings, we share and suffer with them (Hardee 2003) – and cannot help them.

Empathy is a longer-lasting phenomenon than sympathy because empathy is not built solely on emotions but integrates emotion with intelligence.

> "Empathy is concerned with a much higher order of human relationship and understanding: engaged detachment. In empathy, we "borrow" another's feelings to observe, feel, and understand them – but not to take them onto ourselves. By being a participant-observer, we come to understand how the other person feels. An empathetic observer enters into the equation and then is removed." (Hardee 2003)

Empathy leads to long-term, planned action with the ultimate aim of the subjects learning or restarting to help themselves and rebuilding their lives on a sustainable basis. The aid work of established, professional charities, such the Red Cross and UNICEF, is based on empathy.

That is not to say that amateurs could not learn empathy and base their actions on it. On the contrary: individuals and organizations in any walk of life can start empathic responsible behaviour. Managers and companies can build their corporate social responsibility (CSR) on empathy both internally and externally. In this paper a novel CSR action format is introduced. We shall see that CSR is far from one-way charitable actions – even when the subjects (not objects!) of such actions are the most vulnerable individuals of society. Managers and companies can learn invaluable lessons from their CSR actions. This new approach has naturally its own limitations, which will be discussed in the conclusions.

NOVETOS CONSULTING LTD AWAKENED BY THE TSUNAMI

One of those who survived the Asian Tsunami 2004 was a consultant of a Finnish company, Novetos Consulting Ltd, on her holiday in Sri Lanka. After the first few months, most victims became weary of all the questions asked by the concerned people they met. This consultant wrote her reflections on the web pages of the company (http://www.novetos.fi). Her first reflections were titled: "Dare to be frightened". She felt that the reason why she survived, and so many others did not, was the fact that she became frightened by the strange behaviour of the sea from the very beginning and wanted to get as far as possible away from it. She saw a lesson to be learned from this also for SME managers: they should dare to be frightened by alarming messages. They should react quickly and efficiently instead of covering it up under "everything is under control" pretence. She concluded that the ability to read weak signals is possible only if one is ready to be frightened by the message. Hence fear is a healthy feeling. Fear is a messenger. That is why it is valuable to learn to know one's reactions amidst fear. It develops courage to follow one's instincts and act determinedly.

In the chaos following the tsunami, she bumped into a big man riding a small moped. He was a Finn who lived in Sri Lanka and had, with his wife, long been trying to help orphans in the Southern part of the country. This encounter started the idea of turning his attempts to a larger project.

RESPONSIBLE BUSINESS SCRUB BRUSH CAMPS IN SRI LANKA

The direct experience of one consultant of the Asian tsunami changed the course of Novetos Consulting (2006), which started to organize responsible business high-altitude camps in Sri Lanka. These camps are called Scrub Brushes because Finnish business managers go to Sri Lanka as hands-on groups to build something useful for local orphans.

In February 2006 a group of SME managers renovated a children's home in Hikkaduwa for orphaned children. In addition to nailing building materials together they nailed together also shared image of responsible management. The purpose was to build a long-term, sustainable leadership model based on ethics. Instead of playing drop-out games until it is time for us to drop out, we can see the world and its people as a potential of what they can develop into.

Novetos Consulting (2006) emphasize that it is important to take small steps and make sure that the execution of each step is possible and the next step is close enough, so that the outcome does not drain in the sand. The first step at the orphanage was to clean, repair and paint the buildings, so that basic requirements for housing were fulfilled. The second step would be to employ language teachers, which should be easy once the classrooms are in good condition. The third step would be the purchase of shoes and school uniforms for these children. The outcome, orphaned children going to school and being educated, will change the course of these children – and the views of the communities around them.

There are many orphanages in poor condition in that area of Sri Lanka, which means aid work for many years to come. The running of the orphanages, and the schools in them, needs continuous financing, for which a sponsorship system was organized. Companies, work groups and individuals were invited to sponsor a child, group of children or an entire orphanage on a regular basis. Both the givers and the children would feel pleasure for the sponsorships. The actions of the Finnish managers could be seen as building blocks of their own ego and identity; helping others helps them, too.

According to Novetos Consulting (2006), ethical leadership encompasses justice, fairness, reliability, uprightness, consistency and broad-mindedness. These findings are supported by management and leadership literature (see e.g., Ketola 2006ab, Kramer & Tyler 1996, Robertson & Crittenden 2003) and these characteristics belong to Aristotelian (348 BC) virtues. Novetos believe that staff wellbeing, customer satisfaction and profitability are improved by ethical leadership. Hectic business easily narrows the views of even best managers, and as a result, their decisions are not always transparent and may not take all different interests into account. Novetos Consulting is offering the operation Scrub Brush for managers who want to find perspective for the leadership. Scrub Brush allows managers to go deep into developing their ethical leadership, which is a prerequisite for sustainable success. Ethical leadership cannot be faked or learned by heart; it requires subjective experience and insight. A genuinely important issue to a manager turns into genuine action by him/her. Scrub Brush takes managers away from their normal circumstances so that they can find their own line of thought, which they want to follow in their leadership. According to Novetos Consulting (2006), this camp involves a purposeful training process, practical work, personal coaching and a dynamic group. The idea of ethical leadership becomes concrete by taking social responsibility for the orphans. Ideas are immediately put into action.

While small and medium-sized enterprises (SMEs) in many countries are often reported to lag behind large companies in CSR issues (e.g., Jenkins 2004, Studer et al. 2006), many managers of SMEs in Finland have embraced this initiative and learned a great deal about themselves, co-operation and solidarity. They have then brought their individual sense of responsibility into their SME businesses.

One of the participants was the managing director of an information technology (IT) firm FeedbackDialog Ltd. He used the Scrub Brush to develop further his idea of harmonic leadership. The hype of IT business made the IT companies swell from workshops employing a couple of IT enthusiasts to companies with 1,000–2,000 employees. The companies focussed on increasing their share value through acquisitions and market possessions, which involved maneuvering and inhuman leadership, resulting in ill-being, stress and burnout. Such greedy and arrogant behaviour was accepted by the business community: it was business as usual. At the time many people thought that this way of doing business was ethical since the rules were the same for everyone. As a managing director of an IT company he had a choice: either to accept these shared values or to pull himself and his company away from it to more sustainable business principles. It needed courage to pull away from quick profits and immediate need satisfaction. Instead of the earlier command-and control type of leadership and financial motivation he now believes in creating a shared vision and shared experience of doing something significant. He thinks that his own enthusiasm and commitment are invaluable. He finds that the answers to corporate social responsibility issues are not as clear as before: where are the limits of CSR? The new surroundings, different culture, aid work experience and peer group offered by the Scrub Brush allowed the contemplation and reflection of this question.

Novetos Consulting (2006) summarizes the experiences of the first Scrub Brush camp as:

- realizing that ethical leadership is not words but action – constant action;
- adopting a completely different way of thinking;
- understanding that trust improves both business and staff wellbeing;
- finding it easier to pay attention to and even anticipate views of others;
- improving the quality of decision-making;
- taking automatically many more influencing factors into account, and, therefore, seldom
- having to return to the issues, which saves time and energy;
- reacting more holistically to conflicts with more comprehensive outcomes;
- filling up with energy;
- deciding to take one's whole team to a Scrub Brush camp.

The second Scrub Brush camp in Sri Lanka will take place between 28 March and 8 April 2007. Managers of small and medium-sized enterprises (SMEs) have occupied the available places. Managers of large companies seem avoid individual involvement in social responsibility issues. Most large companies simply do what laws and binding agreements require, and donate to charity relatively small amounts of money compared to their turnover. Which "corporate citizen" donates one per cent of its turnover to charity like many individual citizens do? A large number of individuals sponsor a child through Plan, Save the Children Fund, World Vision or other charity by paying 25 € out of the average monthly salary of 2.500 € – not to mention their generous contributions to aid work for disaster victims. Top managers' individual feeling of responsibility could change the course of even large companies, which could change the course of millions of children.

CONCLUSIONS

Social responsibility for an incident that has already taken place may be accepted by both individuals and companies on the basis of retrospective probability, ethnic proximity, magnitude, harm, consensus and retrospective temporal immediacy. These factors together seem to lead to a wave of sympathy, which gradually fades away. A longer-term social responsibility requires empathy, which is possible for individuals and companies alike. This paper has discussed a case of social responsibility arisen from the 2004 Asian tsunami and expanded from a devastating individual experience through novel consultancy action to in-depth CSR for SMEs.

SMEs cannot afford to donate as much money as large companies in absolute terms (although many of them probably donate relatively more). Giving donations to charities seems to be a strategic image issue for large companies: they donate money to gain public visibility, and higher-profile companies donate somewhat more money to keep their profile untarnished (see e.g., Brammer & Millington 2006, Brammer et al. 2006, Campbell & Slack 2006). For many American companies corporate social responsibility (CSR) equals charity donations. For many European, and particularly Northern European, companies, on the other hand, CSR means doing business in a socially responsible way. Many multinationals combine these two approaches by drafting CSR principles for their business activities (such as ethical codes of conduct) and giving donations for activities outside their line of business (such as sports, arts and alleviation of poverty) – and apply each selectively on a global scale.

SMEs could do the same – in their own way. It is usually easier for SMEs to make their business operations responsible, and even sustainable, because they have fewer and less severe issues to change than large companies. Novetos Consulting Ltd has developed a way in which SMEs can think *and* act globally. In their Scrub Brush camps in Sri Lanka, they help Finnish SME managers to re-evaluate their ethical values in totally different circumstances than they are used to *and* to build with their hands something for the orphans: a deed donation to the most disadvantaged of their materially poor society from the most advantaged of their materially rich society. The SMEs are also invited to become sponsors of these orphans, which any SME can afford.

There are many limitations in Novetos Consulting's approach to CSR. The training at the Scrub Brush camps focuses mostly on the internal manager-staff relationships and does not address any burning external stakeholder issues, such as communication (see e.g., Morsing & Schultz 2006) or the roles of company and its stakeholders (see e.g., Pater & van Lierop 2006, Vos 2003). This is most peculiar since the Scrub Brushes takes place in Sri Lanka, far away from the internal stakeholders of the SME managers. It may be the very fact that the scene has been removed so far away even from the usual external stakeholders of these SMEs that the CSR reality becomes blurred. It is almost absurd that the Scrub Brushes do not seem to reflect on the human rights side of CSR (see e.g., Welford 2002) either, despite being held in an area rife with human rights violations. The reports from the first camp do not mention any dialogue between the orphans and the SME managers – the language barrier, of course is a problem, but it can be overcome by a mixture of basic English, sign language and facial expressions. The Scrub Brush camps seem to isolate themselves from both the SME reality in Finland and the local reality in Sri Lanka, and dwell on the personal convictions of the Scrub Brush participants. Maybe complete isolation is needed for silent Finns to find the essence of CSR? (Self-mockery – I am a Finn, too.)

None of the limitations cloud the novelty of the Scrub Brush idea. Novetos Consulting will no doubt develop it further as soon as more practical experience has been gained. The second Scrub Brush camp may take a more culturally holistic approach to the CSR issues contemplated. Since the Scrub Brush camps are already trying to make sense of CSR through thinking and acting, they would probably benefit from the empirical findings by Cramer et al. (2006). The SME managers returning from the Scrub Brush camps are the change agents Cramer et al. describe, initiating the CSR process within their own organizations. Like with Cramer et al., the CSR meaning they develop "stems from their personal and organisational values and frames of reference". Although the SME managers have a great deal of position power and (perhaps) charisma in their companies, which all change agents may not have, also the SME managers must attune the vocabulary of CSR to the language of their colleagues and subordinates they aim to convince.

All companies, whatever size they are, need the support of their staff for their CSR. Employees are both CSR issues and CSR actors. They decide whether their CSR issues become problems or successes, and, by mediating between the employer and the external stakeholders as a part of their job, they also contribute to birth and death of local, regional and global CSR accomplishments. No wonder the SME managers would like to take their teams to Scrub Brush camps.

References

Aristotle 348 BC. Ethics. In J. Barnes (Ed.) 1988. *The Complete Works of Aristotle.* Princeton: Princeton University Press.

Brammer, S. & A. Millington 2006. 'Firm size, organizational visibility and corporate philanthropy: an empirical analysis'. *Business Ethics – A European Review,* 15:1, 6–18.

Brammer, S., A. Millington & S. Pavelin 2006. 'Is philanthropy strategic? An analysis of the management of charitable giving in large UK companies'. *Business Ethics – A European Review,* 15:3, 234–245.

Campbell, D. & R. Slack 2006. 'Public visibility as a determinant of the rate of corporate charitable donations'. *Business Ethics – A European Review,* 15:1, 19–28.

Cramer, J., A. van der Heijden & J. Jonker 2006. 'Corporate social responsibility: making sense through thinking and acting'. *Business Ethics – A European Review,* 15:4, 380–389.

Hardee, J.T. 2003. 'An overview of empathy'. *The Permanente Journal*, 7:4. See: http://xnet.kp.org/permanentejournal/fall03/cpc.html.

Jaffe, E.D. & H. Pasternak 2006. 'Moral intensity as a predictor of social responsibility'. *Business Ethics – A European Review,* 15:1, 53–63.

Jenkins, H. 2004. 'Corporate social responsibility – engaging small and medium sized enterprises in the debate'. *Conference Proceedings,* 98–111. *Corporate Social Responsibility and Environmental Management Conference,* 28–29 June 2004, University of Nottingham.

Ketola, T. 2006a. 'Do you trust your boss? – a Jungian analysis of leadership reliability in CSR.' *Electronic Journal of Business Ethics and Organization Studies,* 11:2, 6–14. See: http://ejbo.jyu.fi/pdf/ejbo_vol11_no2_pages_6-14.pdf.

Ketola, T. 2006b. 'From CR-psychopaths to responsible corporations: waking up the inner Sleeping Beauty of companies'. *Corporate Social Responsibility and Environmental Management*, 13:2, 98–107.

Kramer, R. M. & T. R. Tyler (Eds.) 1996. *Trust in Organizations. Frontiers of Theory and Research.* Thousand Oaks: Sage.

Morsing, M. & M. Schultz 2006. 'Corporate social responsibility communication: stakeholder information, response and involvement strategies'. *Business Ethics: A European Review,* 15:4, 323–338.

Novetos Consulting 2006. See: http://www.novetos.fi. (Visited on 28 December 2006.)

Pater, A. & K. van Lierop 2006. 'Sense and sensitivity: the roles of organisation and stakeholders in managing corporate social responsibility'. *Business Ethics: A European Review,* 15:4, 339–351.

Robertson, C.J. and W.F. Crittenden 2003. Mapping moral philosophies: strategic implications for multinational firms. *Strategic Management Journal*, 24:4, 385–392.

Studer, S., R. Welford & P. Hills 2006. 'Engaging Hong Kong businesses in environmental change: drivers and barriers'. *Business Strategy and the Environment*, 15:6, 416–431.

Welford, R. 2002. 'Globalization, corporate social responsibility and human rights'. *Corporate Social Responsibility and Environmental Management* 9, 1–7.

Vos, J.F.J. 2003. 'Corporate social responsibility and the identification of stakeholders'. *Corporate Social Responsibility and Environmental Management* 10, 141–152.

In: Corporate Social Responsibility
Editor: Adam R. Timpere

ISBN: 978-1-60456-284-2

Chapter 12

LONG-TERM THINKING IN THE SERVICE OF CORPORATE SOCIAL RESPONSIBILITY

Erzsébet Nováky [*] ***and Gergely Tyukodi*** [†]
Futures Studies Department, Corvinus University of Budapest, Hungary

ABSTRACT

The main goal of corporate social responsibility is to make companies not only to act based on a purely economic point of view, but also to involve other aspects into business decisions – like the value of the natural environment or to create a workplace that pays attention to the needs and wishes of its employees. In this chapter we focus on how another tool can assist CSR to achieve its goals. The other tool that we introduce is Futures Studies. It supports CSR with its long-term perspective that tries to investigate possible alternatives of the future more effectively, bringing new values into the decision-making process.

INTRODUCTION

Nowadays, in western culture countries, companies and organizations are judged mainly based on their economic activities. The underlying assumption for emphasizing the economic result of companies lies in current management literature saying that the main goal of companies is to make profit by meeting customers' needs [1]. However, profit as the ultimate driver of companies' success is overemphasized, as western cultures believe that money is the ultimate value in business, thus in society, too. Since there are other values that people follow and that cannot be described in monetary terms, the main assumption of economic theories is not complete. Some sciences have already started to focus on how to involve economic effects of businesses that are not closely related to the contracting parties in economic

[*] erzsebet.novaky@uni-corvinus.hu
[†] gergely.tyukodi@uni-corvinus.hu

models, but the mainstream still believes in the value of money and making profit. This view is much stressed by investors for whom success is measured in stock exchange rates that are closely related to the notion of profitability. Due to high competition on the stock exchange companies translate making profit to maximize profit in order to please investors who are to decide about long-term strategies. The vicious cycle is thus completed: investors stick to stock exchange rates which are indexed to profits that become the guideline for corporate management controlled by investors. Since economic theories don't only focus on maximizing profit, but also say that money in the present is more valuable than money in the future, companies usually prefer to make money on the short run rather than the long run. Thus, the effects of short-term thinking and valuing mainly money in business decisions called the attention of scientists to find new solutions for their problems.

Environmental sciences and Futures Studies (further on: FS) are some of the sciences that try to come up with new theories that deal not only with value as in dollar that is closely related to the contracting parties, but they also try to internalize side effects and other values. In this paper we focus on how long-term thinking and FS tries to answer the new challenge and how it feeds CSR, which has similar goal – make companies not only focus on money, but also on other values. Environmental sciences extend the close environment of business decisions by calculating with the impacts of business activities on the environment at analyzing the possible net profit, as the ultimate driver of business decisions, of the different alternatives. They convince governments to create quotas for air pollution in order to make companies pay the price of the side effects of their activities on the environment.

The concept of FS focuses on the long-term consequences of our decisions and actions. It aims at taking into consideration not only the short-term economic aspects of decisions, but also to draw up different possible alternatives of the future. Another aspect of the focus of FS is how the consequence of these different alternatives probably being realized in the future influence on, and what the impacts of these alternatives have on either the companies or the shareholders. Thus, on the basis of FS we are able to bring new dimensions into business decisions. In the end, companies make their decisions based on economic indicators, but long-term and wider consequences of the alternative decisions are built in the process. If we want to make a conclusion in the end how we can make more responsible decisions, all of us need to be future oriented enough i.e. "a futurist to some extent" in order to understand the more complex impacts of our decisions that enable us to make more realistic analysis in making business decisions.

Futures Studies, Change, Alternatives and Responsibility

But how can we be a futurist? How can one think and act as a futurist? What do we need to do, and with doing it for what can we be responsible? Based on the responsibility of futurists [2], we can say that professional futurists are scientists, experts who:

- focus on finding possible (i.e. not totally unrealistic) alternative futures,
- communicate alternative futures,
- assist in implementing alternative futures, and
- make people to accept changes.

In order to discover alternatives, futurists need to focus on long-term periods where predetermined elements weight less and give space to a wider range of opportunities. Thinking about long-term futures is a concept shared by environmental sciences and sustainability since their objective of satisfying today's need without harming the needs of future generations also relates to long-term thinking. By dealing with long-term alternative futures, making them transparent to the people and communicating it, futurists support the idea of sustainability and even go further, revealing hidden relations and hidden points of view into decision-making. Thus, we would like to introduce the main concept of FS and articulate how each of its characteristics supports sustainability and its main application at companies: CSR. Furthermore we will give suggestions on what we can do in order to make a more responsible society with using the concept of long-term thinking in individual decision-making.

About Futures Studies

FS is a relatively new science, it has a history of only about 50 years. New phenomenon of the 1960's, such as rapidly increasing population, signs of disappearance of non-renewing resources, increasing environmental pollution, world crisis of education insisted that economic growth was not sustainable in its current state; the need of finding new ways of thinking and approaches emerged. All around the world, people started to look more into the future. Towards the end of the 20th century an increasing number of people spoke and wrote about the future, but most of them didn't focus on understanding the future better nor on developing more detailed opportunities about the future. On the other hand, scientists that started to aim at dealing with the future on a scientific level from the 1960's, and have established world wide FS organizations to make easier to exchange approaches, methods and ideas about the future, are more and more expected in many countries.

FS was described from the beginning as a field of science that intends to explore possible futures of different systems of the society or even the possible futures of the whole society. It investigates the field of the future that is related to societies' and individuals' future shaping activities. This way FS emphasizes alternative futures that emerge not only from the changes in the environment, but also as the consequence of human factors and human actions. FS tries – through developing and applying suitable methodologies and methods – to reduce uncertainty that comes from not yet existing processes, events, relations, causalities and states in order to create the chance for people to make less risky decisions.

Investigating changes is one of the bases of FS. Differentiating changes in place and time can bring us closer to understand what the essence of change is: assimilation to the new environment or dissatisfaction with the current situation. The first one pushes us into the future, while we "overtake" the future with the second approach. In both cases we need to prepare ourselves for the coming changes – in what FS can help us. It calls our attention to the changes that are ahead of us, it helps us to find out what to do in order to make favorable changes to come true, or to avoid changes that are unfavorable. Thus, FS is the science of change that sets different goals according to the changing environment. When we set goals, usually we decide on changing the future. We can change processes and events that haven't happened yet, but that are determined to some extent by the past. We can consider this as living in double pressure since the present is limited from both the past and the future. Today FS focuses more to free ourselves from the past in order to lead the world to a new path.

In order to reach our aims it is important to know where our limits are. Mapping the boundaries of forecasts reveals that we need to accept uncertainty, we should not try to dismiss it, but we need to learn facing it. We need to differentiate between different futures in order to leave behind the past and the present, but at the same time not to get far away from the future. Thus, futurists differentiate between plausible, possible, probable and preferable futures. Hence, we are able to tell how to get from the possible to the probable future, or from the preferable to the plausible future: it helps us to make decisions that lead us from one future to another.

Finding Alternative Futures

Now, that we described the basic approach and ideas of FS we should spend some time on focusing through which processes FS can contribute to our understanding of the future. First, we have to stress that one of the main assumption of FS is that there is no such thing as one future but rather there are different possibilities. One of the main goals of FS is to find and describe these alternative futures. It is not an easy activity to do. A critical issue regarding describing alternative futures is that we need to use different methodological approaches in stable and unstable situations. Different methodologies, thus different methods need to be applied in getting to know the future, in determination analysis of the future, in time and place analysis of the future, in complexity analysis and in analysis of the alternatives of the future [3].

In stable circumstances the relation of the past, the present and the future, and how they feed each other gives us the chance to gain information about the future to some extent. In stable times the future appears as more or less the consequence of the past and the present since as time passes the forces that keep up earlier tendencies get stronger. According to the classical philosophical methodological principles the analysis of the past and the present leads us to evaluate the consequences and draw some lessons concerning the future. Thus in stable environment we do have access to information – about the past and present – that enables us to know more about our future. Our task then is to learn how to collect, analyse and evaluate this information. While in unstable times, when the forces that shape the future haven't developed yet in the past and in the present, we cannot rely on facts only about the past and the present. We can only know more about the future if we seek for changes and renewals. We need a positive approach to the future in order to be successful in this activity – we need to be able to continuously revaluate the past and the future according to new phenomenon. The new approach focuses on identifying turning points in the development of different phenomenon, thus it helps to find future states that differ from the past and the present in their main characteristics. This approach also suggests that the future is not so dependent on the past and the present, and thus we can shape the future by human actions to a wider extent.

The probability of the future is one of the most important characteristic of FS in stable times. In case of certain objective conditions, only one concrete future will come true that has a probability between 0 and 1. This probability represents the chance of the future to come true. However, in reality the probability can never reach 1 since none of the processes can be determined to such extent, there is always room for variation, different possible development paths and outcomes. Probability only reflects how much room is left for change, thus possibilities and probabilities of different future alternatives are determined by the relations between the past, the present and the future. The strength and the stability of these relations create the differences between alternative futures. Nowadays, the probability of the future contains new dimensions. In unstable times, the importance of statistical determination decreases, and the role of coincidence increases. From the development of the past and the present, we can not conclude on the future based solely on probabilities. Differently from the past, there is no future with special probability (thus we should not make predictions); however there are many alternative futures with more or less similar probabilities. Sudden and low-probability changes play an important role in shaping the actual outcome that realizes in the future. In unstable situation the internal dynamics of a model such as its feedback loops – as for example our expectations about the future – can also change the course of events.

In FS there is a problem of understanding time and space. According to common sense knowledge time is understood as a linear process. In FS however we need to explore the loops that connect the past, the present and the future through a complex feedback process and self-organizing principles which we call "time-space binding". In unstable times it is especially useful to look into the dynamics of time like this. With this way of thinking about time we can see that the past, the present and the future don't exist only after each other, but they exist together in each moment. Present contains the past, the evolutionary development that led to the present, and the future that relies on further evolutionary decisions. If we analyse the future from the present, we can find various future trends and structures, but if we talk about the effect of the future on the present, we anticipate the future – we bring it back to the present in the forms of wishes, goals, hopes and fears.

We also need to deal with complexity after due consideration in unstable times. In stability it is enough to focus on the key elements that determine the system, and we make predictions on the future development of the whole system based on them. Since the relations between the elements of the system and the influencing factors are simple and there are only a few feedback loops between them, it is reasonable to do accordingly. However in unstable situations we need to take into consideration many elements and components of the system since small changes of single parts can create new situations. When dealing with multidimensional systems that involve many feedback loops it is critical to gain various insights and thus to apply different approaches – like combining top-down and bottom-up perspectives – at the same time. In complex systems we also need to apply different methods for short- and middle-term processes, for linear, exponential and logistic developments and for reversible and irreversible changes.

The issue of alternatives is a key characteristic when we think about the long-term future. We need to pay attention to different possible outcomes when we talk about goals, tools or decisions on possible implementations. In stability we didn't need to focus on alternatives, since the future was mostly determined by the trends; however in unstable times, when future has various ways to develop, we need to think in alternatives. If we involve as many entities, shareholders, parts of the society into decision-making and implementation as it is possible and reasonable, we can increase the source of alternatives since individuals and social groups want to change not only their future, but also their images of the future. In contrary to previous eras, now there is a bigger need to compare the different possibilities that are ahead of us and to decide which ones to accept taking into consideration many points of views.

Participation is a new approach and phenomenon that appears in describing alternative futures [4]. On participation we mean that as many participants as possible should be involved in describing alternative futures whose future is dependent on the decision, who will be involved in the implementation and who will live in the world created accordingly. Without knowing their opinions about the present and their expectations about the future, we cannot aim at bringing a desired future alternative to live. Thus, we need to cooperate with others, if we want to make good decisions in the present regarding the future.

Communication of Alternative Futures

There are three questions that we need to discuss here: what, when and how alternative futures should be communicated. If we want to make better decisions, we need to make our ideas about the future public. We need to talk about ideas that create a positive change in the environment and also that are negative alternatives about the future. We should do it from a reasonable point of view. Positive alternatives about the future mean that we have a chance to lead the society and the economy to a better development path, and that we have a chance to solve a possible problem in the future. Negative alternatives of the future show that current conditions may go worse, changes themselves would lead to a not favourable direction and often if nothing happens, catastrophe could happen. The main reason of the communication of these negative alternatives is to make people understand that current trends are not sustainable, thus we need to do some changes as soon as possible. We should try to be neutral, neither too optimistic nor too pessimistic, when we talk about our ideas about the alternative futures since they can disorient us from what we would like to do otherwise.

The question of when we should communicate alternative futures is more difficult. If we think of a certain decision-making process, we should only communicate the forecasts and the alternatives, when the alternatives are scientifically proven. It is important to reveal also partial forecasts that have statements and consequences that are not totally proven, but according to current scientific approaches they can be verified, and if any kind of strong signal indicates that the forecast can make major consequences on the society. Hence, we should emphasize that in cases like this, the forecasts contain even more uncertainty. In additional questions (e.g. social consequences of global warming) we should start social discussions, thus the society itself can decide on the needed steps.

We often find signals that indicate a possibly critical change in relation to our current situations which can maybe create new futures. Some of these signals are not yet developed but have a restructuring potential: these are the so called weak signals. When we talk about the long-term future, we need to use our best knowledge, to use our methodological experience and intuition in order to identify the seeds of change [5], weak signals and issues that seem to emerge, especially if tendencies continue to develop without any changes. If we think like a futurist we can help making better decisions not by saying there are no changes, but to reveal the opportunities that changes might bring with themselves and to make evaluation of their directions and consequences before they are visible. It is important to make people aware of some processes that have lost dynamics and thus are unable to develop further and of others that are just gaining momentum as soon as possible in order to leave room for developing suitable reactions. In order to recognise that some processes cease to exist or become critical we often have to revaluate our own basic assumptions that were based on the past and present experiences. Self-reflective and self-critic is essential in order to think out of the box of current times as well as imagine difference and create change. Weak signals can appear in objective and in subjective factors, as well. Not only instability of processes, the sensibility for small changes can create weak signals and can give a chance for the seeds of change to appear, but weak signals can appear in forces that shape the future too. If a society is more creative and more sensible for the future, future factors have more opportunities to bring the seeds of change.

When we talk about how to communicate alternative futures, we emphasize that the most effective way for doing it is education among the different communication methods (making scientific essays, introducing results, education, and appearance in the media). With education we can exchange ideas, knowledge about the future, we can discuss different points easily and new ideas, suggestions can more easily emerge given by any of the experts. Participatory FS is an effective way to utilize these opportunities.

Implementing Alternative Futures

Implementing alternative futures is a social activity. We can not assume that the society itself will implement the future that we describe together. Alternative futures are continuously forming, changing during implementation, and they can even miss the direction since many times actual human actions don't follow the set and planned action plans even in the cases of strategies. Human thinking and the complication and unpredictability of current actions don't make it possible to implement exactly the initial ideas. In implementing the future the participation of the whole society is essential. We need to organize social actions not only for avoiding the realization of a catastrophe, but also in order to create a positive future [6].

In forming the actions, future orientation, openness, the need for renewal and responsibility of the society play a great role. Empirical researches among the Hungarian population show that the future orientation of people changed a lot over the last fifteen years. In 1992-93 hope and future shock, in the middle of the 1990's uncertainty and contradiction, and in the 21st century hope, new values and preparing for the future were the most important factors. The last one was the best observed among youth studying at universities. The research proved that positive attitude and the ability to change and shape the future increases with the increase of qualification and training.

"When we think about the future, we need to think about values, too" – said Eleonora Barbieri Masini at the conference of the World Futures Studies Federation [7]. This is a special exercise in an era when old values and questionable new values exist at the same time, and when there is a change in the social and individual values. Information as a factor of growth, respect and love of the environment and long-term commitment appear as new social values. They are not accepted everywhere: the majority hasn't accepted yet that there are more important values than personal wealth (such as the joy of work, knowledge, safe and balanced life, responsibility, etc.).

Making People Accept Changes

We might feel the importance of change, and maybe we prepare the possibly best alternatives, however it doesn't worth a lot if the society is not prepared for them, or if they don't accept them in time. Thus, we need to take responsibility to make people accept required changes. It is our task to call the attention of people to be aware that objective opportunities of change (self organization of processes) and subjective conscious and unconscious relation to change (expectations and actions of individuals and social groups) determine together which alternative future will come true. We can support this process by understanding and recognising people's relation to change and by developing the characteristics that increase the acceptance of change.

At the Futures Studies Department of the Corvinus University of Budapest, empirical researches were carried out in order to get to know students' relation to change [8]. Based on the survey that was took by about 300 students we can say that students at the Corvinus University of Budapest

- think positively about the changes, they accept the existence of change, they are not afraid of change,
- think that they adapt to changes with flexibility, but coming big changes and dangers remain unconscious for them,
- think that stability is important within their families,
- hope that all the previous characteristics give them motivation and power to take unfavourable external changes.

According to the sample we can say that youth accept changes and they look at them positively, but expressed it or not, they would like that changes don't effect their close environment, where they prefer stability. From this inference we can conclude that we have a lot of task to do in order to change the current short-term economy centric approach for being able to create new development path for different countries and for the world. We can only do this with enough responsibility for the future.

The Application of Future Thinking in Business Decisions

As we can see it from the previous part of this chapter futurists are experts who know a lot about change, especially about complex changes. But how can management of a company harmonize this long-term, complex thinking in business decisions with their ultimate goal of long-term profit maximization? Various methods exist that deal with how companies can benefit from collecting more information about the future. The most common among the methods is that they look at the future from different points of view based on the categorization of the different types of the future. These methods also apply the basic concepts and methodological approaches of FS.

The difference between the general approach of FS and applied FS is the same as the difference between sustainability and CSR. Just as everything in real life and in business, companies need a simpler, a more understandable and an easier method to apply scientific theories. CSR tries to involve the main ideas of sustainability into a process that is relatively easy to implement, and results the same: dealing better with the environment, the employees and all the other shareholders. FS at companies has the same role. Using its simpler methods gives an easy, however very innovative process that companies can use for making better decisions on the long run.

The applied concept of FS focuses on change rather than the future. Its main assumption, as it was in the theoretical part, is that the future is change the only question is the pace and the rate of that change. Thus, general applied FS approach deals with change in the following concept [9].

- Understanding and monitoring change
- Critiquing implications
- Imaging difference
- Envisioning preferred future
- Planning and implementing preferred future

If we think back to the section where we described the most important characteristics of FS in general such as long-term thinking, we can see that change is in the focus. Applied FS also deals with change however it puts much more effort into the implementation of the preferred future. It emphasizes the approach of FS that says that the future is less determined by the past and the present and human factors have much more influence on the future in unstable times. The other important difference in applied FS is the point of interest. We said that FS deals with developments, processes that we can observe in the society, the main goal is to create a better future (for different parts of the society or even for the whole society). However, just as other applied sciences, applied FS focuses on to find future alternatives and to make a better future, but from the point of view of the company or the organization. This means that applied FS takes the results of general FS, but it adds a corporate dimension and asks other questions: now that the company or the organization has more information about possible future alternatives, what should be done? How can company decision-makers take advantage from having more information of the coming changes? There seems to be a conflict between the responsibility of sharing expectations and knowledge on the future and the original FS concept of communicating alternative futures. However if we talk about applied FS, companies add their opinions about the future, they input their expectations, and they make reactions according to these modified alternative futures. Thus, their main question changes to what opportunities and threats the changes, the alternative futures bring to the company in the future and how they can benefit from knowing or at least thinking about it in advance.

By recognizing threats and opportunities that arise from different possibilities, they also gain insights to new dimensions of the future other than economic. The decreasing amount of forest for example can in the long run be rephrased as the threat of lack of resources and increasing market prices and costs and thus a seemingly environmental issue can be tackled in business terms. Thus, they can analyze the alternative futures not only from a short-term, profit-oriented point of view but from a wider perspective. CSR can thus be involved in business thinking when the time horizon is longer and the opportunities are wider.

CSR can be used as a guideline for building a future alternative where companies share responsibilities with the communities where they are embedded. In applied FS it is important not to put CSR in the focus based on normative assumptions but rather present it as a possible way of future development that can lead the company to a certain future-situation described by CSR values. When we scan the present for possible changes we should not only look for economic trends and major events but shifts in values and norms as well as paradigms.

Understanding and Monitoring Change

Understanding and monitoring change is the equivalent of seeking the factors that could create change. Thus, in understanding and monitoring change companies should also try to find the influencing factors that determine the future state of the environment of the company; they should look for trends, issues, possible events, images and ideas. Trends help companies to understand the changes that are expected to happen if no other changes are to occur. They describe the expected or the baseline future. The first report of the Club of Rome was basically a trend analysis. The report showed that humanity was going to face a major environmental problem towards 2020 as the consequence of increasing fossil fuel consumption. However, maybe because the report was published, we changed our behavior and we changed our consumption. This is exactly the problem with this analysis: it is very unlikely that existing tendencies remain the same over a long period of time, especially in these unstable times. Thus, we need to focus on other sources of change. Issues or emerging issues, possible events and images and ideas bring renewal and human factor into the future. The common in them is that all of them appear in people's thoughts, thus it is up to us what else will become a major driving force of change. They all take part in creating alternative futures, thus when companies describe alternatives, they should focus on these forces too.

Another important point when talking about understanding and monitoring change is the levels of the environment to analyze. When we talk about the future, we should not forget that it has various fields where changes can come from that could influence the operations of our company. Changes can appear in the economy, in politics, in the applied technology, in the environment and, of course, in society. Thus, companies should analyze all fields in the immediate environment of the company since major changes in any of them could require a reaction from the company. Taking a wider aspect supports bringing CSR in front as one of its main message is that corporate is embedded in the society and in the environment and cannot thrive while others suffer. Bringing in factors of change from different fields and connecting it to the future of the company strengthens the concept of interwoven relations and weakens the individualistic corporate image.

Critiquing Implications

After analyzing the factors of change, company leaders should not forget to make implications regarding what these changes could imply for them. Using these steps, companies should make their own forecasts based on the collected factors that influence the future to some extent. There are also futurists that are experts in certain fields or experts that offer an insight to the development of certain domains, their forecasts can be of point to start from. However, if we are responsible for setting the desired direction for the organization, we should not forget the complexity of the future, thus we should analyze what the effects of a forecast are on other important areas. For instance, if we receive a forecast that says that energy prices will increase, we should think about how others, for example politicians, workers of the enterprise, managers or similar companies will react if it really happens, and how it will effect the operation of the organization. With the expressions of knowledge management theories, forecasts are additional information, but they can be utilized if we make knowledge out of them by analyzing what they mean for the organization.

Imaging Difference

As we said earlier, it is very unlikely that the development of the different systems will remain unchanged. Thus companies should try to imagine what all the changes can imply for them and how the environment would be different as the consequence of these changes. This is the step when we need to talk about alternative futures. Again, we can use forecasts of experts on the future, but we always should find the underlying assumption of the forecasts and check if any alternative assumption could be reasonable. Since alternatives lie behind the assumptions, we should focus on finding them and imagine what their implications would be.

Envisioning Preferred Future

If we created alternative futures based on the changes that we expect to happen or that we believe that can happen, we can turn our focus on finding out which of the alternative futures is the best for us, which one we want to achieve. Of course, this decision depends on our values, but exactly this is the reason why we need to talk about long-term future: it opens the range of possibilities and we can find other important values. This looks like an easy task to do: we have some alternatives and we need to decide on which one is the best for us. In real life this part of applied FS also involves thinking about the preferred situation of the company, not only thinking about the preferred future. Furthermore this step assumes that the organization is aware of its values that are its ultimate deciding factors. Usually it is not the case, thus organizations should work on expressing their values.

Planning and Implementing Preferred Future

The last step of applied FS is a little bit different from the implementation phase of FS; just as implementing a preferred future of the society is different from the preferred future of a company. However in both cases we need to be able to find the direction that leads us to that future, with identifying the milestones to be achieved and creating the priorities to follow and high-level tasks and action plans in order to start moving on the desired path.

Some futurists describe methods of applied FS from a little different point of view, however the logic is the same behind them: we need to find factors that influence the future in order to describe alternative futures; and if we know the most important alternative futures we can decide based on our values which direction we want to start to move. According to other sciences, the last, the implementation part is not the task of futurists; it should be done by managers however it could have an added value to work on the implementation under the lead of someone who knows possible futures possibly better.

FS as a Bridge to CSR

The biggest problem with CSR is that it seems to be an altruistic utopia which is not connected to the present world of profit-chasing. By letting it go to the further future it is easier to think in terms of change towards CSR. Let's see how FS can contribute to CSR.

When we monitor change we see that environmental factors are given more weight – to put it simply the price of oil is on a constant increase. Also environmental protection is not seemed as an act of humanity but rather an act of survival. The same goes for tackling the global problems of poverty and famine: when people on the other side of the globe suffer, we can soon get into trouble (think of international terrorism or immigration).

What are the implications of the changes that we monitored? A company should look out of the economic box to see where the changes that manifest themselves in economic terms come from! In order to see the dynamics it has to investigate social, environmental, political and technical issues. A new assumption is needed: a company should not only focus on the economic factors but on a wider aspect. Politics tend to focus on social responsibility with their tool: laws and taxes on pollution. Technology also focuses on efficient energy savings and renewables. The consequence is that it is more effective to be environmentally sound and more high-tech.

Let's draw up an alternative based on CSR assumptions. It is important however not to position the CSR alternative as a preferred one at this phase, but rather to open it for discussion and evaluation. Developing such an alternative can itself raise awareness about common responsibilities and can give an insight to the operation of a socially responsible company. Imagination is a powerful tool since it helps people to think the unthinkable, to describe a seemingly impossible future and thus to make it more tangible.

This process can guide leaders through the process of putting other values than money in perspective and involving them in the decision-making process. FS also implies the design of a strategy – this brings CSR back to the present through the steps that need to be taken.

Thus, FS can be the bridge that helps us to cross the lake from "profitland" to the "land of socially responsible companies" and a better world.

Acknowledgement

Thanks to the Hungarian Scientific Research Fund (OTKA) for the grant given to the research program (No. T 043522) entitled Change and Future (project coordinator: Erzsébet Nováky)

Conclusion

As we could see, long-term thinking and the concept of FS can bring new ideas and new values to form the present by influencing our expectations about the future that effects our decisions in the present. Our starting point was that the western way of thinking, especially about economies, is short-term oriented and often only one value driven. CSR tries to change this, to bring other values into decision-making. From the better application of the results of

FS we could see that the goal of this new field is the same, to look at decisions from different points of view. FS does it by focusing on long-term thinking since, as time passes, we have more opportunities to create changes. On the other hand, if we think longer ahead, we need to think about alternatives for the reason that we live in an unstable and complex world. And if we think about alternatives, there are lots of situations for new values to emerge, from what companies could benefit. The most difficult problem is that the long-term future doesn't exist without the short-term future and until the main economic theory supports mainly short-term, money driven decisions better, we don't have a chance to create a better world. As we pointed out, long-term thinking contains lots of opportunities for companies that would also bring new values and more responsible and more useful decisions.

REFERENCES

[1] Chikán, A. (2005). *Vállalatgazdaságtan.* [*Business economics*] Budapest, Hungary: AULA.

[2] Nováky, E. (2006). Jövőkutatás és felelősség. [Futures studies and responsibility] *Magyar Tudomány, 167*, 1090-1098.

[3] Nováky, E. (2003). A jövőkutatás módszertana stabilitás és instabilitás mellett. [Futures studies methodology in stability and instability] Budapest, Hungary: BKÁE Jövőkutatási Kutatóközpont.

[4] Nováky, E. (2004). Participative Futures Studies. In E. Nováky, Sz. Fridrik, & B. Szél (Eds.), *Action for the Future* (edition, pp. 67-80). Budapest, Hungary: Futures Studies Centre, University of Economic Sciences and Public Administration.

[5] Hideg, É., Nováky, E., & Vág, A. (2006). Exploration Seeds of Change in the Process of Actualization of Future Images for Hungary. Discussion paper. COST A 22/WG1

[6] Nováky, E. (2006). Action Oriented Futures Studies In Hungary. *Futures, 38*, 685–695.

[7] Masini, E. B. (2004). Values and Actions for the Future. In E. Nováky, Sz. Fridrik, & B. Szél (Eds.), *Action for the Future* (edition, pp. 45-54). Budapest, Hungary: Futures Studies Centre, University of Economic Sciences and Public Administration.

[8] Nováky, E., & Kappéter, I. (2005). How Do Students Relate to Changes? In T. Gáspár, & P. Bakos (Eds.), *Futures Generation for Future Generations.* Budapest, Hungary: Futures Studies Centre, Corvinus University of Budapest. [eBook]. www.budapestfutures.org

[9] Tyukodi, G. (2006). Jövőkutatás a mindennapi életben. [Futures studies in everyday life] In. T. Kristóf, & A. Tóth (Eds.), *Globális és hazai problémák tegnaptól holnapig.* [*Global and national problems from yesterday to tomorrow*] (edition, pp. 322-325). Budapest, Hungary: Arisztotelész Stúdium Bt.

INDEX

A

D

F

G

H

I

J

K

L

M

N

O

P

S

T

U

V

W

Y